Italian

Phrasebook

LAROUSSE

Editors
Debora Mazza, Donald Watt

with
Valerie Grundy, Christy Johnson

Supplement on Italian language and culture
Daphne Day

Publishing manager
Janice McNeillie

Design and typesetting
Sharon McTeir

Achevé d'imprimer en Mai 2006 sur les presses de « La Tipografica Varese S.p.A. » à Varese (Itali

Introduction

This phrasebook is the ideal companion for your trip. It gets straight to the point, helping you to understand and make yourself understood so that you don't miss a thing. Use it like a dictionary to find the exact word you're looking for right away. And at each word we've provided a selection of key phrases that will help you in any situation, no matter how tricky things may have gotten.

The English–Italian section contains all those essential expressions that you'll need to get by in Italy. And because you need to be able to pronounce the words you see on the page properly, we've provided a simple and straightforward phonetic transcription that will enable you to make yourself understood with ease.

The Italian–English section provides all the most important words and expressions that you might read or hear while on vacation.

And that's not all: we've added practical and cultural tips for getting by, a supplement on Italian language, life and culture – everything, in fact, to make your trip go as smoothly as possible.

Buon viaggio!

Pronunciation

So that you can say what you want to say in Italian without running any risk of being misunderstood, we have devised a simple and straightforward phonetic transcription to show how every Italian word or phrase used in this phrasebook is pronounced. This phonetic transcription, which is shown in brackets after each Italian word or phrase, uses as many standard English sounds as possible, so that it is virtually self-explanatory. The following list provides further clarification:

[ay]	as in d**ay**
[ch]	as in **ch**ee**se**
[ee]	as in tr**ee**
[ly]	as in mi**lli**on
[ny]	as in ca**ny**on
[oo]	as in s**oo**n
[ow]	as in n**ow**

Abbreviations

abbr	abbreviation
adj	adjective
adv	adverb
art	article
conj	conjunction
excl	exclamation
f	feminine
m	masculine
n	noun
num	numeral
pl	plural
prep	preposition
pron	pronoun
v	verb

English–Italian phrasebook

a

able

▶ to be able to ... potere ... [potayray]
▶ I'm not able to come tonight non posso venire stasera [non posso vayneeray stasayra]

about circa [cheerka]

▶ I think I'll stay for about an hour penso che rimarrò circa un'ora [penso kay reemarro cheerca oonora]

abroad *(live, travel)* all'estero [allestayro]

▶ I've never been abroad before non sono mai stato all'estero prima [non sono ma-ee stato allestayro preema]

absolutely assolutamente [assolootamentay]

▶ you're absolutely right hai assolutamente ragione [a-ee assolootamentay rajonay]

accept accettare [achettaray]

▶ do you accept traveler's checks? accettate i traveller's cheque? [achettatay ee traveller chek]

access l'accesso *m* [achesso]

▶ is there disabled access? c'è un accesso per disabili? [chay oon achesso per deezabeelee]

accident l'incidente *m* [eencheedentay]

▶ there's been an accident c'è stato un incidente [chay stato oon eencheedentay]

according to secondo [saykondo]

▶ it's well worth seeing, according to the guidebook secondo la guida, vale la pena di vederlo [saykondo la gweeda valay la payna dee vaydayrlo]

address *(details of place)* l'indirizzo *m* [eendeereetso] ◆ *(speak to)* rivolgersi a [reevolgersee a]

▶ could you write down the address for me? mi può scrivere l'indirizzo? [mee poo-o skreevayray leendeereetso]
▶ here is my address and phone number questi sono il mio indirizzo e il mio numero di telefono [kwestee sono eel mee-o eendeereetso ay eel mee-o noomayro dee taylayfono]

adult l'adulto(a) [adoolto(a)]

▶ two adults and one student, please due adulti e uno studente, per favore [doo-ay adooltee ay oono stoodentay per favoray]

advance *(money)* l'anticipo *m* [anteecheepo] ◆ **in advance** *(pay, reserve)* in anticipo [een anteecheepo]

▸ do you have to book in advance? **bisogna prenotare?** [beezonya praynotaray]
▸ do you have to pay for the room in advance? **la camera deve essere pagata in anticipo?** [la kamayra dayvay essayray pagata een anteecheepo]

after dopo [dopo]
▸ we're leaving after lunch **partiamo dopo pranzo** [partee-amo dopo prandzo]
▸ it's twenty after eight **sono le otto e venti** [sono lay otto ay ventee]
▸ the stadium is just after the traffic lights **lo stadio è subito dopo il semaforo** [lo stadee-o ay soobeeto dopo eel saymaforo]

afternoon il pomeriggio [pomayreejo]
▸ is the museum open in the afternoons? **il museo è aperto di pomeriggio?** [eel moozay-o ay aperto dee pomayreejo]

aftershave il dopobarba [dopobarba]
▸ a bottle of aftershave **una bottiglietta di dopobarba** [oona botteelyetta dee dopobarba]

afterwards dopo [dopo]
▸ join us afterwards **raggiungici dopo** [rajoonjeechee dopo]

again di nuovo [dee noo-ovo]
▸ the train is late again **il treno è di nuovo in ritardo** [eel trayno ay dee noo-ovo een reetardo]

age l'età ƒ [ayta]
▸ we've been waiting for ages! **sono secoli che aspettiamo!** [sono saykolee kay aspettee-amo]
▸ what ages are your children? **che età hanno i suoi figli?** [kay ayta anno ee soo-o-ee feelyee]

agency l'agenzia ƒ [ajentsee-a]
▸ what is the contact number for the agency? **qual è il numero per contattare l'agenzia?** [kwal ay eel noomayro per kontattaray lajentsee-a]

ago fa [fa]
▸ I've been before, several years ago **ci sono stato diversi anni fa** [chee sono stato deeversee annee fa]

---

agreement/disagreement

▸ absolutely! **assolutamente sì!** [assolootamentay see]
▸ that's fine by me **per me, va bene** [per may va baynay]
▸ you're right **ha ragione** [a rajonay]
▸ go on, then **allora, faccia pure** [allora facha pooray]
▸ I'm not at all convinced **non sono affatto convinto** [non sono affatto konveento]
▸ I disagree **non sono d'accordo** [non sono dakkordo]

agreement l'accordo *m* [akkordo]

▸ we need to come to some agreement about where we're going next **dobbiamo trovare un accordo su dove andare dopo** [dobbee-amo trovaray oon akkordo soo dovay andaray dopo]

ahead davanti [davantee]

▸ do we carry on straight ahead? **dobbiamo andare sempre dritti?** [dobbee-amo andaray sempray dreettee]

air *(wind)* l'aria *f* [aree-a]

▸ the air is much fresher in the mountains **l'aria è molto più fresca in montagna** [laree-a ay molto pyoo freska een montanya]

air-conditioning l'aria condizionata *f* [aree-a kondeetsee-onata]

▸ do you have air-conditioning? **avete l'aria condizionata?** [avaytay laree-a kondeetsee-onata]

airline la compagnia aerea [kompanyee-a a-ayray-a]

▸ no, we're traveling with a different airline **no, viaggiamo con un'altra compagnia aerea** [no vee-ajamo kon oonaltra kompanyee-a a-ayray-a]

airmail per via aerea [per vee-a a-ayray-a]

▸ I'd like to send it airmail **vorrei spedirlo per via aerea** [vorray-ee spaydeerlo per vee-a a-ayray-a]

airport l'aeroporto *m* [a-ayroporto]

▸ how long does it take to get to the airport? **quanto ci vuole per andare all'aeroporto?** [kwanto chee voo-olay per andaray alla-ayroporto]

airport shuttle la navetta per l'aeroporto [navetta per la-ayroporto]

▸ is there an airport shuttle? **c'è una navetta per l'aeroporto?** [chay oona navetta per la-ayroporto]

air pressure la pressione [pressee-onay]

▸ could you check the air pressure in the tires? **può verificare la pressione dei pneumatici?** [poo-o vayreefeekaray la pressee-onay day-ee pnay-oomateechee]

---

at the airport

▸ where is gate number 2? **dov'è l'uscita numero due?** [dovay loosheeta numayro doo-ay]

▸ where is the check-in desk? **dov'è il banco del check-in?** [dovay eel banko del chekeen]

▸ I'd like an aisle seat **vorrei un posto lato corridoio** [vorray-ee oon posto lato korreedo-yo]

▸ where is the baggage claim? **dov'è il ritiro bagagli?** [dovay eel reeteero bagalyee]

airsick
- to be airsick avere il mal d'aria [avayray eel mal daree-a]
- can I have an airsick bag? posso avere un sacchetto per il mal d'aria? [posso avayray oon sakketto per eel mal daree-a]

aisle *(between plane seats)* il corridoio [korreedo-yo]; *(plane seat)* il posto lato corridoio [posto lato korreedo-yo]
- two seats, please: one window and one aisle due posti, per favore: uno lato finestrino, e uno lato corridoio [doo-ay postee per favoray oono lato feenestreeno ay oono lato korreedo-yo]

aisle seat il posto lato corridoio [posto lato korreedo-yo]
- I'd like an aisle seat vorrei un posto lato corridoio [vorray-ee oon posto lato korreedo-yo]

alarm (clock) la sveglia [zvelya]
- I set the alarm for nine o'clock ho messo la sveglia alle nove [o messo la zvelya allay novay]

alcohol l'alcol *m* [alkol]
- does it contain alcohol? contiene alcol? [kontee-aynay alkol]
- I don't drink alcohol non bevo alcolici [non bayvo alkoleechee]

alcohol-free analcolico(a) [analkoleeko(a)]
- what kind of alcohol-free drinks do you have? che bibite analcoliche avete? [kay beebeetay analkoleekay avaytay]

all tutto(a) [tootto(a)] ✦ *(everybody)* tutti [toottee]
- all the time tutto il tempo [tootto eel tempo]
- all English people tutti gli inglesi [toottee lyee eenglayzee]
- will that be all? è tutto? [ay tootto]

allergic allergico(a) [allerjeeko(a)]
- I'm allergic to aspirin/nuts/wheat/dairy products sono allergico all'aspirina/alla frutta secca/al frumento/ai latticini [sono allerjeeko allaspeereena/alla frootta sekka/al froomento/a-ee latteecheenee]

allow permettere [permettayray]
- are you allowed to smoke here? è permesso fumare qui? [ay permesso foomaray kwee]
- how much luggage are you allowed? qual è il limite autorizzato dei bagagli? [kwal ay eel leemeetay owtoreedzato day-ee bagalyee]

almost quasi [kwazee]
- it's almost one o'clock è quasi l'una [ay kwazee loona]

alone solo(a) [solo(a)]
- leave us alone! ci lasci in pace! [chee lashee een pachay]

along lungo [loongo]
- along the river lungo il fiume [loongo eel fyoomay]

altogether *(in total)* complessivamente [komplesseevamentay]
- how much does it cost altogether? quanto costa complessivamente? [kwanto kosta komplesseevamentay]

always sempre [sempray]
- it's always the same thing è sempre la stessa cosa [ay sempray la stessa kosa]

ambulance l'ambulanza *f* [amboolantsa]
- could you send an ambulance right away to...? potete mandare subito un'ambulanza in ...? [potaytay mandaray soobeeto oonamboolantsa een]

ambulance service il servizio ambulanze [serveetsee-o amboolantsay]
- what's the number for the ambulance service? qual è il numero del servizio ambulanze? [kwal ay eel noomayro del serveetsee-o amboolantsay]

America l'America *f* [amayreeka]
- I live in America vivo in America [veevo een amayreeka]
- I'm from America sono americano(a) [sono amayreekano(a)]
- have you ever been to America? è mai stato in America? [ay ma-ee stato een amayreeka]

American americano(a) [amayreekano(a)] ✦ l'americano/a [amayreekano/a]
- I'm American sono americano(a) [sono amayreekano(a)]
- we're Americans siamo americani [see-amo amayreekanee]

ankle la caviglia [kaveelya]
- I've sprained my ankle mi sono slogato la caviglia [mee sono zlogato la kaveelya]

announcement l'annuncio *m* [annooncho]
- was that an announcement about the Naples train? era un annuncio per il treno per Napoli? [ayra oon annooncho per il treno per napolee]

another un altro *m* [oon altro], un'altra *f* [oonaltra]
- another coffee, please un altro caffè, per favore [oon altro kaffay per favoray]
- (would you like) another drink? (desidera) qualcos'altro da bere? [(dayzeedayra) kwalkozaltro da bayray]

answer la risposta [reesposta] ✦ rispondere [reespondayray]
- there's no answer *(to phone)* non risponde nessuno [non reesponday nessoono]; *(to door)* non c'è nessuno [non chay nessoono]
- I phoned earlier but nobody answered ho telefonato prima, ma non ha risposto nessuno [o taylayfonato preema ma non a reesposto nessoono]

answering machine la segreteria telefonica [saygraytayree-a talayfoneeka]
- I left a message on your answering machine ho lasciato un messaggio sulla sua segreteria telefonica [o lashato oon messajo soolla soo-a saygraytayree-a talayfoneeka]

anti-dandruff shampoo lo shampoo antiforfora [shampoo anteeforfora]
- do you have anti-dandruff shampoo? avete dello shampoo antiforfora? [avaytay dello shampoo anteeforfora]

anybody, anyone *(in questions)* qualcuno [kwalkoono]; *(in negative statements)* nessuno [nessoono]

▸ is there anybody there? c'è qualcuno? [chay kwalkoono]
▸ I didn't see anybody non ho visto nessuno [non o veesto nessoono]

anything *(in questions)* qualcosa [kwalkoza]; *(in negative statements)* niente [nee-entay]

▸ is there anything I can do? posso fare qualcosa? [posso faray kwalkoza]
▸ I haven't bought anything non ho comprato niente [non o komprato nee-entay]

anywhere *(in questions)* da qualche parte [da kwalkay partay]; *(in negative statements)* da nessuna parte [da nessoona partay]

▸ is there anywhere you can buy bus tickets? si possono comprare da qualche parte i biglietti dell'autobus? [see possono comparay da kwalkay partay i beelyettee dellowtoboos]
▸ I can't find my room key anywhere non trovo la chiave della mia camera da nessuna parte [non trovo la kee-avay della mee-a kamayra da nessoona partay]
▸ do you live anywhere near here? abita da queste parti? [abeeta da kwestay partee]

apartment l'appartamento *m* [appartamento]

▸ we'd like to rent an apartment for one week vorremmo affittare un appartamento per una settimana [vorremmo affeettaray oon appartamento per oona setteemana]

apologize scusarsi [skoozarsee]

▸ there's no need to apologize non c'è bisogno di scusarsi [non chay beezonyo dee skoozarsee]

appetizer l'antipasto *m* [anteepasto]

▸ which of the appetizers would you recommend? quali antipasti consiglierebbe? [kwalee anteepastee konseelyayrebbay]

apple la mela [mayla]

▸ could I have half a kilo of apples, please? potrei avere mezzo chilo di mele, per favore? [potray-ee avayray medzo keelo dee maylay per favoray]

---

apologizing

▸ excuse me! mi scusi! [mee skoozee]
▸ I'm sorry, I can't come on Saturday mi dispiace, non posso venire sabato [mee deespee-achay non posso vayneeray sabato]
▸ that's OK non fa niente [non fa nee-entay]
▸ it doesn't matter non importa [non eemporta]
▸ don't mention it si figuri [see feegooree]

apple juice il succo di mela [sooko dee mayla]
- I'd like some apple juice **vorrei del succo di mela** [vorray-ee del sookko dee mayla]

appointment l'appuntamento *m* [appoontamento]
- could I get an appointment for tomorrow morning? **potrei avere un appuntamento per domani mattina?** [potray-ee avayray oon appoontamento per domanee matteena]
- I have an appointment with Doctor ... **ho un appuntamento dal Dottor ...** [o oon appoontamento dal dottor]

April l'aprile *m* [apreelay]
- April 6th **il sei aprile** [eel say-ee apreelay]

area *(region, locality)* la zona [dzona]; *(of knowledge, interest)* il campo [kampo]; *(of town)* il quartiere [kwartee-ayray]
- I'm visiting the area **sto visitando la zona** [sto veezeetando la dzona]
- what walks can you recommend in the area? **quali escursioni può consigliare in zona?** [kwalee eskoorsee-onee poo-o konseelyaray een dzona]

area code *(for telephoning)* prefisso (telefonico) [prayfeesso (taylayfoneeko)]
- what's the area code for Italy? **qual è il prefisso dell'Italia?** [kwal ay eel prayfeesso delleetalee-a]

arm il braccio [bracho]
- I can't move my arm **non riesco a muovere il braccio** [non ree-esko a moo-ovayray eel bracho]

around *(in all directions)* intorno [eentorno]; *(nearby)* nei paraggi [nay-ee parajee]; *(here and there)* in giro [een geero]; *(approximately)* circa [cheerka] ♦ *(encircling)* intorno a [eentorno a]; *(through)* in giro per [een geero per]
- we've been traveling around Europe **siamo andati in giro per l'Europa** [see-amo andatee een geero per lay-ooropa]
- I don't know my way around yet **non mi so ancora orientare da queste parti** [non mee so ankora oree-entaray da kwestay partee]
- I arrived around two o'clock **sono arrivato intorno alle due** [sono arreevato eentorno allay doo-ay]
- I'd like something for around 15 euros **vorrei qualcosa sui quindici euro** [vorray-ee kwalkoza soo-ee kweendeechee ay-ooro]

arrive arrivare [arreevaray]
- my luggage hasn't arrived **i miei bagagli non sono arrivati** [ee mee-ay-ee bagalyee non sono arreevatee]
- we arrived yesterday **siamo arrivati ieri** [see-amo arreevatee ee-ayree]
- we just arrived **siamo appena arrivati** [see-amo appayna arreevatee]

art l'arte *f* [artay]
- I'm not really interested in art **non mi interessa molto l'arte** [non mee eentayressa molto lartay]

as *(while)* mentre [mentray]; *(like)* come [komay]; *(since)* siccome [seekkomay] ♦ *(in comparisons)* come [komay]

- as I said before come ho detto prima [komay o detto preema]
- leave it as it is lascialo così com'è [lashalo kozee komay]
- as it's raining, we won't go today siccome piove, non ci andiamo oggi [seekkomay pee-ovay non chee andee-amo ojee]
- this hotel is not as expensive as the other one questo albergo non è caro come l'altro [kwesto albergo non ay karo komay laltro]
- as much as (tanto) quanto [(tanto) kwanto]
- as many as (tanti) quanti [(tanto) kwantee]

ashtray il posacenere [pozachaynayray]
- could you bring us an ashtray? ci può portare un posacenere? [chee poo-o portaray oon pozachaynayray]

ask *(question)* fare [faray]; *(time)* chiedere [kee-aydayray]
- can I ask you a question? posso farle una domanda? [posso farlay oona domanda]

aspirin l'aspirina *f* [aspeereena]
- I'd like some aspirin vorrei delle aspirine [vorray-ee dellay aspeereenay]

asthma l'asma *f* [azma]
- I have asthma soffro di asma [soffro dee azma]

at a [a]
- our bags are still at the airport i nostri bagagli sono ancora all'aeroporto [ee nostree bagalyee sono ankora alla-ayroporto]
- we arrive at midnight arriviamo a mezzanotte [arreevee-amo a medzanottay]

ATM il Bancomat® [bankomat]
- I'm looking for an ATM sto cercando un Bancomat® [sto cherkando oon bankomat]
- the ATM has eaten my card il Bancomat® mi ha mangiato la carta [eel bankomat mee a manjato la karta]

attack *(of illness)* l'attacco *m* [attakko] ◆ *(person)* aggredire [aggraydeeray]
- he's had an asthma attack ha avuto un attacco d'asma [a avooto oon attakko dazma]

---

asking questions

- is this seat free? è libero questo posto? [ay leebayro kwesto posto]
- where is the station? dov'è la stazione? [dovay la statsee-onay]
- could you help me get my suitcase down, please? mi può aiutare a tirare giù la valigia, per favore? [mee poo-o a-yootaray a teeraray joo la valeeja, per favoray]
- could you give me a hand? mi potrebbe dare una mano? [mee potrebbay daray oona mano]
- could you lend me ten euros? mi può prestare dieci euro? [mee poo-o prestaray dee-aychee ay-ooro]

ATMs

ATMs (*Bancomat*®) are to be found everywhere. Most hotels and restaurants, as well as some gas stations and some stores, will accept cards. Look for the *Carta Sì* sticker.

▸ I've been attacked sono stato aggredito [sono stato aggraydeeto]

attention l'attenzione *f* [attentsee-onay]
▸ may I have your attention for a moment? potrei avere la vostra attenzione per un attimo? [potray-ee avayray la vostra attenstee-onay per oon atteemo]

attractive attraente [attra-entay]
▸ I find you very attractive la trovo molto attraente [la trovo molto attra-entay]

August l'agosto *m* [agosto]
▸ we're arriving on August 29th arriviamo il ventinove agosto [arreevee-amo eel veneenovay agosto]

automatic automatico(a) [owtomateeko(a)] ♦ *(car)* l'auto *f* con il cambio automatico [owto kon eel kambee-o owtomateeko]
▸ I want a car with automatic transmission voglio un'auto con il cambio automatico [volyee-o oonowto kon eel kambee-o owtomateeko]
▸ is it a manual or an automatic? l'auto ha il cambio manuale o automatico? [lowto a eel kambee-o manoo-alay o owtomateeko]

available disponibile [deesponeebeelay]
▸ you don't have a table available before then? non c'è un tavolo disponibile prima? [non chay oon tavolo deesponeebeelay preema]

average medio(a) [maydee-o(a)]
▸ what's the average temperature here in summer? qual è qui la temperatura media in estate? [kwal ay kwee la tempayratoora maydee-a een estatay]

avoid evitare [ayveetaray]
▸ is there a route that would help us avoid the traffic? c'è un percorso che ci permetta di evitare il traffico? [chay oon perkorso kay chee permetta dee ayveetaray eel traffeeko]

away *(indicating movement)* via [vee-a]; *(indicating position)* lontano [lontano]
▸ the village is ten kilometers away il paese è a dieci chilometri [eel pa-ayzay ay a dee-aychee keelometree]
▸ we're looking for a cottage far away from the town cerchiamo una casetta lontano dalla città [cherkee-amo oona cazetta lontano dalla cheetta]
▸ do you have any rooms away from the main road? avete delle camere lontano dalla strada principale? [avaytay dellay kamayray lontano dalla strada preencheepalay]

baby bottle il biberon [beebayron]
- I need to sterilize a baby bottle **devo sterilizzare un biberon** [dayvo stayreeleedzaray oon beebayron]

back *(part of body)* la schiena [skee-ayna]; *(of room)* il fondo [fondo]
- I'll be back in 5 minutes **torno tra cinque minuti** [torno tra cheenkway meenootee]
- I've got a bad back **soffro di mal di schiena** [soffro dee mal dee skee-ayna]
- I prefer to sit at the back of the room **preferisco sedermi in fondo alla sala** [prayfayreesko saydayrmee een fondo alla sala]

backache il mal di schiena [mal dee skee-ayna]
- I've got a backache **ho mal di schiena** [o mal dee skee-ayna]

backpack lo zaino [dza-eeno]
- my passport's in my backpack **il mio passaporto è nel mio zaino** [eel mee-o passaporto ay nel mee-o dza-eeno]

back up fare retromarcia [faray retromarcha]
- I think we have to back up and turn right **penso che dobbiamo fare retromarcia e girare a destra** [penso kay dobbee-amo faray retromarcha ay geeraray a destra]

bad *(experience, news, weather)* brutto(a) [brootto(a)]; *(restaurant)* cattivo(a) [katteevo(a)]
- the weather's bad today **oggi c'è brutto tempo** [ojee chay brootto tempo]

bag il bagaglio [bagalyo]; *(suitcase)* la valigia [valeeja]; *(purse)* la borsa [borsa]
- are these the bags from flight 502? **questi bagagli provengono dal volo cinquecentodue?** [kwestee bagalyee provengono dal volo cheenkwaychentodoo-ay]
- can someone take our bags up to the room, please? **qualcuno può portarci le valigie in camera, per favore?** [kwalkoono poo-o portarchee le valeejay een kamayra per favoray]
- someone's stolen my wallet from my bag **mi hanno rubato il portafoglio dalla borsa** [mee anno roobato eel portafolyo dalla borsa]

baggage i bagagli [bagalyee]
- my baggage hasn't arrived **i miei bagagli non sono arrivati** [ee mee-ay-ee bagalyee non sono arreevatee]
- I'd like to report the loss of my baggage **vorrei fare una denuncia di smarrimento bagagli** [vorray-ee faray oona daynooncha dee zmarreemento bagalyee]

baggage cart il carrello portabagagli [karrello portabagalyee]
> I'm looking for a baggage cart **sto cercando un carrello portabagagli** [sto cherkando oon karrello portabagalyee]

bakery la panetteria [panettayree-a]
> is there a bakery nearby? **c'è una panetteria qui vicino?** [chay oona panettayree-a kwee veecheeno]

balcony il balcone [balkonay]
> do you have any rooms with a balcony? **avete delle camere con balcone?** [avaytay dellay kamayray kon balkonay]

banana la banana [banana]
> a kilo of bananas, please **un chilo di banane, per favore** [oon keelo dee bananay per favoray]

bandage la benda [benda]
> I need a bandage for my ankle **ho bisogno di una benda per la caviglia** [o beezonyo dee oona benda per la kaveelya]

Band-Aid® il cerotto [chayrotto]
> can I have a Band-Aid® for my cut? **posso avere un cerotto per la ferita?** [posso avayray oon chayrotto per la fayreeta]

bank *(for money)* la banca [banka]
> is there a bank nearby? **c'è una banca da queste parti?** [chay oona banka da kwestay partee]
> are banks open on Saturdays? **le banche sono aperte di sabato?** [lay bankay sono apertay dee sabato]

bank card la carta di credito [karta dee craydeeto]
> I've lost my bank card **ho perso la carta di credito** [o perso la karta dee craydeeto]

---

at the bank

> I'd like to change 200 dollars into euros **vorrei cambiare duecento dollari in euro** [vorray-ee kambee-aray doo-aychento dollaree een ay-ooro]
> in small bills, please **in banconote di piccolo taglio, per favore** [een bankonotay dee peekolo talyo per favoray]
> what is the exchange rate for the euro? **qual è il tasso di cambio dell'euro?** [kwal ay eel tasso dee kambee-o dellay-ooro]
> how much is that in dollars? **quanto fa in dollari?** [kwanto fa een dollaree]
> do you take traveler's checks? **prendete i traveller's cheque?** [prendaytay ee traveler chek]
> do you charge a commission? **c'è una commissione?** [chay oona kommeessee-onay]

bar *(establishment serving alcohol)* il bar [bar]; *(counter)* il banco [banko]; *(of chocolate)* la barretta [barretta]

» are there any good bars around here? ci sono dei bei bar nei dintorni? [chee sono day-ee bay-ee bar nay-ee deentornee]

» I'd like a bar of soap vorrei una saponetta [vorray-ee oona saponetta]

base la base [bazay]

» the base of the lamp got broken la base della lampada si è rotta [la bazay della lampada see ay rotta]

» we're going to use the village as our base to explore the area useremo il paese come base per esplorare la zona [oozayraymo eel pa-ayzay komay bazay per esploraray la dzona]

basic elementare [aylaymentaray]

» does the staff speak at least basic English? il personale parla un inglese almeno elementare? [eel personalay parla oon eenglayzay almayno aylaymentaray]

» the basics le nozioni basilari [lay notsee-onee bazeelaree]

» I know the basics, but no more than that ho delle nozioni basilari, niente di più [o dellay notsee-onee bazeelaree nee-entay dee pyoo]

basis

» the price per night is on a double-occupancy basis il prezzo per notte è per due persone [eel pretso per nottay ay per doo-ay personay]

» on a weekly/monthly basis settimanalmente/mensilmente [setteemanalmentay/menseelmentay]

bat *(for table tennis)* la racchetta [rakketta]

» can you rent bats? si possono affittare delle racchette? [see possono affeettaray dellay rakkettay]

bath il bagno [banyo]

» to take a bath fare il bagno [faray eel banyo]

bathroom il bagno [banyo]

» where's the bathroom? dov'è il bagno? [dovay eel banyo]

bathtub la vasca da bagno [vaska da banyo]

» there's no plug for the bathtub non c'è il tappo nella vasca da bagno [non chay eel tappo nella vaska da banyo]

battery *(for radio, flashlight)* la pila [peela]; *(in car, for mobile, laptop)* la batteria [battayree-a]

» I need new batteries mi servono delle pile nuove [mee servono dellay peelay noo-ovay]

» the battery needs to be recharged bisogna ricaricare la batteria [beezonya reekareekaray la battayree-a]

» the battery's dead la batteria è scarica [la battayree-a ay skareeka]

be essere [essayray]

» where are you from? di dov'è? [dee dovay]

» I'm a teacher sono insegnante [sono eensenyantay]

- I'm happy sono contento [sono kontento]
- what day is it? che giorno è? [kay jorno ay]
- it's eight o'clock sono le otto [sono lay otto]
- how are you? come sta? [komay sta]
- I'm fine sto bene [sto baynay]
- where is terminal 1? dov'è il terminale uno? [dovay eel termeenalay oona]
- could you show me where I am on the map? mi può far vedere dove mi trovo sulla cartina? [mee poo-o far vaydayray dovay mee trovo soolla karteena]
- have you ever been to the United States? è mai stato negli Stati Uniti? [ay ma-ee stato nelyee statee ooneetee]
- it's the first time I've been here è la prima volta che vengo qui [ay la preema volta kay vengo kwee]
- how old are you? quanti anni hai? [kwantee annee a-ee]
- I'm 18 (years old) ho diciott'anni [o deechottannee]
- it was over thirty-five degrees c'erano più di trentacinque gradi [chayrano pyoo dee trentacheenkway gradee]
- it's cold in the evenings fa freddo di sera [fa freddo dee sayra]
- how much is it? quanto costa? [kwanto kosta]
- I'm 1.68 meters tall sono alto un metro e sessantotto [sono alto oon metro ay sessantotto]

beach la spiaggia [spee-aja]
- is it a sandy beach? è una spiaggia di sabbia fina? [ay oona spee-aja dee sabbee-a feena]
- is it a quiet beach? è una spiaggia tranquilla? [ay oona spee-aja trankweella]

beach umbrella l'ombrellone [ombrellonay]
- can you rent beach umbrellas? si possono noleggiare degli ombrelloni? [see possono nolejaray delyee ombrellonee]

beautiful bello(a) [bello(a)]
- isn't the weather beautiful today? oggi il tempo è proprio bello! [ojee eel tempo ay propree-o bello]

bed il letto [letto]
- is it possible to add an extra bed? è possibile aggiungere un letto? [ay posseebeelay ajoonjayray oon letto]
- do you have a children's bed? avete un lettino da bambini? [avaytay oon letteeno da bambeenee]
- I went to bed late sono andato a letto tardi [sono andato a letto tardee]
- I need to put my children to bed now devo mettere i bambini a letto ora [dayvo mettayray ee bambeenee a letto ora]

bedroom la camera (da letto) [kamayra (da letto)]
- how many bedrooms does the apartment have? quante camere da letto ci sono nell'appartamento? [kwantay kamayray da letto chee sono nellapartemento]

bedside lamp la lampada del letto [lampada del letto]
- the bedside lamp doesn't work **la lampada del letto non funziona** [la lampada del letto non foontsee-ona]

beef il manzo [mandzo]
- I don't eat beef **non mangio manzo** [non manjo mandzo]

beer la birra [beerra]
- two beers, please **due birre, per favore** [doo-ay beerray per favoray]

begin *(start)* cominciare [komeencharay]
- when does the performance begin? **quando comincia la rappresentazione?** [kwando komeencha la rapprayzentatsee-onay]

beginner il/la principiante [preencheepee-antay]
- I'm a complete beginner **sono del tutto principiante** [sono del tootto preencheepee-antay]

behind dietro [dee-aytro]
- from behind **da dietro** [da dee-aytro]
- the rest of our party is in the car behind **il resto del nostro gruppo è nella macchina dietro** [eel resto del nostro grooppo ay nella makkeena dee-aytro]

berth *(on ship)* la cuccetta [koochetta]
- I'd prefer the upper berth **preferirei la cuccetta superiore** [prayfayreeray-ee la koochetta soopayree-oray]

beside accanto a [akkanto a]
- is there anyone sitting beside you? **c'è qualcuno seduto accanto a lei?** [chay kwalkoono saydooto akkanto a lay-ee]

best migliore [meelyoray]
- what's the best restaurant in town? **qual è il miglior ristorante della città?** [kwal ay eel meelyor reestorantay della cheetta]

better migliore [meelyoray] ◆ meglio [melyo]
- I've been on antibiotics for a week and I'm not any better **sono sotto antibiotici da una settimana e non va affatto meglio** [sono sotto anteebee-oteechee da oona setteemana ay non va affatto melyo]
- the better situated of the two hotels **l'albergo con la posizione migliore tra i due** [lalbergo kon la pozeetsee-onay meelyoray tra ee doo-ay]

between tra [tra]
- a bus runs between the airport and the hotel **c'è un autobus che effettua il collegamento tra l'aeroporto e l'albergo** [chay oon owtobus kay effettoo-a eel collagamento tra la-ayroporto ay lalbergo]

bicycle la bicicletta [beecheekletta]
- is there a place to leave bicycles? **c'è un posto per lasciare le biciclette?** [chay oon posto per lasharay lay beecheeklettay]

bicycle lane la pista ciclabile [peesta cheeklabeelay]
  ▸ are there any bicycle lanes? ci sono delle piste ciclabili? [chee sono dellay peestay cheeklabeelee]

bicycle pump la pompa per biciclette [pompa per beecheeklettay]
  ▸ do you have a bicycle pump? ha una pompa per biciclette? [a oona pompa per beecheeklettay]

big grande [granday]
  ▸ do you have it in a bigger size? ce l'avete in una taglia più grande? [chay lavaytay een oona talya pyoo granday]
  ▸ it's too big è troppo grande [ay troppo granday]

bike la bici [beechee]
  ▸ I'd like to rent a bike for an hour vorrei noleggiare una bici per un'ora [vorray-ee nolejaray oona beechee per oonora]
  ▸ I'd like to do a bike tour mi piacerebbe fare una gita in bici [mee pee-achayrebbay faray oona geeta een beechee]

bill (in hotel) il conto [konto]; (paper money) la banconota [bankonota]
  ▸ I think there's a mistake with the bill credo che ci sia un errore nel conto [craydo kay chee see-a oon erroray nel konto]
  ▸ put it on my bill me lo metta sul conto [may lo metta sool konto]
  ▸ can you make up my bill, please? mi può fare il conto, per favore? [mee poo-o faray eel konto per favoray]

birthday il compleanno [komplay-anno]
  ▸ Happy Birthday! buon compleanno! [boo-on komplay-anno]

bite (of animal) il morso [morso]; (of insect) la puntura [poontoora] ◆ (animal) mordere [mordayray]; (insect) pungere [poonjayray]
  ▸ do you have a cream for mosquito bites? avete una pomata per le punture di zanzara? [avaytay oona pomata per lay poontooray dee dzandzara]
  ▸ I've been bitten by a mosquito mi ha punto una zanzara [mee a poonto oona dzandzara]

black nero(a) [nayro(a)]; (coffee, tea) senza latte [sentsa lattay]
  ▸ I'm looking for a little black dress sto cercando un vestito semplice nero [sto cherkando oon vesteeto sempleechay nayro]

black-and-white in bianco e nero [een bee-anko ay nayro]
  ▸ I like black-and-white movies mi piacciono i film in bianco e nero [mee pee-achono ee feelm een bee-anko ay nayro]

black ice il ghiaccio sulla strada [ghee-acho soolla strada]
  ▸ there's black ice c'è del ghiaccio sulla strada [chay del ghee-acho soolla strada]

blanket la coperta [koperta]
  ▸ I'd like an extra blanket vorrei una coperta supplementare [vorray-ee oona koperta sooplaymentaray]

bleed sanguinare [sangweenaray]
▸ it won't stop bleeding continua a sanguinare [konteenoo-a a sangweenaray]

blind *(on window)* la tapparella [tapparella]
▸ can we pull down the blinds? possiamo abbassare le tapparelle? [possee-amo abbassaray lay tapparellay]

blister la vescica [vesheeka]
▸ I've got a blister ho una vescica [o oona vesheeka]

block *(pipe, sink)* intasare [eentazaray]; *(road)* bloccare [blokkaray]
▸ the toilet's blocked il water è intasato [eel vatayr ay eentazato]
▸ my ears are completely blocked ho le orecchie completamente tappate [o lay orekkee-ay komplaytamentay tappatay]

blond biondo(a) [bee-ondo(a)]
▸ she has blond hair ha i capelli biondi [a ee capellee bee-ondee]

blood il sangue [sangway]
▸ traces of blood tracce di sangue [trachay dee sangway]

blood pressure la pressione (sanguigna) [pressee-onay (sangweenya)]
▸ I have high blood pressure ho la pressione alta [o la pressee-onay alta]

blood type il gruppo sanguigno [grooppo sangweenyo]
▸ my blood type is A positive il mio gruppo sanguigno è A positivo [eel mee-o grooppo sangweenyo ay a pozeeteevo]

blue blu [bloo]
▸ the blue one quello blu [kwello bloo]

board *(plane)* imbarcarsi su [eembarkarsee soo] ◆ effettuare l'imbarco [effettoo-aray leembarko]
▸ what time will the plane be boarding? a che ora è l'imbarco? [a kay ora ay leembarko]
▸ where is the flight to Dublin boarding? dov'è l'imbarco per Dublino? [dovay leembarko per doobleeno]

boarding pass la carta d'imbarco [karta deembarko]
▸ I can't find my boarding pass non trovo la mia carta d'imbarco [non trovo la mee-a karta deembarko]

boat la nave [navay]
▸ can we get there by boat? ci si può andare in nave? [chee see poo-o andaray een navay]

boat trip la gita in barca [jeeta een barka]
▸ are there boat trips on the river? ci sono gite in barca sul fiume? [chee sono jeetay een barka sool fyoomay]

book *(for reading)* il libro [leebro]; *(of tickets, stamps)* il carnet [karnay]; *(of matches)* la bustina [boosteena] ◆ *(ticket, room)* prenotare [praynotaray]
▸ do you sell English-language books? vendete libri in inglese? [vendaytay leebree een eenglayzay]

‣ is it more economical to buy a book of tickets? il carnet di biglietti è più conveniente? [eel karnay dee beelyeettee ay pyoo konvaynee-entay]

‣ I'd like to book a ticket vorrei prenotare un biglietto [vorray-ee praynotaray oon beelyetto]

‣ do you need to book in advance? è necessario prenotare? [ay naychessaree-o praynotaray]

born nato(a) [nato(a)]

‣ to be born nascere [nashayray]

‣ I was born on March 3rd, 1985 sono nato il tre marzo millenovecentottanta-cinque [sono nato eel tray martso meellaynovaychentottantacheenkway]

bottle la bottiglia [botteelya]

‣ a bottle of red wine, please una bottiglia di vino rosso, per favore [oona botteelya dee veeno rosso per favoray]

bottle opener l'apribottiglie *m* [apreebotteelyay]

‣ can you pass me the bottle opener? mi può passare l'apribottiglie? [mee poo-o passaray lapreebotteelyay]

bottom *(of well, of box)* il fondo [fondo]

‣ my passport's at the bottom of my suitcase il mio passaporto è in fondo alla mia valigia [eel mee-o passaporto ay een fondo alla mee-a valeeja]

box la scatola [skatola]

‣ could I have a box of matches, please? potrei avere una scatola di fiammiferi, per favore? [potray-ee avayray oona skatola dee fee-ammeefayree per favoray]

boy *(young male)* il ragazzo [ragatso]; *(son)* il figlio (maschio) [feelyo (maskee-o)]

‣ he seems like a nice boy sembra un ragazzo simpatico [sembra oon ragatso seempateeko]

‣ she has two boys ha due figli maschi [h doo-ay feelyee maskee]

boyfriend il ragazzo [ragatso]

‣ my boyfriend is a biologist il mio ragazzo è biologo [eel mee-o ragatso ay bee-ologo]

brake il freno [frayno]

‣ the brakes aren't working properly i freni non funzionano bene [ee fraynee non foontsee-ano baynay]

brake fluid l'olio *m* dei freni [olee-o day-ee fraynee]

‣ could you check the brake fluid? può controllare l'olio dei freni? [poo-o kontrollaray lolee-o day-ee fraynee]

branch *(of bank)* la filiale [feelee-alay]

‣ which branch should I visit to get the replacement traveler's checks? in quale filiale devo andare per avere i nuovi traveller's cheque? [een kwalay feelee-alay dayvo andaray per avayray ee noo-ovee traveller chek]

bread il pane [panay]

- do you have any bread? **ha del pane?** [a del panay]
- could we have some more bread? **potremmo avere altro pane?** [potremmo avayray altro panay]

break *(pause)* la **pausa** [powza] ♦ **rompere** [rompayray]

- should we take a break? **facciamo una pausa?** [fachamo oona powza]
- be careful you don't break it **stai attento a non romperlo** [sta-ee attento a non romperlo]
- I think I've broken my ankle **penso di essermi rotto la caviglia** [penso dee essermee rotto la kaveelya]

break down **rompersi** [rompersee]

- my car has broken down **mi si è rotta la macchina** [mee see ay rotta la makkeena]

breakdown il **guasto** [gwasto]

- to have a breakdown **rimanere in panne** [reemanayray een pannay]
- we had a breakdown on the way to the airport **siamo rimasti in panne andando all'aeroporto** [see-amo reemastee een pannay andando alla-ayroporto]

breakfast la **colazione** [kolatsee-onay]

- to have breakfast **fare colazione** [faray kolatsee-onay]
- what time is breakfast served? **a che ora è servita la colazione?** [a kay ora ay serveeta la kolatsee-onay]

bridge *(over river)* il **ponte** [pontay]; *(on ship)* il **ponte di comando** [pontay dee komando]

- do you have to pay a toll to use the bridge? **bisogna pagare un pedaggio per attraversare il ponte?** [beezonya pagaray oon paydajo per attraversaray eel pontay]

bring **portare** [portaray]

- what should we bring to drink? **cosa portiamo da bere?** [koza portee-amo da bayray]

bring down *(bags, luggage)* **portare giù** [portaray joo]

- could you get someone to bring down our luggage, please? **ci può mandare qualcuno per portare giù i nostri bagagli, per favore?** [chee poo-o mandaray kwalkoono per portaray joo ee nostree bagalyee per favoray]

bring in *(bags, luggage)* **portare dentro** [portaray dentro]

- can you bring in my bags, please? **può portare dentro i miei bagagli, per favore?** [poo-o portaray dentro ee mee-ay-ee bagalyee per favoray]

broken **rotto(a)** [rotto(a)]

- the lock is broken **la serratura è rotta** [la serratoora ay rotta]
- I think I've got a broken leg **penso di avere una gamba rotta** [penso dee avayray oona gamba rotta]

bronchitis la **bronchite** [bronkeetay]

- do you have anything for bronchitis? **avete qualcosa contro la bronchite?** [avaytay kwalkoza kontro la bronkeetay]

brother il fratello [fratello]

> this is my brother **questo è mio fratello** [kwesto ay mee-o fratello]
> I don't have any brothers or sisters **non ho fratelli o sorelle** [non o fratellee o sorellay]

brown marrone [marronay]; *(hair, eyes)* castano(a) [kastano(a)]

> he has brown hair **ha i capelli castani** [a ee kapellee kastanee]
> I'm looking for a brown leather belt **sto cercando una cintura di pelle marrone** [sto cherkando oona cheentoora dee pellay marronay]

brush *(for hair, clothes)* la spazzola [spatsola]; *(broom)* la scopa [skopa]; *(with short handle)* la scopetta [skopetta] ♦ *(hair)* spazzolare [spatsolaray]

> can I borrow a brush? **posso prendere in prestito una spazzola?** [posso prendayray een presteeto oona spatsola]
> where are the brush and dustpan? **dove sono la scopetta e la paletta?** [dovay sono la skopetta ay la paletta]
> to brush one's teeth **lavarsi i denti** [lavarsee ee dentee]

bulb *(light)* la lampadina [lampadeena]

> the bulb's out in the bathroom **la lampadina del bagno è bruciata** [la lampadeena del banyo ay broochata]

bunk beds i letti a castello [lettee a kastello]

> are there bunk beds for the children? **ci sono dei letti a castello per i bambini?** [chee sono day-ee lettee a kastello per ee bambeenee]

burn bruciare [broocharay]

> the chicken's completely burned **il pollo è completamente bruciato** [eel pollo ay komplaytamentay broochato]
> I've burned my hand **mi sono bruciato la mano** [mee sono broochato la mano]

burst far scoppiare [far skoppee-aray] ♦ scoppiare [skoppee-aray]

> one of my tires burst **mi è scoppiata una gomma** [mee ay skoppee-ata oona gomma]

bus l'autobus *m* [owtoboos]

> does this bus go downtown? **questo autobus va in centro?** [kwesto owtoboos va een chentro]
> which bus do I have to take to go to the station? **quale autobus devo prendere per andare alla stazione** [kwale owtoboos dayvo prendayray per andaray alla statsee-onay]

bus driver il conducente dell'autobus [kondoochentay dellowtoboos]

> can you buy tickets from the bus driver? **si possono comprare i biglietti dal conducente dell'autobus?** [see possono kompraray ee beelyettee dal kondoochentay dellowtoboos]

business *(commerce)* gli affari [affaree]; *(company)* l'azienda f [atsee-enda]; *(affair, matter)* la faccenda [fachenda]

> I'm here on business **sono qui per lavoro** [sono kwee per lavoro]
> it's none of your business **non sono affari tuoi** [non sono affaree too-o-ee]

business card il biglietto da visita [beelyetto da veezeeta]

> here's my business card ecco il mio biglietto da visita [ekko eel mee-o beelyetto da veezeeta]

business class la classe affari [klassay affaree], la business (class) [beezneez (klas)]

+ in classe affari [een klassay affaree], in business (class) [een beezneez (klas)]

> are there any seats in business class? ci sono posti in classe affari? [chee sono postee een klassay affaree]

> I prefer to travel business class preferisco viaggiare in business [prayfayreesko vee-ajaray een beezneez]

bus station la stazione degli autobus [statsee-onay delyee owtoboos]

> I'm looking for the bus station sto cercando la stazione degli autobus [sto cherkando la statsee-onay delyee owtoboos]

bus stop la fermata dell'autobus [fermata dellowtoboos]

> where's the nearest bus stop? dov'è la fermata dell'autobus più vicina? [dovay la fermata dellowtoboos pyoo veecheena]

busy *(person)* impegnato(a) [eempenyato(a)]; *(town, street)* animato(a) [anee-mato(a)]; *(beach)* affollato(a) [affollato(a)]; *(period)* pieno(a) di impegni [pee-ayno(a) dee eempenyee]; *(phone line)* occupato(a) [okkoopato(a)]

> I'm afraid I'm busy tomorrow mi dispiace, domani sono impegnato [mee deespee-achay domanee sono eempenyato]

> the line's busy la linea è occupata [la leenay-a ay okkoopata]

butter il burro [boorro]

> could you pass the butter please? mi può passare il burro, per favore? [mee poo-o passaray eel boorro per favoray]

buy comprare [kompraray]

> where can I buy tickets? dove posso comprare i biglietti? [dovay posso kompraray ee beelyettee]

> can I buy you a drink? posso offrirle da bere? [posso offreerlay da bayray]

bye ciao [chow]

> bye, see you tomorrow! ciao, a domani! [chow a domanee]

C

cab il taxi [taxee]

> can you order me a cab to the airport? mi può chiamare un taxi per l'aeroporto? [mee poo-o kee-amaray oon taxee per la-ayroporto]

cab driver il/la tassista [tasseesta]

> does the cab driver speak English? il tassista parla inglese? [eel tasseesta parla eenglayzay]

cabin la cabina [kabeena]

  ▸ can I have breakfast in my cabin? posso fare colazione in cabina? [posso faray kolatsee-onay een kabeena]

cable *(TV)* la tv via cavo [teevoo vee-a cavo]

  ▸ does the hotel have cable? c'è la tv via cavo in albergo? [chay la teevoo vee-a cavo een albergo]

café il caffè [kaffay]

  ▸ is there a café near here? c'è un caffè qui vicino? [chay oon kaffay kwee veecheeno]

cake il dolce [dolchay]

  ▸ a piece of that cake, please una fetta di quel dolce, per favore [oona fetta dee kwel dolchay per favoray]

call *(on phone)* la telefonata [taylayfonata] ♦ *(name)* chiamare [kee-amaray]; *(on phone)* telefonare a [taylayfonaray a]

  ▸ I have to make a call devo fare una telefonata [dayvo faray oona taylayfonata]

  ▸ what is this called? come si chiama? [komay see kee-ama]

  ▸ who's calling? chi parla? [kee parla]

call back richiamare [reekee-amaray]

  ▸ could you ask her to call me back? le può chiedere di richiamarmi? [lay poo-o kee-aydayray dee reekee-amarmee]

  ▸ I'll call back (later) richiamo io (più tardi) [reekee-amo ee-o (pyoo tardee)]

calm calmo(a) [kalmo (a)]

  ▸ keep calm! si calmi! [see kalmee]

camera *(for taking photos)* la macchina fotografica [makkeena fotografeeka]; *(for filming)* la cinepresa [cheenayprayza]

  ▸ can I use my camera here? posso usare la macchina fotografica qui? [posso oozaray la makkeena fotografeeka kwee]

camper il camper [kamper]

  ▸ do you have a space left for a camper? vi resta un posto camper? [vee resta oon posto kamper]

  ▸ I'd like to book space for a camper for the night of August 15th vorrei prenotare un posto camper per la notte del quindici agosto [vorray-ee praynotaray oon posto kamper per la nottay del kweendeechee agosto]

in a café

  ▸ is this table/seat free? è libero questo tavolo/posto? [ay leebayro kwesto tavolo/posto]

  ▸ excuse me! scusi! [skoozee]

  ▸ two black/white coffees, please due caffè/caffè con latte, per favore [doo-ay kaffay/kaffay kon lattay per favoray]

campground il campeggio [kampejo]
- ▶ I'm looking for a campground **sto cercando un campeggio** [sto cherkando oon kampejo]

camping il campeggio [kampejo]
- ▶ I love going camping **adoro andare in campeggio** [adoro andaray een kampejo]

can *(of food)* la scatola [skatola]; *(of drink)* la lattina [latteena]; *(of oil)* la latta [latta]; *(of paint)* il bidone [beedonay]
- ▶ a can of oil, please **una latta d'olio, per favore** [oona latta dolee-o per favoray]

can *(be able to)* potere [potayray]; *(know how to)* sapere [sapayray]
- ▶ can I help you? **posso esserle d'aiuto?** [posso esserlay da-yooto]
- ▶ I can't swim **non so nuotare** [non so noo-otaray]
- ▶ can you speak English? **parla inglese?** [parla eenglayzay]

Canada il Canada [kanada]
- ▶ I live in Canada **vivo in Canada** [veevo een kanada]
- ▶ I'm from Canada **sono canadese** [sono kanadayzay]
- ▶ have you ever been to Canada? **è mai stato in Canada?** [ay ma-ee stato een kanada]

Canadian canadese [kanadayzay]
- ▶ I'm Canadian **sono canadese** [sono kanadayzay]
- ▶ we're Canadians **siamo canadesi** [see-amo kanadese]

cancel annullare [annoollaray]
- ▶ is it possible to cancel a reservation? **è possibile annullare una prenotazione?** [ay posseebeelay annoollaray oona praynotatsee-onay]

canoeing la canoa [kano-a]
- ▶ I was told we could go canoeing **mi avevano detto che avremmo potuto fare canoa** [mee avayvano detto kay avremmo potooto faray kano-a]

car *(automobile)* l'auto *f* [owto], la macchina [makkeena]; *(on train)* la carrozza [carrotsa]
- ▶ I'd like to rent a car for a week **vorrei noleggiare un'auto per una settimana** [vorray-ee nolejaray oonowto per oona setteemana]
- ▶ I've just crashed my car **ho appena avuto un incidente con la mia auto** [o appayna avooto oon eencheedentay kon la mee-a owto]

renting a car

- ▶ with comprehensive insurance **con polizza kasko** [kon poleetsa kasko]
- ▶ can I leave the car at the airport? **posso lasciare la macchina all'aeroporto?** [posso lasharay la makkeena alla-ayroporto]
- ▶ here's my driver's license **ecco la mia patente di guida** [ekko la mee-a patentay dee gweeda]

▶ can you help us to push the car? **ci potete aiutare a spingere la macchina?** [chee potaytay a-yootaray a speenjayray la makkeena]

▶ my car's been towed away **mi hanno rimosso la macchina** [mee anno reemosso la makkeena]

▶ my car's broken down **la mia auto è in panne** [la mee-a owto ay een pannay]

carafe la caraffa [karaffa]

▶ a large carafe of water, please **una grande caraffa d'acqua, per favore** [oona granday karaffa dakkwa per favoray]

▶ a carafe of house wine **una caraffa del vino della casa** [oona karaffa del veeno della kaza]

car crash l'incidente *m* automobilistico [eencheedentay owtomobeeleesteeko]

▶ he's been killed in a car crash **è morto in un incidente automobilistico** [ay morto een oon eencheedentay owtomobeeleesteeko]

card *(credit card)* la carta di credito [karta dee kraydeeto]; *(greeting card)* il biglietto d'auguri [beelyetto dowgooree]; *(business card)* il biglietto da visita [beelyetto da veezeeta]

▶ the waiter hasn't brought my card back **il cameriere non mi ha riportato la carta di credito** [eel kamayree-ayray non mee a reeportato la karta dee kraydeeto]

▶ I need to get a card for my parents for their anniversary **devo comprare un biglietto d'auguri per i miei genitori per il loro anniversario** [dayvo kompraray oon beelyetto dowgooree per ee mee-ay-ee jayneetoree per eel loro anneeversaree-o]

▶ can I give you my card? **posso darle il mio biglietto da visita?** [posso darlay eel mee-o beelyetto da veezeeta?]

cardigan il golf [golf]

▶ should I take a cardigan for the evening? **devo prendere un golf per la sera?** [dayvo prendayray oon golf per la sayra]

carpet *(rug)* il tappeto [tappayto]; *(fitted)* la moquette [moket]

▶ the carpet hasn't been vacuumed **non è stato passato l'aspirapolvere sulla moquette** [non ay stato passato laspeerapolvayray soolla moket]

car rental il noleggio auto [nolejo owto]

▶ is car rental expensive? **costa molto noleggiare una macchina?** [kosta molto nolejaray oona makkeena]

car rental agency l'autonoleggio *m* [owtonolejo]

▶ do you know of any car rental agencies? **conosce qualche autonoleggio?** [konoshay kwalkay owtonolejo]

carry *(baggage)* portare [portaray] ◆ *(sound)* sentirsi [senteersee]

▶ could you help me to carry something? **mi può aiutare a portare qualcosa?** [mee poo-o a-yootaray a portaray kwalkoza]

carry-on bag il bagaglio a mano [bagalyo a mano]

▶ am I only allowed one carry-on bag? **posso prendere solo un bagaglio a mano?** [posso prendayray solo oon bagalyo a mano]

cart il carrello [karrello]
- where can I get a cart? dove posso trovare un carrello? [dovay posso trovaray oon karrello]

carton *(of cigarettes)* la stecca [stekka]
- I'd like a carton of cigarettes vorrei una stecca di sigarette [vorray-ee oona stekka dee seegarettay]

case il caso [kazo] • **in case** nel caso [nel kazo]
- it's better to call, in case the restaurant is closed è meglio telefonare, nel caso il ristorante fosse chiuso [ay melyo taylayfonare nel kazo eel reestorantay fossay kee-oozo]
- just in case per ogni evenienza [per onyee ayvaynee-entsa]

cash *(notes and coins)* i contanti [kontantee] • *(check)* incassare [eenkassaray]
- I'll pay cash pago in contanti [pago een kontantee]
- I want to cash this traveler's check voglio incassare questo traveller's cheque [volyo eenkassaray questo traveller's chek]

castle il castello [kastello]
- is the castle open to the public? il castello è aperto al pubblico? [eel kastello ay aperto al poobbleeko]

catalog il catalogo [katalogo]
- do you have a catalog? avete un catalogo? [avaytay oon katalogo]

catch *(with hands)* afferrare [afferraray]; *(cold)* prendere [prendayray]; *(hear clearly)* capire [kapeeray]
- I've caught a cold ho preso il raffreddore [o prayzo eel raffreddoray]
- I'm sorry, I didn't quite catch your name mi scusi, non ho capito bene il suo nome [mee skoozee non o kapeeto baynay eel soo-o nomay]

Catholic cattolico(a) [kattoleeko(a)] • il cattolico [kattoleeko], la cattolica [kattoleeka]
- where is there a Catholic church? dove c'è una chiesa cattolica? [dovay chay oona kee-ayza kattoleeka]

CD il cd [cheedee]
- how much does this CD cost? quanto costa questo cd? [kwanto kosta kwesto cheedee]

cellphone il (telefono) cellulare [(taylayfono) chelloolaray]
- what's your cellphone number? qual è il suo numero di cellulare? [kwal ay eel soo-o noomayro dee chelloolaray]

center il centro [chentro]
- we'd like to be based near the center of the region vorremmo alloggiare vicino al centro della regione [vorremmo allojaray veecheeno al chentro della rayjonay]

chair la sedia [saydee-a]

▸ could we have another chair in our room? potremmo avere un'altra sedia nella nostra camera? [potremmo avayray oonaltra saydee-a nella nostra kamayra]

change il cambiamento [kambee-amento]; *(money)* gli spiccioli [speecholee]

• cambiare [kambee-aray]; *(baby)* cambiare il pannolino a [kambee-aray eel pannoleeno a]

▸ do you have any change? ha degli spiccioli? [a delyee speecholee]

▸ keep the change tenga pure il resto [tenga pooray eel resto]

▸ I don't have exact change non ho la moneta giusta [non o la monayta joosta]

▸ could you give me change for ten euros? mi può cambiare dieci euro? [mee poo-o kambee-aray dee-aychee ay-ooro]

▸ is it possible to change a reservation? è possibile cambiare una prenotazione? [ay posseebeelay kambee-aray oona praynotatsee-onay]

▸ I'd like to change 200 dollars into euros vorrei cambiare duecento dollari in euro [vorray-ee kambee-aray doo-aychento dollaree een ay-ooro]

▸ I'd like to change these traveler's checks vorrei cambiare questi traveller's cheque [vorray-ee kambee-aray questee traveller chek]

▸ could you change a 10 euro bill? ha da cambiare una banconota da dieci euro? [a da kambee-aray oona bankonota da dee-aychee ay-ooro]

▸ can you help me to change the tire? mi può aiutare a cambiare la gomma? [mee poo-o a-yootaray a kambee-aray la gomma]

▸ the oil needs to be changed bisogna cambiare l'olio [beezonya kambee-aray lolee-o]

changing table il fasciatoio [fashato-yo]

▸ is there a changing table? c'è un fasciatoio? [chay oon fashato-yo]

charge

▸ is there a charge for the parking lot? il parcheggio è a pagamento? [eel parkejo ay a pagamanto]

▸ is there a charge for using the facilities? bisogna pagare per utilizzare gli impianti? [beezonya pagaray per ooteeleedzaray lyee eempee-antee]

▸ is there a charge for cancellations? c'è una penale in caso di annullamento? [chay oona paynalay een kazo dee annoollamento]

▸ I'd like to speak to the person in charge vorrei parlare con il responsabile [vorray-ee parlaray kon eel responsabeelay]

charter flight il volo charter [volo charter]

▸ where do we board the charter flight to Milan? dov'è l'imbarco del volo charter per Milano? [dovay leembarko del volo charter per meelano]

cheap economico(a) [aykonomeeko(a)]

▸ I'm trying to find a cheap flight home sto cercando di trovare un volo di ritorno economico [sto cherkando dee trovaray oon volo dee reetorno aykonomeeko]

check *(for paying)* l'assegno *m* [assenyo]; *(in restaurant)* il conto [konto] ♦ *(test, verify)* controllare [kontrollaray]

▶ can I pay by check? **posso pagare con un assegno?** [posso pagaray kon oon assenyo]

▶ the check, please! **il conto, per favore!** [eel konto per favoray]

▶ can you check the oil? **può controllare l'olio?** [poo-o kontrollaray lolee-o]

checkbook il libretto degli assegni [leebretto delyee asenyee]

▶ my checkbook's been stolen **mi hanno rubato il libretto degli assegni** [mee anno roobato eel leebretto delyee asenyee]

check in *(baggage)* registrare [raygeestraray] ♦ *(at airport)* fare il check-in [fare eel chekeen]; *(at hotel)* registrarsi [raygeestrarsee]

▶ I'd like to check in both these bags, please **vorrei registrare questi due bagagli, per favore** [vorray-ee raygeestraray kwestee doo-ay bagalyee per favoray]

▶ what time do you have to be at the airport to check in? **a che ora bisogna essere all'aeroporto per il check-in?** [a kay ora beezonya essayray alla-ayroporto per eel chekeen]

check-in desk *(at airport)* il banco del check-in [banko del chekeen]

▶ where is the United Airlines check-in desk? **dov'è il banco del check-in della United Airlines?** [dovay eel banko del chekeen della yoona-eeted ayrla-eenz]

check out *(pay hotel bill)* pagare il conto [pagaray eel konto]; *(leave hotel)* lasciare la camera [lasharay la kamayra]

▶ what time do you have to check out by? **entro che ora bisogna lasciare la camera?** [entro kay ora beezonya lasharay la kamayra]

cheers salute [salootay]

▶ cheers and all the best! **salute e tanti auguri!** [salootay ay tantee owgooree]

cheese il formaggio [formajo]

▶ what are the best local cheeses? **quali sono i migliori formaggi locali?** [kwalee sono ee meelyoree formajee localee]

---

checking

▶ is it right and then left? **bisogna girare prima a destra e poi a sinistra?** [beezonya geeraray preema a destra ay po-ee a seeneestra]

▶ is this the train for Naples? **è il treno per Napoli?** [ay eel trayno per Napolee]

▶ could you tell me where to get off, please? **mi può dire dove devo scendere, per favore?** [mee poo-o deeray dovay dayvo shendayray per favoray]

▶ is this the right stop for ...? **è la fermata giusta per ...?** [ay la fermata justa per]

▶ are you sure that he'll be able to come? **è sicuro che potrà venire?** [ay seekooro kay potra vayneeray]

cheese

Italy has almost 300 different types of cheese. There are soft cheeses such as *robiola*, *caciotta*, *mozzarella*, *gorgonzola*, and *Belpaese*®. And there are hard cheeses such as *caciocavallo*, *provolone*, *grana*, or Parmesan and *pecorino* that you can grate on top of pasta or soups. If a recipe calls for melted cheese, the natural choice is *fontina*.

chicken il pollo [pollo]
▸ I'll have the roast chicken prendo il pollo arrosto [prendo eel pollo arrosto]
▸ a chicken salad un'insalata di pollo [ooneensalata dee pollo]

child il bambino [bambeeno], la bambina [bambeena]; *(son, daughter)* il figlio [feelyo], la figlia [feelya]
▸ two adults and two children, please due adulti e due bambini, per favore [doo-ay adooltee ay doo-ay bambeenee per favoray]
▸ do you have discounts for children? ci sono riduzioni per i bambini? [chee sono reedootsee-onee per ee bambeenee]
▸ do you have children? ha figli? [a feelyee]

children's menu il menu per bambini [maynoo per bambeenee]
▸ do you have a children's menu? c'è un menu per bambini? [chay oon maynoo per bambeenee]

chilled *(wine)* fresco(a) [fresko(a)]
▸ this wine isn't chilled enough questo vino non è abbastanza fresco [kwesto veeno non ay abbastantsa fresko]

chocolate il cioccolato [chokkolato]; *(hot drink)* la cioccolata [chokkolata]
▸ I'd like a bar of chocolate vorrei una barretta di cioccolato [vorray-ee oona barretta dee chokkolato]

choose scegliere [shelyayray]
▸ I don't know which one to choose non so quale scegliere [non so kwalay shelyayray]

christmas il Natale [natalay]
▸ Merry Christmas! buon Natale! [boo-on natalay]
▸ I wish you a very merry Christmas le faccio tanti auguri di buon Natale [lay facho tantee owgooree dee boo-on natalay]

christmas Day il giorno di Natale [jorno dee natalay]
▸ are you closed on Christmas Day? siete chiusi il giorno di Natale? [see-aytay kee-oozee eel jorno dee natalay]

church la chiesa [kee-ayza]
▸ how old is the church? a quando risale la chiesa? [a kwando reesalay la kee-ayza]
▸ where can we find a Protestant church? dove possiamo trovare una chiesa

protestante? [dovay possee-amo trovaray oona kee-ayza protestantay]
- where is there a Catholic church? dov'è una chiesa cattolica? [dovay oona kee-ayza kattoleeka]

cigarette la sigaretta [seegaretta]
- can I ask you for a cigarette? posso chiederle una sigaretta? [posso kee-aydayrlay oona seegaretta]
- where can I buy cigarettes? dove posso comprare delle sigarette? [dovay possay kompraray dellay seegarettay]

cigarette lighter l'accendino m [achendeeno]
- do you have a cigarette lighter? ha un accendino? [a oon achendeeno]

city la città [cheetta]
- what's the nearest big city? qual è la città grande più vicina? [kwal ay la cheetta granday pyoo veecheena]

class (on train, plane) la classe [klassay]
- which class are your seats in? in quale classe siete? [een kwalay klassay see-aytay]

clean pulito(a) [pooleeto(a)] ◆ pulire [pooleeray]
- the sheets aren't clean le lenzuola non sono pulite [lay lentsoo-ola non sono pooleetay]
- do we have to clean the apartment before leaving? dobbiamo pulire l'appartamento prima di partire? [dobbee-amo pooleeray lappartamento preema dee parteeray]
- could you clean the windshield? mi potrebbe pulire il parabrezza? [mee potrebbay pooleeray eel parabredza]

cleaning le pulizie [pooleetsee-ay]
- who does the cleaning? chi fa le pulizie? [kee fa lay pooleetsee-ay]

clear (easily understood) chiaro(a) [kee-aro(a)]; (way) libero(a) [leebayro(a)] ◆ (road, path) sgombrare [zgombraray]
- is that clear? è chiaro? [ay kee-aro]
- is the road clear? è libera la strada? [ay leebayra la strada]
- when will the road be cleared? quando verrà sgombrata la strada? [kwando verra zgombrata la strada]

climb (mountaineer) arrampicarsi [arrampeekarsee]; (plane, road) salire [saleeray]
- the road climbs steadily after you leave the village la strada sale progressivamente una volta usciti dal paese [la strada salay progresseevamentay oona volta oosheetay dal pa-ayzay]

climbing l'alpinismo m [alpeeneezmo]
- can you go climbing here? si può fare alpinismo qui? [see poo-o fare alpeeneezmo kwee]

cloakroom (in museum, theater) il guardaroba [gwardaroba]
- is there a charge for the cloakroom? si paga per il guardaroba? [see paga per eel gwardaroba]

coffee

No one needs to be reminded just how good Italian coffee is. Throughout Italy, if you order a *caffè*, you'll be served a strong black coffee. If you want there to be a bit more of it, add the word *lungo*. For coffee with milk, say *con latte* or *macchiato* (with a dash of milk). Or you can have coffee with a splash of alcohol, *corretto*. A real *cappuccino* is topped with frothy milk (not cream) and sometimes sprinkled with chocolate.

▸ I'd like to leave my things in the cloakroom vorrei lasciare le mie cose nel guardaroba [vorray-ee lasharay lay mee-ay kozay nel gwardaroba]

close chiudere [kee-oodayray] ♦ chiudersi [kee-oodayrsee]
▸ what time do the stores close? a che ora chiudono i negozi? [a kay ora kee-oodono ee negotsee]
▸ what time do you close? a che ora chiudete? [a kay ora kee-oodaytay]
▸ the door won't close la porta non si chiude [la porta non see kee-ooday]

closed chiuso(a) [kee-oozo(a)]
▸ are the stores closed on Sundays? i negozi sono chiusi di domenica? [ee negotsee sono kee-oozee dee domayneeka]

clothes i vestiti [vesteetee]
▸ where can we wash our clothes? dove possiamo lavare i vestiti? [dovay possee-amo lavaray ee vesteetee]

club *(nightclub)* la discoteca [deeskotayka]
▸ we could go to a club afterwards potremmo andare in discoteca dopo [potremmo andaray een deeskotayka dopo]

coach la classe turistica [klassay tooreesteeka]
▸ we'd like to fly coach vorremmo viaggiare in classe turistica [vorremmo vee-ajaray een klassay tooreesteeka]

coast la costa [kosta]
▸ an island off the coast of Tuscany un'isola vicino alla costa della Toscana [ooneezola veecheeno alla kosta della toskana]

coffee *(drink, beans)* il caffè [kaffay]
▸ I'd like a coffee vorrei un caffè [vorray-ee oon kaffay]
▸ would you like some coffee? gradisce un caffè? [gradeeshay oon kaffay]
▸ coffee with milk or cream caffè con latte o panna [kaffay kon lattay o panna]
▸ black coffee caffè (senza latte) [kaffay (sentsa lattay)]

coin la moneta [monayta]
▸ the machine only takes coins la macchina funziona solo con le monete [la makkeena fontsee-ona solo kon lay monaytay]

cold freddo(a) [freddo(a)] ◆ *(illness)* il raffreddore [raffreddoray]; *(low temperature)* il freddo [freddo]

▸ it's cold today **oggi fa freddo** [ojee fa freddo]
▸ I'm very cold **ho molto freddo** [o molto freddo]
▸ the soup's cold: can you heat it up? **la minestra è fredda: la può riscaldare?** [la meenestra ay fredda la poo-o reeskaldaray]
▸ to have a cold **avere il raffreddore** [avayray eel raffreddoray]
▸ I've caught a cold **ho preso il raffreddore** [o preso eel raffreddoray]

collect con chiamata a carico del destinatario [kon kee-amata a kareeko del desteenataree-o]

▸ I have to call my parents collect **devo telefonare ai miei genitori con chiamata a carico del destinatario** [dayvo taylayfonaray a-ee mee-ay-ee jayneetoree kon kee-amata a kareeko del desteenataree-o]

collect call la chiamata a carico del destinatario [kee-amata a kareeko del desteenataree-o]

▸ to make a collect call **fare una chiamata a carico del destinatario** [fare oona kee-amata a kareeko del desteenataree-o]

color il colore [koloray]

▸ do you have it in another color? **ce l'avete in un altro colore?** [chay lavaytay een oon altro koloray]

color film il rullino a colori [roolleeno a koloray]

▸ I'd like a roll of color film **vorrei un rullino a colori** [vorray-ee oon roolleeno a koloray]

come *(move here)* venire [vayneeray]; *(arrive)* arrivare [arreevaray]; *(pass by)* passare [passaray]

▸ come here! **vieni qui!** [vee-aynee kwee]
▸ coming! **arrivo!** [arreevo]
▸ when does the bus come? **quando passa l'autobus?** [kwando passa lowtoboos]

come from venire da [vayneeray da]

▸ where do you come from? **da dove viene?** [da dovay vee-aynay]

come in *(enter)* entrare [entraray]; *(train)* arrivare [arreevaray]; *(tide)* salire [saleeray]

▸ may I come in? **posso entrare?** [posso entraray]
▸ come in! **si accomodi!** [see akkomodee]
▸ what time does the Rome train come in? **a che ora arriva il treno da Roma?** [a kay ora arreeva eel trayno da roma]
▸ the tide's coming in **sta salendo la marea** [sta salendo la maray-a]

come on *(light, heating)* accendersi [achendersee]

▸ the heating hasn't come on **il riscaldamento non si è acceso** [eel reeskaldamento non see ay achayzo]
▸ come on! **su!** [soo]

come with *(go with)* accompagnare [akkompanyaray]; *(be served with)* essere servito con [essayray serveeto kon]

▸ could you come with me to the station? mi accompagnerebbe alla stazione? [mee akkompanyayrebbay alla statsee-onay]

▸ what does it come with? con che cosa è servito? [kon kay koza ay serveeto]

comfortable *(person)* comodo(a) [komodo(a)]

▸ make yourself comfortable si metta comodo [see metta komodo]

▸ we're very comfortable here stiamo molto bene qui [stee-amo molto baynay kwee]

commission la commissione [kommeessee-onay]

▸ what commission do you charge? quanto prendete di commissione? [kwanto prendaytay dee kommeessee-onay]

company *(firm)* l'azienda *f* [atsee-enda]

▸ is it a big company? è una grande azienda? [ay oona granday atsee-enda]

compartment lo scompartimento [skomparteemento]

▸ which compartment are our seats in? in quale scompartimento siamo? [een kwalay skomparteemento see-amo]

complain reclamare [rayklamaray]

▸ I will be writing to your head office to complain scriverò alla vostra sede centrale per reclamare [skreevayro alla vostra sayday per rayklamaray]

complaint il reclamo [rayklamo]

▸ I'd like to make a complaint vorrei fare un reclamo [vorray-ee faray oon rayklamo]

complete *(form)* compilare [kompeelaray]

▸ here's the completed form ecco il modulo compilato [ekko eel modoolo kompeelato]

---

complaints

▸ I'd like to see the manager, please vorrei vedere il direttore, per favore [vorray-ee vaydayray eel deerettoray per favoray]

▸ I have a complaint ho un reclamo [o oon rayklamo]

▸ there's a problem with the heating c'è un problema con il riscaldamento [chay oon problayma kon eel reeskaldamento]

▸ I am counting on you to sort this problem out conto su di lei per risolvere questo problema [konto soo dee lay-ee per reesolvayray kwesto problayma]

▸ I expect the cost of the camera to be fully reimbursed mi sembra giusto che il costo della macchina fotografica mi venga interamente rimborsato [mee sembra joosto kay eel kosto della makkeena fotografeeka mee venga eentayramentay reemborsato]

comprehensive insurance la polizza kasko [poleetsa kasko]
- how much extra is the comprehensive insurance coverage? quanto costa in più la polizza kasko? [kwanto kosta een pyoo la poleetsa kasko]

computer il computer [kompyooter]
- is there a computer I can use? c'è un computer che posso utilizzare? [chay oon kompyooter kay posso ooteeleedzaray]

concert il concerto [koncherto]
- did you like the concert? le è piaciuto il concerto? [lay ay pee-achooto eel koncherto]

condom il preservativo [prayzervateevo]
- do you have any condoms? avete dei preservativi? [avaytay day-ee prayzervateevee]

confirm confermare [konfermaray]
- I confirmed my reservation by phone ho confermato la mia prenotazione per telefono [o konfermato la mee-a praynotatsee-onay per taylayfono]
- I'd like to confirm my return flight vorrei confermare il volo di ritorno [vorray-ee konfermaray eel volo dee reetorno]

congratulations complimenti [kompleementee]
- congratulations! complimenti! [kompleementee]

connecting flight la coincidenza [co-eencheedentsa]
- does the connecting flight leave from the same terminal? la coincidenza parte dallo stesso terminale? [la co-eencheedentsa partay dallo stesso termeenalay]

connection (on phone) la linea [leenay-a]; (transportation) la coincidenza [co-eencheedentsa]
- the connection is very bad: I can't hear very well la linea è molto disturbata: non sento bene [la leenay-a ay molto deestoorbata non sento baynay]
- I've missed my connection ho perso la coincidenza [o perso la co-eencheedentsa]

consulate il consolato [konsolato]
- where is the American consulate? dov'è il consolato americano? [dovay eel konsolato amayreekano]

contact (communication) il contatto [kontatto] ◆ contattare [kontattaray]
- I need to contact my family in the States devo contattare la mia famiglia negli Stati Uniti [dayvo kontattaray la mee-a fameelya nelyee statee ooneetee]
- do you know how to get in contact with him? sa come mettersi in contatto con lui? [sa komay mettersee een kontatto kon loo-ee]

contact lens la lente a contatto [lentay a kontatto]
- I've lost a contact lens ho perso una lente a contatto [ho perso oona lentay a kontatto]

cookie (food) il biscotto [beeskotto]
- a box of cookies, please una scatola di biscotti, per favore [oona skatola dee beeskottee per favoray]

cooking la cucina [koocheena]

> I love Italian cooking adoro la cucina italiana [adoro la koocheena eetalee-ana]

> we prefer to do our own cooking preferiamo prepararci noi da mangiare [prayfayree-amo praypararchee no-ee da manjaray]

cork *(for bottle)* il tappo [tappo]

> where's the cork for the bottle? dov'è il tappo della bottiglia? [dovay eel tappo della botteelya]

corked

> this wine is corked questo vino sa di tappo [kwesto veeno sa dee tappo]

corner l'angolo *m* [angolo]

> stop at the corner si fermi all'angolo [see fermee allangolo]

coronary l'infarto *m* (cardiaco) [eenfarto (kardee-ako)]

> he's had a coronary ha avuto un infarto [a avooto oon eenfarto]

correct *(check)* esatto(a) [ayzatto(a)]

> that's correct è esatto [ay ayzatto]

cost costare [kostaray]

> how much will it cost to go to the airport? quanto verrà a costare andare all'aeroporto? [kwanto verra a kostaray andaray alla-ayroporto]

> it cost us 150 euros ci è costato centocinquanta euro [chee ay kostato chentocheenkwanta ay-ooro]

cot il letto pieghevole [letto pee-aygayvolay]

> can you put a cot in the room for us? può mettere nella nostra camera un letto pieghevole? [poo-o mettayray nella nostra kamayra oon letto pee-aygayvolay?]

cough la tosse [tossay] ♦ tossire [tosseeray]

> I've got a cough ho la tosse [o la tossay]

> I need something for a cough mi serve qualcosa per la tosse [mee servay kwalkoza per la tossay]

could

> she couldn't come non poteva venire [non potayva vayneeray]

> could you help me? mi potrebbe aiutare? [mee potrebbay a-yootaray]

count contare [kontaray]

> that doesn't count questo non conta [kwesto non konta]

counter *(in store)* il banco [banko]; *(in bank)* lo sportello [sportello]

> which counter do I have to go to? a quale sportello devo andare? [a kwalay sportello dayvo andaray]

> do you sell this medication over the counter? vendete questa medicina senza ricetta medica? [vendaytay kwesta maydeecheena sentsa reechetta maydeeka]

country il paese [pa-ayzay]

> what country do you come from? da che paese viene? [da kay pa-ayzay vee-aynay]

couple la coppia [koppee-a]
- ▸ it's for a couple and two children è per una coppia con due bambini [ay per oona koppee-a kon doo-ay bambeenee]
- ▸ a couple of friends un paio di amici [oon pa-yo dee ameechee]

course *(of meal)* la portata [portata]; *(of ship, plane)* la rotta [rotta]; *(for race)* il percorso [perkorso]; *(in yoga, sailing)* il corso [korso]
- ▸ is the set meal three courses? il menu a prezzo fisso comprende tre portate? [eel maynoo a pretso feesso komprenday tray portatay]
- ▸ how much does the sailing course cost? quanto costa il corso di vela? [kwanto kosta eel korso dee vayla]
- ▸ of course! certo! [cherto]
- ▸ of course not! certo che no! [cherto kay no]
- ▸ of course he'll come certo che verrà [cherto kay verra]

cream *(for skin)* la crema [krayma]
- ▸ I need some cream for my sunburn mi serve una crema per una scottatura da sole [mee servay oona krayma per oona skottatoora del solay]

credit card la carta di credito [karta dee kraydeeto]
- ▸ do you take credit cards? prendete le carte di credito? [prendaytay lay kartay dee kraydeeto]

cross *(street, river)* attraversare [attraversaray]; *(border)* passare [passaray]
+ *(roads, streets)* incrociarsi [eenkrocharsee]
- ▸ how do we cross this street? come si fa ad attraversare questa strada? [komay see fa ad attraversaray kwesta strada]

cross-country skiing lo sci di fondo [shee dee fondo]
- ▸ where can I go cross-country skiing around here? dove posso fare sci di fondo in questa zona? [dovay posso faray shee dee fondo een kwesta dzona]

crosswalk il passaggio pedonale [passajo paydonalay]
- ▸ I always cross at the crosswalk attraverso sempre sul passaggio pedonale [attraverso sempray sool passajo paydonalay]

cruise la crociera [krochayra]
- ▸ how much does a Mediterranean cruise cost? quanto costa una crociera sul Mediterraneo? [kwanto kosta oona krochayra sool maydeeterranay-o]

cry piangere [pee-anjayray]
- ▸ don't cry non piangere [non pee-anjayray]

cup la tazza [tatsa]
- ▸ I'd like a cup of tea vorrei una tazza di tè [vorray-ee oona tatsa dee tay]
- ▸ a coffee cup una tazza da caffè [oona tatsa da kaffay]
- ▸ could we have an extra cup? potremmo avere una tazza in più? [potremmo avayray oona tatsa een pyoo]

currency *(money)* la valuta [valoota]
- how much local currency do you have? quanto avete in valuta locale? [kwanto avaytay een valoota lokalay]

cut tagliare [talyaray]
- I cut my finger mi sono tagliato un dito [mee sono talyato oon deeto]

d

daily giornaliero(a) [jornalee-ayro(a)] ◆ *(newspaper)* il quotidiano [kwoteedee-ano]
- there are daily flights to New York i voli per New York hanno frequenza giornaliera [ee volee per nyoo york anno fraykwentsa jornalee-ayra]
- what's the name of the local daily newspaper? come si chiama il quotidiano locale? [komay see kee-ama eel kwoteedee-ano lokalay]

damage danneggiare [dannejaray]
- my suitcase was damaged in transit la mia valigia è stata danneggiata nel trasporto [la mee-a valeeja ay stata dannejata nel trasporto]

damp umido(a) [oomeedo(a)]
- it's damp today oggi è umido [ojee ay oomeedo]

dance ballare [ballaray]
- shall we dance? balliamo? [ballee-amo]
- I can't dance non so ballare [non so ballaray]

dancing il ballo [ballo]
- will there be dancing? si potrà anche ballare? [see potra ankay ballaray]
- where can we go dancing? dove si può andare a ballare? [dovay see poo-o andaray a ballaray]

dandruff la forfora [forfora]
- I have bad dandruff ho molta forfora [o molta forfora]

danger il pericolo [payreekolo]
- hurry! someone's in danger! presto! c'è qualcuno in pericolo! [presto chay kwalkoono een payreekolo]

dangerous pericoloso(a) [payreekolozo(a)]
- this stretch of the river is quite dangerous questo tratto di fiume è piuttosto pericoloso [kwesto tratto dee fee-oomay ay pyoottosto payreekolozo]

dark *(room, night)* buio(a) [boo-yo(a)]; *(hair)* scuro(a) [skooro(a)]
- it's dark è buio [ay boo-yo]
- she has dark hair ha i capelli scuri [a ee kapellee skooree]

dark chocolate il cioccolato fondente [chokkolato fondentay]
  ▸ I prefer dark chocolate preferisco il cioccolato fondente [prayfayreesko eel chokkolato fondentay]

date *(in time)* la data [data]; *(appointment)* l'appuntamento *m* [appoontamento]
  ▸ I've got a date tonight stasera ho un appuntamento [stasayra o oon appoontamento]

date-stamp timbrare (con ora e data) [teembraray (kon ora ay data)]
  ▸ do I have to date-stamp this ticket? devo timbrare questo biglietto? [dayvo teembraray kwesto beelyetto]

daughter la figlia [feelya]
  ▸ this is my daughter questa è mia figlia [kwesta ay mee-a feelya]

day il giorno [jorno]; *(expressing duration)* la giornata [jornata]
  ▸ what day is it? che giorno è? [kay jomo ay]
  ▸ I arrived three days ago sono arrivato tre giorni fa [sono arreevato tray jornee fa]
  ▸ I'd like to do a round trip in a day vorrei fare l'andata e ritorno in giornata [vorray-ee faray landata ay reetorno een jornata]
  ▸ how much is it per day? quanto costa al giorno? [kwanto kosta al jorno]

dead morto(a) [morto(a)]
  ▸ he was pronounced dead at the scene hanno constatato la sua morte sul luogo dell'incidente [anno konstatato la soo-a mortay sool loo-ogo deleencheedentay]
  ▸ the battery's dead la batteria è scarica [la battayree-a ay skareeka]

dead end il vicolo cieco [veekolo chayko]
  ▸ it's a dead end è un vicolo cieco [ay oon veekolo chayko]

deal *(business agreement)* l'affare *m* [affaray]
  ▸ I got a good deal on the room ho fatto un buon affare con la camera [o fatto oon boo-on affaray kon la kamayra]

death *(state)* la morte [mortay]; *(person)* la vittima [veetteema]
  ▸ there were two deaths ci sono state due vittime [chee sono statay doo-ay veetteemay]

decaf, decaffeinated il decaffeinato [daykafay-eenato] ◆ decaffeinato(a) [daykafay-eenato(a)]
  ▸ a decaf/decaffeinated coffee, please un caffè decaffeinato, per favore [oon kaffay daykafay-eenato per favoray]

December il dicembre [deechembray]
  ▸ December 10th il dieci dicembre [eel dee-aychee deechembray]

decide decidere [daycheedayray]
  ▸ we haven't decided yet non abbiamo ancora deciso [non abbee-amo ankora daycheezo]

deck *(of ship)* il ponte [pontay]; *(of cards)* il mazzo [matso]
  ▸ how do I get to the upper deck? come si sale in coperta? [komay see salay een koperta]

deckchair la sdraio [zdra-yo]
- I'd like to rent a deckchair vorrei noleggiare una sdraio [vorray-ee nolejaray oona zdra-yo]

declare dichiarare [deekee-araray]
- I have nothing to declare non ho niente da dichiarare [non o nee-entay da deekee-araray]
- I have a bottle of spirits to declare ho un superalcolico da dichiarare [o oon sooperalkoleeko da deekee-araray]

definitely sicuramente [seekooramentay]
- we'll definitely come back here torneremo sicuramente qui [tornayraymo seekooramentay kwee]

degree il grado [grado]
- it's 5 degrees below freezing ci sono cinque gradi sotto zero [chee sono cheenkway gradee sotto dzayro]

delay il ritardo [reetardo]
- is there a delay for this flight? c'è un ritardo su questo volo? [chay oon reetardo soo kwesto volo]

delayed in ritardo [een reetardo]
- how long will the flight be delayed? di quanto sarà in ritardo il volo? [dee kwanto sara een reetardo eel volo]

delighted molto contento(a) [molto kontento(a)]
- we're delighted you could make it siamo molto contenti che lei sia potuto venire [see-amo molto kontentee kay lay-ee see-a potooto vayneeray]

dentist il/la dentista [denteesta]
- I need to see a dentist urgently ho bisogno urgente di un dentista [o beezonyo oorjentay dee oon denteesta]

department *(in store)* il reparto [rayparto]
- I'm looking for the menswear department sto cercando il reparto di abbigliamento da uomo [sto cherkando eel rayparto dee abbeelyamento da oo-omo]

department store il grande magazzino [granday magadzeeno]
- where are the department stores? dove sono i grandi magazzini? [dovay sono ee grandee magadzeenee]

departure la partenza [partentsa]
- which way is departures? *(in airport)* da che parte sono le partenze? [da kay partay sono lay partentsay]

departure lounge la sala partenze [sala partentsay]
- where's the departure lounge? dov'è la sala partenze? [dovay la sala partentsay]

deposit *(against loss or damage)* la cauzione [kowtsee-onay]; *(down payment)* l'anticipo *m* [anteecheepo]
- is there a deposit to pay on the equipment? bisogna pagare una cauzione per

l'attrezzatura? [beezonya pagaray oona kowtsee-onay per lattretsattoora]

▶ how much is the deposit? quant'è la cauzione? [kwantay la kowtsee-onay]

▶ do you have to pay a deposit? bisogna versare un anticipo? [beezonya versaray oon anteecheepo]

desk *(in office, home)* la scrivania [skreevanee-a]; *(at hotel)* la reception [raysepshon]; *(for cashier)* la cassa [kassa]; *(at airport)* il banco [banko]

▶ where can I find the American Airlines desk ? dove posso trovare il banco dell'American Airlines? [dovay posso trovaray eel banko dellamayreekan ayrla-eenz]

dessert il dolce [dolchay], il dessert [daysser]

▶ what desserts do you have? cosa avete come dolce? [koza avaytay komay dolchay]

dessert wine il vino da dessert [veeno da daysser]

▶ can you recommend a good dessert wine? ci può consigliare un buon vino da dessert? [chee poo-o konseelyaray oon boo-on veeno da daysser]

detour la deviazione [dayvee-atsee-onay]

▶ is there a detour ahead? c'è una deviazione più avanti? [chay oona dayvee-atsee-onay pyoo avantee]

develop sviluppare [zveeloopparay]

▶ how much does it cost to develop a roll of 36 photos? quanto costa sviluppare un rullino da trentasei pose? [kwanto kosta zveeloopparay oon roolleeno da trentasay-ee pozay]

diabetic diabetico(a) [dee-abayteeko(a)] ♦ il diabetico [dee-abayteeko], la diabetica [dee-abayteeka]

▶ I'm diabetic and I need a prescription for insulin sono diabetico e ho bisogno di una ricetta medica per l'insulina [sono dee-abayteeko e o beezonyo dee oona reechetta maydeeka per leensooleena]

diarrhea la diarrea [dee-array-a]

▶ I'd like something for diarrhea vorrei qualcosa per la diarrea [vorray-ee kwalkoza per la dee-array-a]

difference *(in price, cost)* la differenza [deeffayrentsa]

▶ will you pay the difference? paga la differenza? [paga la deeffayrentsa]

difficult difficile [deeffeecheelay]

▶ I find some sounds difficult to pronounce trovo che alcuni suoni siano difficili da pronunciare [trovo kay alkoonee soo-onee see-ano deeffeecheelee da pronooncharay]

difficulty la difficoltà [deeffeekolta]

▶ I'm having difficulty finding the place ho qualche difficoltà a trovare il posto [o kwalkay deeffeekolta a trovaray eel posto]

digital camera la macchina fotografica digitale [makkeena fotografeeka deejeetalay]

▶ my digital camera's been stolen mi hanno rubato la macchina fotografica digitale [mee anno roobato la makkeena fotografeeka deejeetalay]

dining room la sala ristorante [sala reestorantay]

> do you have to have breakfast in the dining room? bisogna far colazione nella sala ristorante? [beezonya far kolatsee-onay nella sala reestorantay]

dinner la cena [chayna]

> up to what time do they serve dinner? fino a che ora servono la cena? [feeno a kay ora servono la chayna]

direct diretto(a) [deeretto(a)]

> is that train direct? questo treno è diretto? [kwesto trayno ay deeretto]

direction *(heading)* la direzione [deeretsee-onay]

> am I going in the right direction for the train station? sto andando nella direzione giusta per la stazione (ferroviaria)? [sto andando nella deeretsee-onay joosta per la statsee-onay ferrovee-aree-a]

directory assistance il servizio ricerca elenco abbonati [serveetsee-o reecherka aylenko abbonatee]

> what's the number for directory assistance? qual è il numero del servizio ricerca elenco abbonati? [kwal ay eel noomayro del serveetsee-o reecherka aylenko abbonatee]

dirty *(room, tablecloth)* sporco(a) [sporko(a)]

> the sheets are dirty le lenzuola sono sporche [lay lentsoo-ola sono sporkay]

disability l'invalidità *f* [eenvaleedeeta]

> do you have facilities for people with disabilities? il posto è attrezzato per i disabili? [eel posto ay attretsato per ee deezabeelee]
> people with disabilities i disabili [ee deezabeelee]

disabled *(person)* disabile [deezabeelay]; *(parking)* per (i) disabili [per (ee) deezabeelee]

> where's the nearest disabled parking spot? dov'è il posteggio più vicino per i disabili? [dovay eel postejo pyoo veecheeno per ee deezabeelee]

disco *(club)* la discoteca [deeskotayka]

> are there any discos around here? ci sono delle discoteche qui vicino? [chee sono dellay deeskotaykay kwee veecheeno]

discount lo sconto [skonto]

> is there any chance of a discount? è possibile avere uno sconto? [ay posseebeelay avayray oono skonto]

dish il piatto [pee-atto]

> what's the dish of the day? qual è il piatto del giorno? [kwal ay eel pee-atto del jorno]
> can I help you with the dishes? posso aiutarla a lavare i piatti? [posso a-yootarla a lavaray ee pee-attee]

disposable usa e getta [ooza ay jetta]

> I need some disposable razors mi servono dei rasoi usa e getta [mee servono day-ee razo-ee ooza ay jetta]

▸ do you sell disposable cameras? vendete macchine fotografiche usa e getta? [vendaytay makkeenay fotografeekay ooza ay jetta]

distance la distanza [deestantsa]

▸ the hotel is only a short distance from here l'albergo è a poca distanza da qui [lalbergo ay a poka deestantsa da kwee]

district *(of town)* il quartiere [kwartee-ayree]

▸ which district do you live in? in quale quartiere abita? [een kwalay kwartee-ayree abeeta]

dive tuffarsi [tooffarsee] ♦ *(into water)* il tuffo [tooffo]; *(scuba)* l'immersione *f* [eemersee-onay]

▸ are you not allowed to dive in this pool? è vietato tuffarsi in questa piscina? [ay vee-aytato tooffarsee een kwesta peesheena]

▸ can we do a night dive? possiamo fare un'immersione notturna? [possee-amo faray ooneemersee-onay nottoorna]

diving *(scuba diving)* l'immersione *f* [eemersee-onay]

▸ I'd like to take diving lessons vorrei prendere lezioni di immersione [vorray-ee prendayray letsee-onee dee eemersee-onay]

▸ what's the diving like around here? si possono fare delle belle immersioni da queste parti? [see possono faray dellay bellay eemersee-onee da kwestay partee]

▸ do you rent out diving equipment? noleggiate attrezzatura da sub? [nolejatay attretsatoora da soob]

diving board il trampolino [trampoleeno]

▸ is there a diving board? c'è un trampolino? [ay oon trampoleeno]

dizzy spell il giramento di testa [jeeramento dee testa]

▸ I've been having dizzy spells ho avuto dei giramenti di testa [o avooto day-ee jeeramentee dee testa]

do fare [faray]

▸ what do you do for a living? che lavoro fa? [kay lavoro fa]

▸ is there anything I can do (to help)? posso fare qualcosa (per aiutare)? [posso faray kwalkoza (per a-yootaray)]

▸ what are you doing tonight? cosa fai stasera? [koza fa-ee stasayra]

▸ what is there to do here on Sundays? cosa c'è da fare qui di domenica? [koza chay da faray kwee dee domayneeka]

doctor il medico [maydeeko]

▸ I have to see a doctor devo andare da un medico [dayvo andaray da oon maydeeko]

dollar il dollaro [dollaro]

▸ I'd like to change some dollars into euros vorrei cambiare dei dollari in euro [vorray-ee kambee-aray day-ee dollaree een ay-ooro]

door la porta [porta]

▸ do you want me to answer the door? vuole che vada io ad aprire la porta? [voo-olay kay vada ee-o ad apreeray la porta]

having a drink

In Italy, what we call 'cafés' are called *bar* and what we call 'bars' are *osterie*, *birrerie* or *American bar*. If you want to try some of the excellent Italian wines, ask where the town's *enoteche* (wine bars) are. If you're planning a late night out, you can go to a nightclub (*discoteca*).

dormitory *(in youth hostel)* il dormitorio [dormeetoree-o]; *(for students)* il pensionato [pensee-onato]

▸ are you staying in the dormitory? alloggi nel pensionato? [allojee nel pensee-onato]

double doppio(a) [doppee-o(a)] ♦ il doppio [eel doppee-o] ♦ raddoppiare [raddoppee-aray]

▸ it's spelled with a double l si scrive con due elle [see skreevay kon doo-ay ellay]
▸ prices have doubled since last year i prezzi sono raddoppiati rispetto all'anno scorso [ee pretsee sono raddoppee-atee reespetto allanno skorso]

double bed il letto matrimoniale [letto matreemonee-alay]

▸ does the room have a double bed? c'è un letto matrimoniale nella camera? [chay oon letto matreemonee-alay nella kamayra]

double room la camera doppia [kamayra doppee-a]

▸ I'd like a double room for 5 nights, please vorrei una camera doppia per cinque notti, per favore [vorray-ee oona kamayra doppee-a per cheenkway nottee per favoray]

downtown il centro [chentro] ♦ in centro [een chentro]

▸ we're looking for a good downtown hotel cerchiamo un buon albergo in centro [cherkee-amo oon bo-on albergo een chentro]
▸ does this bus go downtown? questo autobus va in centro? [kwesto owtoboos va een chentro]

draft beer la birra alla spina [beerra alla speena]

▸ a draft beer, please una birra alla spina, per favore [oona beerra alla speena per favoray]

dream il sogno [sonyo] ♦ sognare [sonyaray]

▸ to have a dream fare un sogno [faray oon sonyo]
▸ I dreamed (that)... ho sognato che ... [o sonyato kay]

drink la bevanda [bayvanda] ♦ bere [bayray]

▸ what kind of hot drinks do you have? cosa avete come bevande calde? [koza avaytay komay bayvanday kalday]
▸ I'll have a cold drink prendo qualcosa di fresco [prendo kwalkoza dee fresko]
▸ I could do with a drink mi andrebbe qualcosa da bere [mee andrebbay kwalkoza da bayray]

‣ shall we go for a drink? andiamo a bere qualcosa? [andee-amo a bayray kwalkoza]

‣ can I buy you a drink? posso offrirle da bere? [posso offreerlay da bayray]

drinking water l'acqua potabile *f* [akkwa potabeelay]

‣ is it drinking water? è potabile l'acqua? [ay potabeelay lakkwa]

drive *(in vehicle)* il giro (in macchina) [jeero (een makkeena)] ◆ *(vehicle)* guidare [gweederay]

‣ is it a long drive? ci vuole molto (in macchina)? [chee voo-olay molto (een makkeena)]

‣ could you drive me home? mi potrebbe dare un passaggio fino a casa? [mee potrebbay daray oon passajo feeno a kasa]

‣ she was driving too close guidava a distanza troppo ravvicinata [gweedava a deestantsa troppo ravveecheenata]

driver *(of car)* il guidatore [gweedatoray], la guidatrice [gweedatreechay]; *(of bus)* il/la conducente [kondoochentay]; *(of taxi)* il/la tassista [tasseesta]

‣ the other driver wasn't looking where he was going l'altro guidatore non guardava dove andava [latro gweedatoray non gwardava dovay andava]

driver's license la patente (di guida) [patentay (dee gweeda)]

‣ here's my driver's license ecco la mia patente [ekko la mee-a patentay]

drop *(of liquid)* la goccia [gocha]; *(small amount)* il goccio [gocho] ◆ *(let fall)* lasciar cadere [lashar kadayray]; *(let out of vehicle)* lasciare [lasharay]

‣ could I just have a drop of milk? potrei avere un goccio di latte? [potray-ee avayray oon gocho dee lattay]

‣ I dropped my scarf mi è caduta la sciarpa [mee ay kadoota la sharpa]

‣ could you drop me at the corner? mi può lasciare all'angolo? [mee poo-o lasharay allangolo]

drop off *(let out of vehicle)* lasciare [lasharay]

‣ could you drop me off here? mi può lasciare qui? [mee poo-o lasharay kwee]

drown annegare [annaygaray]

‣ he's drowning: somebody call for help sta annegando: qualcuno chiami aiuto [sta annaygando kwalkoono kee-amee a-yooto]

---

at the drugstore

‣ I'd like something for a headache/a sore throat/diarrhea vorrei qualcosa per il mal di testa/il mal di gola/la diarrea [vorray-ee kwalkoza per eel mal dee testa/eel mal dee gola/la dee-array-a]

‣ I'd like some aspirin/some Band-Aids® vorrei delle aspirine/dei cerotti [vorray-ee dellay aspeereenay/day-ee chayrottee]

‣ could you recommend a doctor? mi può consigliare un medico? [mee poo-o konseelyaray oon maydeeko]

drugstore la farmacia [farmachee-a]
- where is the nearest drugstore? dov'è la farmacia più vicina? [dovay la farmachee-a pyoo veecheena]

drunk ubriaco(a) [oobree-ako(a)]
- he's very drunk è molto ubriaco [ay molto oobree-ako]

dry secco(a) [sekko(a)]; *(clothing)* asciutto(a) [ashootto(a)] ♦ asciugare [ashoogaray] ♦ asciugarsi [ashoogarsee]
- a glass of dry white wine un bicchiere di vino bianco secco [oon beekee-ayray dee veeno bee-anko sekko]
- where can I put my towel to dry? dove posso mettere ad asciugare il mio asciugamano? [dovay posso mettayray ad ashoogaray eel mee-o ashoogamano]

dry cleaner's la lavanderia [lavandayree-a]
- is there a dry cleaner's nearby? c'è una lavanderia qui vicino? [chay oona lavandayree-a kwee veecheeno]

dryer *(for laundry)* l'asciugatrice f [ashoogatreechay]
- is there a dryer? c'è un'asciugatrice? [chay oona ashoogatreechay]

dub *(movie)* doppiare [doppee-aray]
- do they always dub English-language movies? i film in inglese sono sempre doppiati? [ee feelm een eenglayzay sono sempray doppee-atee]

during durante [doorantay]
- is there restricted parking during the festival? ci sono restrizioni di parcheggio durante il festival? [chee sono raystreetsee-onee dee parkejo doorantay eel festeeval]

duty *(tax)* il dazio (doganale) [datsee-o (doganalay)]
- do I have to pay duty on this? devo pagare il dazio doganale su questo? [dayvo pagaray eel datsee-o doganalay soo kwesto]

duty-free shop il duty free shop [dyootee free shop]
- where are the duty-free shops? dove sono i duty free shop? [dovay sono ee dyootee free shop]

DVD il DVD [deeveedee]
- which region is this DVD coded for? per quale area è codificato questo DVD? [per kwalay aray-a ay kodeefeekato kwesto deeveedee]

ear l'orecchio *m* [orekkee-o]
- I have a ringing in my ears ho un ronzio nelle orecchie [o oon rondzee-o nellay orekkee-ay]

earache il male alle orecchie [malay allay orekkee-ay]
- he has an earache ha male alle orecchie [a malay allay orekkee-ay]

ear infection l'otite *f* [oteetay]

▶ I think I have an ear infection penso di avere un'otite [penso dee avayray oonoteetay]

early *(before the expected time)* prima [preema], in anticipo [een anteecheepo]; *(in the day)* presto [presto]; *(at the beginning)* primo(a) [preemo(a)]

▶ is there an earlier flight? c'è un volo prima? [chay oon volo preema]

▶ we arrived early siamo arrivati in anticipo [see-amo arreevatee een anteecheepo]

▶ we'll be leaving early in the morning partiremo al mattino presto [parteeraymo al matteeno presto]

Easter la Pasqua [paskwa]

▶ Happy Easter! buona Pasqua! [boo-ona paskwa]

easy facile [facheelay]

▶ is it easy to use? è facile da usare? [ay facheelay da oozaray]

▶ I'd like something easy to carry vorrei qualcosa che si possa trasportare facilmente [vorray-ee kwalkoza kay see possa trasportaray facheelmentay]

eat mangiare [manjaray]

▶ I'm afraid I don't eat meat mi dispiace, non mangio carne [mee deespee-achay non manjo karnay]

▶ where can we get something to eat? dove possiamo mangiare qualcosa? [dovay possee-amo manjaray kwalkoza]

economy (class) la classe economica [classay aykonomeeka], l'economy (class) *f* [aykonomee (klass)] ♦ in classe economica [een classay aykonomeeka], in economy [een aykonomee]

▶ are there any seats in economy class? ci sono posti in economy? [chee sono postee een aykonomee]

▶ I'd prefer to go economy preferirei viaggiare in economy [prayfayreeray-ee vee-ajaray een aykonomee]

egg l'uovo *m* [oo-ovo]

▶ I'd like my eggs sunny side up, please vorrei le uova all'occhio di bue, per favore [vorray-ee le oo-ova allokkee-o dee boo-ay per favoray]

eight otto [otto]

▶ there are eight of us siamo in otto [see-amo een otto]

electric heater *(portable)* la stufa elettrica [stoofa aylettreeka]; *(fixed)* il radiatore elettrico [radee-atoray aylettreeko]

▶ do you have an electric heater? avete una stufa elettrica? [avaytay oona stoofa aylettreeka]

electricity l'elettricità *f* [aylettreecheeta]

▶ there's no electricity in the room non c'è la corrente in camera [non chay la correntay een kamayra]

electric razor, electric shaver il rasoio elettrico [razo-yo aylettreeko]

▶ where can I plug in my electric razor? dove c'è una presa per il rasoio elettrico? [dovay chay oona prayza per eel razo-yo aylettreeko]

elevator l'ascensore *m* [ashensoray]
 ▸ is there an elevator? c'è un ascensore? [chay oon ashensoray]
 ▸ the elevator is out of order l'ascensore è rotto [lashensoray ay rotto]

eleven undici [oondeechee]
 ▸ there are eleven of us siamo in undici [see-amo een oondeechee]

e-mail l'e-mail *f* [eemayl]
 ▸ I'd like to send an e-mail vorrei spedire un'e-mail [vorray-ee spaydeeray ooneemayl]
 ▸ where can I check my e-mail? dove posso consultare le mie e-mail? [dovay posso konsooltaray lay mee-y eemayl]

e-mail address l'indirizzo *m* e-mail [eendeereetso eemayl]
 ▸ do you have an e-mail address? ha un indirizzo e-mail? [a oon eendeereetso eemayl]

emergency l'emergenza *f* [aymerjentsa]
 ▸ it's an emergency! è un'emergenza! [ay oonaymerjentsa]
 ▸ what number do you call in an emergency? che numero bisogna fare in caso di emergenza? [kay noomayro beezonya faray een kazo dee aymerjentsa]

emergency brake il freno a mano [frayno a mano]
 ▸ I'm sure I put the emergency brake on sono sicuro di aver messo il freno a mano [sono seekooro dee avayr messo eel frayno a mano]

emergency cord la maniglia dell'allarme [maneelya dellallarmay]
 ▸ someone's pulled the emergency cord qualcuno ha tirato la maniglia dell'allarme [kwalkoono a teerato la maneelya dellallarmay]

emergency exit l'uscita *f* di emergenza [oosheeta dee aymerjentsa]
 ▸ where's the nearest emergency exit? dov'è l'uscita di emergenza più vicina? [dovay loosheeta dee aymerjentsa pyoo veecheena]

emergency room il pronto soccorso [pronto sokkorso]
 ▸ I need to go to the emergency room right away devo andare subito al pronto soccorso [dayvo andaray soobeeto al pronto sokkorso]

emergency services i servizi di soccorso [serveetsee dee sokkorso]
 ▸ do you a have a listing of emergency services numbers? avete una lista dei numeri dei servizi di soccorso? [avaytay oona leesta day-ee noomayree day-ee serveetsee dee sokkorso]

end *(conclusion, finish)* la fine [feenay]
 ▸ at the end of July alla fine di luglio [alla feenay dee loolyo]

engine il motore [motoray]
 ▸ the engine is making a funny noise il motore fa uno strano rumore [eel motoray fa oono strano roomoray]

English inglese [eenglayzay] ♦ *(language)* l'inglese *m* [eenglayzay]
 ▸ he's English è inglese [ay eenglayzay]
 ▸ do you understand English? capisce l'inglese? [kapeeshay leenglayzay]

enjoy

▶ to enjoy oneself **divertirsi** [deeverteersee]
▶ enjoy your meal! **buon appetito!** [boo-on appayteeto]
▶ did you enjoy your meal? **ha mangiato bene?** [a manjato baynay]
▶ I enjoyed the film **il film mi è piaciuto** [eel feelm mee ay pee-achooto]

enough **abbastanza** [abbastantsa]

▶ I don't have enough money **non ho abbastanza soldi** [non o abbastantsa soldee]
▶ that's enough! **basta!** [basta]
▶ no thanks, I've had quite enough **no grazie, sto bene così** [no gratsee-ay sto baynay cozee]

enter *(type in)* **inserire** [eensayreeray]

▶ do I enter my PIN number now? **ora devo inserire il mio codice segreto?** [ora dayvo eensayreeray eel mee-o kodeechay saygrayto]

entrance **l'entrata** *f* [entrata]

▶ where's the entrance to the subway? **dov'è l'entrata della metropolitana?** [dovay lentrata della metropoleetana]

entry *(to place)* **l'ingresso** *m* [eengresso]

▶ is entry to the exhibit free? **l'ingresso per la mostra è gratuito?** [leengresso per la mostra ay gratoo-eeto]

envelope **la busta** [boosta]

▶ I'd like a pack of envelopes **vorrei una confezione di buste** [vorray-ee oona konfetsee-onay dee boostay]

equipment **l'attrezzatura** *f* [attretsatoora]

▶ do you provide the equipment? **fornite l'attrezzatura?** [forneetay lattretsatoora]

escalator **la scala mobile** [skala mobeelay]

▶ is there an escalator? **c'è una scala mobile?** [chay oona skala mobeelay]

euro **l'euro** *m* [ay-ooro]

▶ I'd like to change some dollars into euros **vorrei cambiare alcuni dollari in euro** [vorray-ee kambiaray alkoonee dollaree een ay-ooro]

evening **la sera** [sayra]; *(expressing duration)* **la serata** [sayrata]

▶ in the evening **di sera** [dee sayra]
▶ why don't we meet up this evening? **perché non ci vediamo stasera?** [perkay non chee vaydee-amo stasayra]

event *(cultural)* **la manifestazione** [maneefestatsee-onay]

▶ what's the program of events? **qual è il programma delle manifestazioni?** [kwal ay eel programma dellay maneefestatsee-onee]

ever **mai** [ma-ee]

▶ have you ever been to Boston? **è mai stato a Boston?** [ay ma-ee stato a Boston]

everything tutto [tootto]
- that's everything, thanks è tutto, grazie [ay tootto gratsee-ay]
- we didn't have time to see everything non abbiamo avuto il tempo di vedere tutto [non abbee-amo avooto eel tempo dee vaydrayray tootto]

excess baggage il bagaglio in eccedenza [bagalyo een echaydentsa]
- what's your policy on excess baggage? cos'è previsto in caso di bagaglio in eccedenza? [kozay prayveesto een kazo dee bagalyo een echaydentsa]

exchange cambiare [kambee-aray]
- I'd like to exchange this T-shirt vorrei cambiare questa maglietta [vorray-ee kambee-aray kwesta malyetta]

exchange rate il tasso di cambio [tasso dee kambee-o]
- what is today's exchange rate? qual è il tasso di cambio odierno? [kwal ay eel tasso dee kambee-o odee-erno]

excursion l'escursione f [eskoorsee-onay]
- I'd like to sign up for the excursion on Saturday vorrei iscrivermi all'escursione di sabato [vorray-ee eeskreeveermee alleskoorsee-onay dee sabato]

excuse (behavior, person) scusare [skoozaray]
- excuse me? (asking for repetition) prego? [praygo]
- excuse me! (mi) scusi! [(mee) skoozee]
- you'll have to excuse my (poor) Italian le chiedo scusa per il mio (cattivo) italiano [lay kee-aydo skooza per eel mee-o (katteevo) eetalee-ano]

exhaust il tubo di scappamento [toobo dee skappamento]
- the exhaust is making a strange noise il tubo di scappamento fa uno strano rumore [eel toobo dee skappamento fa oono strano roomoray]

exhausted (tired) sfinito(a) [sfeeneeto(a)]
- I'm exhausted sono sfinito [sono sfeeneeto]

exhibit la mostra [mostra]
- I'd like a ticket for the temporary exhibit vorrei un biglietto per la mostra temporanea [vorray-ee oon beelyetto per la mostra temporanea-a]
- is this ticket valid for the exhibit too? questo biglietto vale anche per la mostra? [questo beelyetto valay ankay per la mostra]

exit l'uscita f [oosheeta]
- where's the exit? dov'è l'uscita? [dovay loosheeta]
- is it far to the next exit? è lontana la prossima uscita? [ay lontana la prosseema oosheeta]

expect (baby, letter) aspettare [aspettaray]
- I'll be expecting you at eight o'clock at... la aspetto alle otto a ... [la aspetto allay otto a]
- when do you expect it to be ready? quando pensa che sarà pronto? [kwando pensa kay sara pronto]

expensive caro(a) [karo(a)]

▸ do you have anything less expensive? non ha niente di meno caro? [non a nee-entay dee mayno karo]

▸ is the round-trip ticket less expensive? costa meno il biglietto di andata e ritorno? [kosta mayno eel beelyotto dee andata ay reetorno]

expire *(visa)* scadere [skadayray]

▸ my passport has expired il mio passaporto è scaduto [eel mee-o passaporto ay skadooto]

explain spiegare [spee-aygaray]

▸ please explain how to get to the airport per favore, mi spiega come andare all'aeroporto? [per favoray mee spee-ayga komay andaray alla-ayroporto]

▸ can you explain what this means? mi può spiegare cosa vuol dire questo? [mee poo-o spee-aygaray koza voo-ol deeray kwesto]

express (train) il (treno) rapido [(trayno) rapeedo]

▸ how long does it take by express train? quanto ci vuole con il rapido? [kwanto chee voo-olay kon eel rapeedo]

extension *(phone line)* l'interno *m* [eenterno]; *(cord)* la prolunga [proloonga]

▸ could I have extension 358, please? mi passa l'interno tre cinque otto, per favore? [mee passa leenterno tray cheenkway otto per favoray]

extra supplementare [sooplaymentaray]

▸ is it possible to add an extra bed? è possibile mettere un letto supplementare? [ay posseebeelay mettayray oon letto sooplaymentaray]

▸ would it be possible to stay an extra night? sarebbe possibile rimanere una notte in più? [sarebbay posseebeelay reemanayray oona notte een pyoo]

extra charge il costo aggiuntivo [kosto ajoonteevo]

▸ at no extra charge senza costi aggiuntivi [sentsa kostee ajoonteevee]

▸ what would the extra charge be for this service? quanto verrebbe a costare in più questo servizio? [kwanto verrebbay a kostaray een pyoo kwesto serveetsee-o]

eye l'occhio *m* [okkee-o]

▸ she has blue eyes ha gli occhi azzurri [a lyee okkee adzoorree]

▸ can you keep an eye on my bag for a few minutes? può tenermi d'occhio la borsa per qualche minuto? [poo-o taynayrmee dokkee-o la borsa per kwalkay meenooto]

eye drops il collirio [kolleeree-o]

▸ do you have any eye drops? avete del collirio? [avaytay del kolleeree-o]

eye shadow l'ombretto *m* [ombretto]

▸ is this the only eye shadow you've got? è l'unico ombretto che avete? [ay looneeko ombretto kay avaytay]

eyesight la vista [vista]

▸ I don't have very good eyesight non ho la vista molto buona [non o la vista molto boo-ona]

face *(of person)* la faccia [facha], il viso [veezo]
- the attacker had a broad face l'aggressore aveva una faccia larga [lagressoray avayva una facha larga]

facilities le attrezzature [attretsatooray]
- what kind of exercise facilities do you have here? che tipo di attrezzature avete qui per la ginnastica? [kay teepo dee attretsatooray avaytay kwee per la geenasteeka]
- are there facilities for cooking? c'è la possibilità di cucinare? [chay la posseebeeleeta dee koocheenaray]
- do you have facilities for people with disabilities? il posto è attrezzato per i disabili? [eel posto ay attretsato per ee deezabeelee]
- are there facilities for children? ci sono attrezzature per bambini? [chee sono attretsatooray per bambeenee]

faint svenire [zvayneeray]
- I fainted twice last week sono svenuto due volte la settimana scorsa [sono zvaynooto doo-ay voltay la setteemana skorsa]

fair *(person, situation)* giusto(a) [joosto(a)]; *(price)* equo(a) [aykwo(a)]; *(hair)* biondo(a) [bee-ondo(a)]; *(skin, complexion)* chiaro(a) [kee-aro(a)]
- this isn't a fair price non è un prezzo equo [non ay oon pretso aykwo]
- it's not fair! non è giusto! [non ay joosto]

fall cadere [kadayray]
- I fell on my back sono caduto sulla schiena [sono kadooto soolla skee-ayna]

family la famiglia [fameelya]
- a family of five una famiglia di cinque persone [oona fameelya dee cheenkway personay]
- do you have any family in the area? ha dei parenti in questa zona? [a day-ee parentee een kwesta dzona]

fan il ventilatore [venteelatoray]
- how does the fan work? come funziona il ventilatore? [omay foontsee-ona eel venteelatoray]

far lontano [lontano]
- am I far from the village? sono lontano dal paese? [sono lontano dal pa-ayzay]
- is it far to walk? è lontano a piedi? [ay lontano a pee-aydee]
- is it far by car? è lontano in macchina? [ay lontano een makkeena]
- how far is the market from here? quanto dista da qui il mercato? [kwanto deesta da kwee eel merkato]

▸ far away/off lontano [lontano]
▸ so far finora [feenora]

fast veloce [vaylochay] ◆ velocemente [vaylochaymentay]
▸ as fast as possible il più velocemente possibile [eel pyoo vaylochaymentay posseebeelay]
▸ please don't drive so fast per favore, non vada così veloce [per favoray non vada cozee vaylochay]
▸ to be fast *(watch, clock)* essere avanti [essayray avantee]
▸ my watch is five minutes fast il mio orologio è avanti di cinque minuti [eel mee-o orolojo ay avantee dee cheenkwe meenootee]

fat *(in diet)* i grassi [grassee]
▸ it's low in fat ha pochi grassi [a pokee grassee]

father il padre [padray]
▸ this is my father questo è mio padre [kwesto ay mee-o padray]

fault *(responsibility)* la colpa [kolpa]
▸ it was my fault è stata colpa mia [ay stata kolpa mee-a]

favor *(kind act)* il favore [favoray]
▸ can I ask you a favor? posso chiederle un favore? [posso kee-ayderlay oon favoray]

favorite preferito(a) [prayfayreeto(a)] ◆ il preferito [prayfayreeto], la preferita [prayfayreeta]
▸ it's my favorite book è il mio libro preferito [ay eel mee-o libro prayfayreeto]

feather la piuma [pyooma]
▸ are these feather pillows? sono guanciali di piuma? [sono gwanchalee dee pyooma]

February il febbraio [febbra-yo]
▸ February 8th l'otto febbraio [lotto febbra-yo]

feed *(breastfeed)* allattare [allattaray]
▸ where can I feed the baby? dove posso allattare il bimbo? [dovay posso allattaray eel beembo]

feel *(touch)* toccare [tokkaray]; *(sense)* sentire [senteeray] ◆ *(physically)* sentirsi [senteersee]
▸ I can't feel my feet non mi sento più i piedi [non mee sento pyoo ee pee-aydee]
▸ I don't feel well non mi sento bene [non mee sento baynay]

ferry il traghetto [traghetto]
▸ when does the next ferry leave? quando parte il prossimo traghetto? [kwando partay eel prosseemo traghetto]

ferry terminal il terminal traghetti [termeenal traghettee]
▸ which way is the ferry terminal? da che parte è il terminal traghetti? [da kay partay ay eel termeenal traghettee]

fever la febbre [febbray]
▸ the baby's got a fever il bambino ha la febbre [eel bambeeno a la febbray]

few poco(a) [poko(a)] ♦ **a few** qualche [kwalkay]
  ▸ there are few sights worth seeing around here ci sono poche cose da vedere da queste parti [chee sono pokay kozay da vaydayray da kwestay partee]
  ▸ we're thinking of staying a few more days stiamo pensando di restare qualche giorno in più [stee-amo pensando dee restaray kwalkay jorno een pyoo]
  ▸ I spent a month in Italy a few years ago ho trascorso un mese in Italia qualche anno fa [o traskorso oon mayzay een eetalee-a kwalkay anno fa]

fifth quinto(a) [kweento(a)] ♦ *(gear)* la quinta [kweenta]
  ▸ I can't get it into fifth non riesco a ingranare la quinta [non ree-esko a eengranaray la kweenta]

filling *(in tooth)* l'otturazione *f* [ottooratsee-onay]
  ▸ one of my fillings has come out mi è saltata un'otturazione [mee ay saltata oonottooratsee-onay]

fill up fare il pieno (a) [fare eel pee-ayno (a)]
  ▸ fill it up, please il pieno, per favore [eel pee-ayno per favoray]

film *(for camera)* il rullino [roolleeno] ♦ filmare [feelmaray]
  ▸ I'd like to have this film developed vorrei far sviluppare questo rullino [vorray-ee far zveeloopparay kwesto roolleeno]
  ▸ do you have black-and-white film? avete dei rullini in bianco e nero? [avaytay day-ee roolleenee een bee-anko ay nayro]
  ▸ is filming allowed in the museum? si può filmare nel museo? [see poo-o feelmaray nel moozay-o]

find trovare [trovaray]
  ▸ has anyone found a watch? qualcuno ha trovato un orologio? [kwalkoono a trovato oon orolojo]
  ▸ where can I find a doctor on a Sunday? dove posso trovare un medico di domenica? [dovay posso trovaray oon maydeeko dee domayneeka]

find out scoprire [skopreeray]; *(find information on)* informarsi su [eenformarsee soo]
  ▸ I need to find out the times of trains to Florence devo informarmi sugli orari dei treni per Firenze [dayvo eenformarmee soolyee oraree day-ee traynee per feerentsay]

fine *(weather)* bello(a) [bello(a)]; *(food)* buono(a) [boo-on(a)] ♦ *(financial penalty)* la multa [moolta]
  ▸ I'm fine thanks, and you? sto bene, grazie, e lei? [sto baynay gratsee-ay ay lay-ee]
  ▸ how much is the fine? di quant'è la multa? [dee kwantay la moolta]

finger il dito [deeto]
  ▸ I've cut my finger mi sono tagliato un dito [mee sono talyato oon deeto]

finish finire [feeneeray]
  ▸ can we leave as soon as we've finished our meal? possiamo andarcene appena abbiamo finito di mangiare? [possee-amo andarchaynay appayna abbee-amo feeneeto dee manjaray]

fire il fuoco [foo-oko]; *(out of control)* l'incendio *m* [eenchendee-o]
  ▶ to make a fire fare un fuoco [faray oon foo-oko]

fire department i pompieri [pompee-ayree]
  ▶ call the fire department! chiamate i pompieri! [kee-amatay ee pompee-ayree]

fireworks i fuochi d'artificio [foo-okee darteefeecho]
  ▶ what time do the fireworks start? a che ora cominciano i fuochi d'artificio? [a kay ora komeenchano ee foo-okee darteefeecho]

first primo(a) [preemo(a)] ◆ *(before all others)* il primo [preemo], la prima [preema]; *(gear)* la prima [preema]; *(class)* la prima (classe) [preema (klassay)]
  ▶ it's the first time I've been here è la prima volta che vengo qui [ay la preema volta kay vengo kwee]
  ▶ you have to take the first left after the lights deve prendere la prima a sinistra dopo il semaforo [dayvay prendayray la preema a seeneestra dopo eel saymaforo]
  ▶ are our seats first? i nostri posti sono in prima classe? [ee nostree postee sono een preema klassay]
  ▶ put it into first metti la prima [metteela la preema]

first-aid kit la valigetta del pronto soccorso [valeejetta del pronto sokkorso]
  ▶ do you have a first-aid kit? ha una valigetta del pronto soccorso? [a oona valeejetta del pronto sokkorso]

first class la prima classe [preema klassay] ◆ in prima classe [een preema klassay]
  ▶ are there any seats in first class? ci sono posti in prima classe? [chee sono postee een preema klassay]
  ▶ I'd like to send this first class vorrei spedire questo tramite posta celere [vorray-ee spaydeeray kwesto trameetay posta chaylayray]
  ▶ I prefer to travel first class preferisco viaggiare in prima classe [prayfayreesko vee-ajaray een preema klassay]

fish il pesce [payshay]
  ▶ I don't eat fish non mangio pesce [non manjo payshay]

fishing permit la licenza di pesca [leechentsa dee payska]
  ▶ do you need a fishing permit to fish here? ci vuole la licenza (di pesca) per pescare qui? [chee voo-olay la leechentsa (dee payska) per payskaray kwee]

fit *(of laughter, tears)* l'attacco *m* [attakko] ◆ *(clothes)* andare bene a [andaray baynay a]
  ▶ I think she's having some kind of fit penso che le sia venuto una specie di attacco [penso kay lay see-a vaynooto oona spaychay dee attakko]
  ▶ those pants fit you better questi pantaloni le vanno meglio [kwestee pantalonee lay vanno melyo]
  ▶ the key doesn't fit in the lock la chiave non entra nella serratura [la kee-avay non entra nella serratoora]
  ▶ we won't all fit around one table non ci stiamo tutti a un tavolo [non chee stee-amo toottee a oon tavolo]

fit in *(go in)* stare [staray] ✦ *(put in)* far stare [far staray]

- I can't get everything to fit in my suitcase non riesco a far stare tutto nella mia valigia [non ree-esko a far staray tootto nella mee-a valeeja]
- how many people can you fit in this car? quante persone può trasportare questa macchina? [kwantay personay poo-o trasportaray kwesta makkeena]

fitting room la cabina di prova [kabeena dee prova]

- where are the fitting rooms? dove sono le cabine di prova? [dovay sono le kabeenay dee prova]

five cinque [cheenkway]

- there are five of us siamo in cinque [see-amo een cheenkway]

fix riparare [reepararay]

- where can I find someone to fix my bike? dove posso trovare qualcuno che mi ripari la bici? [dovay posso trovaray kwalkoono kay me reeparee la beechee]

fixed price il prezzo fisso [pretso feesso]

- do taxis to the airport charge a fixed price? i taxi per l'aeroporto fanno un prezzo fisso? [ee taxee per la-ayroporto fanno oon pretso feesso]

flash *(on camera)* il flash [flash]

- I'd like some batteries for my flash mi servono delle pile per il flash [mee servono dellay peelay per eel flash]

flash photography la fotografia con il flash [fotografee-a kon eel flash]

- is flash photography allowed here? si può usare il flash qui? [see poo-o oozare eel flash kwee]

flat *(tire)* a terra [a terra]

- the tire's flat la gomma è a terra [la gomma ay a terra]

flavor il gusto [goosto]

- I'd like to try a different flavor of ice cream vorrei provare un altro gusto di gelato [vorray-ee provaray oon altro goosto dee jaylato]

flight il volo [volo]

- how many flights a day are there? quanti voli ci sono al giorno? [kwantee volee chee sono al jorno]
- has our flight been canceled? il nostro volo è stato annullato? [eel nostro volo ay stato annoollato]
- what time is the flight? a che ora è il volo? [a kay ora ay eel volo]

flight of stairs la rampa (di scale) [rampa (dee skalay)]

- is our room up that flight of stairs? la nostra camera è in cima a questa rampa? [la nostra kamayra ay een cheema a kwesta rampa]

floor *(story)* il piano [pee-ano]

- which floor is it on? a che piano è? [a kay pee-ano ay]
- it's on the top floor è all'ultimo piano [ay alloolteemo pee-ano]

flower il fiore [fee-oray]

▶ do you sell flowers? vendete dei fiori? [vendetay day-ee fee-oree]

flu l'influenza *f* [eenfloo-entsa]
▶ I'd like something for the flu vorrei qualcosa per l'influenza [vorray-ee kwalkoza per leenfloo-entsa]

flush lo sciacquone [shakwonay] ♦ *(toilet)* tirare l'acqua di [teeraray lakwa dee] ♦ *(person)* diventare rosso(a) [deeventaray rosso (a)]
▶ the toilet won't flush lo sciacquone non funziona [lo shakwonay non foontsee-ona]

fog la nebbia [nebbee-a]
▶ is there a lot of fog today? c'è molta nebbia oggi? [chay molta nebbee-a ojee]

food il cibo [cheebo]
▶ is there someplace to buy food nearby? c'è un posto qui vicino dove si possa comprare da mangiare? [chay oon posto kwee veecheeno dovay see possa kompraray da manjaray]
▶ the food here is excellent qui si mangia benissimo [kwee see manja bayneesseemo]
▶ dog/cat food cibo per cani/gatti [cheebo per kanee/gattee]
▶ health food alimenti macrobiotici [aleementee makrobee-oteechee]

food cart *(on train)* il carrello delle bevande [carrello dellay bayvanday]; *(on plane)* il carrello dei pasti [carrello day-ee pastee]
▶ is there food cart service on this train? c'è un servizio bar su questo treno? [chay oon serveetsee-o bar soo kwesto trayno]

food section *(in store)* il reparto alimentari [rayparto aleementaree]
▶ where's the food section? dov'è il reparto alimentari? [dovay eel rayparto aleementaree]

foot il piede [pee-aydee]
▶ on foot a piedi [a pee-aydee]

for per [per]; *(since)* da [da]
▶ the flight for Milan il volo per Milano [eel volo per meelano]
▶ is this the right train for Pisa? è questo il treno per Pisa? [ay kwesto eel trayno per peeza]
▶ what's that for? a cosa serve? [a koza servay]
▶ I'm staying for two months mi fermo due mesi [mee fermo doo-ay mayzee]
▶ I need something for a cough mi serve qualcosa per la tosse [mee servay kwalkoza per la tossay]
▶ I've been here for a week sono qui da una settimana [sono kwee da oona setteemana]

foreign *(country, language)* straniero(a) [stranee-ayro(a)]
▶ I don't speak any foreign languages non parlo nessuna lingua straniera [non parlo nessoona leengwa stranee-ayra]

foreign currency la valuta estera [valoota estayra]
▶ do you change foreign currency? cambiate valuta estera? [kambee-atay valoota estayra]

foreigner lo straniero [stranee-ayro], la straniera [stranee-ayra]
 ▸ as a foreigner, this custom seems a bit strange to me come straniero, trovo quest'usanza un po' strana [komay stranee-ayro trovo kwestoozantsa oon po' strana]

forever per sempre [per sempray]
 ▸ our money won't last forever i nostri soldi non dureranno per sempre [ee nostree soldee non doorayranno per sempray]

fork la forchetta [forketta]
 ▸ could I have a fork? potrei avere una forchetta? [potray-ee avayray oona forketta]

forward inoltrare [eenoltraray]
 ▸ can you forward my mail? può inoltrarmi la corrispondenza? [poo-o eenoltrarmee la korreespondentsa]

four quattro [kwattro]
 ▸ there are four of us siamo in quattro [see-amo een kwattro]

fourth quarto(a) [kwarto(a)] ♦ (gear) la quarta [kwarta]
 ▸ it's hard to get it into fourth è difficile ingranare la quarta [ay deeffeecheelay eengranaray la kwarta]

four-wheel drive la quattro per quattro [kwattro per kwattro]
 ▸ I'd like a four-wheel drive vorrei una quattro per quattro [vorray-ee oona kwattro per kwattro]

fracture la frattura [frattoora]
 ▸ is it a hairline fracture? è una microfrattura? [ay oona meekrofrattoora]

free (offered at no charge) gratis [gratees], gratuito(a) [gratoo-eeto(a)]; (not occupied, available) libero(a) [leebayro(a)]
 ▸ is it free? è gratis? [ay gratees]
 ▸ is this seat free? è libero questo posto? [ay leebayro kwesto posto]
 ▸ are you free on Thursday evening? è libero giovedì sera? [ay leebayro jovaydee sayra]

freeway l'autostrada f [owtostrada]
 ▸ what is the speed limit on freeways? qual è il limite di velocità in autostrada? [kwal ay eel leemeetay dee vaylocheeta een owtostrada]
 ▸ how do I get onto the freeway? come si arriva all'autostrada? [komay see arreeva allowtostrada]

freezing (cold) (room, day) gelato(a) [jaylato(a)]
 ▸ I'm freezing (cold) sono gelato [sono jaylato]

frequent frequente [fraykwentay]
 ▸ I get frequent headaches ho frequenti mal di testa [o fraykwentee mal dee testa]
 ▸ how frequent are the trains to the city? con quale frequenza partono i treni per la città? [kon kwalay fraykwentsa partono ee traynee per la cheetta]

fresh (food) fresco(a) [fresko(a)]
 ▸ is the fish fresh or frozen? il pesce è fresco o surgelato? [eel payshay ay fresko o soorjaylato]

▶ I'd like some fresh orange juice vorrei una spremuta d'arancia [vorray-ee oona spraymoota darancha]

freshly *(ironed)* appena [appayna]

▶ freshly baked bread pane appena sfornato [panay appayna sfornato]
▶ freshly squeezed orange juice spremuta d'arancia appena fatta [spraymoota darancha appayna fatta]

Friday il venerdì [vaynerdee]

▶ we're arriving/leaving on Friday arriviamo/partiamo venerdì [arreevee-amo/ partee-amo vaynerdee]

fried egg l'uovo fritto *m* [oo-ovo freetto]

▶ I'd prefer a fried egg preferirei un uovo fritto [prayfayreeray-ee oon oo-ovo freetto]

friend l'amico [ameeko], l'amica [ameeka]

▶ are you with friends? è insieme a degli amici? [ay eensee-aymee a delyee ameechee]
▶ I've come with a friend sono venuto con un amico [sono vaynooto kon oon ameeko]
▶ I'm meeting some friends devo incontrarmi con degli amici [dayvo eenkontrarmee kon delyee ameechee]

from *(expressing origin)* di [dee]; *(leaving from)* da [da]

▶ I'm from Chicago sono di Chicago [sono dee sheekago]
▶ how many flights a day are there from Malpensa Airport to JFK? quanti voli al giorno ci sono da Malpensa per New York, JFK? [kwantee volee al jorno chee sono da malpensa per nyoo york jay-efkay]

front *(of train)* la testa [testa] ◆ **in front** davanti [davantee] ◆ **in front of** davanti a [davantee a]

▶ I'd like a seat toward the front of the train vorrei un posto verso la testa del treno [vorray-ee oon posto verso la testa del trayno]
▶ the car in front braked suddenly la macchina davanti ha frenato di colpo [la makkeena davantee a fraynato dee kolpo]
▶ I'll meet you in front of the museum ci vediamo davanti al museo [chee vaydee-amo davantee al moozay-o]

front door la porta d'ingresso [porta deengresso]

▶ which is the key to the front door? qual è la chiave della porta d'ingresso? [kwal ay la kee-avay della porta deengresso]
▶ the front door is closed la porta d'ingresso è chiusa [la porta deengresso ay kee-ooza]

frozen *(person, pipes)* gelato(a) [jaylato(a)]; *(food)* surgelato(a) [soorjaylato(a)]

▶ I'm absolutely frozen sono completamente gelato [sono complaytamentay jaylato]
▶ the lock is frozen la serratura è gelata [la serratoora ay jaylata]

frozen food i surgelati [soorjaylatee]

▶ is that all the frozen food you have? sono tutti qui i surgelati che avete? [sono toottee kwee ee soorjaylatee kay avaytay]

fruit juice il succo di frutta [sookko dee frootta]
- what types of fruit juice do you have? che succhi di frutta avete? [kay sookkee dee frootta avaytay]

full pieno(a) [pee-ayno(a)]; *(hotel, restaurant, train)* completo(a) [komplayto(a)]
- is the flight full? il volo è completo? [eel volo ay komplayto]
- I'm quite full, thank you sono abbastanza pieno, grazie [sono abbastantsa pee-ayno gratsee-ay]

full up *(with food)* strapieno(a) [strapee-ayno(a)]
- I'm full up sono strapieno [sono strapee-ayno]

fun *(pleasure, amusement)* il divertimento [deeverteemento]
- to be fun essere divertente [essayray deevertentay]
- to have fun divertirsi [deeverteersee]

gallery *(for art)* la galleria [gallayree-a]
- what time does the gallery open? a che ora apre la galleria? [a kay ora apray la gallayree-a]

game *(fun activity)* il gioco [joko]; *(of sport)* la partita [parteeta]
- do you want to play a game of tennis tomorrow? vuoi fare una partita a tennis domani? [voo-o-ee faray oona parteeta a tennees domanee]

garage *(for car repair)* l'officina *f* (di riparazione) [offeecheena (dee reeparatsee-onay)]
- is there a garage near here? c'è un'officina qui vicino? [chay oonoffeecheena kwee veecheeno]
- could you tow me to a garage? mi può rimorchiare la macchina fino a un'officina? [mee poo-o reemorkee-aray la makkeena feeno a oonoffeecheena]

garbage can il bidone della spazzatura [beedonay della spatsatoora]
- where is the garbage can? dov'è il bidone della spazzatura? [dovay eel beedonay della spatsatoora]

gas *(for vehicle)* la benzina [bendzeena]; *(for domestic use)* il gas [gas]; *(for medical use)* il gas anestetico [gas anestayteeko]
- where can I get gas? dove posso far benzina? [dovay posso far bendzeena]
- I've run out of gas sono rimasto senza benzina [sono reemasto sentsa bendzeena]

gas pump la pompa di benzina [pompa dee bendzeena]
- how do you use this gas pump? come si usa questa pompa di benzina? [komay see ooza kwesta pompa dee bendzeena]

gas burner il fornello a gas [fornello a gas]
> do you have gas burners for sale? **vendete dei fornelli a gas?** [vendaytay day-ee fornellee a gas]

gas station il distributore di benzina [deestreebootoray dee bendzeena]
> where can I find a gas station? **dove posso trovare un distributore di benzina?** [dovay posso trovaray oon deestreebootoray dee bendzeena]

gas stove la cucina a gas [koocheena a gas]
> do you have a gas stove we could borrow? **avrebbe una cucina a gas da prestarci?** [avrebbay oona koocheena a gas da prestarchee]

gas tank il serbatoio [serbato-yo]
> the gas tank is leaking **il serbatoio perde** [eel serbato-yo perday]

gate (of garden) il cancello [kanchello]; (of town) la porta [porta]; (at airport) l'uscita f [oosheeta]
> where is Gate 2? **dov'è l'uscita due?** [dovay loosheeta doo-ay]

gear (of car, bike) la marcia [marcha]
> how many gears does the bike have? **quante marce ha la bici?** [kwantay marchay a la beechee]

get (obtain) ottenere [ottaynayray]; (understand) capire [kapeeray] ♦ (make one's way) andare [andaray]
> where can we get something to eat this time of night? **dove possiamo trovare qualcosa da mangiare a quest'ora?** [dovay possee-amo trovaray kwalkoza da manjaray a kwestora]
> I can't get it into reverse **non riesco a ingranare la retromarcia** [non ree-esko a eengranaray la retromarcha]
> now I get it **adesso capisco** [adesso capeesko]
> I got here a month ago **sono arrivato qui un mese fa** [sono arreevato kwee oon mayzay fa]
> can you get there by car? **ci si può andare in macchina?** [chee see poo-o andaray een makkeena]
> how can I get to...? **come si fa per andare a ...?** [komay see fa per andaray a]
> could you tell me the best way to get to Rimini? **mi può dire qual è la strada migliore per andare a Rimini?** [mee poo-o deeray kwal ay la strada meelyoray per andaray a reemeenee]
> how do we get to Terminal 2? **come si va al terminale 2?** [komay see va al termeenalay doo-ay]

get back (money) riavere [reeavayray]
> I just want to get my money back **voglio solo riavere i miei soldi** [volyo solo reeavayray ee mee-ay-ee soldee]

get back onto (road) ritornare su [reetornaray soo]
> how can I get back onto the freeway? **come posso ritornare sull'autostrada?** [komay posso reetornaray soolowtostrada]

get in *(arrive)* arrivare [arreevaray]; *(gain entry)* entrare [entraray] ✦ *(car)* salire in [saleeray een]

- ▸ what time does the train get in to Perugia? **a che ora arriva a Perugia il treno?** [a kay ora arreeva a perooja eel trayno]
- ▸ what time does the flight get in? **a che ora arriva il volo?** [a kay ora arreeva eel volo]
- ▸ do you have to pay to get in? **bisogna pagare per entrare?** [beezonya pagaray per entraray]

get off *(bus, train, bike)* scendere da [shendayray da]; *(road)* uscire da [oosheeray da] ✦ *(leave)* partire [parteeray]; *(from bus)* scendere [shendayray]

- ▸ where do we get off the bus? **dove dobbiamo scendere dall'autobus?** [dovay dobbee-amo shendayray dallowtoboos]
- ▸ where do I get off the freeway? **dove devo uscire dall'autostrada?** [dovay dayvo oosheeray dallowtostrada]

get on *(enter)* salire su [saleeray soo]; *(travel on)* prendere [prendayray]

- ▸ when can we get on the plane? **quando possiamo salire sull'aereo?** [kwando possee-amo saleeray soolla-ayray-o]
- ▸ which bus should we get on to go downtown? **quale autobus dobbiamo prendere per andare in centro?** [kwalay owtoboos dobbee-amo prendayray per andaray een chentro]

get past passare [passaray]

- ▸ sorry, can I get past, please? **scusi, posso passare, per favore?** [skoozee posso passaray per favoray]

get up *(in morning)* alzarsi [altsarsee]

- ▸ I got up very early **mi sono alzato prestissimo** [mee sono altsato presteeseemo]

gift-wrap

- ▸ could you gift-wrap it for me? **mi può fare un pacco regalo?** [mee poo-o faray oon pakko raygalo]

girl *(young female)* la ragazza [ragatsa]; *(daughter)* la figlia [feelya]

- ▸ who is that girl? **chi è quella ragazza?** [kee ay kwella ragatsa]
- ▸ I've got two girls **ho due figlie** [o doo-ay feelyee]

girlfriend la ragazza [ragatsa]

- ▸ is she your girlfriend? **è la tua ragazza?** [ay la too-a ragatsa]

give dare [daray]

- ▸ I can give you my e-mail address **le posso dare il mio indirizzo e-mail** [lay posso daray eel mee-o eendeeretso eemayl]
- ▸ can you give me a hand? **mi può dare una mano?** [mee poo-o daray oona mano]

glass *(material)* il vetro [vaytro]; *(for drinking)* il bicchiere [beekee-ayray] ✦ **glasses** gli occhiali [okkee-alee]

- ▸ can I have a clean glass? **posso avere un bicchiere pulito?** [posso avayray oon beekee-ayray pooleeto]

> ▶ would you like a glass of champagne? gradisce un bicchiere di champagne? [gradeeshay oon beekee-ayray dee shampanye]
> ▶ I've lost my glasses ho perso gli occhiali [o perso lyee okkee-alee]

glove il guanto [gwanto]

> ▶ I've lost a brown glove ho perso un guanto marrone [o perso oon gwanto marronay]

go andare [andaray]

> ▶ let's go to the beach andiamo in spiaggia [andee-amo een spee-aja]
> ▶ where can we go for breakfast? dove possiamo andare per la colazione? [dovay possee-amo andaray per la kolatsee-onay]
> ▶ where does this path go? dove va questo sentiero? [dovay va kwesto sentee-ayro]
> ▶ I must be going devo andare [dayvo andaray]
> ▶ we're going home tomorrow andiamo a casa domani [andee-amo a kaza domanee]

go away *(person)* andare via [andaray vee-a]; *(pain)* passare [passaray]

> ▶ go away and leave me alone! vai via e lasciami in pace! [va-ee vee-a ay lashamee een pachay]

go back *(return)* tornare [tornaray]

> ▶ we're going back home tomorrow torniamo a casa domani [tornee-amo a kaza domanee]

go down *(stairs)* scendere [shendayray]; *(street)* prendere [prendayray]

> ▶ go down that street and turn left at the bottom prenda questa strada e in fondo giri a sinistra [prenda kwesta strada ay een fondo jeeree a seeneestra]

gold *(metal)* l'oro *m* [oro]

> ▶ is it made of gold? è d'oro? [ay doro]

golf il golf [golf]

> ▶ I play golf gioco a golf [joko a golf]

golf club la mazza da golf [matsa da golf]

> ▶ where can I rent golf clubs? dove posso noleggiare delle mazze da golf? [dovay posso nolejaray delle matsay da golf]

golf course il campo da golf [kampo da golf]

> ▶ is there a golf course nearby? c'è un campo da golf nei paraggi? [chay oon kampo da golf nay-ee parajee]

good buono(a) [boo-ono(a)]; *(skilled)* bravo(a) [bravo(a)]; *(enjoyable)* bello(a) [bello(a)]

> ▶ this isn't a very good restaurant questo ristorante non è molto buono [kwesto reestorantay non ay molto boo-ono]
> ▶ you're really good at surfing! sei davvero bravo a fare surf! [say-ee davvayro bravo a faray surf]
> ▶ we had a good time siamo stati molto bene [see-amo statee molto baynay]

saying goodbye

When you're leaving, say *arrivederci* (or *arrivederla*, if you're on more formal terms). If you've already arranged to meet up again, you can say *a più tardi* (see you later). If you're saying goodbye to friends, say *ciao* or *ci vediamo* (see you later). If you're going to bed, say *buonanotte* (goodnight).

▸ we've had a good vacation abbiamo passato delle belle vacanze [abbee-amo passato dellay bellay vakantsay]

good afternoon buon pomeriggio [boo-on pomayreejo]

▸ good afternoon! isn't it a beautiful day? buon pomeriggio: non è una magnifica giornata? [boo-on pomayreejo non ay oona manyeefeeka jornata]

goodbye arrivederci [arreevayderchee]

▸ goodbye! see you soon! arrivederci, a presto! [arreevayderchee a presto]

▸ to say goodbye salutare [salootaray]

good evening buonasera [boo-onasayra]

▸ good evening! how are you tonight? buonasera: come si sente stasera? [boo-onasayra komay see sentay stasayra]

good morning buongiorno [boo-onjorno]

▸ good morning! how are you today? buongiorno: come si sente oggi? [boo-onjorno komay see sentay ojee]

good night buonanotte [boo-onanottay]

▸ I'll say good night, then allora, buonanotte [allora boo-onanottay]

go out uscire [oosheeray]; *(tide)* salire [saleeray]

▸ what's a good place to go out for a drink to? qual è un bel posto per uscire a bere qualcosa? [kwal ay oon bel posto per oosheeray a bayray kwalkoza]

▸ the tide's going out la marea sta salendo [la maray-a sta salendo]

grapefruit il pompelmo [pompelmo]

▸ I'll just have the grapefruit prendo solo il pompelmo [prendo solo eel pompelmo]

great *(very good)* fantastico(a) [fantasteeko(a)]

▸ that's great! è fantastico! [ay fantasteeko]

▸ it was great! è stato fantastico! [ay stato fantasteeko]

green verde [verday]

▸ the green one quello verde [kwello verday]

grocery store la drogheria [drogayree-a]

▸ is there a grocery store around here? c'è una drogheria da queste parti? [chay oona drogayree-a da kwestay partee]

ground cloth il telone impermeabile [taylonay eempermay-abeelay]
- I brought a ground cloth ho portato un telone impermeabile [o portato oon taylonay eempermay-abeelay]

group il gruppo [grooppo]
- there's a group of 12 of us siamo un gruppo di dodici [see-amo oon grooppo dee dodeechee]
- are there reductions for groups? ci sono sconti per comitive? [chee sono skontee per komeeteevay]

group rate la tariffa per comitive [tareeffa per komeeteevay]
- are there special group rates? ci sono delle tariffe speciali per comitive? [chee sono dellay tareeffay spaychalee per komeeteevay]

guarantee *(for purchased product)* la garanzia [garantsee-a]
- it's still under guarantee è ancora sotto garanzia [ay ankora sotto garantsee-a]

guesthouse la pensione [pensee-onay]
- we're looking for a guesthouse for the night stiamo cercando una pensione per la notte [stee-amo cherkando oona pensee-onay per la nottay]

guide *(person, book)* la guida [gweeda]
- does the guide speak English? la guida parla inglese? [la gweeda parla eenglayzay]

guidebook la guida [gweeda]
- do you have a guidebook in English? avete una guida in inglese? [avaytay oona gweeda een eenglayzay]

guided tour la visita guidata [veezeeta gweedata]
- what time does the guided tour begin? a che ora inizia la visita guidata? [a kay ora eeneetsee-a la veezeeta gweedata]
- is there a guided tour in English? c'è una visita guidata in inglese? [chay oona veezeeta gweedata een eenglayzay]
- are there guided tours of the museum? ci sono visite guidate del museo? [chee sono veezeetay gweedatay del moozay-o]

h

hair i capelli [kapellee]
- she has short hair ha i capelli corti [a ee kapellee cortee]
- he has red hair ha i capelli rossi [a ee kapellee rossee]

hairbrush la spazzola per capelli [spatsola per kapellee]
- do you sell hairbrushes? vendete spazzole per capelli? [vendaytay spatsolay per kapellee]

hairdryer il fon [fon], l'asciugacapelli *m* [ashoogakapellee]
- do the rooms have hairdryers? c'è il fon nelle camere? [chay eel fon nellay kamayray]

hair salon il parrucchiere [parrookee-ayray]
- does the hotel have a hair salon? c'è un parrucchiere in albergo? [chay oon parrookee-ayray een albergo]

half mezzo(a) [medzo(a)] ◆ la metà [mayta]
- half the cake mezza torta [medza torta]
- it's only half a block away è solo a mezzo isolato da qui [ay solo a medzo eezolato da kwee]
- I'm only half dressed non sono ancora del tutto vestito [non sono del tootto vesteeto]
- shall we meet in half an hour? ci vediamo tra mezzora? [chee vaydee-amo tra medzora]
- it's half past eight sono le otto e mezza [sono lay otto ay medza]

half-bottle la bottiglia piccola [botteelya peekola]
- a half-bottle of red wine, please una bottiglia piccola di vino rosso, per favore [oona botteelya peekola dee veeno rosso per favoray]

ham il prosciutto [proshootto]
- I'd like five slices of ham vorrei cinque fette di prosciutto [vorray-ee cheenkway fettay dee proshootto]

hand la mano [mano]
- where can I wash my hands? dove posso lavarmi le mani? [dovay posso lavarmee lay manee]

handbag la borsa [borsa], la borsetta [borsetta]
- someone's stolen my handbag mi hanno rubato la borsa [mee anno roobato la norsa]

hand baggage i bagagli a mano [bagalyee a mano]
- I have one suitcase and one piece of hand baggage ho una valigia e un bagaglio a mano [o oona valeeja ay oon bagalyo a mano]

handkerchief il fazzoletto [fatsoletto]
▸ do you have a spare handkerchief? ha un fazzoletto da prestarmi? [a oon fatsoletto da prestarmee]

handle *(of door)* la maniglia [maneelya]; *(of suitcase)* il manico [maneeko]
▸ the handle's broken il manico è rotto [eel maneeko ay rotto]

handmade fatto(a) a mano [fatto(a) a mano]
▸ is this handmade? è fatto a mano? [ay fatto a mano]

happen *(occur)* succedere [soochaydaray], capitare [kapeetaray]
▸ what happened? cos'è successo? [kozay soochesso]
▸ these things happen sono cose che capitano [sono kozay kay kapeetano]

happy contento(a) [kontento(a)]
▸ we're not very happy with the accomodations non siamo molto contenti della sistemazione [non see-amo molto kontentee della seestaymatsee-onay]
▸ I'd be happy to help sarei lieto di aiutare [saray-ee lee-ayto dee a-yootaray]
▸ Happy Birthday! buon compleanno! [boo-on komplay-anno]
▸ Happy New Year! buon anno! [boo-on anno]

hat il cappello [kappello]
▸ I think I left my hat here penso di aver dimenticato qui il cappello [penso dee avayr deementeekato kwee eel kappello]

hate detestare [daytestaray]
▸ I hate golf detesto il golf [detesto eel golf]

have avere [avayray]; *(meal, drink)* prendere [prendayray] ♦ *(be obliged)* dovere [dovayray]
▸ do you have any bread? avete del pane? [avaytay del panay]
▸ do you have them in red? ce li avete rossi? [chay lee avaytay rossee]
▸ he has brown hair ha i capelli castani [a ee kapellee kastanee]
▸ where should we go to have a drink? dove possiamo andare a bere qualcosa? [dovay possee-amo andaray a bayray kwalkoza]
▸ I have to be at the airport by six (o'clock) devo essere all'aeroporto per le sei [dayvo essayray alla-ayroporto per lay say-ee]
▸ we have to go dobbiamo andare [dobbee-amo andaray]

head la testa [testa]
▸ I hit my head when I fell ho battuto la testa cadendo [o battooto la testa kadendo]

headache il mal di testa [mal dee testa]
▸ I've got a headache ho mal di testa [o mal dee testa]
▸ do you have anything for a headache? avete qualcosa per il mal di testa? [avaytay kwalkoza per eel mal dee testa]

headlight il faro [faro], il fanale [fanalay]
▸ one of my headlights got smashed ho un fanale fracassato [o oon fanalay frakassato]

headphones le cuffie [kooffee-ay]
▸ did you find my headphones? avete trovato le mie cuffie? [avaytay trovato lay mee-ay kooffee-ay]

health la salute [salootay]
▸ in good/poor health in buona/cattiva salute [een boo-ona/katteeva salootay]

hear sentire [senteeray]
▸ I've heard a lot about you ho sentito molte cose su di lei [o senteeto moltay kozay soo dee lay-ee]

heart il cuore [koo-oray]
▸ he's got a weak heart ha dei problemi di cuore [a day-ee problaymee dee koo-oray]

heart attack l'infarto *m* [eenfarto]
▸ he had a heart attack ha avuto un infarto [a avooto oon eenfarto]
▸ I nearly had a heart attack! mi è quasi venuto un infarto! [mee ay kwazee vaynooto oon eenfarto]

heart condition
▸ to have a heart condition essere malato/a di cuore [essayray malato/a dee koo-oray]

heat *(hot quality)* il calore [kaloray]; *(weather)* il caldo [kaldo]; *(for cooking)* il fuoco [foo-oko]
▸ I can't stand this heat non sopporto questo caldo [non sopporto kwesto kaldo]
▸ there's no heat from the radiator in my room il termosifone nella mia camera non scalda per niente [eel termoseefonay nella mee-a kamayra non skalda per nee-entay]

heating il riscaldamento [reeskaldamento]
▸ how does the heating work? come funziona il riscaldamento? [komay foontsee-ona eel reeskaldamento]

heavy pesante [payzantay]
▸ my bags are very heavy i miei bagagli pesano molto [ee mee-ay-ee bagalyee payzano molto]

heel *(of foot)* il tallone [tallonay]; *(of shoe)* il tacco [takko]
▸ can you put new heels on these shoes? può sostituire i tacchi a queste scarpe? [poo-o sosteetoo-eeray ee takkee a kwestay skarpay]

hello *(as greeting)* salve [salvay]; *(on phone)* pronto [pronto]
▸ hello, is this ...? pronto, parlo con... ? [pronto parlo kon]

helmet il casco [kasko]
▸ do you have a helmet you could lend me? ha un casco da prestarmi? [a oon kasko da prestarmee]

help l'aiuto *m* [a-yooto] ◆ aiutare [a-yootaray]
▸ help! aiuto! [a-yooto]

hi!

Young Italians usually say *ciao* both when they meet and when they go. It's quite an informal word, so avoid using it with people you don't know or older people, and also in shops. In these cases say *buongiorno* (hello/goodbye) or *arrivederci* (goodbye).

- go and get help quickly! vada subito a cercare aiuto! [vada soobeeto a cherkaray a-yooto]
- thank you for your help grazie per il suo aiuto [gratsee-ay per eel soo-o a-yooto]
- could you help me? mi potrebbe aiutare? [mee potrebbay a-yootaray]
- could you help us push the car? ci potrebbe aiutare a spingere la macchina? [chee potrebbay a-yootaray a speenjayray la makkeena]
- let me help you with that lasci che l'aiuti [lashee kay la-yootee]
- could you help me with my bags? mi potrebbe aiutare con i bagagli? [mee potrebbay a-yootaray kon ee bagaglyee]

herbal tea la tisana [teezana]
- I'd like an herbal tea vorrei una tisana [vorray-ee oona teezana]

here qui [kwee] ◆ *(giving)* ecco [ekko]
- I've been here two days sono qui da due giorni [sono kwee da doo-ay jornee]
- I came here three years ago sono venuto qui tre giorni fa [sono vaynooto kwee tray jornee fa]
- are you from around here? è di queste parti? [ay dee kwestay partee]
- I'm afraid I'm a stranger here myself mi dispiace, ma non sono di qui neanch'io [mee deespee-achay ma non sono dee kwee nay-ankee-o]
- it's five minutes from here è a cinque minuti da qui [ay a cheenkway meenootee da kwee]
- here is/are... ecco ... [ekko]
- here are my passport and ticket ecco il mio passaporto e il biglietto [ekko eel mee-o passaporto ay eel beelyetto]

hi ciao [chow]
- hi, I'm Julia ciao, sono Julia [chow sono jool-ee-a]

high beam
- put your lights on high beam metti gli abbaglianti [mettee lyee abbalyantee]

high chair il seggiolone [sejolonay]
- could we have a high chair for the baby? potremmo avere un seggiolone per il bambino? [potremmo avayray oon sejolonay per eel bambeeno]

high season l'alta stagione *f* [alta stajonay]
- is it very expensive in the high season? costa molto in alta stagione? [kosta molto een alta stajonay]

high tide l'alta marea *f* [alta maray-a]
> what time is high tide? a che ora c'è l'alta marea? [a kay ora chay lalta maray-a]

hike l'escursione *f* a piedi [eskoorsee-onay a pee-aydee]
> are there any good hikes around here? ci sono delle belle escursioni da fare a piedi in zona? [chee sono dellay bellay eskoorsee-onee da faray a pee-aydee een dzona]

hiking l'escursionismo *m* [eskoorsee-oneezmo]
> to go hiking fare escursionismo [faray eskoorsee-oneezmo]
> are there any hiking trails? ci sono dei sentieri da escursioni? [chee sono day-ee sentee-ayree da eskoorsee-onee]

hiking boot lo scarpone da montagna [skarponay da montagna]
> do you need to wear hiking boots? bisogna portare scarponi da montagna? [beezonya portaray skarponee da montagna]

hitchhike fare autostop [faray owtostop]
> we hitchhiked here siamo arrivati qui in autostop [see-amo arreevatee kwee een owtostop]

holiday la festa [festa]
> is tomorrow a holiday? è festa domani? [ay festa domanee]

home *(house)* la casa [kaza] ♦ a casa [a kaza]
> to stay at home rimanere a casa [reemanayray a kaza]
> we're going home tomorrow torniamo a casa domani [tornee-amo a kaza domanee]

homemade fatto(a) in casa [fatto(a) een kaza]
> is it homemade? è fatto in casa? [ay fatto een kaza]

hood *(of car)* il cofano [kofano]
> I've dented the hood ho ammaccato il cofano [o ammakkato eel kofano]

horrible *(weather, day)* orribile [orreebeelay]; *(person)* antipatico(a) [anteepateeko(a)]
> what horrible weather! che tempo orribile! [kay tempo orreebeelay]

horseback riding
> can we go horseback riding? possiamo andare a cavallo? [possee-amo andaray a cavallo]

hospital l'ospedale *m* [ospaydalay]
> where is the nearest hospital? dov'è l'ospedale più vicino? [dovay lospaydalay pyoo veecheeno]

hot *(in temperature)* caldo(a) [kaldo(a)]; *(spicy)* piccante [peekkantay]
> I'm too hot ho troppo caldo [o troppo kaldo]
> this dish is really hot questo piatto è veramente piccante [kwesto pee-atto ay vayramentay peekkantay]
> there's no hot water non c'è l'acqua calda [non chay lakkwa calda]

at the hotel

- we'd like a double room/two single rooms **vorremmo una camera doppia/due camere singole** [vorremmo oona kamayra doppee-a/doo-ay kamayray seengolay]
- I have a reservation in the name of Jones **ho una prenotazione a nome Jones** [o oona praynotatsee-onay a nomay Jonz]
- what time is breakfast/dinner served? **a che ora servite la colazione/la cena?** [a kay ora serveetay la kolatsee-onay/la chayna]
- could I have a wake-up call at 7 a.m.? **mi potete svegliare alle sette?** [mee potaytay zvelyaray allay settay]

hotel l'albergo *m* [albergo], l'hotel *m* [otel]
- do you have a list of hotels in this area? **ha una lista degli alberghi in questa zona?** [a oona leesta delyee alberghee een kwesta dzona]
- are there any reasonably priced hotels near here? **ci sono degli alberghi non troppo cari qui vicino?** [chee sono delyee alberghee non troppo karee kwee veecheeno]
- is the hotel downtown? **l'albergo è in centro?** [lalbergo ay een chentro]
- could you recommend another hotel? **mi può consigliare un altro albergo?** [mee poo-o konseelyaray oon altro albergo]

hour l'ora *f* [ora]
- I'll be back in an hour **torno tra un'ora** [torno tra oonora]
- the flight takes three hours **il volo dura tre ore** [eel volo doora tray oray]

house la casa [kaza]
- is this your house? **è casa sua?** [ay kaza soo-a]

house wine il vino della casa [veeno della kaza]
- a bottle of house wine, please **una bottiglia di vino della casa, per favore** [oona botteelya dee veeno della kaza per favoray]

how come [komay]
- how are you? **come va?** [komay va]

how are you?

The equivalent of 'hello, how are you?' is *buongiorno, come va?* or *buongiorno, tutto bene?* The reply to *come va?* often goes into quite a bit more detail than you would expect in answer to 'how are you?' in English. Italians also often use *salve*, which is a useful alternative to *buongiorno* (which is rather formal) when you don't know whether you should be saying *lei* or *tu* to someone.

- ▶ how do you spell it? come si scrive? [komay see skreevay]
- ▶ how about a drink? e se andassimo a bere qualcosa? [ay say andasseemo a bayray kwalkoza]

humid umido(a) [oomeedo(a)]

- ▶ it's very humid today è molto umido oggi [ay molto oomeedo ojee]

hungry

- ▶ to be hungry aver fame [avayr famay]
- ▶ I'm starting to get hungry comincio ad aver fame [komeencho ad avayr famay]

hurry

- ▶ to be in a hurry essere di fretta [essayray dee fretta]

hurry up sbrigarsi [zbreegarsee]

- ▶ hurry up! sbrigati! [zbreegatee]

hurt far male (a) [far malay (a)]

- ▶ you're hurting me! mi sta facendo male! [mee sta fachendo malay]
- ▶ to hurt oneself farsi male [farsee malay]
- ▶ I hurt myself mi sono fatto male [mee sono fatto malay]
- ▶ I hurt my hand mi sono fatto male alla mano [mee sono fatto malay alla mano]
- ▶ it hurts fa male [fa malay]

ice il ghiaccio [ghee-acho]

- ▶ the car skidded on the ice l'auto è slittata sul ghiaccio [lowto ay zleetata sool ghee-acho]
- ▶ a Diet Coke® without ice, please una Coca Cola® light senza ghiaccio, per favore [oona koka kola la-eet sentsa ghee-acho per favoray]

ice cream il gelato [jaylato]

- ▶ I'd like some ice cream vorrei del gelato [vorray-ee del jaylato]

---

ice cream

Go into any of Italy's famous *gelaterie* and you'll find a huge variety of ice-cream flavors only Italians seem to know the secret of. You can have your *gelato* in a cone (*cono*) or a carton (*coppetta*), and even top the whole thing off with a dollop of thick cream (*con panna*).

ice cube il cubetto di ghiaccio [koobetto dee ghee-acho]

▶ could I have a carafe of water with no ice cubes in it? potrei avere una caraffa d'acqua senza cubetti di ghiaccio? [potray-ee avayray oona karaffa dakkwa sentsa koobettee dee ghee-acho]

iced coffee il caffè freddo [kafffay freddo]

▶ I'd like an iced coffee vorrei un caffè freddo [vorray-ee oon kafffay freddo]

ice rink la pista di pattinaggio [peesta dee patteenajo]

▶ is there an ice rink nearby? c'è una pista di pattinaggio qui vicino? [chay oona peesta dee patteenajo kwee veecheeno]

ice skate il pattino da ghiaccio [patteeno da ghee-acho]

▶ I'd like to rent some ice skates vorrei noleggiare dei pattini da ghiaccio [vorray-ee nolejaray day-ee patteenee da ghee-acho]

ice-skate

▶ would you like to go ice-skating tomorrow? ti andrebbe di andare a pattinare sul ghiaccio domani? [tee andrebbay dee andaray a patteenaray sool ghee-acho domanee]

ID card la carta d'identità [karta deedenteeta]

▶ I don't have an ID card: will a passport work? non ho la carta d'identità: va bene il passaporto ? [non o la karta deedenteeta va baynay eel passaporto]

if se [say]

▶ we'll go if you want andiamo noi, se vuoi [andee-amo no-ee say voo-o-ee]

ill malato(a) [malato(a)]

▶ my son is ill mio figlio è malato [mee-o feelyo ay malato]

immediately immediatamente [eemmaydee-atamentay]

▶ can you do it immediately? lo può fare immediatamente? [lo poo-o faray eemmaydee-atamentay]

improve migliorare [meelyoraray]

▶ I'm hoping to improve my Italian while I'm here spero di migliorare il mio italiano durante il mio soggiorno [spayro dee meelyoraray eel mee-o eetalee-ano doorantay eel mee-o sojorno]

in in [een]; *(with towns)* a [a]

▶ our bags are still in the room i nostri bagagli sono ancora in camera [ee nostree bagalyee sono ankora een kamayra]

▶ do you live in Rome? vive a Roma? [veevay a roma]

included compreso(a) [komprayzo(a)]

▶ is breakfast included? la colazione è compresa? [la kolatsee-onay ay komprayza]

▶ is sales tax included? l'IVA è compresa? [leeva ay komprayza]

▶ is service included? il servizio è compreso? [eel serveetsee-o ay komprayzo]

indoor *(swimming pool, tennis court)* coperto(a) [koperto(a)]

▶ is there an indoor pool? c'è una piscina coperta? [chay oona peesheena koperta]

infection l'infezione *f* [eenfetsee-onay]

▶ I have an eye infection **ho un'infezione all'occhio** [o ooneenfetsee-onay allokkee-o]

information *(facts)* le informazioni *f* [eenformatsee-onee]; *(service, department)* l'ufficio *m* informazioni [ooffeecho eenformatsee-onee]; *(directory assistance)* la ricerca elenco abbonati [reecherka aylenko abbonatee]

▶ a piece of information **un'informazione** [ooneenformatsee-onay]

▶ may I ask you for some information? **posso chiederle alcune informazioni?** [posso kee-ayderlay alkoonay eenformatsee-onee]

▶ where can I find information on...? **dove posso trovare delle informazioni su ...?** [dovay posso trovaray dellay eenformatsee-onee soo]

injection *(medicine)* l'iniezione *f* [eenyetsee-onay]

▶ am I going to need an injection? **devo fare un'iniezione?** [dayvo faray ooneenyetsee-onay]

injure ferire [fayreeray]

▶ to injure oneself **ferirsi** [fayreersee]

▶ I injured myself **mi sono ferito** [mee sono fayreeto]

inside dentro a [dentro a] ♦ all'interno [alleenterno], dentro [dentro]

▶ we'd prefer a table inside **preferiremmo un tavolo all'interno** [prayfayreeremmo oon tavolo alleenterno]

▶ are you allowed inside the castle? **si può entrare nel castello?** [see poo-o entraray nel kastello]

insurance l'assicurazione *f* [asseekooratsee-onay]

▶ what does the insurance cover? **cosa copre l'assicurazione?** [koza kopray lasseekooratsee-onay]

insure *(house, car)* assicurare [asseekooraray]

▶ yes, I'm insured **sì, sono assicurato** [see sono asseekoorato]

interesting interessante [eentayressantay]

▶ it's not a very interesting place **non è un posto molto interessante** [non ay oon posto molto eentayressantay]

international call la chiamata internazionale [kee-amata eenternatsee-onalay]

▶ I'd like to make an international call **vorrei fare una chiamata internazionale** [vorray-ee faray oona kee-amata eenternatsee-onalay]

Internet Internet *m* [eenternet]

▶ where can I connect to the Internet? **dove mi posso connettere a Internet?** [dovay mee posso konnettayray a eenternet]

introduce *(present)* presentare [prayzentaray]

▶ to introduce oneself **presentarsi** [prayzentarsee]

▶ allow me to introduce myself: I'm Michael **lasci che mi presenti: sono Michael** [lashee kay mee prayzentee sono ma-eekel]

invite invitare [eenveetaray]

▸ I'd like to invite you to dinner next weekend **vorrei invitarvi a cena il prossimo fine settimana** [vorray-ee eenveetarvee a chayna eel prosseemo feenay setteemana]

iron *(for ironing)* il ferro da stiro [ferro da steero] ◆ *(clothes)* stirare [steeraray]
▸ I need an iron **mi serve un ferro da stiro** [mee servay oon ferro da steero]

itch il prurito [prooreeto]
▸ I've got an itch on my left leg **ho un prurito alla gamba sinistra** [o oon prooreeto alla gamba seeneestra]

itinerary l'itinerario *m* [eeteenayraree-o]
▸ is it possible to modify the planned itinerary? **è possibile modificare l'itinerario previsto?** [ay posseebeelay modeefeekaray leeteenayraree-o prayveesto]

j

January il gennaio [jenna-yo]
▸ January 4th **il quattro gennaio** [eel kwattro jenna-yo]

Jet Ski® l'acquascooter *m* [akkwaskooter]
▸ I'd like to rent a Jet Ski® **vorrei noleggiare un acquascooter** [vorray-ee nolejaray oon akkwaskooter]

job *(employment)* il lavoro [lavoro]
▸ I'm looking for a summer job in the area **sto cercando un lavoro estivo in questa zona** [sto cherkando oon lavoro esteevo een kwesta dzona]

joke lo scherzo [skertso] ◆ scherzare [skertsaray]
▸ it was just a joke! **era solo uno scherzo!** [ayra solo oono skertso]
▸ it's beyond a joke! **la cosa si fa seria!** [la koza see fa sayree-a]
▸ I was just joking **stavo solo scherzando** [stavo solo skertsando]

journey il viaggio [vee-ajo]
▸ how long does the journey take? **quanto dura il viaggio?** [kwanto doora eel vee-ajo]

juice *(from fruit)* il succo [sookko]
▸ what types of juice do you have? **che succhi avete?** [kay sookkee avaytay]

July il luglio [loolyo]
▸ July 4th **il quattro luglio** [eel kwattro loolyo]

June il giugno [joonyo]
▸ June 2nd **il due giugno** [eel doo-ay joonyo]

just *(recently)* appena [appayna]; *(at that moment)* proprio [propree-o]; *(only, simply)* solo [solo]
▸ he just left **è appena andato via** [ay appayna andato vee-a]
▸ I'll just have one **ne prendo uno solo** [nay prendo oono solo]

k

kayak il kayak [ka-yak]

- can we rent kayaks? **possiamo noleggiare dei kayak?** [possee-amo nolejaray day-ee ka-yak]

keep *(retain)* tenere [taynayray]; *(promise)* mantenere [mantaynayray]

- keep the change **tenga pure il resto** [tenga pooray eel resto]
- can you keep an eye on my bag for me? **mi può tener d'occhio la borsa, per favore?** [mee poo-o taynayr dokkee-o la borsa per favoray]
- I'm sorry, I won't be able to keep the appointment **mi dispiace, devo annullare l'appuntamento** [mee deespee-achay dayvo annoollaray lappoontamento]

key *(for door, container)* la chiave [kee-avay]; *(on keyboard, phone)* il tasto [tasto]

- which is the key to the front door? **qual è la chiave della porta di ingresso?** [kwal ay la kee-avay della porta dee eengresso]

kilometer il chilometro [keelometro]

- how much is it per kilometer? **quanto costa al chilometro?** [kwanto kosta al keelometro]

kind *(nice)* gentile [jenteelay] ◆ *(sort, type)* il genere [jaynayray]

- that's very kind of you **è molto gentile da parte sua** [ay molto jenteelay da partay soo-a]
- what's your favorite kind of music? **qual è il suo genere musicale preferito?** [kwal ay eel soo-o jaynayray moozeekalay prayfayreeto]

kitchen la cucina [koocheena]

- is the kitchen shared? **la cucina è comune?** [la koocheena ay komoonay]

Kleenex® il fazzoletto di carta [fatsoletto dee karta]

- do you have any Kleenex®? **ha dei fazzoletti di carta?** [a day-ee fatsolettee dee karta]

knife il coltello [koltello]

- could I have a knife? **potrei avere un coltello?** [potray-ee avayray oon koltello]

know *(fact)* sapere [sapayray]; *(person, place)* conoscere [konoshayray]

- I don't know **non lo so** [non lo so]
- I don't know this town very well **non conosco molto bene questa città** [non konosko molto baynay kwesta cheetta]
- I know the basics but no more than that **ho delle nozioni di base, niente di più** [o dellay notsee-onee dee bazay nee-entay dee pyoo]
- do you know each other? **vi conoscete?** [vee konoshaytay]

knowledge la conoscenza [konoshentsa]

▸ she has a good knowledge of Italian **ha una buona conoscenza dell'italiano** [a oona boo-na konoshentsa delleetalee-ano]

▸ without my knowledge **a mia insaputa** [a me-a eensapoota]

ladies' room il bagno delle donne [banyo dellay donnay]

▸ where's the ladies' room? **dov'è il bagno delle donne?** [dovay eel banyo dellay donnay]

lake il lago [lago]

▸ can you go swimming in the lake? **si può nuotare nel lago?** [see poo-o noo-otaray nel lago]

lamp la lampada [lampada]

▸ the lamp doesn't work **la lampada non funziona** [la lampada non foontsee-ona]

land *(plane)* atterrare [atterraray]

▸ what time is the plane scheduled to land? **a che ora è previsto che atterri l'aereo?** [a kay ora ay prayveesto kay atterree la-ayray-o]

landmark il punto di riferimento [poonto dee reefayreemento]

▸ do you recognize any landmarks? **ritrova qualche punto di riferimento?** [reetrova kwalkay poonto dee reefayreemento]

lane *(on highway, for bus)* la corsia [korsee-a]

▸ a four-lane highway **un'autostrada a quattro corsie** [oonowtostrada a kwattro korsee-ay]

laptop il PC portatile [peechee portateelay]

▸ my laptop's been stolen **mi hanno rubato il PC portatile** [mee anno roobato eel peechee portateelay]

last *(final)* ultimo(a) [oolteemo(a)] ◆ *(continue)* durare [dooraray]

▸ when does the last bus go? **a che ora parte l'ultimo autobus?** [a kay ora partay loolteemo owtoboos]

▸ when is the last subway train? **a che ora è l'ultima metropolitana?** [a kay ora ay loolteema metropoleetana]

last name il cognome [konyomay]

▸ could I have your last name? **posso avere il suo cognome?** [posso avayray eel soo-o konyomay]

late *(not on time)* in ritardo [een reetardo]; *(after usual time)* tardi [tardee]

▸ the plane was two hours late **l'aereo era in ritardo di due ore** [la-ayray-o ayra een reetardo dee doo-ay oray]

▸ could you tell me if the 1:17 to Rome is running late? **mi potrebbe dire se il treno dell'una e diciassette per Roma ha del ritardo?** [mee potrebbay deeray say eel trayno delloona ay deechassettay per roma a del reetardo]

later più tardi [pyoo tardee]

▸ is there a later train? **c'è un treno più tardi?** [chay oon trayno pyoo tardee]

▸ see you later! **a dopo!** [a dopo]

latest ultimo(a) [oolteemo(a)]

▸ what's the latest time we can check out? **a che ora dobbiamo lasciare la camera al più tardi?** [a kay ora dobbee-amo lasharay la kamayra al pyoo tardee]

laugh la risata [reezata] ♦ ridere [reedayray]

▸ we has a good laugh **ci siamo fatti una bella risata** [chee see-amo fattee oona bella reezata]

▸ I just did it for a laugh **l'ho fatto solo per scherzare** [lo fatto solo per skertsaray]

Laundromat® la lavanderia a gettoni [lavandayree-a a jettonee]

▸ is there a Laundromat® nearby? **c'è una lavanderia a gettoni nei paraggi?** [chay oona lavandayree-a a jettonee nay-ee parajee]

laundry (clothes) il bucato [bookato]; (business, room) la lavanderia [lavandayree-a]

▸ where can we do our laundry? **dove possiamo fare il bucato?** [dovay possee-amo faray eel bookato]

▸ where's the nearest laundry? **dov'è la lavanderia più vicina?** [dovay la lavandayree-a pyoo veecheena]

lawyer l'avvocato *m* [avvokato]

▸ I'm a lawyer **sono avvocato** [sono avvokato]

▸ I need a lawyer **ho bisogno di un avvocato** [o beezonyo dee oon avvokato]

leaflet il dépliant [dayplee-on]

▸ do you have any leaflets in English? **avete dei dépliant in inglese?** [avaytay day-ee dayplee-on een eenglayzay]

learn imparare [eempararay]

▸ I've just learned a few words from a book **ho imparato solo qualche parola da un libro** [o eemparato solo kwalkay parola da oon leebro]

least minimo(a) [meeneemo(a)] ♦ il minimo [meeneemo] ♦ meno [mayno] ♦ **at least** almeno [almayno]

▸ it's the least I can do **è il minimo che io possa fare** [ay eel meeneemo kay ee-o possa faray]

▸ not in the least **per niente** [per nee-entay]

▸ to say the least **per non dire altro** [per non deeray altro]

▸ it's at least a three-hour drive **ci vogliono almeno tre ore in macchina** [chee volyono almayno tray oray een makkeena]

leave (go away from) partire da [parteeray da]; (let stay) lasciare [lasharay]; (forget to take) dimenticare [deementeekaray] ♦ (go away) partire [parteeray]

- can I leave my backpack at the reception desk? **posso lasciare lo zaino alla reception?** [posso lasharay lo dza-eeno alla raysepshon]
- can I leave the car at the airport? **posso lasciare la macchina all'aeroporto?** [posso lasharay la makkeena alla-ayroporto]
- leave us alone! **lasciaci in pace!** [lashachee een pachay]
- I've left something on the plane **ho dimenticato una cosa sull'aereo** [o deementeekato oona koza soolla-ayray-o]
- I'll be leaving at nine o'clock tomorrow morning **partirò domani mattina alle nove** [parteero domanee matteena allay novay]
- what platform does the train for Palermo leave from? **da quale binario parte il treno per Palermo?** [da kwalay beenaree-o partay eel trayno per palermo]

left *(not right)* sinistro(a) [seeneestro(a)] ◆ la sinistra [seeneestra]

- to be left **rimanere** [reemanayray], **esserci ancora** [esserchee ankora]
- are there any tickets left for...? **ci sono ancora dei biglietti per ...?** [chee sono ankora day-ee beelyettee per]
- to the left (of) **a sinistra (di)** [a seeneestra (dee)]

left-hand a sinistra [a seeneestra]

- on your left-hand side **alla sua sinistra** [alla soo-a seeneestra]

leg la gamba [gamba]

- I have a pain in my left leg **ho un dolore alla gamba sinistra** [o oon doloray alla gamba seeneestra]
- I can't move my leg **non riesco a muovere la gamba** [non ree-esko a moo-ovayray la gamba]

lemon il limone [leemonay]

- can I have half a kilo of lemons? **posso avere mezzo kilo di limoni?** [posso avayray medzo keelo dee leemonee]

lend prestare [prestaray]

- could you lend us your car? **ci può prestare la sua macchina?** [chee poo-o prestaray la soo-a makkeena]

lens *(of camera)* la lente [lentay]; *(contact lens)* la lente a contatto [lentay a kontatto]

- there's something on the lens **c'è qualcosa sulla lente** [chay kwalkoza soolla lentay]
- I have hard lenses **porto lenti a contatto rigide** [porto lentee a kontatto reejeeday]
- I have soft lenses **porto lenti a contatto morbide** [porto lentee a kontatto morbeeday]

less meno [mayno]

- less and less **sempre meno** [sempray mayno]
- a little less **un po' (di) meno** [oon po (dee) mayno]

lesson la lezione [letsee-onay]

- how much do lessons cost? **quanto costano le lezioni?** [kwanto kostano lay letsee-onee]

▶ can we take lessons? possiamo prendere lezioni? [possee-amo prendayray letsee-onee]

let off *(allow to disembark)* lasciare [lasharay]
  ▶ could you let me off here, please? mi può lasciare qui, per favore? [me poo-o lasharay kwee per favoray]

letter la lettera [lettayra]
  ▶ I would like to send this letter to the States vorrei spedire questa lettera negli Stati Uniti [vorray-ee spaydeeray kwesta lettayra nelyee statee ooneetee]
  ▶ I confirmed my reservation by letter ho confermato la mia prenotazione per lettera [o konfeermato la mee-a praynotatsee-onay per lettayra]

level *(amount)* il livello [leevello]; *(of building, ship)* il piano [pee-ano]
  ▶ do you know if cabin 27 is on this level? sa se la cabina ventisette è su questo piano? [sa say la kabeena venteesettay ay soo kwesto pee-ano]

license il permesso [permesso]; *(for driving)* la patente [patentay]
  ▶ do you need a license to hunt here? ci vuole un permesso per cacciare qui? [chee voo-olay oon permesso per kacharay kwee]
  ▶ I left my license in my hotel room ho dimenticato la patente nella mia camera in albergo [o deementeekato la patentay nella mee-a kamayra een albergo]

license number il numero di targa [noomayro dee targa]
  ▶ I got the license number ho preso il numero di targa [o prayzo eel noomayro dee targa]

license plate la targa [targa]
  ▶ the license plate was damaged la targa era danneggiata [la targa ayra dannejata]

lifebelt il salvagente [salvagentay]
  ▶ throw me a lifebelt! gettatemi un salvagente! [jettataymee oon salvagentay]

lifeboat la scialuppa (di salvataggio) [shalooppa (dee salvatajo)]
  ▶ how many lifeboats are there? quante scialuppe ci sono? [kwantay shalooppay chee sono]

lifejacket il giubbotto salvagente [joobotto salvagentay]
  ▶ are there any lifejackets? ci sono dei giubbotti salvagente? [chee sono day-ee joobottee salvagentay]

light la luce [loochay]; *(on car)* la luce [loochay], il faro [faro]; *(regulating traffic)* il semaforo [saymaforo]
  ▶ the light doesn't work la luce non funziona [la loochay non foontsee-ona]
  ▶ could you check the lights? può controllare i fari? [poo-o kontrollaray ee faree]
  ▶ stop at the next light si fermi al prossimo semaforo [see fermee al prosseemo saymaforo]
  ▶ do you have a light? ha da accendere? [a da achendayray]

lighter l'accendino *m* [achendeeno]
  ▶ can I borrow your lighter? mi presta il suo accendino? [mee presta eel soo-o achendeeno]

liking versus loving

In Italian, if you want to say 'I like pizza,' you use the verb *piacere* (*mi piace la pizza*). If you want to say 'I love you,' you use the verb *amare* (*ti amo*). If, on the other hand, you want to say you are really fond of someone, you use the formula *voler bene* (*ti voglio bene*).

lighthouse il faro [faro]
▸ are there boat trips to the lighthouse? ci sono gite in barca al faro? [chee sono jeetay een barka al faro]

like come [komay] ✦ *(want)* volere [volayray]
▸ it's quite like English è un po' come l'inglese [ay oon po komay leenglayzay]
▸ I'd like to speak to the manager vorrei parlare con il direttore [vorray-ee parlaray kon eel deerettoray]
▸ I like it mi piace [mee pee-achay]
▸ I don't like it non mi piace [non mee pee-achay]
▸ do you like it here? le piace qui? [lay pee-achay kwee]
▸ I like Chinese food very much mi piace moltissimo la cucina cinese [mee pee-achay molteesseemo la koocheena cheenayzay]
▸ do you like the movies? le piace il cinema? [lay pee-achay eel cheenayma]
▸ would you like a drink? gradisce qualcosa da bere? [gradeeshay kwalkoza da bayray]

lime il lime [la-eem]
▸ can I have half a kilo of limes? posso avere mezzo kilo di lime? [posso avayray medzo keelo dee la-eem]

limit il limite [leemeetay] ✦ limitare [leemeetaray]
▸ is that area off limits? è vietato l'accesso a questa zona? [ay vee-aytato lachesso a kwesta dzona]

line la linea [leenay-a]; *(of people waiting)* la coda [koda]
▸ the line's busy il telefono è occupato [eel taylayfono ay okkoopato]

likes

▸ I really love that painting mi piace moltissimo quel quadro [mee pee-achay molteesseemo kwel kwadro]
▸ I like your brother tuo fratello mi è simpatico [too-o fratello mee ay seempateeko]
▸ I've got a soft spot for her ho un debole per lei [o oon daybolay per lay-ee]
▸ I think she's very nice la trovo molto simpatica [la trovo molto seempateeka]

▶ we had to stand in line for 15 minutes siamo rimasti quindici minuti in coda [see-amo reemastee kweendeechee meenootee een koda]

▶ which line do I take to get to via Roma? che linea devo prendere per andare in via Roma? [kay leenay-a dayvo prendayray per andaray een vee-a roma]

lipstick il rossetto [rossetto]

▶ I need to buy some lipstick devo comprare un rossetto [dayvo kompraray oon rossetto]

listen ascoltare [askoltaray]

▶ listen, I really need to see a doctor ascolti, ho davvero bisogno di un medico [askoltee o davvayro beezonyo dee oon maydeeko]

▶ listen to me carefully mi ascolti attentamente [mee askoltee attentamentay]

liter il litro [leetro]

▶ a two-liter bottle of mineral water una bottiglia d'acqua minerale da due litri [oona botteelya dakkwa meenayralay da doo-ay leetree]

little piccolo(a) [peekkolo(a)] ♦ poco [poko] ♦ **a little** poco(a) [poko(a)] ♦ un po' [oon po]

▶ it's for a little girl è per una bambina [ay per oona bambeena]

▶ as little as possible il meno possibile [eel mayno posseebeelay]

▶ I speak a little Italian parlo un po' l'italiano [parlo oon po leetalee-ano]

▶ we've only got a little money left ci restano solo pochi soldi [chee restano solo pokee soldee]

▶ a little bit un po' [oon po]

▶ a little less un po' di meno [oon po dee mayno]

▶ a little more un po' di più [oon po dee pyoo]

live vivere [veevayray]

▶ do you live around here? vive da queste parti? [veevay da kwestay partee]

▶ I live in Dallas vivo a Dallas [veevo a dallas]

live music la musica dal vivo [moozeeka dal veevo]

▶ I'd like to go to a bar with live music vorrei andare in un bar con della musica dal vivo [vorray-ee andaray een oon bar kon della moozeeka dal veevo]

living room il soggiorno [sojorno]

---

dislikes

▶ I hate football detesto il calcio [daytesto eel kalcho]

▶ I can't stand him non lo sopporto [non lo sopporto]

▶ I don't really like him/her non mi è molto simpatico/a [non mee ay molto seempateeko/a]

▶ I'm not really into modern art non sono proprio un patito dell'arte contemporanea [non sono propree-o oon pateeto dellartay kontemporanay-a]

> I can sleep in the living room posso dormire in soggiorno [posso dormeeray een sojorno]

loaf (of bread) il pane [panay]
> I'd like one of those large loaves vorrei uno di quei pani grossi [vorray-ee oono dee kway-ee panee grossee]

local locale [lokalay]
> is there a local newspaper? c'è un quotidiano locale? [chay oon kwoteedee-ano lokalay]
> what's the local specialty? qual è la specialità del posto? [kwal ay la spaychaleeta del posto]

lock la serratura [serratoora] ◆ chiudere a chiave [kee-oodayray a kee-avay]
> the lock's broken la serratura è rotta [la serratoora ay rotta]
> I locked the door ho chiuso la porta a chiave [o kee-oozo la porta a kee-avay]

lock out
> to lock oneself out rimanere chiuso fuori [reemanayray kee-oozo foo-oree]
> I've locked myself out sono rimasto chiuso fuori [sono reemasto kee-oozo foo-oree]

long lungo [loongo]
> it's 10 feet long è lungo tre metri [ay loongo tray metree]
> I waited for a long time ho aspettato a lungo [o aspettato a loongo]
> how long? quanto tempo? [kwanto tempo]
> how long will it take? quanto ci vorrà? [kwanto chee vorra]
> we're not sure how long we're going to stay non sappiamo bene quanto ci fermeremo [non sappee-amo baynay kwanto chee fermayraymo]

look (with eyes) l'occhiata f [okkee-ata]; (appearance) l'aspetto m [aspetto]
◆ (with eyes) guardare [gwardaray]; (seem) sembrare [sembraray]
> could you have a look at my car? potrebbe dare un'occhiata alla mia macchina? [potrebbay daray oonokkee-ata alla mee-a makkeena]
> no, thanks, I'm just looking no grazie, sto solo guardando [no gratsee-ay, sto solo gwardando]
> what does she look like? com'è fatta? [komay fatta]
> you look like your brother assomiglia a suo fratello [assomeelya a soo-o fratello]
> it looks like it's going to rain sembra che pioverà [sembra kay pee-ovayra]

look after (child, ill person) occuparsi di [okkooparsee dee]; (luggage) sorvegliare [sorvelyaray]
> can someone look after the children for us? qualcuno può occuparsi dei bambini per noi? [kwalkoono poo-o okkooparsee day-ee bambeenee per no-ee]
> can you look after my things for a minute? può sorvegliare un attimo le mie cose? [poo-o sorvelyaray oon atteemo lay mee-ay kozay]

look for cercare [cherkaray]

▸ I'm looking for a good restaurant **sto cercando un buon ristorante** [sto cherkando oon boo-on reestorantay]

lose *(be unable to find)* **perdere** [perdayray]

▸ I've lost the key to my room **ho perso la chiave della mia camera** [o perso la kee-avay della mee-a kamayra]

▸ I've lost my way **mi sono perso** [mee sono perso]

lost smarrito(a) [zmarreeto(a)]

▸ who do you have to see about lost luggage? **a chi bisogna rivolgersi per dei bagagli smarriti?** [a kee beezonya reevoljersee per day-ee bagalyee zmarreetee]

▸ could you help me? I seem to be lost **mi può aiutare? credo di essermi perso** [mee poo-o a-yootaray craydo dee essermee perso]

▸ to get lost **perdersi** [perdersee]

▸ get lost! **togliti dai piedi!** [tolyeetee da-ee pee-aydee]

lost-and-found l'ufficio *m* **oggetti smarriti** [ooffeecho ojettee zmarreetee]

▸ where's the lost-and-found? **dov'è l'ufficio oggetti smarriti?** [dovay looffeecho ojettee zmarreetee]

lot

▸ a lot of ... **molto/a ...** [molto/a]

▸ are there a lot of things to see around here? **ci sono molte cose da vedere da queste parti?** [chee sono moltay kozay da vaydayray da kwestay partee]

▸ will there be a lot of other people there? **ci sarà molta altra gente?** [chee sara molta altra jentay]

▸ a lot **molto** [molto]

▸ thanks a lot **grazie mille** [gratsee-ay meeellay]

loud *(noise)* **forte** [fortay]; *(voice, music)* **alto(a)** [alto(a)]

▸ the television is too loud **la televisione è troppo alta** [la taylayveezee-onay ay troppo alta]

loudly *(speak)* **forte** [fortay]

▸ can you speak a little more loudly? **può parlare un po' più forte?** [poo-o parlaray oon po pyoo fortay]

love amare [amaray]

▸ I love you **ti amo** [tee amo]

▸ I love the movies **adoro il cinema** [adoro eel cheenayma]

▸ I love cooking **adoro cucinare** [adoro koocheenaray]

lovely bello(a) [bello(a)]

▸ what a lovely room! **che bella camera!** [kay bella kamayra]

▸ it's lovely today **il tempo è bello oggi** [eel tempo ay bello ojee]

low *(temperature)* **basso(a)** [basso (a)]; *(speed)* **ridotto(a)** [reedotto(a)]

▸ the ceiling is very low in this room **il soffitto è molto basso in questa camera** [eel soffeetto ay molto basso een kwesta kamayra]

low beam
- keep your lights on low beam lascia gli anabbaglianti [lasha lyee anabbalyantee]

lower abbassare [abbassaray] ◆ inferiore [infayree-oray]
- is it OK if I lower the blind a little? va bene se abbasso un po' la tapparella? [va baynay say abasso oon po la tapparella]
- how do we get to the lower level? come si fa per andare al piano inferiore? [komay see fa per andaray al pee-ano infayree-oray]

low-fat *(yogurt)* magro(a) [magro(a)]
- do you have any low-fat yogurt? avete dello yogurt magro? [avaytay dello yogoort magro]

low season la bassa stagione [bassa stajonay]
- what are prices like in the low season? come sono i prezzi in bassa stagione? [komay sono ee pretsee een bassa stajonay]

low tide la bassa marea [bassa maray-a]
- what time is low tide today? a che ora c'è oggi la bassa marea? [a kay ora chay ojee la bassa maray-a]

luck la fortuna [fortoona]
- good luck! buona fortuna! [boo-ona fortoona]

luggage i bagagli [bagalyee]
- my luggage hasn't arrived i miei bagagli non sono arrivati [ee mee-ay-ee bagalyee non sono arreevatee]
- I'd like to report the loss of my luggage vorrei fare una denuncia di smarrimento bagagli [vorray-ee faray oona daynooncha dee zmarreemento bagalyee]

luggage cart il carrello bagagli [karrello bagalyee]
- I'm looking for a luggage cart sto cercando un carrello bagagli [sto cherkando oon karrello bagalyee]

lunch il pranzo [prandzo]
- to have lunch pranzare [prandzaray]
- what time is lunch served? a che ora è servito il pranzo? [a kay ora ay serveeto ee prandzo]

m

machine-washable lavabile in lavatrice [lavabeelay een lavatreechay]
- is it machine-washable? si può lavare in lavatrice? [see poo-o lavaray een lavatreechay]

maid la cameriera [kamayree-ayra]
- what time does the maid come? a che ora arriva la cameriera? [a kay ora arreeva la kamayree-ayra]

mail

Local post offices are generally open from 8 a.m. to 1:30 p.m. (but only until 12:30 p.m. on Saturdays). Only main post offices are open in the afternoon, up until 6:30 or 7 p.m. In small villages the post office is often open only every other day. Mailboxes are red or blue.

maid service il servizio di pulizia in camera [serveetsee-o dee pooleetsee-a een kamayra]
▶ is there maid service? c'è il servizio di pulizia in camera? [chay eel serveetsee-o dee pooleetsee-a een kamayra]

mailbox la buca delle lettere [booka dellay lettayray]
▶ where's the nearest mailbox? dov'è la buca delle lettere più vicina? [dovay la booka dellay lettayray pyoo veecheena]

main course il secondo (piatto) [saykondo (pee-atto)]
▶ what are you having for your main course? cosa prende di secondo? [koza prenday dee saykondo]

mainline la linea principale [leenay-a preencheepalay]
▶ where are the mainline trains? dove sono i treni della linea principale? [dovay sono ee traynee della leenay-a preencheepalay]

make (create, produce) fare [faray]; (cause to become) rendere [rendayray]
▶ how is this dish made? come è fatto questo piatto? [komay ay fatto kwesto pee-atto]
▶ I hope to make new friends here spero di farmi nuovi amici qui [spayro dee farmee noo-ovee ameechee kwee]
▶ that would make me very happy questo mi renderebbe molto felice [kwesto mee rendayrebbay molto fayleechay]

make up (compensate for) recuperare [raykoopayraray]; (invent) inventare [eenventaray]
▶ will we be able to make up the time we've lost? riusciremo a recuperare il tempo che abbiamo perso? [re-oosheeraymo a raykoopayraray eel tempo kay abbee-amo perso]

man l'uomo *m* [oo-omo]
▶ that man is bothering me quell'uomo mi sta importunando [kwelloo-omo mee sta eemportoonando]
▶ where's the men's changing room? dov'è lo spogliatoio degli uomini? [dovay lo spolyato-yo delyee oo-omeenee]

man-made (fibers) sintetico(a) [seentayteeko(a)]
▶ is it man-made? è sintetico? [ay seentayteeko]

many molti(e) [moltee(ay)]
▶ are there many good restaurants here? ci sono molti buoni ristoranti qui? [chee sono moltee boo-onee reestorantee kwee]

▶ how many? quanti/e? [kwantee/ay]

▶ how many days will you be staying? quanti giorni si ferma? [kwantee jornee see ferma]

map la mappa [mappa]

▶ where can I buy a map of the area? dove posso comprare una mappa della zona? [dovay posso kompraray oona mappa della dzona]

▶ can you show me where we are on the map? mi può far vedere dove siamo sulla mappa? [mee poo-o far vaydayray dovay see-amo soolla mappa]

▶ can I have a map of the subway? posso avere una mappa della metropolitana? [posso avayray oona mappa della metropoleetana]

March il marzo [martso]

▶ March 1st il primo marzo [eel preemo martso]

market il mercato [merkato]

▶ is there a market in the square every day? c'è il mercato in piazza tutti i giorni? [chay eel merkato een pee-atsa toottee ee jornee]

married sposato(a) [spozato(a)]

▶ are you married? è sposato? [ay spozato]

mass *(religious service)* la messa [messa]

▶ what time is mass? a che ora è la messa? [a kay ora ay la messa]

match *(for lighting)* il fiammifero [fee-ammeefayro]

▶ do you have any matches? ha dei fiammiferi? [a day-ee fee-ammeefayree]

matter importare [eemportaray]

▶ it doesn't matter non importa [non eemporta]

mattress il materasso [matayrasso]

▶ the mattresses are saggy i materassi sono deformati [ee matayrassee sono dayformatee]

May il maggio [majo]

▶ May 9th il nove maggio [eel novay majo]

maybe forse [forsay]

▶ maybe the weather will be better tomorrow forse il tempo sarà migliore domani [forsay eel tempo sara meelyoray domanee]

meal il pasto [pasto]

▶ are meals included? i pasti sono compresi? [ee pastee sono komprayzee]

mean *(signify)* significare [seenyeefeekaray], voler dire [volayr deeray]; *(matter)* significare [seenyeefeekaray]; *(intend)* volere [volayray]

▶ what does that word mean? cosa significa quella parola? [koza seenyeefeeka kwella parola]

▶ I mean it dico sul serio [deeko sool sayree-o]

▶ I didn't mean it non l'ho fatto apposta [non lo fatto apposta]

---

meals (i)

The food is one of the reasons why people come to Italy. Meals can have up to four courses: an *antipasto* (hors d'oeuvre), a *primo* (pasta or risotto), a *secondo* (meat or fish) accompanied by *contorni* (side orders) and finally the *dolce* (dessert). Of course, if you go to a restaurant, you don't have to eat all four courses: you can have as many or as few as you like.

---

meat la carne [karnay]
- I don't eat meat non mangio carne [non manjo karnay]

mechanic il meccanico [mekkaneeko]
- what did the mechanic say was wrong with the car? cos'è che non va nella macchina secondo il meccanico? [kozay kay non va nella makkeena saykondo eel mekkaneeko]

medication il farmaco [farmako]
- I'm not taking any other medication at the moment non sto prendendo altri farmaci al momento [non sto prendendo altree farmachee al momento]

medicine la medicina [maydeecheena]
- how many times a day do I have to take the medicine? quante volte al giorno devo prendere la medicina? [kwantay voltay al jorno dayvo prendray la maydeecheena]

medium *(size)* medio(a) [maydee-o(a)]; *(steak)* non troppo cotto(a) [non troppo kotto(a)] ♦ *(in size)* la (taglia) media [(talya) maydee-a]
- I'd like my steak medium, please vorrei la bistecca non troppo cotta [vorray-ee la beestekka non troppo kotta]
- do you have this shirt in a medium? avete la media di questa maglietta? [avaytay la maydee-a dee kwesta malyetta]

meet *(by chance)* incontrare [eenkontraray]; *(by arrangement)* incontrarsi con [eenkontrarsee kon]; *(make the acquaintance of)* conoscere [konoshayray] ♦ *(by chance)* incontrarsi [eenkontrarsee]; *(by arrangement)* trovarsi [trovarsee], vedersi [vaydersee]; *(become acquainted)* conoscersi [konoshersee]
- meet you at 9 o'clock in front of the town hall ci troviamo alle nove di fronte al municipio [chee trovee-amo allay novay dee frontay al mooneecheepee-o]
- I have to meet my friend at 9 o'clock devo incontrarmi con il mio amico alle nove [dayvo eenkontrarmee kon eel mee-o ameeko allay novay]
- pleased to meet you piacere (di conoscerla) [pee-achayray (dee konosherla)]
- goodbye! it was nice meeting you arrivederci! è stato un piacere conoscerti [arreevayderchee ay stato oon pee-achayray konoshertee]
- Claudio, I'd like you to meet Mr. Dalton Claudio, vorrei presentarti il signor Dalton [clowdee-o vorray-ee prayzentartee eel seenyor dolton]

‣ where shall we meet? dove ci troviamo? [dovay cee trov-eeamo]
‣ what time are we meeting tomorrow? a che ora ci vediamo domani? [a kay ora chee vaydee-amo domanee]

member *(of club)* il socio [socho], la socia [socha]
‣ do you have to be a member? bisogna essere soci? [beezonya essayray sochee]

men's room il bagno degli uomini [banyo delyee oo-omeenee]
‣ where's the men's room? dov'è il bagno degli uomini? [dovay eel banyo delyee oo-omeenee]

menu il menu [maynoo]
‣ can we see the menu? possiamo vedere il menu? [possee-amo vaydrayray eel maynoo]
‣ do you have a menu in English? avete un menu in inglese? [avaytay oon maynoo een eenglayzay]
‣ do you have a children's menu? avete un menu per bambini? [avaytay oon maynoo per bambeenee]

message il messaggio [messajo]
‣ can I leave a message? posso lasciare un messaggio? [posso lasharay oon messajo]
‣ can you give him a message? può riferirgli qualcosa? [poo-o reefayreerlyee kwalkoza]
‣ did you get my message? ha ricevuto il mio messaggio? [a reechayvooto eel mee-o messajo]

meter *(measurement)* il metro [metro]; *(device)* il contatore [kontatoray]
‣ it's about five meters long è lungo circa cinque metri [ay loongo cheerka cheenkway metree]

midday mezzogiorno m [medzojorno]
‣ we have to be there by midday dobbiamo essere lì per mezzogiorno [dobbeeamo essayray lee per medzojorno]

midnight la mezzanotte [medzanottay]
‣ it's midnight è mezzanotte [ay medzanottay]

mileage *(distance)* il chilometraggio [keelometrajo]
‣ is there unlimited mileage? c'è il chilometraggio illimitato? [chay eel keelometrajo eelleemeetato]

milk il latte [lattay]
‣ a liter of milk un litro di latte [oon leetro dee lattay]
‣ tea with milk tè al latte [tay al lattay]

milk chocolate il cioccolato al latte [chokkolato al lattay]
‣ I prefer milk chocolate preferisco il cioccolato al latte [prayfayreesko eel chokkolato al lattay]

mind
‣ I don't mind per me è lo stesso [per may ay lo stesso]

- do you mind if I smoke? **le dispiace se fumo?** [lay deespee-achay say foomo]
- do you mind if I open the window? **le dispiace se apro il finestrino?** [lay deespee-achay say apro eel feenestreeno]
- never mind **non fa niente** [non fa nee-entay]

mineral water l'acqua *f* minerale [akkwa meenayralay]

- could I have a bottle of mineral water, please? **potrei avere una bottiglia d'acqua minerale, per favore?** [potray-ee avayray oona botteelya dee akkwa meenayralay per favoray]

minus meno [mayno]

- it's minus two degrees outside! **fa meno due fuori!** [fa mayno doo-ay foo-oree]

minute il minuto [meenooto]

- we're going in a minute **andiamo tra un minuto** [andee-amo tra oon meenooto]

mirror lo specchio [spekkee-o]

- the mirror's cracked **lo specchio è rotto** [lo spekkee-o ay rotto]

miss *(be too late for)* perdere [perdayray]

- I've missed my connection **ho perso la coincidenza** [o perso la co-eencheedentsa]
- we're going to miss the train **perderemo il treno** [perdayraymo eel trayno]
- I missed you **mi sei mancato** [mee say-ee mankato]

missing

- to be missing **mancare** [mankaray]
- one of my suitcases is missing **manca una delle mie valigie** [manka oona dellay mee-ay valeejay]

mistake l'errore *m* [erroray]

- I think there's a mistake with the bill **credo che ci sia un errore nel conto** [craydo kay chee see-a oon erroray nel konto]
- you've made a mistake with my change **si è sbagliato a darmi il resto** [see ay zbalyato a darmee eel resto]

moment il momento [momento]

- for the moment, we prefer staying in Rome **per il momento, preferiamo rimanere a Roma** [per eel momento prayfayree-amo reemanayray a roma]

Monday il lunedì [loonaydee]

- we're arriving/leaving on Monday **arriviamo/partiamo lunedì** [arreevee-amo/partee-amo loonaydee]

money i soldi [soldee]

- I don't have much money **non ho molti soldi** [non o moltee soldee]
- where can I change money? **dove posso cambiare dei soldi?** [dovay posso kambee-aray day-ee soldee]
- I want my money back **rivoglio i miei soldi** [reevolyo ee mee-ay-ee soldee]

money order il vaglia [valya]

- I'm expecting a money order **sto aspettando un vaglia** [sto aspettando oon valya]

month il mese [mayzay]
- I'm leaving in a month parto tra un mese [parto tra oon mayzay]

monument il monumento [monoomento]
- what does this monument commemorate? cosa commemora questo monumento? [koza kommaymora kwesto monoomento]

more più [pyoo]
- I don't want any more, thank you non ne voglio più, grazie [non nay volyo pyoo gratsee-ay]
- a little more un po' di più [oon po dee pyoo]
- can we have some more bread? possiamo avere ancora un po' di pane? [possee-amo avayray ankora oon po dee panay]
- could I have a little more wine? potrei avere ancora un po' di vino? [potray-ee avayray ankora oon po dee veeno]
- I don't want to spend any more non voglio spendere di più [non volyo spendayray dee pyoo]
- should we allow more than 20 euros a person? dobbiamo contare più di venti euro a testa? [dobbee-amo kontaray pyoo dee ventee ay-ooro a testa]

morning il mattino [matteeno]; (expressing duration) la mattinata [matteenata]
- is the museum open in the morning? il museo è aperto al mattino? [eel moozay-o ay aperto al matteeno]

morning-after pill la pillola del giorno dopo [peellola del jorno dopo]
- I need the morning-after pill ho bisogno della pillola del giorno dopo [o beezonyo della peellola del jorno dopo]

mosque la moschea [moskay-a]
- where's the nearest mosque? dov'è la moschea più vicina? [dovay la moskay-a pyoo veecheena]

most (the majority of) la maggior parte di [la major partay dee]; (the largest amount of) più [pyoo] ◆ (the majority) la maggior parte [la major partay]; (the largest amount) il massimo [masseemo] ◆ (to the greatest extent) di più [dee pyoo]; (very) molto [molto]
- are you here most days? è qui quasi tutti i giorni? [ay kwee kwazee toottee ee jornee]
- that's the most I can offer questo è il massimo che posso offrire [kwesto ay eel masseemo kay posso offreeray]

mother la madre [madray]
- this is my mother questa è mia madre [kwesta ay mee-a madray]

motorboat il motoscafo [motoskafo]
- can we rent a motorboat? possiamo noleggiare un motoscafo? [possee-amo nolejaray oon motoskafo]

motorcycle la motocicletta [motocheekletta]
- I'd like to rent a motorcycle vorrei noleggiare una motocicletta [vorray-ee nolejaray oona motocheekletta]

mountain la montagna [montanya]

> in the mountains in montagna [een montanya]

mountain hut il rifugio [reefujo]

> we slept in a mountain hut abbiamo dormito in un rifugio [abbee-amo dormeeto een oon reefujo]

mouth la bocca [bokka]

> I've got a strange taste in my mouth ho uno strano gusto in bocca [o oono strano goosto een bokka]

move *(movement)* il movimento [moveemento]; *(step, measure)* la mossa [mossa] ◆ *(part of body)* muovere [moo-ovayray]; *(object)* spostare [spostaray] ◆ *(shift)* muoversi [moo-oversee]; *(step aside)* spostarsi [spostarsee]

> I can't move my leg non riesco a muovere la gamba [non ree-esko a moo-ovayray la gamba]
> don't move him non lo spostate [non lo spostatay]
> why aren't we moving? perché non ci muoviamo? [perkay non chee moo-ovee-amo]

movie il film [feelm]

> have you seen ...'s latest movie? ha visto l'ultimo film di ...? [a veesto loolteemo feelm dee]
> is it a subtitled movie? è un film sottotitolato? [ay oon feelm sottoteetolato]

movie theater il cinema [cheenayma]

> where is there a movie theater? dove c'è un cinema? [dovay chay oon cheenayma]
> what's on at the movie theater? cosa danno al cinema? [koza danno al cheenayma]

much molto(a) [molto(a)]

> I don't have much money non ho molti soldi [non o moltee soldee]
> how much is it? *(asking price)* quanto costa? [kwanto kosta]; *(asking total)* quanto fa? [kwanto fa]
> how much is it for one night? quanto costa una notte? [kwanto kosta oona nottay]
> how much is it per day and per person? quanto costa a testa per giorno? [kwanto kosta a testa per jorno]
> how much does it cost per hour? quanto costa all'ora? [kwanto kosta allora]
> how much is a ticket to Rome? quanto costa un biglietto per Roma? [kwanto kosta oon beelyetto per roma]

museum il museo [moozay-o]

> what time does the museum open? a che ora apre il museo? [a kay ora apray eel moozay-o]

music la musica [moozeeka]

> what kind of music do they play in that club? che genere di musica c'è in quella discoteca? [kay jaynayray dee moozeeka chay een kwella deeskotayka]

must dovere [dovayray]
- that must cost a lot **deve costare parecchio** [dayvay kostaray parekkee-o]

mustard la senape [saynapay]
- is it strong mustard? **è forte la senape?** [ay fortay la saynapay]

nail *(on finger, toe)* l'unghia *f* [oonghee-a]
- I need to cut my nails **devo tagliarmi le unghie** [dayvo talyarmee lay oonghee-ay]

nail polish lo smalto [zmalto]
- I'd like to find nail polish in a dark shade of red **vorrei trovare uno smalto in una tonalità rosso scuro** [vorray-ee trovaray oono zmalto een oona tonaleeta rosso skooro]

name il nome [nomay]
- what is your name? **come si chiama?** [komay see kee-ama]
- my name is Patrick **mi chiamo Patrick** [mee kee-amo patreek]
- hello, my name's Jane **salve, mi chiamo Jane** [salvay, mee kee-amo jayn]
- I have a reservation in the name of Jackson **ho una prenotazione a nome Jackson** [o oona praynotatsee-onay a nomay dee jakson]

napkin il tovagliolo [tovalyolo]
- could I have a clean napkin, please? **potrei avere un tovagliolo pulito, per favore?** [potray-ee avayray oon tovalyolo pooleeto per favoray]

national holiday la festa nazionale [festa natsee-onalay]
- tomorrow is a national holiday **domani è una festa nazionale** [domanee ay oona festa natsee-onalay]

nationality la nazionalità [natsee-onaleeta]
- what nationality are you? **di che nazionalità è?** [dee kay natsee-onaleeta ay]

nature la natura [natoora]
- I like to take long walks outdoors and enjoy nature **mi piace fare lunghe passeggiate all'aria aperta e godermi la natura** [mee pee-achay faray loongay passejatay allaree-a aperta ay godermee la natoora]

nausea la nausea [nowzay-a]
- I've had nausea all day **ho avuto la nausea tutto il giorno** [o avooto la nowzay-a tootto eel jorno]

near *(close)* vicino(a) [veecheeno(a)] ◆ *(close by)* vicino [veecheeno] ◆ *(close to)* vicino a [veecheeno a]
- where's the nearest subway station? **dov'è la stazione della metropolitana più vicina?** [dovay la statsee-onay della metropoleetana pyoo veecheena]
- it's near the station **è vicino alla stazione** [ay veecheeno alla statsee-onay]
- very near the airport **vicinissimo all'aeroporto** [veecheeneessemo alla-ayroporto]

nature

If you're a nature lover, be sure to go hiking in one of Italy's five national parks: *Gran Paradiso* and *Stelvio*, in the Alps, where protected species like the ibex and the chamois live; *Abruzzo* and *Calabria*, in the Apennine mountains, the last refuge of the Italian wolf; or the *Circeo*, a forest near the ocean in Lazio.

nearby nei paraggi [nay-ee parajee]
> is there a supermarket nearby? c'è un supermercato nei paraggi? [chay oon soopermerkato nay-ee parajee]

neck il collo [kollo]
> I have a sore neck ho il torcicollo [o eel torcheekollo]

need il bisogno [beezonyo] ◆ aver bisogno di [avayr beezonyo dee] ◆ dovere [dovayray]
> I need something for a cough ho bisogno di qualcosa per la tosse [o beezonyo dee kwlakoza per la tossay]
> I need to be at the airport by six (o'clock) devo essere all'aeroporto per le sei [dayvo essayray alla-ayroporto per lay say-ee]
> we need to go dobbiamo andare [dobbee-amo andaray]

neither nessuno(a) [nessoono(a)] ◆ né [nay] ◆ nemmeno [nemmayno]
> neither of us nessuno di noi (due) [nessoono dee no-ee (doo-ay)]
> neither... nor... né ... né ... [nemmayno ee-o]
> me neither nemmeno io [nemmayno ee-o]

neutral
> to be in neutral essere in folle [essayray een follay]
> make sure the car's in neutral assicurati che l'auto sia in folle [asseekooratee kay lowto see-a een follay]

never mai [ma-ee]
> I've never been to Italy before non sono mai stato in Italia prima [non sono ma-ee stato een eetalee-a preema]

new nuovo(a) [noo-ovo(a)]
> could we have a new tablecloth, please? possiamo avere una nuova tovaglia, per favore [possee-amo avayray oona noo-ova tovalya per favoray]

news *(information)* le notizie [noteetsee-ay]; *(on TV)* il telegiornale [taylayjornalay]; *(on radio)* il giornale radio [jornalay radee-o]
> a piece of news una notizia [oona noteetsee-a]
> that's great news! è fantastico! [ay fantasteeko]
> I heard it on the news l'ho sentito al giornale radio [lo senteeto al jornalay radee-o]

where to spend the night

In addition to campgrounds (*campeggi*), youth hostels (*ostelli della gioventù*), and guesthouses and farms in the country (*agriturismi*), there are family-run bed-and-breakfasts (*pensioni* or *locande*), which may offer up to three meals a day. Hotels (*hotel* or *alberghi*) have from 1 to 5 stars and are naturally more expensive.

newspaper il giornale [jornalay]
 ▸ do you have any English-language newspapers? **avete dei giornali in inglese?** [avaytay day-ee jornalee een eenglayzay]

New Year l'anno nuovo *m* [anno noo-ovo]
 ▸ Happy New Year! **buon anno (nuovo)!** [boo-on anno (noo-ovo)]

New Year's Day il (giorno di) capodanno [(jorno dee) capodanno]
 ▸ are stores open on New Year's Day? **i negozi sono aperti il giorno d capodanno?** [ee negotsee sono apertee eel jorno dee capodanno]

next prossimo(a) [prosseemo(a)] ◆ **next to** vicino a [veecheeno a]
 ▸ when is the next guided tour? **a che ora è la prossima visita guidata?** [a kay ora ay la prosseema veezeeta gweedata]
 ▸ when is the next train to Venice? **a che ora è il prossimo treno per Venezia?** [a kay ora ay eel prosseemo trayno per vaynetsee-a]
 ▸ what time is the next flight to London? **a che ora è il prossimo volo per Londra?** [a kay ora ay eel prosseemo volo per londra]
 ▸ can we park next to the tent? **possiamo parcheggiare vicino alla tenda?** [possee-amo parkejaray veecheeno alla tenda]

nice *(vacation, food)* buono(a) [boo-ono(a)]; *(kind)* gentile [jenteelay]; *(likable,* simpatico(a) [seempateeko(a)]
 ▸ have a nice vacation! **buone vacanze!** [boo-onay vakantsay]
 ▸ we found a really nice little hotel **abbiamo trovato un alberghetto davvero simpatico** [abbee-amo trovato oon alberghetto davvayro seempateeko]
 ▸ goodbye! it was nice meeting you **arrivederci! è stato un piacere conoscerla** [arreevayderchee ay stato oon pee-acharay konosherla]

night la notte [nottay]
 ▸ how much is it per night? **quanto costa a notte?** [kwanto kosta a nottay]
 ▸ I'd like to stay an extra night **vorrei fermarmi un'altra notte** [vorray-ee fermarme oonaltra nottay]

nightclub la discoteca [deeskotayka]
 ▸ are there any good nightclubs in this town? **ci sono delle belle discoteche in questa città?** [chee sono dellay bellay deeskotaykay een kwesta cheetta]

nine nove [novay]

▸ there are nine of us **siamo in nove** [see-amo een novay]

▸ we have a reservation for nine (o'clock) **abbiamo prenotato per le nove** [abbee-amo praynotato per lay novay]

no no [no] ◆ nessuno(a) [nessoono(a)]

▸ no, thanks! **no, grazie!** [no gratsee-ay]

▸ a cup of tea with no milk or sugar, please **una tazza di tè senza latte né zucchero, per favore** [oona tatsa dee tay sentsa lattay nay tsookkayro per favoray]

nobody nessuno [nessoono]

▸ there's nobody at the reception desk **non c'è nessuno alla reception** [non chay nessoono alla raysepshon]

noise il rumore [roomoray]

▸ to make a noise **far rumore** [far roomoray]

▸ I heard a funny noise **ho sentito uno strano rumore** [o senteeto oono strano roomoray]

noisy rumoroso(a) [roomorozo(a)]

▸ I'd like another room: mine is too noisy **vorrei un'altra camera: la mia è troppo rumorosa** [vorray-ee oonaltra kamayra la mee-a ay troppo roomoroza]

nonsmoker il non fumatore [non foomatoray], la non fumatrice [non foomatreechay]

▸ we're nonsmokers **non fumiamo** [non foomee-amo]

nonsmoking non fumatori [non foomatoree]

▸ aren't restaurants nonsmoking? **i ristoranti non sono non fumatori?** [ee reestorantee non sono non foomatoree]

nonsmoking compartment lo scompartimento non fumatori [skomparteemento non foomatoree]

▸ are there only nonsmoking compartments? **ci sono solo scompartimenti non fumatori?** [chee sono solo skomparteementee non foomatoree]

nonstop diretto(a) [deeretto(a)] ◆ direttamente [deerettamentay]

▸ I'd like a nonstop flight from Milan to Chicago **vorrei un volo diretto da Milano a Chicago** [vorray-ee oon volo deeretto da meelano a sheekago]

noon mezzogiorno m [medzojorno]

▸ we leave at noon **partiamo a mezzogiorno** [partee-amo a medzojorno]

no one nessuno [nessoono]

▸ there's no one there **non c'è nessuno lì** [non chay nessoono lee]

normal normale [normalay] ◆ la norma [norma]

▸ is it normal for it to rain as much as this? **è normale che piova così tanto?** [ay normalay kay pee-ova kozee tanto]

not non [non]

▸ I don't like spinach **non mi piacciono gli spinaci** [non mee pee-achono lyee speenachee]

- I don't think so non credo [non kraydo]
- not at all per niente [per nee-entay]

note *(short letter)* il biglietto [beelyetto]; *(written reminder)* l'appunto *m* [appoonto]
- could I leave a note for him? posso lasciargli un biglietto? [posso lasharlyee oon beelyetto]

nothing niente [nee-entay]
- there's nothing to do here in the evening non c'è niente da fare qui la sera [non chay nee-entay da faray kwee la sayra]
- there's nothing I can do about it non ci posso fare niente [non chee posso faray nee-entay]

November il novembre [novembray]
- November 7th il sette novembre [eel settay novembray]

now ora [ora], adesso [adesso]
- what should we do now? cosa facciamo ora? [koza fachamo ora]

number il numero [noomayro]
- my name is... and my number is... mi chiamo ... e il mio numero è ... [mee kee-amo ay eel mee-o noomayro ay]

occupied *(bathroom)* occupato(a) [okkoopato(a)]
- the restroom's occupied il bagno è occupato [eel banyo ay okkoopato]

o'clock
- it's eight o'clock sono le otto [sono lay otto]

October l'ottobre *m* [ottobray]
- October 12th il dodici ottobre [eel dodeechee ottobray]

of di [dee]
- one of us uno di noi [oono dee no-ee]

off *(indicating movement)* via [vee-a] ♦ *(at a distance from)* da [da]
- my hotel is just off the main square il mio albergo è a pochi passi dalla piazza principale [eel mee-o albergo ay a pokee passee dalla pee-atsa preencheepalay]
- we're going to an island off the coast of Sicily andiamo su un'isola vicino alla costa siciliana [andee-amo soo ooneezola veecheeno alla kosta seecheelee-ana]
- isn't it 10 percent off the marked price? non c'è uno sconto del dieci percento sul prezzo indicato? [non chay oono skonto del dee-aychee perchento sool pretso eendeekato]

offer offrire [offreeray]

▸ can I offer you a cigarette? posso offrirle una sigaretta? [posso offreerlay oona seegaretta]

office l'ufficio *m* [oofeecho]

▸ where is the hotel office? dov'è l'ufficio dell'albergo? [dovay loofeecho dellalbergo]

often spesso [spesso]

▸ how often does the ferry sail? con che frequenza salpa il traghetto? [kon kay fraykwentsa salpa eel traghetto]

oil l'olio *m* [olee-o]

▸ could you check the oil, please? può controllare l'olio, per favore? [poo-o kontrollaray lolee-o per favoray]

OK okay [okay], va bene [va baynay]

▸ that's OK va bene [va baynay]

▸ do you think it's still OK? pensa che vada ancora bene? [pensa kay vada ankora baynay]

old vecchio(a) [vekkee-o]

▸ how old are you? quanti anni hai? [kwantee annee a-ee]

▸ I'm 18 years old ho diciott'anni [o deechottannee]

▸ my brother is older than me mio fratello è più vecchio di me [mee-o fratello ay pyoo vekkee-o dee may]

▸ my guidebook's rather old and not up to date la mia guida è un po' vecchia e non è aggiornata [la mee-a gweeda ay oon po vekkee-a ay non ay ajornata]

▸ have you visited the old town? ha visitato il centro storico? [a veezeetato eel chentro storeeko]

on *(working)* acceso(a) [achayzo(a)]

▸ you've left the light on ha lasciato la luce accesa [a lashato la loochay achayza]

▸ how long is it on for? quanto dura? [kwanto doora]

once una volta [oona volta] ✦ **at once** subito [soobeeto]

▸ I've been here once before sono già stato qui una volta [sono ja stato kwee oona volta]

▸ please do it at once per favore, lo faccia subito [per favoray lo facha soobeeto]

one uno(a) [oono (a)]

▸ a table for one, please un tavolo per una persona, per favore [oon tavolo per oona persona per favoray]

one-way (ticket) il biglietto di sola andata [beelyetto dee sola andata]

▸ how much is a one-way ticket to Perugia? quanto costa un biglietto di sola andata per Perugia? [kwanto kosta oon beelyetto dee sola andata per payrooja]

▸ a second-class one-way ticket to Messina un biglietto di sola andata in seconda classe per Messina [oon beelyetto dee sola andata een saykonda klassay per messeena]

only solo [solo]

- ▶ we're staying only two days ci fermiamo solo due giorni [chee fermee-amo solo doo-ay jornee]
- ▶ that's the only one left è l'ultimo [ay loolteemo]

open aperto(a) [aperto(a)] ✦ aprire [apreeray] ✦ aprirsi [apreersee]

- ▶ is the museum open all day? il museo è aperto tutto il giorno? [eel moozay-o ay aperto tootto eel jorno]
- ▶ is the bank open at lunchtime? la banca fa l'orario continuato? [la banka fa loraree-o konteenoo-ato]
- ▶ at what time is ... open? a che ora è aperto ...? [a kay ora ay aperto]
- ▶ can I open the window? posso aprire il finestrino? [posso appreeray eel feenestreeno]
- ▶ what time do you open? a che ora aprite? [a kay ora apreetay]

open-air scoperto(a) [skoperto(a)]

- ▶ is there an open-air swimming pool? c'è una piscina scoperta? [chay oona peesheena skoperta]

operating room la sala operatoria [sala opayratoree-a]

- ▶ is she still in the operating room? è ancora in sala operatoria? [ay ankora een sala opayratoree-a]

opinion l'opinione f [opeenee-onay]

- ▶ what's your opinion? qual è la sua opinione? [kwal ay la soo-a opeenee-onay]
- ▶ in my opinion, ... secondo me, ... [saykondo may]

orange arancione [aranchonay] ✦ (fruit) l'arancia f [arancha]; (color) l'arancione m [aranchonay]

- ▶ I'd like a kilo of oranges vorrei un chilo di arance [vorray-ee oon keelo dee aranchay]

orange juice il succo d'arancia [sookko darancha]

- ▶ I'll have a glass of orange juice prendo un bicchiere di succo d'arancia [prendo oon beekee-ayray dee sookko darancha]
- ▶ I'd like a freshly squeezed orange juice vorrei una spremuta d'arancia [vorray-ee oona spraymoota darancha]

---

opinions

- ▶ personally, I don't think it's fair personalmente, non credo sia giusto [personalmentay non kraydo see-a joosto]
- ▶ I think he's right penso che abbia ragione [penso kay abbee-a rajonay]
- ▶ I don't want to say non voglio pronunciarmi [non volyo pronooncharmee]
- ▶ I'm not sure non ne sono sicuro [non nay sono seekooro]
- ▶ no idea! non ne ho idea! [non nay o eeday-a]
- ▶ it depends dipende [deependay]

order l'ordinazione f [ordeenatsee-onay] ◆ ordinare [ordeenaray]
- this isn't what I ordered: I asked for... non è quello che ho ordinato: ho chiesto ... [non ay kwello kay o ordeenato o kee-esto]
- I ordered a coffee ho ordinato un caffè [o ordeenato oon kaffay]
- we'd like to order now vorremmo ordinare adesso [vorremmo ordeenaray adesso]

organize organizzare [organeedzaray]
- can you organize the whole trip for us? ci può organizzare tutto il viaggio? [chee poo-o organeedzaray tootto eel vee-ajo]

other altro(a) [altro(a)]
- I'll have the other one prendo l'altro [prendo laltro]
- on the other side of the street dall'altra parte della strada [dallaltra partay della strada]
- go ahead; I'm going to wait for the others vai avanti; io aspetto gli altri [va-ee avantee ee-o aspetto lyee altree]

out-of-date scaduto(a) [skadooto(a)]
- I think my passport is out-of-date credo che il mio passaporto sia scaduto [kraydo kay eel mee-o passaporto see-a skadooto]

outside call la chiamata esterna [kee-amata esterna]
- I'd like to make an outside call vorrei fare una chiamata esterna [vorray-ee faray oona kee-amata esterna]

outside line la linea esterna [leeney-a esterna]
- how do you get an outside line? come si prende la linea esterna? [komay see prenday la leeney-a esterna]

overheat surriscaldarsi [soorreeskaldarsee]
- the engine is overheating il motore si sta surriscaldando [eel motore see sta soorreeskaldando]

owner il proprietario [propree-aytaree-o], la proprietaria [propree-aytaree-a]
- do you know who the owner is? sa chi è il proprietario? [sa kee ay eel propree-aytaree-o]

p

pack *(of cigarettes, chewing gum)* il pacchetto [pakketto] ◆ *(for trip)* fare i bagagli [faray ee bagalyee]
- how much is a pack of cigarettes? quanto costa un pacchetto di sigarette? [kwanto kosta oon pakketto dee seegarettay]
- I need to pack devo fare i bagagli [dayvo faray ee bagalyee]

package *(wrapped object)* il pacco [pakko]; *(of butter)* il pacchetto [pakketto]; *(vacation deal)* il viaggio tutto compreso [vee-ajo tootto komprayzo]

▸ I'd like to send this package to Boston by airmail vorrei mandare questo pacco a Boston per via aerea [vorray-ee mandaray kwesto pakko a boston per vee-a a-ayray-a]
▸ do you have weekend packages? avete dei viaggi tutto compreso per il fine settimana? [avaytay day-ee vee-ajee tootto komprayzo per eel feenay setteemana]

package tour il viaggio organizzato [vee-ajo organeedzato]
▸ it's my first time on a package tour è la prima volta che faccio un viaggio organizzato [ay la preema volta kay facho oon vee-ajo organeedzato]

padlock il lucchetto [lookketto]
▸ I'd like to buy a padlock for my bike vorrei comprare un lucchetto per la bici [vorray-ee kompraray oon lookketto per la beechee]

pain *(physical)* il dolore [doloray]
▸ I'd like something for pain vorrei qualcosa contro il dolore [vorray-ee kwalkoza kontro eel doloray]
▸ I have a pain here ho un dolore qui [o oon doloray kwee]

painkiller l'analgesico *m* [analjayzeeko]
▸ I have a really bad toothache: can you give me a painkiller, please? ho un mal di denti fortissimo: mi può dare un analgesico, per favore? [o oon mal dee dentee forteesseemo mee poo-o daray oon analjayzeeko per favoray]

pair *(of gloves, socks)* il paio [pa-yo]
▸ a pair of shoes un paio di scarpe [oon pa-yo dee skarpay]
▸ a pair of pants un paio di pantaloni [oon pa-yo dee pantalonee]
▸ do you have a pair of scissors? ha un paio di forbici? [a oon pa-yo dee forbeechee]

pants i pantaloni [pantalonee]
▸ a pair of pants un paio di pantaloni [oon pa-yo dee pantalonee]
▸ there is a hole in these pants c'è un buco in questi pantaloni [chay oon booko een kwestee pantalonee]

pantyhose il collant [kollan]
▸ I've got a run in my pantyhose ho il collant smagliato [o eel kollan zmalyato]

paper *(for writing on)* la carta [carta]; *(newspaper)* il giornale [jornalay]
♦ **papers** *(official documents)* i documenti [dokoomentee]
▸ a piece of paper un foglietto [oon folyetto]
▸ can I take a look at the paper? posso dare un'occhiata al giornale?el [posso daray oonokkee-ata al jornalay]
▸ here are my papers ecco i miei documenti [ekko ee mee-ay-ee dokoomentee]

parasol l'ombrellone *m* [ombrellonay]
▸ can you rent parasols? si possono noleggiare degli ombrelloni? [see possono nolejaray delyee ombrellonee]

pardon *(forgiveness)* la scusa [skooza] ♦ *(forgive)* scusare [skoozaray]
▸ I beg your pardon? *(asking for repetition)* chiedo scusa? [kee-aydo skooza]
▸ I beg your pardon! (mi) scusi! [(mee) skoozee]

‣ pardon me? *(asking for repetition)* (mi) scusi? [(mee) skoozee]

‣ pardon me! (mi) scusi! [(mee) skoozee]

park parcheggiare [parkejaray]

‣ can we park our trailer here? possiamo parcheggiare qui la nostra roulotte? [possee-amo parkejaray kwee la nostra roolot]

‣ am I allowed to park here? posso parcheggiare qui? [posso parkejaray kwee]

parking il posto per parcheggiare [posto per parkejaray]

‣ is there any parking near the hostel? c'è posto per parcheggiare vicino all'ostello? [chay posto per parkejaray veecheeno allostello]

parking lot il parcheggio [parkejo]

‣ is there a parking lot nearby? c'è un parcheggio qui vicino? [chay oon parkejo kwee veecheeno]

parking space il posto per parcheggiare [posto per parkejaray]

‣ is it easy to find a parking space in town? si trova facilmente posto per parcheggiare in centro? [see trova facheelmentay posto per parkejaray een chentro]

part la parte [partay]

‣ what part of Italy are you from? di che parte dell'Italia è? [dee kay partay delleetalee-a ay]

‣ I've never been to this part of Italy before non sono mai stato in questa parte dell'Italia prima [non sono ma-ee stato een kwesta partay delleetalee-a preema]

party la festa [festa] ✦ divertirsi [deeverteersee]

‣ I'm planning a little party tomorrow sto organizzando una piccola festa per domani [sto organeedzando oona peekkola festa per domanee]

pass *(hand)* passare [passaray]; *(in car)* passare davanti a [passaray davantee a] ✦ *(in car)* passare [passaray]

‣ can you pass me the salt? mi può passare il sale? [mee poo-o passaray eel salay]

‣ can you pass on this road? si può passare su questa strada? [see poo-o passaray soo kwesta strada]

passage *(corridor)* il corridoio [korreedo-yo]

‣ I heard someone outside in the passage ho sentito qualcuno fuori in corridoio [o senteeto kwalkoono foo-oree een korreedo-yo]

passenger il passeggero [passejayro], la passeggera [passejayra]

‣ is this where the passengers from the Genoa flight arrive? è qui che arrivano i passeggeri del volo da Genova? [ay kwee kay arreevano ee passejayree del volo da jaynova]

passport il passaporto [passaporto]

‣ I've lost my passport ho perso il passaporto [o perso eel passaporto]

‣ I forgot my passport ho dimenticato il passaporto [o deementeekato eel passaporto]

‣ my passport has been stolen mi hanno rubato il passaporto [mee anno roobato eel passaporto]

paying

In a restaurant, you ask for *il conto* (the check). In a café or a snack bar, it's better to ask *quanto viene?* ('how much does it come to?'). In most bars, especially in cities, you pay when leaving. In some large establishments that tend to be crowded, e.g. at train stations, airports or service plazas, if you want to drink an *espresso* up at the counter, you first have to pay at the register and then show your *scontrino* (receipt) to the barista. If you're in a group of Italians and someone says *facciamo alla romana?*, they're suggesting that you split the check equally.

past dopo [dopo]
- ▸ do you mean the hotel just past the cathedral? intende l'albergo subito dopo la cattedrale? [eentenday lalbergo soobeeto dopo la kattedralay]
- ▸ twenty past twelve le dodici e venti [lay dodeechee ay ventee]

path *(track)* il sentiero [sentee-ayro]
- ▸ is the path well-marked? è segnato bene il sentiero? [ay senyato baynay eel sentee-ayro]

pay pagare [pagaray]
- ▸ can you pay by credit card? si può pagare con la carta di credito? [see poo-o pagaray kon la karta dee kraydeeto]
- ▸ we're going to pay separately paghiamo separatamente [paghee-amo sayparatamentay]
- ▸ do I have to pay a deposit? devo versare un anticipo? [dayvo versaray oon anteecheepo]
- ▸ do you have to pay to get in? l'ingresso è a pagamento? [leengresso ay a pagamento]

pay-per-view TV la tv pay-per-view [teevoo pay per vyoo]
- ▸ is there pay-per-view TV in the room? c'è la tv pay-per-view in camera? [chay la teevoo pay per vyoo een kamayra]

pay-per-view channel il canale pay-per-view [kanalay pay per vyoo]
- ▸ are there any pay-per-view channels? ci sono dei canali pay-per-view? [chee sono day-ee kanalee pay per vyoo]

pedestrian il pedone [paydonay] ◆ pedonale [paydonalay]
- ▸ is this just a pedestrian street? è una via esclusivamente pedonale? [ay oona vee-a eskloozeevamentay paydonalay]

pedestrian mall l'area pedonale *f* [aray-a paydonalay]
- ▸ can you direct me to the pedestrian mall? mi può dire come andare all'area pedonale? [mee poo-o deeray komay andaray alllaray-a paydonalay]

pen la penna [penna]
- can you lend me a pen? mi può prestare una penna? [mee poo-o prestaray oona penna]

pencil la matita [mateeta]
- can you lend me a pencil? mi può prestare una matita? [mee poo-o prestaray oona mateeta]

penicillin la penicillina [payneecheelleena]
- I'm allergic to penicillin sono allergico alla penicillina [sono allerkeeko alla payneecheelleena]

pepper il pepe [paypay]
- pass the pepper, please passami il pepe, per favore [passamee eel paypay per favoray]

percent percento [perchento]
- could you knock 10 percent off the price? può farmi uno sconto del dieci percento? [poo-o farmee ono skonto del dee-aychee perchento]

performance (show) la rappresentazione [rapprayzentatsee-onay]; (in movie theater) la proiezione [pro-yetsee-onay]
- what time does the performance begin? a che ora comincia la rappresentazione? [a kay ora komeencha la rapprayzentatsee-onay]

perfume il profumo [profoomo]
- how much is this perfume? quanto costa questo profumo? [kwanto kosta kwesto profoomo]

perhaps forse [forsay]
- perhaps we'll stay another night forse ci fermiamo un'altra notte [forsay chee fermee-amo oonaltra nottay]
- perhaps you can help me? mi potrebbe aiutare? [mee potrebbay a-yootaray]

person la persona [persona]
- how much is it per hour and per person? quanto costa all'ora a persona? [kwanto kosta allora a persona]

pet l'animale domestico *m* [aneemalay domesteeko]
- are pets allowed? gli animali domestici sono ammessi? [lyee aneemalee domesteechee sono ammessee]

phone il telefono [taylayfono] ✦ telefonare (a) [taylayfonaray (a)]
- can I use the phone? posso usare il telefono? [posso oozaray eel taylayfono] ▸ see boxes on p. 102

phone booth la cabina telefonica [kabeena taylayfoneeka]
- is there a phone booth near here? c'è una cabina telefonica qui vicino? [chay oona kabeena taylayfoneeka kwee veecheeno]

phone call la telefonata [taylayfonata]
- I'd like to make a phone call vorrei fare una telefonata [vorray-ee faray oona taylayfonata]

phoning

When you're giving someone your phone number, you pronounce each number separately. When you call someone, they might ask you *con chi parlo?* (who's speaking?). The number you dial to call collect (*a carico del destinatario*) is 170 (*centosettanta*). All operators speak English.

phonecard la scheda telefonica [skayda taylayfoneeka]
▸ where can I buy a phonecard? dove posso comprare una scheda telefonica? [dovay posso kompraray oona skayda taylayfoneeka]

photo la foto [foto]
▸ can I take photos in here? posso scattare delle foto qui? [posso skattaray dellay foto kwee]
▸ could you take a photo of us? ci potrebbe fare una foto? [chee potrebbay faray oona foto]
▸ I'd like copies of some photos vorrei delle copie di alcune foto [vorray-ee dellay koppee-ay dee alkoonay foto]

photography la fotografia [fotografee-a]
▸ is photography allowed in the museum? si possono scattare delle fotografie nel museo? [see possono skattaray dellay fotografee-ay nel moozay-o]

picnic il picnic [peekneek]
▸ could we go for a picnic by the river? possiamo andare a fare un picnic in riva al fiume? [possee-amo andaray a faray oon peekneek een reeva al fee-oomay]

piece *(of chocolate, paper, wood)* il pezzo [petso]; *(of cake)* la fetta [fetta]; *(of apple)* lo spicchio [speekkee-o]

on the phone

▸ hello? pronto? [pronto]
▸ Joe Stewart speaking sono Joe Stewart [sono jo styoo-art]
▸ I'd like to speak to Anna Rossi vorrei parlare con Anna Rossi [vorray-ee parlaray kon anna rossee]
▸ hold the line resti in linea [restee een leenay-a]
▸ can you call back in ten minutes? può richiamare tra dieci minuti? [poo-o reekee-amaray tra dee-aychee meenootee]
▸ would you like to leave a message? vuole lasciare un messaggio? [voo-olay lasharay oon messajo]
▸ you have the wrong number ha sbagliato numero [a zbalyato noomayro]

pizza

You can eat pizza in a *pizzeria*, of course, or in *tavole calde* (snack bars), where you can buy it by the slice (*al taglio*). Some places, mostly in Rome and southern Italy, sell *pizza al metro*, which means that you can buy as big a portion of pizza as you like.

▸ a piece of cake, please una fetta di torta, per favore [oona fetta dee torta per favoray]

▸ a piece of advice un consiglio [oon konseelyo]

▸ a piece of news una notizia [oona noteetsee-a]

pill la pillola [peellola]

▸ a bottle of pills un flacone di pillole [oon flakonay dee peellolay]

▸ the Pill (*contraceptive*) la pillola [la peellola]

pillow il guanciale [gwanchalay]

▸ could I have another pillow? potrei avere un altro guanciale? [potray-ee avayray oon altro gwanchalay]

pizza la pizza [peetsa]

▸ I'd like a large mushroom pizza vorrei una pizza grande ai funghi [vorray-ee oona peetsa granday a-ee foonghee]

place il posto [posto]; (*house*) la casa [kaza]; (*place setting*) il coperto [koperto]

▸ can you recommend a nice place to eat? ci può consigliare un buon posto per mangiare? [chee poo-o konseelyaray oon boo-on posto per manjaray]

▸ do you want to change places with me? vuoi scambiare il tuo posto con il mio? [voo-o-ee skambee-aray eel too-o posto kon eel mee-o]

plain (*clear*) chiaro(a) [kee-aro(a)]; (*with nothing added*) semplice [sempleechay]

▸ I'm looking for a plain black dress sto cercando un vestito nero semplice [sto cherkando oon vesteeto nayro sempleechay]

▸ do you have any plain yogurt? avete dello yogurt nature? [avaytay dello yogoort natoor]

plan (*strategy*) il piano [pee-ano]; (*intention, idea*) il programma [programma]
♦ (*organize*) preparare [praypararay]; (*intend*) prevedere [prayvaydayray]

▸ do you have any plans for tonight? avete programmi per stasera? [avaytay programmee per stasayra]

▸ I'm planning to stay for just one night prevedo di fermarmi una notte sola [prayvaydo dee fermarmee oona nottay sola]

plane l'aereo *m* [a-ayray-o]

▸ which gate does the plane depart from? da quale uscita parte l'aereo? [da kwalay oosheeta partay la-ayray-o]

▸ when's the next plane to Milan? **a che ora è il prossimo aereo per Milano?** [a kay ora ay eel prosseemo a-ayray-o per meelano]

plate il piatto [pee-atto]

▸ this plate's got a crack in it **questo piatto è incrinato** [kwesto pee-atto ay eenkreenato]

platform *(at station)* il binario [beenaree-o]

▸ which platform does the train leave from? **da che binario parte il treno?** [da kay beenaree-o partay eel trayno]

play *(at theater)* la rappresentazione [rapprayzentatsee-onay] ◆ *(sport, game)* giocare a [jokaray a]; *(instrument, music)* suonare [soo-onaray]

▸ what time does the play start ? **a che ora comincia la rappresentazione?** [a kay ora komeencha la rapprayzentatsee-onay]

▸ do you play tennis? **gioca a tennis?** [joka a tennees]

▸ I play the cello **suono il violoncello** [soo-ono eel vee-olonchello]

playroom la stanza (dei) giochi [stantsa (day-ee) jokee]

▸ is there a children's playroom here? **c'è una stanza (dei) giochi per i bambini qui?** [chay oona stantsa (day-ee) jokee per ee bambeenee kwee]

please *(requesting)* per favore [per favoray]; *(encouraging)* prego [praygo]; *(accepting)* grazie [gratsee-ay]

▸ can you help me, please? **mi può aiutare, per favore?** [mee poo-o a-yootaray per favoray]

▸ please sit down **prego, si accomodi** [praygo see akkomodee]

▸ can I come in? – please do **posso entrare? – prego** [posso entraray – praygo]

▸ would you like some more wine? – yes, please **vuole ancora un po' di vino? – sì, grazie** [voo-olay ankora oon po dee veeno – see gratsee-ay]

pleased soddisfatto(a) [soddeesfatto(a)]

▸ I'm very pleased with the room **sono molto soddisfatto della camera** [sono molto soddeesfatto della kamayra]

▸ pleased to meet you **molto lieto (di conoscerla)** [molto lee-ayto (dee konosherla)]

pleasure il piacere [pee-achayray]

▸ with pleasure! **con piacere!** [kon pee-achayray]

▸ it's a pleasure **è un piacere** [ay oon pee-achayray]

plug *(on electrical equipment)* la spina [speena]

▸ where can I find an adaptor for the plug on my hairdryer? **dove posso trovare un adattatore per la spina del mio fon?** [dovay posso trovaray oon adattoray per la speena del mee-o fon]

plug in attaccare (alla presa) [attakkaray (alla prayza)]

▸ can I plug my cellphone in here to recharge it? **posso attaccare qui il mio cellulare per ricaricarlo?** [posso attakkaray kwee eel mee-o chelloolaray per reekareekarlo]

point il punto [poonto] ◆ *(way)* indicare [eendeekaray]

- points of the compass **punti cardinali** [poontee cardeenalee]
- can you point me in the direction of the freeway? **mi può indicare la direzione dell'autostrada?** [mee poo-o indeekaray la deeretsee-onay dellowtostrada]

police la polizia [poleetsee-a]

- call the police! **chiamate la polizia!** [kee-amatay la poleetsee-a]
- what's the number for the police? **qual è il numero della polizia?** [kwal ay eel noomayro della poleetsee-a]

police station il commissariato (di polizia) [kommeessaree-ato (dee poleetsee-a)]

- where is the nearest police station? **dov'è il commissariato più vicino?** [dovay eel kommeessaree-ato pyoo veecheeno]

pool (for swimming) la piscina [peesheena]

- main pool **piscina principale** [peesheena preencheepalay]
- children's pool **piscina per bambini** [peesheena per bambeenee]
- is the pool heated? **è riscaldata la piscina?** [ay reeskaldata la peesheena]
- is there an indoor pool? **c'è una piscina coperta?** [chay oona peesheena koperta]

pork il maiale [ma-yalay]

- I don't eat pork **non mangio (carne di) maiale** [non manjo (karnay dee) ma-yalay]

portable portatile [portateelay]

- do you have a portable heater I could borrow? **ha una stufa portatile da prestarmi?** [a oona stoofa portateelay da prestarmee]

portion la porzione [portsee-onay]

- the portions at that restaurant are just right **le porzioni in quel ristorante sono giuste** [lay portsee-onay een kwel reestorantay sono joostay]

possible possibile [posseebeelay]

- without sauce, if possible **senza salsa, se possibile** [sentsa salsa say posseebeelay]

postcard la cartolina [kartoleena]

- where can I buy postcards? **dove posso comprare delle cartoline?** [dovay posso kompraray dellay kartoleenay]
- how much are stamps for postcards to the States? **quanto costano i francobolli da cartolina per gli Stati Uniti?** [kwanto kostano ee frankobollee da kartoleena per lyee statee ooneetee]

post office l'ufficio postale *m* [ooffeecho postalay]

- where is the nearest post office? **dov'è l'ufficio postale più vicino?** [dovay l'ooffeecho postalay pyoo veecheeno]

power (electricity) la corrente [correntay]

- there's no power **non c'è corrente** [non chay correntay]

power failure il blackout [blakkowt]

- there's a power failure **c'è un blackout** [chay oon blakkowt]
- how long is the power failure expected to last? **quanto dovrebbe durare il blackout?** [kwanto dovrebbay dooraray eel blakkowt]

prawn il gambero [gambayro]

> I'd like to try a dish with prawns vorrei assaggiare un piatto a base di gamberi [vorray-ee assajaray oon pee-atto a bazay dee gambayree]

prefer preferire [prayfayreeray]

> I'd prefer black tea preferirei il tè senza latte [prayfayreeray-ee eel tay sentsa lattay]
> I'd prefer you not smoke preferirei che non fumasse [prayfayreeray-ee kay non foomassay]

preference la preferenza [prayfayrentsa]

> my preference would be for red wine avrei una preferenza per il vino rosso [avray-ee oona prayfayrentsa per eel veeno rosso]

prescription (medicine) la ricetta (medica) [reechetta (maydeeka)]

> is it only available by prescription? si può avere solo dietro ricetta medica? [see poo-o avayray solo dee-aytro reechetta maydeeka]

present (gift) il regalo [raygalo]

> where can we buy presents around here? dove possiamo comprare dei regali qui intorno? [dovay possee-amo kompraray day-ee raygalee kwee eentorno]

pretty carino(a) [kareeno(a)]

> she's a very pretty girl è una ragazza molto carina [ay oona ragatsa molto kareena]

price (cost) il prezzo [pretso]

> what's the price of gas here? qual è il prezzo della benzina attualmente? [kwal ay eel pretso della bendzeena kwee]
> if the price is right se il prezzo è corretto [say eel pretso ay korretto]

price list il listino dei prezzi [leesteeno day-ee pretsee]

> do you have a price list? avete un listino dei prezzi? [avaytay oon leesteeno day-ee pretsee]

print (photograph) la stampa [stampa]

> could I have another set of prints? potrei avere un'altra serie di stampe? [potray-ee avayray oonaltra sayree-ay dee stampay]

private (not public) privato(a) [preevato(a)]; (personal) personale [personalay]

> is it a private beach? è una spiaggia privata? [ay oona spee-aja preevata]

expressing a preference

> I prefer red wine to white wine preferisco il vino rosso al vino bianco [prayfayreesko eel veeno rosso al veeno bee-anko]
> I'd rather fly than go by train preferisco andare in aereo piuttosto che in treno [prayfayreesko andaray een a-ayray-o pyoottosto kay een trayno]
> Saturday would suit me better sabato mi andrebbe meglio [sabato mee andrebbay melyo]

public transportation

In towns, people usually get around by bus or streetcar. The subway in Rome has only two lines, which operate until 11:30 in the evening (12:30 on Saturdays). The Milan subway has three lines, which run from 6 a.m. till 1 a.m. After that, there's a replacement bus service (called *corse sostitutive*) for the red and yellow lines; the green line serves the downtown area, so you can just use regular buses, which run all night, when it's closed.

problem il problema [problayma]

▸ there's a problem with with the central heating c'è un problema con il riscaldamento centrale [chay oon problayma kon eel reeskaldamento chentralay]

▸ no problem nessun problema [nessoon problayma]

program *(for event)* il programma [programma]

▸ could I see a program? potrei vedere un programma? [potray-ee vaydayray oon programma]

pronounce *(word)* pronunciare [pronooncharay]

▸ how is that pronounced? come si pronuncia? [komay see pronooncha]

public pubblico(a) [poobbleeko(a)] ◆ il pubblico [poobbleeko]

▸ I'm looking for a public phone sto cercando un telefono pubblico [sto cherkando oon taylayfono poobbleeko]

▸ let's go somewhere less public andiamo in un posto più tranquillo [andee-amo een oon posto pyoo trankweello]

▸ is the castle open to the public? il castello è aperto al pubblico? [eel kastello ay aperto al poobbleeko]

public holiday il giorno festivo [jorno festeevo]

▸ is tomorrow a public holiday? domani è un giorno festivo? [domanee ay jorno festeevo]

public transportation i mezzi (di trasporto) pubblici [medzee (dee trasporto) poobleechee]

▸ can you get there by public transportation? ci si può andare con i mezzi pubblici? [chee see poo-o andaray kon ee medzee poobleechee]

pull *(muscle)* stirarsi [steerarsee]; *(tooth)* estrarre [estrarray]

▸ I've pulled a muscle mi sono stirato un muscolo [mee sono steerato oon mooskolo]

puncture

▸ the tire's been punctured c'è un foro nella gomma [chay oon foro nella gomma]

purpose lo scopo [skopo] ◆ **on purpose** apposta [apposta]

▸ sorry, I didn't do it on purpose scusi, non l'ho fatto apposta [skoozee non lo fatto apposta]

purse *(handbag)* la borsetta [borsetta]; *(change purse)* il portamonete [portamonaytay]

▸ my purse was stolen mi hanno rubato la borsetta [mee anno roobato la borsetta]

push spingere [speenjayray]

▸ can you help us push the car? ci può aiutare a spingere la macchina? [chee poo-o a-yootaray a speenjayray la makkeena]

put *(into place, position)* mettere [mettayray]

▸ is there somewhere I can put my bags? c'è un posto dove posso mettere i miei bagagli? [chay oon posto dovay posso mettayray ee mee-ay-ee bagalyee]

put down *(set down)* posare [posaray]

▸ can we put our things down in the corner? possiamo posare le nostre cose nell'angolo? [possee-amo posaray lay nostray kozay nellangolo]

put on *(clothes)* mettersi [mettersee]; *(TV, radio, heating)* accendere [achendayray]; *(on telephone)* passare [passaray]

▸ can you put the heat on? può accendere il riscaldamento? [poo-o achendayray eel reeskaldamento]

▸ can you put Mrs. Martin on, please? mi può passare la signora Martin, per favore? [mee poo-o passaray la seenyora marteen per favoray]

put out *(cigarette, fire)* spegnere [spenyayray]

▸ can you please put your cigarette out? può spegnere la sigaretta, per favore? [poo-o spenyayray la seegaretta per favoray]

put up *(tent)* montare [montaray]; *(person)* ospitare [ospeetaray]

▸ can we put up our tent here? possiamo montare la tenda qui? [possee-amo montaray la tenda kwee]

q

quarter *(fourth)* il quarto [kwarto]

▸ I'll be back in a quarter of an hour sarò di ritorno tra un quarto d'ora [saro dee reetorno tra oon kwarto dora]

▸ a quarter past/after one l'una e un quarto [loona ay oon kwarto]

▸ a quarter to/of one l'una meno un quarto [loona mayno oon kwarto]

quay il molo [molo]

▸ is the boat at the quay? la barca è al molo? [la barka ay al molo]

question la domanda [domanda]

▸ can I ask you a question? posso farle una domanda? [posso farlay oona domanda]

quickly *(rapidly)* velocemente [vaylochaymentay]; *(hurriedly)* in fretta [een fretta]

▸ we need to get him to the hospital as quickly as possible dobbiamo portarlo all'ospedale il più velocemente possibile [dobbee-amo portarlo allospaydalay eel pyoo vaylochaymentay posseebeelay]

▶ everyone speaks so quickly **parlano tutti così in fretta** [parlano toottee kozee een fretta]

quiet *(not noisy)* silenzioso(a) [seelentsee-ozo(a)]; *(peaceful)* calmo(a) [kalmo(a)], tranquillo(a) [trankweello(a)]

▶ is it a quiet beach? **è una spiaggia tranquilla?** [ay oona spee-aja trankweella]

▶ do you have anything quieter? **non avete niente di più calmo?** [non avaytay nee-entay dee pyoo kalmo]

quite *(rather)* piuttosto [pyoottosto]

▶ it's quite expensive around here **è piuttosto caro da queste parti** [ay pyoottosto karo da kwestay partee]

racket *(for tennis)* la racchetta [rakketta]

▶ can you rent rackets? **si possono noleggiare delle racchette?** [see possono nolejaray dellay rakkettay]

radiator il radiatore [radee-atoray]

▶ the radiator's leaking **il radiatore perde** [eel radee-atoray perday]

radio *(set)* la radio [radee-o]

▶ the radio doesn't work **la radio non funziona** [la radee-o non foontsee-ona]

radio station la stazione radiofonica [statsee-onay radee-ofoneeka]

▶ can you get any English-language radio stations here? **si prendono stazioni radiofoniche in inglese qui?** [see prendono statsee-onee radee-ofoneekay een eenglayzay kwee]

railroad *(system)* la ferrovia [ferrovee-a]; *(organization)* le ferrovie [ferrovee-ay]; *(track)* il binario [beenaree-o]

▶ what region does this railroad cover? **che zona serve questa ferrovia?** [kay dzona servay kwesta ferrovee-a]

rain piovere [pee-ovayray]

▶ it's raining **piove** [pee-ovay]

random

▶ at random **a caso** [a kazo]

rare *(meat)* al sangue [al sangway]

▶ rare, please **al sangue, per favore** [al sangway per favoray]

rate *(price)* la tariffa [tareeffa]

▶ what's your daily rate? **qual è la sua tariffa giornaliera?** [kwal ay la soo-a tareeffa jornalee-ayra]

receipts

When you make a purchase, make sure you get a receipt (*scontrino*). You need to have one for any purchase you make and retailers are obliged to give you one by law.

rate of exchange il tasso di cambio [tasso dee kambee-o]
  ▸ do they offer a good rate of exchange? propongono un buon tasso di cambio? [propongono oon boo-on tasso dee kambee-o]

razor il rasoio [razo-yo]
  ▸ where can I buy a new razor? dove posso comprare un nuovo rasoio? [dovay posso kompraray oon noo-ovo razo-yo]

razor blade la lametta (da barba) [lametta (da barba)]
  ▸ I need to buy some razor blades devo comprare delle lamette da barba [dayvo kompraray dellay lamettay da barba]

ready pronto(a) [pronto(a)]
  ▸ when will it be ready? quando sarà pronto? [kwando sara pronto]

really (*actually*) davvero [davvayro]; (*very*) molto [molto]
  ▸ really? davvero? [davvayro]
  ▸ your sneakers are really trendy! le tue scarpe da ginnastica sono davvero all'ultimo grido! [lay too-ay skarpay da jeennasteeka sono davvayro alloolteemo greedo]

rear (*of train*) la coda [koda]
  ▸ are our seats in the rear of the train? i nostri posti sono in coda al treno? [ee nostree postee sono een koda al trayno]

receipt la ricevuta [reechayvoota]
  ▸ can I have a receipt, please? mi può fare una ricevuta, per favore? [mee poo-o faray oona reechayvoota per favoray]

receive (*package, letter*) ricevere [reechayvayray]
  ▸ I should have received the package this morning avrei dovuto ricevere il pacco stamattina [avray-ee dovooto reechayvayray eel pakko stamatteena]

reception (*welcome*) l'accoglienza *f* [akkolyentsa]; (*party*) il ricevimento [reechayveemento]; (*for TV, radio, cellphone*) la ricezione [reechetsee-onay]
  ▸ there's no reception (*for cellphone*) non prende [non prenday]

reception desk (*in hotel, office*) la reception [raysepshon]
  ▸ can I leave my backpack at the reception desk? posso lasciare lo zaino alla reception? [posso lasharay lo dza-eeno alla raysepshon]

recline reclinare [raykleenaray]
  ▸ do you mind if I recline my seat? le dispiace se reclino il mio schienale? [lay deespee-achay say raykleeno eel mee-o skee-aynalay]

recommend consigliare [konseelyaray]
- could you recommend another hotel? mi potrebbe consigliare un altro albergo? [mee potrebbay konseelyaray oon altro albergo]
- could you recommend a restaurant? mi potrebbe consigliare un ristorante? [mee potrebbay konseelyaray oon reestorantay]
- what do you recommend? cosa consiglia? [koza konseelya]

record store il negozio di dischi [naygotsee-o dee deeskee]
- I'm looking for a record store sto cercando un negozio di dischi [sto cherkando oon naygotsee-o dee deeskee]

rec center, recreation center il centro attività ricreative [chentro atteeveeta reecray-ateevay]
- what kinds of activities does the recreation center offer? che tipo di attività propone il centro attività ricreative? [kay teepo dee atteeveeta proponay eel chentro atteeveeta reecray-ateevay]

red (in color) rosso(a) [rosso(a)] ◆ (color, wine) il rosso [rosso]
- she was dressed in red era vestita di rosso [era vesteeta dee rosso]

redhead il rosso [rosso], la rossa [rossa]
- a tall redhead wearing glasses una rossa alta con gli occhiali [oona rossa alta kon lyee okkee-alee]

red light il (semaforo) rosso [(saymaforo) rosso]
- you failed to stop at a red light non si è fermato con il rosso [non see ay fermato kon eel rosso]

reduced (price, rate) ridotto(a) [reedotto(a)]
- is there a reduced rate for students? c'è una tariffa ridotta per studenti? [chay oona tareeffa reedotta per stoodentee]

reduced-price (ticket) ridotto(a) [reedotto(a)]
- two reduced-price tickets and one full-price due biglietti ridotti e uno intero [doo-ay beelyettee reedottee ay oono eentayro]

reduction la riduzione [reedootsee-onay]
- do you have reductions for groups? ci sono riduzioni per comitive? [chee sono reedootsee-onee per komeeteevay]

red wine il vino rosso [veeno rosso]
- a bottle of red wine una bottiglia di vino rosso [oona botteelya dee veeno rosso]
- what kinds of red wine do you have? che vini rossi avete? [kay veenee rossee avaytay]

refresher course il corso di aggiornamento [korso dee ajornamento]
- I need a refresher course ho bisogno di un corso di aggiornamento [o beezonyo dee oon korso dee ajornamento]

refundable rimborsabile [reemborsabeelay]

▸ are the tickets refundable? i biglietti sono rimborsabili? [ee beelyettee sono reemborsabeelee]

regard il riguardo [reegwardo] ◆ **regards** i saluti [salootee] ◆ **with regard to** in relazione a [een ralylatsee-onay a]

▸ they showed no regard for our safety non hanno mostrato nessun riguardo per la nostra sicurezza [non anno mostrato nessoon reegwardo per la nostra seekooretsa]

▸ give my regards to your parents! trasmetta i miei saluti ai suoi genitori! [trazmetta ee mee-ay-ee salootee a-ee soo-o-ee jayneetoree]

▸ I'm calling you with regard to ... la chiamo in relazione a ... [la kee-amo een ralylatsee-onay a]

region la regione [rayjonay]

▸ in the Alps region nella regione alpina [nella rayjonay alpeena]

registered mail

▸ I would like to send a letter by registered mail vorrei spedire una lettera raccomandata [vorray-ee spaydeeray oona lettayra rakkomandata]

registration *(of car)* il libretto (di circolazione) [leebretto (dee cheerkolatsee-onay)]

▸ here's the car's registration ecco il libretto dell'auto [ekko eel leebretto dellowto]

regret *(be sorry about)* essere spiacente di [essayray spee-achentay dee] ◆ **regrets** le scuse [skoozay]

▸ I regret that I won't be able to come sono spiacente di non poter venire [sono spee-achentay dee non potayr vayneeray]

▸ please give her my regrets la prego di farle le mie scuse [la praygo dee farlay lay mee-ay skoozay]

relative il/la parente [parentay]

▸ I have relatives in Sicily ho dei parenti in Sicilia [o day-ee parentee een seecheelee-a]

remember ricordarsi (di) [reekordarsee (dee)]

▸ I can't remember his name non riesco a ricordarmi il suo nome [non ree-esko a reekordarmee eel soo-o nomay]

▸ do you remember me? si ricorda di me? [see reekorda dee may]

remote (control) il telecomando [taylaykomando]

▸ I can't find the remote for the TV non trovo il telecomando della tv [non trovo eel taylaykomando della teevoo]

rent *(of house, apartment)* l'affitto *m* [affeetto]; *(of car, bike, DVD)* il noleggio [nolejo] ◆ *(house, apartment)* affittare [affeettaray]; *(car, bike, DVD)* noleggiare [nolejaray]

▸ how much is the rent per week? quant'è l'affitto alla settimana? [kwantay laffeetto alla setteemana]

▶ I'd like to rent a car for a week **vorrei noleggiare un'auto per una settimana** [vorray-ee nolejaray oonowto per oona setteemana]

▶ I'd like to rent a boat **vorrei noleggiare una barca** [vorray-ee nolejaray oon barka]

▶ is it cheaper to rent the equipment by the week? **costa meno noleggiare l'attrezzatura a settimana?** [kosta mayno nolejaray lattretsatoora a setteemana]

rental *(of house, apartment)* **l'affitto** *m* [affeetto]; *(of car, bike)* **il noleggio** [nolejo]; *(house)* **la casa in affitto** [kaza een affeetto]; *(apartment)* **l'appartamento** *m* **in affitto** [appartamento een affeetto]; *(car)* **la macchina a noleggio** [makkeena a nolejo]

▶ we have the rental for two weeks **abbiamo la macchina a noleggio per due settimane** [abbee-amo la makkeena a nolejo per doo-ay setteemanay]

repair **la riparazione** [reeparatsee-onay] ◆ **riparare** [reepararay]

▶ will you be able to make the repairs today? **riuscirà a fare le riparazioni in giornata?** [ree-oosheera a faray lay reeparatsee-onee een jornata]

▶ how long will it take to repair? **quanto ci vorrà per ripararlo?** [kwanto chee vorra per reepararlo]

repeat **ripetere** [reepaytayray]

▶ can you repeat that, please? **può ripetere, per favore?** [poo-o reepaytayray per favoray]

report *(theft)* **denunciare** [daynooncharay]

▶ I'd like to report something stolen **vorrei denunciare un furto** [vorray-ee daynooncharay oon foorto]

▶ I'd like to report the loss of my credit cards **vorrei denunciare lo smarrimento delle mie carte di credito** [vorray-ee daynooncharay lo zmarreemento delle mee-ay kartay dee craydeeto]

reservation **la prenotazione** [praynotatsee-onay]

▶ I have a reservation in the name of Jones **ho una prenotazione a nome Jones** [o oona praynotatsee-onay a nomay jonz]

▶ do you have to make a reservation? **bisogna prenotare?** [beezonya praynotaray]

reserve *(ticket, room)* **prenotare** [praynotaray]

▶ hello, I'd like to reserve a table for two for tomorrow night at 8 **buongiorno, vorrei prenotare un tavolo per due per domani sera alle otto** [boo-onjorno vorray-ee praynotaray oon tavolo per doo-ay per domanee sayra allay otto]

reserved *(booked)* **prenotato(a)** [praynotato(a)]

▶ is this table reserved? **è prenotato questo tavolo?** [ay praynotato kwesto tavolo]

rest *(relaxation)* **il riposo** [reepozo] ◆ *(relax)* **riposarsi** [reepozarsee]

▶ I've come here to get some rest **sono venuto per riposarmi un po'** [sono vaynooto per reepozarmee oon po]

restaurants

If you want to eat cakes or sandwiches (*panini, tramezzini*) that aren't too expensive, go to a *caffè*, *panetteria* (bakery) or *tavola calda* (snack bar). Some *tavole calde* still sell pizzas and pasta but more and more *rosticcerie* (grills), *pizzerie-bar*, *trattorie* and *osterie* (cheaper family-run bistros) are springing up. *Ristorante* is the term that covers them all.

restaurant il ristorante [reestorantay]
  ▸ are there any good restaurants around here? ci sono dei buoni ristoranti nei dintorni? [chee sono day-ee boo-onee reestorantee nay-ee deentornee]

restriction la limitazione [leemeetatsee-onay]
  ▸ are there restrictions on how much luggage you can take? ci sono delle limitazioni sul numero dei bagagli che si possono portare? [chee sono dellay leemeetatsee-onee sool noomayro day-ee bagalyee kay see possono portaray]

restroom il bagno [banyo]
  ▸ is there a restroom on the bus? c'è un bagno sul pullman? [chay oon banyo sool poollman]

retired in pensione [een pensee-onay]
  ▸ I'm retired now sono in pensione ora [sono een pensee-onay ora]

return *(arrival back)* il ritorno [reetorno] ◆ *(rental car)* restituire [raysteetoo-eeray]
  ▸ when do we have to return the car? quando dobbiamo restituire la macchina? [kwando dobbee-amo raysteetoo-eeray la makkeena]

return trip il viaggio di ritorno [vee-ajo dee reetorno]
  ▸ the return trip is scheduled for 6 o'clock il viaggio di ritorno è previsto per le sei [eel vee-ajo dee reetorno ay prayveesto per lay say-ee]

at a restaurant

  ▸ I'd like to reserve a table for tonight vorrei prenotare un tavolo per stasera [vorray-ee praynotaray oon tavolo per stasayra]
  ▸ can we see the menu? possiamo avere il menu? [possee-amo avayray eel maynoo]
  ▸ do you have a set menu? avete un menu a prezzo fisso? [avaytay oon maynoo a pretso feesso]
  ▸ rare/medium/well done, please al sangue/non troppo cotto/ben cotto, per favore [al sangway/non troppo kotto/ben kotto per favoray]
  ▸ can I have the check, please? posso avere il conto, per favore? [posso avayray eel konto per favoray]

rice il riso [reezo]

▸ I'd like some rice, please vorrei del riso, per favore [vorray-ee del reezo per favoray]

ride *(trip in car)* il giro (in macchina) [jeero (een makkeena)]; *(lift)* il passaggio [pasajo]; *(on bike)* il giro (in bici) [jeero (een beechee)]; *(on motorcycle)* il giro (in moto) [jeero (een moto)]

▸ do you want a ride? vuole un passaggio? [voo-olay oon pasajo]

▸ where can we go for a ride around here? dove possiamo fare un giro nei dintorni? [dovay possee-amo faray oon jeero nay-ee deentornee]

riding

▸ to go riding andare a cavallo [andaray a kavallo]

▸ where can we go riding around here? dove possiamo andare a cavallo da queste parti? [dovay possee-amo andaray a kavallo da kwestay partee]

right *(correct)* giusto(a) [joosto(a)], esatto(a) [ayzatto(a)]; *(not left)* destro(a) [destro(a)] ◆ la destra [destra] ◆ a destra [a destra]

▸ to the right (of) a destra (di) [a destra (dee)]

▸ that's right (è) esatto [(ay) ayzatto]

▸ I don't think the check's right non mi sembra che il conto sia giusto [non mee sembra kay eel konto see-a joosto]

▸ is this the right train for Turin? è questo il treno per Torino? [ay kwesto eel trayno per toreeno]

▸ is this the right number? è il numero giusto? [ay eel noomayro joosto]

▸ take the next right prenda la prossima a destra [prenda la prosseema a destra]

▸ you have to turn right deve girare a destra [dayvay jeeraray a destra]

right-hand a destra [a destra]

▸ it's on the right-hand side of the steering column è a destra del piantone del volante [ay a destra del pee-antonay del volantay]

right of way la precedenza [praychaydentsa]

▸ who has the right of way here? chi ha la precedenza qui? [kee a la praychaydentsa kwee]

road la strada [strada]

▸ which road do I take for Rome? che strada prendo per Roma? [kay strada prendo per roma]

▸ what is the speed limit on this road? qual è il limite di velocità su questa strada? [kwal ay eel leemeetay dee vaylocheeta soo kwesta strada]

rob *(person)* derubare [dayroobaray]

▸ I've been robbed sono stato derubato [sono stato dayroobato]

rock climbing

▸ to go rock climbing fare roccia [faray rocha]

▸ can you go rock climbing here? si può fare roccia qui? [see poo-o faray rocha kwee]

roller skate il pattino a rotelle [patteeno a rotellay]

▶ where can we rent roller skates? dove possiamo noleggiare dei pattini a rotelle? [dovay possee-amo nolejaray day-ee patteenee a rotellay]

room *(bedroom)* la camera [kamayra]; *(in house)* la stanza [stantsa]; *(in building)* la sala [sala]; *(space)* lo spazio [spatsee-o]

▶ do you have any rooms available? avete delle camere libere? [avaytay dellay kamayray leebayray]

▶ how much is an en suite room? quanto costa una camera con bagno? [kwanto kosta oona kamayra kon banyo]

▶ I've reserved a room for tonight under the name Pearson ho prenotato una camera per stanotte a nome Pearson [o praynotato oona kamayra per stanottay a nomay peerson]

▶ can I see the room? posso vedere la camera? [posso vaydayray la kamayra]

rosé rosé [rozay], rosato [rozato] ✦ il rosé [rozay], il rosato [rozato]

▶ could you recommend a good rosé? potrebbe consigliarmi un buon rosé? [potrebbay konseelyarmee oon boo-on rozay]

round trip il viaggio di andata e ritorno [vee-ajo dee andata ay reetorno]

▶ how long will the round trip take? quanto dura il viaggio di andata e ritorno? [kwanto doora eel vee-ajo dee andata ay reetorno]

round-trip ticket il biglietto di andata e ritorno [beelyetto dee andata ay reetorno]

▶ two round-trip tickets to Rome, please due biglietti di andata e ritorno per Roma [doo-ay beelyettee dee andata ay reetorno per roma]

▶ I'd like a round-trip ticket to Cosenza, leaving on the 3rd and coming back on the 9th vorrei un biglietto di andata e ritorno per Cosenza, con partenza il tre e ritorno il nove [vorray-ee oon beelyetto dee andata ay reetorno per kozentsa kon partentsa eel tray ay reetorno eel novay]

▶ a round-trip ticket for one car, two adults and two children, please un biglietto di andata e ritorno per una macchina, due adulti e due bambini, per favore [oon beelyetto dee andata ay reetorno per oona makkeena doo-ay adooltee ay doo-ay bambeenee per favoray]

route *(itinerary)* il percorso [perkorso]; *(of bus, train, plane)* la linea [leenay-a]

▶ is there an alternative route we could take? c'è un percorso alternativo che potremmo fare? [chay oon perkorso alternateevo kay potremmo faray]

row *(of seats)* la fila [feela]

▶ can we have seats in the front row? possiamo avere dei posti in prima fila? [possee-amo avayray day-ee postee een preema feela]

rowboat la barca a remi [barka a raymee]

▶ can we rent a rowboat? possiamo noleggiare una barca a remi? [possee-amo nolejaray oona barka a raymee]

rubber ring la ciambella salvagente [chambella salvajentay]

▶ where can I buy a rubber ring? dove posso comprare una ciambella salvagente? [dovay posso kompraray oona chambella salvajentay]

run *(on foot)* la corsa [korsa]; *(in car)* il giro (in macchina) [jeero (een makkeena)]; *(for skiing)* la pista [peesta] ♦ *(on foot)* correre [korrayray]; *(bus, train)* viaggiare [vee-ajaray]; *(engine)* funzionare [foontsee-onaray] ♦ *(traffic light)* passare con [passaray kon]

▶ I'm going for a run **vado a correre** [vado a korrayray]

▶ do buses run on Sundays **gli autobus viaggiano di domenica** [lyee owtoboos vee-ajono dee domayneeka]

▶ the bus runs every half hour **l'autobus passa ogni mezzora** [lowtoboos passa onyee medzora]

running

▶ to go running **andare a correre** [andaray a korrayray]

▶ where can I go running here? **dove posso andare a correre qui?** [dovay posso andaray a korrayray kwee]

run out of rimanere senza [reemanayray sentsa]

▶ I've run out of gas **sono rimasto senza benzina** [sono reemasto sentsa bendzeena]

S

safe non pericoloso(a) [non payreekolozo(a)] ♦ *(for valuables)* la cassaforte [kassafortay]

▶ is it safe to swim here? **non è pericoloso nuotare qui?** [non ay payreekolozo noo-otaray kwee]

▶ is it safe to camp here? **non è pericoloso accamparsi qui?** [non ay payreekolozo akkamparsee kwee]

▶ is there a safe in the room? **c'è una cassaforte in camera?** [chay oona kassafortay een kamayra]

sail *(of boat)* la vela [vayla]

▶ we need to adjust that sail **dobbiamo regolare quella vela** [dobbee-amo raygolaray kwella vayla]

sailboat la barca a vela [barka a vayla]

▶ can we rent a sailboat? **possiamo noleggiare una barca a vela?** [possee-amo nolejaray oona barka a vayla]

sailing la vela [vayla]

▶ to go sailing **fare vela** [faray vayla]

▶ I'd like to take beginners' sailing classes **vorrei fare un corso di vela per principianti** [vorray-ee faray oon korso dee vayla per preencheepee-antee]

salad l'insalata *f* [eensalata]

▶ can I just have a salad? **posso avere solo un'insalata?** [posso avayray solo ooneensalata]

sale *(selling)* la vendita [vendeeta]; *(at reduced prices)* i saldi [saldee]
- is it for sale? è in vendita? [ay een vendeeta]
- can you get your money back on sale items? si può avere il rimborso per gli articoli in saldo? [see poo o avayray eel reemborso per lyee arteekolee een saldo]

sales tax l'IVA *f* [eeva]
- is sales tax included? l'IVA è compresa? [leeva at komprayza]
- can you deduct the sales tax? si può detrarre l'IVA? [see poo-o daytrarray leeva]

salt il sale [salay] ◆ *(food)* salare [salaray]; *(road)* spargere il sale su [sparjayray eel salay soo]
- can you pass me the salt? mi può passare il sale? [mee poo-o passaray eel salay]
- it doesn't have enough salt non c'è abbastanza sale [non chay abbastantsa salay]

salty salato(a) [salato(a)]
- it's too salty è troppo salato [ay troppo salato]

same stesso(a) [stesso(a)]
- the same (as) lo stesso/la stessa (di) [lo stesso/la stessa (dee)]
- I'll have the same prendo lo stesso [prendo lo stesso]
- it's the same as yours è lo stesso del tuo [ay lo stesso del too-o]

sandwich il panino [paneeno]
- a chicken sandwich, please un panino al pollo, per favore [oon paneeno al pollo per favoray]

Saturday il sabato [sabato]
- Saturday, September 13th sabato tredici settembre [sabato traydeechee settembray]
- is it closed on Saturdays? è chiuso di sabato? [ay kee-oozo dee sabato]

sauce la salsa [salsa]; *(for pasta)* il sugo [soogo]
- do you have a sauce that isn't too strong? avete una salsa non troppo forte? [avaytay oona salsa non troppo fortay]

sauna la sauna [sowna]
- is there a sauna? c'è una sauna? [chay oona sowna]

sausage la salsiccia [salseecha]
- I'd like to try some of the sausage vorrei assaggiare un po' di salsiccia [vorray-ee assajaray oon po dee salseecha]

say dire [deeray]
- how do you say "good luck" in Italian? come si dice ''good luck'' in italiano? [komay see deechay good luk een eetalee-ano]

scared
- to be scared aver paura [avayr pa-oora]
- I'm scared of spiders ho paura dei ragni [o pa-oora day-ee ranyee]

scheduled flight il volo di linea [volo dee leenay-a]
- when is the next scheduled flight to Cagliari? a che ora è il prossimo volo di linea per Cagliari? [a kay ora ay eel prosseemo volo dee leenay-a per kalyaree]

school *(for children)* la scuola [skoo-ola]; *(college, university)* l'università *f* [ooneeverseeta]
▸ are you still in school? studi ancora? [stoodee ankora]

scoop *(of ice cream)* la pallina (di gelato) [palleena (dee jaylato]
▸ I'd like a cone with two scoops vorrei un cono con due palline di gelato [vorray-ee oon kono kon doo-ay palleenay dee jaylato]

scooter lo scooter [skooter]
▸ I'd like to rent a scooter vorrei noleggiare uno scooter [vorray-ee nolejaray oono skooter]

Scotch *(whiskey)* lo scotch [skotsh]
▸ a Scotch on the rocks, please uno scotch on the rocks, per favore [oono skotsh on thay rox per favoray]

Scotch tape® lo Scotch® [skotsh]
▸ do you have any Scotch tape®? ha dello Scotch®? [a dello skotsh]

scrambled eggs le uova strapazzate [oo-ova strapatsatay]
▸ I'd like scrambled eggs for breakfast vorrei delle uova strapazzate per colazione [vorray-ee dellay oo-ova strapatsatay per kolatsee-onay]

screen *(room in movie theater)* la sala (di proiezione) [sala (dee pro-yetsee-onay)]
▸ how many screens does the movie theater have? quante sale ha il cinema? [kwantay salay a eel cheenayma]

scuba diving l'immersione *f* [eemersee-onay]
▸ can we go scuba diving? possiamo fare immersione? [possee-amo faray eemersee-onay]

sea il mare [maray]
▸ the sea is rough il mare è mosso [eel maray ay mosso]
▸ how long does it take to walk to the sea? quanto ci vuole per andare a piedi al mare? [kwanto chee voo-olay per andaray a pee-aydee al maray]

seasick
▸ I feel seasick ho il mal di mare [o eel mal dee maray]

seasickness il mal di mare [mal dee maray]
▸ can you give me something for seasickness, please? mi può dare qualcosa per il mal di mare, per favore? [mee poo-o daray kwalkoza per eel mal dee maray per favoray]

seaside resort la stazione balneare [statsee-onay balnay-aray]
▸ what's the nearest seaside resort? qual è la stazione balneare più vicina? [kwal ay la statsee-onay balnay-aray pyoo veecheena]

season *(of year)* la stagione [stajonay]
▸ what is the best season to come here? qual è la migliore stagione per venire qui? [kwal ay la meelyor stajonay per vayneeray kwee]

season ticket l'abbonamento *m* [abbonamento]
▸ how much is a season ticket? quanto costa l'abbonamento? [kwanto kosta labbonamento]

seat il posto (a sedere) [posto (a saydayray)]; *(in car)* il sedile [saydeelay]; *(in theater, movie theater)* la poltrona [poltrona]
▸ is this seat taken? è occupato questo posto? [ay okkoopato kwesto posto]
▸ excuse me, I think you're (sitting) in my seat mi scusi, credo che si sia seduto al mio posto [mee skoozee kraydo kay see see-a saydooto al mee-o posto]

second *(unit of time)* il secondo [saykondo]; *(gear)* la seconda [saykonda]
♦ secondo(a) [saykondo(a)]
▸ wait a second! aspetta un secondo! [aspetta oon saykondo]
▸ are you in second? sei in seconda? [say-ee een saykonda]
▸ it's the second street on your right è la seconda via sulla sua destra [ay la saykonda vee-a soolla soo-a destra]

second class la seconda (classe) [saykonda (klassay)] ♦ in seconda (classe) [een saykonda (klassay)]
▸ my seat's in second class il mio posto è in seconda classe [eel mee-o posto ay een saykonda klassay]
▸ to travel second class viaggiare in seconda [vee-ajaray een saykonda]

see vedere [vaydayray]
▸ I'm here to see Dr. Arena devo vedere il Dottor Arena [dayvo vaydayray eel dottor arayna]
▸ can I see the room? posso vedere la camera? [posso vaydayray la kamayra]
▸ I'd like to see the dress in the window vorrei vedere il vestito in vetrina [vorray-ee vaydayray eel vesteeto een vetreena]
▸ see you soon! a presto! [a presto]
▸ see you around! ci vediamo! [chee vaydee-amo]
▸ see you later! a dopo! [a dopo]
▸ see you (on) Thursday! a giovedì! [a jovaydee]

self-service *(restaurant, gas station)* self-service [selfservees] ♦ il self-service [selfservees]
▸ is it self-service? è self-service? [ay selfservees]

sell vendere [vendayray]
▸ do you sell stamps? vendete francobolli? [vendaytay frankobollee]
▸ the radio I was sold is defective la radio che mi hanno venduto è difettosa [la radee-o kay mee anno vendooto ay deefettoza]

send mandare [mandaray]
▸ I'd like to send this package to Boston by airmail vorrei mandare questo pacco a Boston per via aerea [vorray-ee mandaray kwesto pakko a boston per vee-a a-ayray-a]
▸ could you send a tow truck? può mandare un carro attrezzi? [poo-o mandaray oon karro attretsee]

service charge

As well as *servizio* (service charge), which you pay for the staff who serve you, a supplement, *coperto* (cover charge), is added in some restaurants. This is for the preparation of the table and includes bread. Count on 1 to 3 euros on average. This should be stated on the menu, but that doesn't always happen.

---

separately *(individually)* separatamente [sayparatamentay]
▸ is it sold separately? è venduto separatamente? [ay vendooto sayparatamentay]

September il settembre [settembray]
▸ September 9th il nove settembre [eel novay settembray]

serve *(meal, drink, customer)* servire [serveeray]; *(town, station)* fermare in [fermaray een]
▸ when is breakfast served? a che ora è servita la colazione? [a kay ora ay serveeta la kolatsee-onay]
▸ are you still serving lunch? servite ancora il pranzo? [serveetay ankora eel prandzo]

service *(in restaurant)* il servizio [serveetsee-o] ✦ *(car)* fare la revisione a [faray la rayveezee-onay a]
▸ the service was terrible il servizio era pessimo [eel serveetsee-o ayra pesseemo]
▸ we have to have the car serviced dobbiamo far fare la revisione alla macchina [dobbee-amo far faray la rayveezee-onay alla makkeena]

service charge il servizio [serveetsee-o]
▸ is the service charge included? il servizio è compreso? [eel serveetsee-o ay komprayzo]

set *(of cookware)* la batteria [battayree-a]; *(of keys)* il mazzo [matso] ✦ *(sun)* tramontare [tramontaray]
▸ do you have a spare set of keys? ha un mazzo di chiavi di riserva? [a oon matso dee kee-avee dee reezerva]
▸ what time does the sun set? a che ora tramonta il sole? [a kay ora tramonta eel solay]

seven sette [settay]
▸ there are seven of us siamo in sette [see-amo een settay]

several *(some)* alcuni(e) [alkoonee(ay)], diversi(e) [deeversee(ay)] ✦ *(some people)* alcuni(e) [alkoonee(ay)]
▸ I've been before, several years ago ci sono già stato, diversi anni fa [chee sono ja stato deeversee annee fa]

shade *(shadow)* l'ombra *f* [ombra]
▸ can we have a table in the shade? possiamo avere un tavolo all'ombra? [possee-amo avayray oon tavolo allombra]

shaking hands

When meeting someone for the first time, shake hands and say *piacere* ('pleased to meet you') or *molto lieto* ('delighted to meet you'). Friends, however, usually kiss each other on both cheeks.

shake *(bottle)* agitare [ajeetaray]
- to shake hands stringersi la mano [streengersee la mano]
- let's shake qua la mano [kwa la mano]

shame *(remorse, humiliation)* la vergogna [vergonya]; *(pity)* il peccato [pekkato]
- (what a) shame! (che) peccato! [(kay) pekkato]

shampoo lo shampoo [shampoo]
- do you have any shampoo? avete dello shampoo? [avaytay dello shampoo]

share dividere [deeveedayray]
- we're going to share it: can you bring us two plates? lo dividiamo: ci può portare due piatti? [lo deeveedee-amo chee poo-o portaray doo-ay pee-attee]

shared *(bathroom, kitchen)* in comune [een komoonay]
- is the bathroom shared? il bagno è in comune? [eel banyo ay een komoonay]

shaver il rasoio elettrico [razo-yo aylettreeko]
- where can I buy a new shaver? dove posso comprare un altro rasoio elettrico? [dovay posso kompraray oon altro razo-yo aylettreeko]

sheet *(for bed)* il lenzuolo [lentsoo-olo]; *(of paper)* il foglio [folyo]
- could you change the sheets? può cambiare le lenzuola? [poo-o kambee-aray lay lentsoo-ola]

ship la nave [navay]
- when does the ship dock? quando entra in porto la nave? [kwando entra een porto la navay]

shoe la scarpa [skarpa]
- what sort of shoes should you wear? che tipo di scarpe si devono portare? [kay tipo dee skarpay see dayvono portaray]

shoe size il numero di scarpe [noomayro dee skarpay]
- my shoe size is 8 porto il quarantadue [porto eel kwarantadoo-ay]

shop *(store)* il negozio [naygotsee-o]
- what time do the shops downtown close? a che ora chiudono i negozi in centro? [a kay ora kee-oodono ee naygotsee een chentro]

shopping lo shopping [shoppeen]
- where can you go shopping around here? dove si può fare shopping nei dintorni? [dovay see poo-o faray shoppeen nay-ee deentornee]

shopping

The usual shopping hours are 9 a.m. to 7:30 p.m. Small stores usually close for lunch between 1 and 4 p.m. All stores are generally closed on Monday mornings, apart from grocery stores and bakeries, which are closed on Wednesday afternoons.

shopping bag il sacchetto [sakketto]
- can I have a plastic shopping bag, please? posso avere un sacchetto di plastica, per favore? [posso avayray oon sakketto dee plasteeka per favoray]

shopping center il centro commerciale [chentro kommerchalay]
- I'm looking for a shopping center sto cercando un centro commerciale [sto cherkando oon chentro kommerchalay]

shop window la vetrina [vetreena]
- we've just been peeking in the shop windows abbiamo dato solo una rapida occhiata alle vetrine [abbee-amo dato solo oona rapeeda okkee-ata allay vetreenay]

short *(in time)* breve [brayvay]; *(in length)* corto(a) [korto(a)]; *(in height)* basso(a) [basso(a)]
- we'd like to do a shorter trip vorremmo fare un viaggio più breve [vorremmo faray oon vee-ajo pyoo brayvay]
- we're only here for a short time ci fermiamo poco [chee fermee-amo poko]
- I'm two euros short mi mancano due euro [mee mankano doo-ay ay-ooro]

shortcut la scorciatoia [skorchato-ya]
- is there a shortcut? c'è una scorciatoia? [chay oona skorchato-ya]

short wave le onde corte [onday kortay]
- can you get any English stations on short wave? si prendono delle stazioni inglesi sulle onde corte? [see prendono dellay statsee-onee eenglayzee soollay onday kortay]

should dovere [dovayray]
- what should I do? cosa devo fare? [koza dayvo faray]

show *(at theater, movies)* lo spettacolo [spettakolo] ♦ *(let see)* far vedere [far vaydayray], mostrare [mostraray]
- what time does the show begin? a che ora comincia lo spettacolo? [a kay ora komeencha lo spettakolo]
- could you show me where that is on the map? mi può far vedere dov'è sulla mappa? [mee poo-o far vaydayray dovay soolla mappa]
- could you show me the room? mi può mostrare la camera? [mee poo-o mostraray la kamayra]

shower *(device, act)* la doccia [docha]; *(of rain)* l'acquazzone *m* [akkwatsonay]

- I'd like a room with a shower, please vorrei una camera con doccia, per favore [vorray-ee oona kamayra kon docha per favoray]
- how does the shower work? come funziona la doccia? [komay foontsee-ona la docha]
- the shower is leaking la doccia perde [la docha perday]

shower head il soffione della doccia [soffee-onay della docha]

- the shower head is broken il soffione della doccia è rotto [eel soffee-onay della docha ay rotto]

shrimp il gamberetto [gambayretto]

- I'm allergic to shrimp sono allergico ai gamberetti [sono allerjeeko a-ee gambayrettee]

shut chiudere [kee-ooderay] ◆ chiudersi [kee-oodersee]

- the window won't shut la finestra non si chiude [la feenestra non see kee-ooday]

shutter (on window) la persiana [persee-ana]; (on camera) l'otturatore *m* [ottooratoray]

- are there shutters on the windows? ci sono le persiane alle finestre? [chee sono lay persee-anay allay feenestray]

shuttle (vehicle) la navetta [navetta]

- is there a shuttle to the airport? c'è una navetta per l'aeroporto? [chay oona navetta per la-ayroporto]

sick (unwell) malato(a) [malato(a)]

- I feel sick mi sento male [mee sento malay]
- to be sick (be unwell) essere malato [essayray malato]; (vomit) vomitare [vomeetaray]

side il lato [lato]; (of the body) il fianco [fee-anko]; (edge) il bordo [bordo]

- I have a pain in my right side ho un dolore al fianco destro [o oon doloray al fee-anko destro]
- could we have a table on the other side of the room? potremmo avere un tavolo dall'altro lato della sala? [potremmo avayray oon tavolo dallaltro lato della sala]
- which side of the road do we drive on here? su che lato della strada dobbiamo guidare qui? [soo kay lato della strada dobbee-amo gweedaray kwee]

sidewalk il marciapiede [marchape-ayday]

- the sidewalks are very clean here i marciapiedi sono molto puliti qui [ee marchape-ayde sono molto pooleetee kwee]

sight (seeing) la vista [veesta] ◆ **sights** (of place) i posti da visitare [postee da veezeetaray]

- I'm having problems with my sight ho qualche problema di vista [o kwalkay problayma dee veesta]
- what are the sights that are most worth seeing? quali sono i posti più interessanti da visitare? [kwalee sono ee postee pyoo eentayressantee da veezeetaray]

sign firmare [feermaray]

▶ do I sign here? **firmo qui?** [feermo kwee]

signpost il cartello (stradale) [kartello (stradalay)]

▶ what does that signpost say? **cosa dice quel cartello?** [koza deechay kwel kartello]
▶ does the route have good signposts? **è buona la segnalazione sulla strada?** [ay boo-ona la senyalatsee-onay soolla strada]

silver *(metal)* l'argento *m* [arjento]

▶ is it made of silver? **è d'argento?** [ay darjento]

since *(starting from)* da [da] ♦ *(from the time that)* da quando [da kwando]; *(because)* dato che [dato kay]

▶ I've been here since Tuesday **sono qui da martedì** [sono kwee da martaydee]
▶ it hasn't rained once since we've been here **non è piovuto una volta da quando siamo qui** [non au pee-ovooto oona volta da kwando see-amo kwee]

single *(only one)* solo(a) [solo(a)]; *(unmarried)* single [seengol] ♦ *(CD)* il singolo [seengolo]

▶ not a single one **nemmeno uno/a** [nemmayno oono/a]
▶ I'm single **sono single** [sono seengol]
▶ she's a single woman in her thirties **è una single sulla trentina** [ay oona seengol soolla trenteena]

single bed il letto singolo [letto seengolo]

▶ we'd prefer two single beds **preferiremmo due letti singoli** [prayfayreeremmo doo-ay lettee seengolee]

single room la camera singola [kamayra seengola]

▶ I'd like to book a single room for 5 nights **vorrei prenotare una camera singola per cinque notti** [vorray-ee praynotaray oona kamayra seengola per cheenkway nottee]

sister la sorella [sorella]

▶ I have two sisters **ho due sorelle** [o doo-ay sorellay]

sit sedersi [saydayrsee]

▶ may I sit at your table? **posso sedermi al vostro tavolo?** [posso saydayrmee al vostro tavolo]
▶ is anyone sitting here? **c'è qualcuno seduto qui?** [chay kwalkoono saydooto kwee]

site *(construction site)* il cantiere [kantee-ayray]; *(archaeological)* il sito [seeto]

▶ can we visit the site? **possiamo visitare il sito?** [possee-amo veezeetaray eel seeto]

sitting

▶ is there more than one sitting for lunch? **il pranzo è servito in più di una tranche oraria?** [eel prandzo ay serveeto een pyoo dee oona transh orararee-a]

six sei [say-ee]

▶ there are six of us **siamo in sei** [see-amo een say-ee]

sixth sesto(a) [sesto(a)]

▶ our room is on the sixth floor **la nostra camera è al settimo piano** [la nostra kamayra ay al setteemo pee-ano]

sizes

You have to get used to Italian sizes when you are shopping. Bear in mind that an Italian 42 is the equivalent of an American 8, 44 is a 10, etc.

size *(of person, clothes)* la taglia [talya]
 ▸ do you have another size? avete un'altra taglia? [avaytay oonaltra talya]
 ▸ do you have it in a smaller size? ce l'avete in una taglia più piccola? [chay lavaytay een oona talya pyoo peekkola]
 ▸ I take or I'm a size 8 *(shoes)* porto il trentanove (di scarpe) [porto eel trentanovay (dee skarpay)]; *(clothes)* porto la (taglia) quarantadue [porto la (talya) kwarantadoo-ay]

skate *(for skating)* il pattino [patteeno] ◆ pattinare [patteenaray]
 ▸ how much is it to rent skates? quanto costa noleggiare dei pattini? [kwanto kosta nolejaray day-ee patteenee]
 ▸ can you skate? sa pattinare? [sa patteenaray]

skating il pattinaggio [patteenajo]
 ▸ where can we go skating? dove possiamo andare a pattinare? [dovay possee-amo andaray a patteenaray]

ski lo sci [shee] ◆ sciare [shee-aray]
 ▸ I'd like to rent a pair of skis for the week, please vorrei noleggiare un paio di sci per la settimana, per favore [vorray-ee nolejaray oon pa-yo dee shee per la setteemana per favoray]
 ▸ can you ski? sa sciare? [sa shee-aray]

ski boots gli scarponi da sci [skarponee da shee]
 ▸ I'd like to rent ski boots vorrei noleggiare degli scarponi da sci [vorray-ee nolejaray delyee skarponee da shee]

skiing lo sci [shee]
 ▸ where can we take skiing lessons? dove possiamo prendere delle lezioni di sci? [dovay possee-amo prendayray dellay letsee-onee dee shee]
 ▸ where can we go skiing near here? dove possiamo andare a sciare qui vicino? [dovay possee-amo andaray a shee-aray kwee veecheeno]

sleep dormire [dormeeray]
 ▸ I slept well ho dormito bene [o dormeeto baynay]
 ▸ I can't sleep non riesco a dormire [non ree-esko a dormeeray]

sleeping bag il sacco a pelo [sakko a paylo]
 ▸ where can I buy a new sleeping bag? dove posso comprare un nuovo sacco a pelo? [dovay posso kompraray oon noo-ovo sakko a paylo]

sleeping pill il sonnifero [sonneefayro]

smoking

Since January 2005, smoking has been banned in Italy in all enclosed public places such as offices, cafés, bars and restaurants. People may still smoke in their homes and outdoors, but in places open to the public, smoking is allowed only in special smoking rooms, where these have been provided.

▸ I'd like some sleeping pills vorrei dei sonniferi [vorray-ee day-ee sonneefayree]

slice *(of bread, ham)* la fetta [fetta] ◆ affettare [affettaray]

▸ a thin slice of ham una fetta sottile di prosciutto [oona fetta sotteelay dee proshootto]

slim *(person)* snello(a) [znello(a)]

▸ she's slim è snella [ay znella]

slow lento(a) [lento(a)]; *(clock, watch)* indietro [eendee-aytro]

▸ the service in this restaurant is rather slow il servizio in questo ristorante è un po' lento [eel serveetsee-o een kwesto reestorantay ay oon po lento]

▸ is that clock slow? quell'orologio è indietro? [kwellorolojo ay eendee-aytro]

slowly lentamente [lentamentay]

▸ could you speak more slowly, please? potrebbe parlare più lentamente, per favore? [potrebbay parlaray pyoo lentamentay per favoray]

small piccolo(a) [peekkolo(a)]

▸ do you have anything smaller? non ha qualcosa di più piccolo? [non a kwalkoza dee pyoo peekkolo]

smell *(notice a smell of)* sentire odore di [senteeray odoray dee] ◆ *(have a smell)* odorare [odoraray]; *(have a bad smell)* puzzare [pootsaray]

▸ can you smell something burning? non sente odore di bruciato? [non sentay odoray dee broochato]

▸ it smells in here puzza qui [pootsa kwee]

smoke il fumo [foomo] ◆ *(person)* fumare [foomaray]

▸ is the smoke bothering you? il fumo le dà fastidio? [eel foomo lay da fasteedee-o]

▸ do you mind if I smoke? le dispiace se fumo? [lay deespee-achay say foomo]

▸ no thanks, I don't smoke no grazie, non fumo [no gratsee-ay non foomo]

smoker il fumatore [foomatoray], la fumatrice [foomatreechay]

▸ are you smokers or nonsmokers? siete fumatori o non fumatori? [see-aytay foomatoree o non foomatoree]

smoking il fumo [foomo]

▸ I can't stand smoking non sopporto il fumo [non sopporto eel foomo]

▸ is smoking allowed here? si può fumare qui? [see poo-o foomaray kwee]

smoking section la zona fumatori [dzona foomatoree]

> I'd like a table in the smoking section vorrei un tavolo nella zona fumatori [vorray-ee oon tavolo nella dzona foomatoree]

sneaker la scarpa da ginnastica [skarpa da jeennasteeka]

> your sneakers are really trendy! le tue scarpe da ginnastica sono davvero all'ultimo grido! [lay too-ay skarpay da jeennasteeka sono davvayro alloolteemo greedo]

snorkel il boccaglio [bokkalyo]

> I'd like to rent a snorkel and mask, please vorrei noleggiare una maschera con boccaglio, per favore [vorray-ee nolejaray oona maskayra kon bokkalyo per favoray]

snow nevicare [nayveekaray]

> it's snowing nevica [nayveeka]

snowboard lo snowboard [snobord]

> I'd like to rent a snowboard vorrei noleggiare uno snowboard [vorray-ee nolejaray oono snobord]

snowboarding lo snowboard [snobord]

> where can we go snowboarding near here? dove possiamo fare snowboard qui vicino? [dovay possee-amo faray snobord kwee veecheeno]

snow tire la gomma da neve [gomma da nayvay]

> do I need snow tires? devo avere le gomme da neve? [dayvo avayray lay gommay da nayvay]

so *(to such a degree, consequently)* così [kozee]; *(also)* anche [ankay]

> it's so big! è così grande! [ay kozee granday]

> there are so many choices I don't know what to have c'è così tanta scelta che non so cosa prendere [chay kozee tanta shelta kay non so koza prendayray]

> I'm hungry – so am I! ho fame – anch'io! [o famay – ankee-o]

soap il sapone [saponay]

> there's no soap non c'è sapone [non chay saponay]

socket *(in wall)* la presa (di corrente) [prayza (dee correntay)]

> is there a socket I can use to recharge my cell? c'è una presa che posso usare per ricaricare il mio cellulare? [chay oona prayza kay posso oozaray per reekareekaray eel mee-o chelloolaray]

solution la soluzione [solootsee-onay]

> that seems to be the best solution sembra la soluzione migliore [sembra la solootsee-onay meelyoray]

> I'd like some contact lens solution vorrei una soluzione per lenti a contatto [vorray-ee oona solootsee-onay per lentee a kontatto]

some *(an amount of)* del (della) [del (della)], un po' di [oon po dee]; *(a number of)* alcuni(e) [alkoonee(ay)] ♦ *(an amount)* un po' [oon po]; *(a number)* alcuni(e) [alkoonee(ay)]

> I'd like some coffee vorrei del caffè [vorray-ee del kaffay]

- some friends recommended this place **alcuni amici mi hanno consigliato questo posto** [alkoonee ameechee mee anno konseelyato kwesto posto]
- can I have some? **ne posso avere un po'?** [nay posso avayray oon po]

somebody, someone qualcuno [kwalkoono]
- somebody left this for you **qualcuno ha lasciato questo per lei** [kwalkoono a lashato kwesto per lay-ee]

something qualcosa [kwalkoza]
- is something wrong? **c'è qualcosa che non va?** [chay kwalkoza kay non va]

somewhere da qualche parte [da kwalkay partay]
- somewhere near here **da qualche parte qui vicino** [da kwalkay partay kwee veecheeno]
- I'm looking for somewhere to stay **sto cercando un posto in cui stare** [sto cherkando oon posto in koo-ee staray]
- somewhere else **da qualche altra parte** [da kwalkay altra partay]

son il figlio [feelyo]
- this is my son **questo è mio figlio** [kwesto ay mee-o feelyo]

soon presto [presto]
- see you soon! **a presto!** [a presto]
- as soon as possible **il prima possibile** [eel preema posseebeelay]

sore throat il mal di gola [mal dee gola]
- I have a sore throat **ho mal di gola** [o mal dee gola]

sorry
- I'm sorry **mi dispiace** [mee deespee-achay], **(mi) scusi** [(mee) skoozee]
- sorry I'm late **mi dispiace, sono in ritardo** [mee deespee-achay sono een reetardo]
- I'm sorry, but this seat is taken **mi dispiace, ma questo posto è occupato** [mee deespee-achay ma kwesto posto ay okkoopato]
- sorry to bother you **scusi se la disturbo** [skoozee say la deestoorbo]
- sorry? *(asking for repetition)* **scusi?** [skozee]
- no, sorry no, **mi dispiace** [no mee deespee-achay]

sound il suono [soo-ono]; *(TV, radio volume)* il volume [voloomay]
- can you turn the sound down? **può abbassare il volume?** [poo-o abbassaray eel voloomay]

souvenir il souvenir [soovayneer]
- where can we buy souvenirs? **dove possiamo comprare dei souvenir?** [dovay possee-amo kompraray day-ee soovayneer]

souvenir shop il negozio di souvenir [naygotsee-o dee soovayneer]
- I'm looking for a souvenir shop **sto cercando un negozio di souvenir** [sto cherkando oon naygotsee-o dee soovayneer]

spa *(town)* la località termale [lokaleeta termalay]; *(health club)* il centro benessere [chentro baynessayray]; *(bathtub)* l'idromassaggio m [eedromassajo]

sparkling wine

If you want to make your evening go with a zing, try a glass of *spumante*. This Italian bubbly comes in sweet, medium-dry or dry, and you can drink it as an aperitif or with your dessert. The best vintages are given the initials *V.S.Q.R.D.: vino spumante di qualità prodotto in regioni delimitate*, which guarantees their origin.

▸ the spa's not working l'idromassaggio non funziona [leedromassajo non foontsee-ona]

space *(room)* lo spazio [spatsee-o]; *(for car, tent, trailer)* il posto [posto]

▸ is there space for another bed in the room? c'è spazio per un altro letto nella camera? [chay spatsee-o per oon altro letto nella kamayra]

▸ I'd like a space for one tent for two days vorrei un posto tenda per due giorni [vorray-ee oon posto tenda per doo-ay jornee]

▸ do you have any spaces farther from the road? avete dei posti più lontani dalla strada? [avaytay day-ee postee pyoo lontane dalla strada]

spade *(child's toy)* la paletta [paletta]

▸ my son's left his spade at the beach mio figlio ha dimenticato la paletta in spiaggia [mee-o feelyo a deementeekato la paletta een spee-aja]

spare *(clothes, battery)* di ricambio [dee reekambee-o] ◆ *(tire)* la ruota di scorta [roo-ota dee skorta]; *(part)* il (pezzo di) ricambio [(petso dee) reekambee-o]

▸ should I take some spare clothes? devo prendere dei vestiti di ricambio? [dayvo prendayray day-ee vesteetee dee reekambee-o]

▸ I don't have any spare cash non ho disponibilità [non o deesponeebeeleeta]

▸ I've got a spare ticket for the game ho un biglietto in più per la partita [o oon beelyetto een pyoo per la parteeta]

spare part il pezzo di ricambio [petso dee reekambee-o]

▸ where can I get spare parts? dove posso trovare i pezzi di ricambio? [dovay posso trovaray ee petsee dee reekambee-o]

spare tire la ruota di scorta [roo-ota dee skorta]

▸ the spare tire's flat too anche la ruota di scorta è a terra [ankay la roo-ota dee skorta ay a terra]

spare wheel la ruota di scorta [roo-ota dee skorta]

▸ there's no spare wheel non c'è la ruota di scorta [non chay la roo-ota dee skorta]

sparkling *(water, wine)* frizzante [freedzantay]

▸ could I have a bottle of sparkling water, please? posso avere una bottiglia d'acqua frizzante, per favore? [posso avayray oona botteelya dakkwa freedzantay per favoray]

speak parlare [parlaray]

- I speak hardly any Italian parlo pochissimo l'italiano [parlo pokeesseemo leetalee-ano]
- is there anyone here who speaks English? c'è qualcuno qui che parla inglese? [chay kwalkoono kwee kay parla eenglayzay]
- could you speak more slowly? potrebbe parlare più lentamente? [potrebbay parlaray pyoo lentamentay]
- hello, I'd like to speak to Mr...; this is... pronto, vorrei parlare con il signor ...; sono ... [pronto vorray-ee parlaray kon eel seenyor sono]
- who's speaking please? chi parla, per favore? [kee parla per favoray]
- hello, Gary speaking pronto, sono Gary [pronto sono garee]

special il piatto del giorno [pee-atto del jorno]

- what's today's special? qual è il piatto del giorno? [kwal ay eel pee-atto del jorno]

specialist lo/la specialista [spaychaleesta]

- could you refer me to a specialist? mi può indirizzare da uno specialista? [mee poo-o eendeereetsaray da oono spaychaleesta]

specialty la specialità [spaychaleeta]

- what are the local specialties? quali sono le specialità del posto? [kwalee sono lay spaychaleeta del posto]

speed limit il limite di velocità [leemeetay dee vaylocheeta]

- what's the speed limit on this road? qual è il limite di velocità su questa strada? [kwal ay eel leemeetay dee vaylocheeta soo kwesta strada]

speedometer il tachimetro [takeemetro]

- the speedometer's broken il tachimetro è rotto [eel takeemetro ay rotto]

speed trap il radar [radar]

- are there lots of speed traps in the area? ci sono molti radar nella zona? [chee sono moltee radar nella dzona]

spell scrivere [skreevayray]

- how do you spell your name? come si scrive il suo nome? [komay see skreevay eel soo-o nomay]
- can you spell your name for me, please? mi può scandire il suo nome lettera per lettera, per favore? [mee poo-o skandeeray eel soo-o nomay lettayra per lettayra, per favoray]

spend (money) spendere [spendayray]; (time, vacation) passare [passaray]

- we are prepared to spend up to 200 euros siamo disposti a spendere fino a duecento euro [see-amo deespostee a spendayray feeno a doo-aychento ay-ooro]
- I spent a month in Italy a few years ago ho passato un mese in Italia qualche anno fa [o passato oon mayzay een eetalee-a kwalkay anno fa]

spicy piccante [peekkantay]

- is this dish spicy? è piccante questo piatto? [ay peekkantay kwesto pee-atto]

spoon il cucchiaio [kookkee-a-yo]
- could I have a spoon? **potrei avere un cucchiaio?** [potray-ee avayray oon kookkee-a-yo]

sport lo sport [sport]
- do you play any sports? **fa qualche sport?** [fa kwalkay sport]
- I play a lot of sports **faccio molti sport** [facho molti sport]

sporty *(person)* sportivo(a) [sporteevo(a)]
- I'm not very sporty **non sono molto sportivo** [non sono molto sporteevo]

sprain slogarsi [zlogarsee]
- I think I've sprained my ankle **penso di essermi slogato la caviglia** [penso dee essermee zlogato la kaveelya]
- my wrist is sprained **ho il polso slogato** [o eel polso zlogato]

square *(in town)* la piazza [pee-atsa]
- where is the main square? **dov'è la piazza principale?** [dovay la pee-atsa preencheepalay]

stain la macchia [makkee-a]
- can you remove this stain? **può mandar via questa macchia?** [poo-o mandar vee-a kwesta makkee-a]

stairs le scale [skalay]
- where are the stairs? **dove sono le scale?** [dovay sono lay skalay]

stall *(car, engine)* spegnersi [spenyersee]
- the engine keeps stalling **il motore continua a spegnersi** [eel motoray konteenoo-a a spenyersee]

stamp *(for letter, postcard)* il francobollo [frankobollo]
- a stamp for a postcard to the United States, please **un francobollo da cartolina per gli Stati Uniti, per favore** [oon frankobollo da kartoleena per lyee statee ooneetee per favoray]

stand *(in market)* la bancarella [bankarella]; *(in street)* il chiosco [kee-osko]; *(at exhibit)* lo stand [stand]; *(in stadium)* la tribuna [treeboona] ♦ *(tolerate)* sopportare [sopportaray] ♦ *(be upright)* stare in piedi [staray een pee-aydee]; *(get up)* alzarsi [altsarsee]
- where's stand number five? **dov'è lo stand numero cinque?** [dovay lo stand noomayro cheenkway]

start *(begin)* iniziare [eeneetsee-aray]; *(function)* partire [parteeray]
- when does the concert start? **a che ora inizia il concerto?** [a kay ora eeneetsee-a eel koncherto]
- the car won't start **la macchina non parte** [la makkeena non partay]

starving affamato(a) [affamato(a)]
- I'm absolutely starving **sto letteralmente morendo di fame** [sto lettayralmentay morendo dee famay]

States

- the States gli Stati Uniti [lyee statee ooneetee]
- I live in the States vivo negli Stati Uniti [veevo nelyee statee ooneetee]
- I'm from the States sono statunitense [sono statooneetensay]
- have you ever been to the States? è mai stato negli Stati Uniti? [ay ma-ee stato nelyee statee ooneetee]

station la stazione [statsee-onay]; *(police)* il commissariato [kommeessaree-ato]

- to the train station, please! alla stazione (ferroviaria), per favore! [alla statsee-onay (ferrovee-aree-a) per favoray]
- where is the nearest subway station? dov'è la stazione della metropolitana più vicina? [dovay la statsee-onay della metropoleetana pyoo veecheena]

stay *(in place)* rimanere [reemanayray], fermarsi [fermarsee] ◆ *(visit)* il soggiorno [sojorno]

- we're planning to stay for two nights abbiamo intenzione di rimanere due notti [abbee-amo eententsee-onay dee reemanayray doo-ay nottee]
- a two-week stay un soggiorno di due settimane [oon sojorno dee doo-ay setteemanay]

steak la bistecca [beestekka]

- I'd like a steak and fries vorrei una bistecca con patate fritte [vorray-ee oona beestekka kon patatay freettay]

steal *(money, wallet, necklace)* rubare [roobaray]

- my passport was stolen mi hanno rubato il passaporto [mee hanno roobato eel passaporto]
- our car has been stolen ci hanno rubato la macchina [chee hanno roobato la makkeena]

steering lo sterzo [stertso]

- there's a problem with the steering c'è un problema con lo sterzo [chay oon problayma kon lo stertso]

steering wheel il volante [volantay]

- the steering wheel is very stiff il volante è molto rigido [eel volantay ay molto reejeedo]

stick shift *(lever)* la leva del cambio [layva del kambee-o]; *(car)* l'auto *f* col cambio manuale [owto kol kambee-o manoo-alay]

- is it a stick shift or an automatic? l'auto ha il cambio manuale o automatico? [lowto a eel kambee-o manoo-alay o owtomateeko]

sticky note il Post-it® [posteet]

- do you sell sticky notes? vendete dei Post-it®? [vendaytay day-ee posteet]

still ancora [ankora]

- how many miles are there still to go? quanti chilometri mancano ancora? [kwantee keelometree mankano ankora]

▸ we're still waiting to be served stiamo ancora aspettando di essere serviti [stee-amo ankora aspettando dee essayray serveetee]

sting *(wasp, nettle)* pungere [poonjayray]

▸ I've been stung by a wasp mi ha punto una vespa [mee a poonto oona vespa]

stomach lo stomaco [stomako]

▸ my stomach hurts mi fa male lo stomaco [mee fa malay lo stomako]

stomachache il mal di stomaco [mal dee stomako]

▸ I have a really bad stomachache ho un forte mal di stomaco [o oon fortay mal dee stomako]

stop *(for buses)* la fermata [fermata]; *(for trains)* la stazione [statsee-onay]; *(on journey, flight)* la sosta [sosta] ♦ fermare [fermaray] ♦ fermarsi [fermarsee]

▸ is this the right stop for ...? è la fermata giusta per ...? [ay la fermata joosta per]

▸ stop it! smettila! [zmetteela]

▸ where in town does the shuttle stop? dove ferma in città la navetta? [dovay ferma een cheetta la navetta]

▸ please stop here si fermi qui, per favore [see fermee kwee per favoray]

▸ which stations does this train stop at? in quali stazioni ferma questo treno? [een kwalee statsee-onee ferma kwesto trayno]

▸ do we stop at Pisa? ci fermiamo a Pisa? [chee fermee-amo a peeza]

store *(place selling goods)* il negozio [naygotsee-o]

▸ are there any bigger stores in the area? ci sono dei negozi più grandi in zona? [chee sono day-ee naygotsee pyoo grandee een dzona]

store window la vetrina [vetreena]

▸ the store windows are very beautiful le vetrine sono molto belle [lay vetreenay sono molto bellay]

storm il temporale [temporalay]

▸ is there going to be a storm? ci sarà un temporale? [chee sara oon temporalay]

---

in a store

▸ no, thanks, I'm just looking no, grazie, sto solo guardando [no gratsee-ay sto solo gwardando]

▸ how much is this? quanto costa? [kwanto kosta]

▸ I take/I'm a size 8 *(shoes)* porto il trentanove (di scarpe) [porto eel trentanovay (dee skarpay)]; *(clothes)* porto la (taglia) quarantadue [porto la (talya) kwarantadoo-ay]

▸ can I try this coat on? posso provare questo giaccone? [posso provaray kwesto jakkonay]

▸ can it be exchanged? si può cambiarlo? [see poo-o kambee-arlo]

straight *(line, road)* dritto(a) [dreetto(a)]; *(hair)* liscio(a) [leesho(a)] ♦ *(in straight line)* dritto [dreetto]

▶ you have to keep going straight on deve andare sempre dritto [dayvay andaray sempray dreetto]

street la via [vee-a]

▶ will this street take me to the station? se prendo questa via arrivo alla stazione? [say prendo kwesta vee-a arrevo alla statsee-onay]

streetcar il tram [tram]

▶ can you buy tickets on the streetcar? si possono comprare i biglietti sul tram? [see possono kompraray ee beelyettee sool tram]

▶ which streetcar line do we have to take? che linea di tram dobbiamo prendere? [kay leenay-a dee tram dobbee-amo prendayray]

▶ where is the nearest streetcar stop? dov'è la fermata del tram più vicina? [dovay la fermata del tram pyoo veecheena]

street map la piantina [pee-anteena]

▶ where can I buy a street map? dove posso comprare una piantina? [dovay posso kompraray oona pee-anteena]

strong forte [fortay]

▶ is the current very strong here? è molto forte la corrente qui? [ay molto fortay la korrentay kwee]

stuck

▶ to be stuck *(jammed)* essere incastrato(a) [essayray eenkastrato(a)]; *(trapped)* rimanere bloccato(a) [reemanayray blokkato(a)]

▶ someone is stuck in the elevator qualcuno è rimasto bloccato nell'ascensore [kwalkoono ay reemasto blokkato nellashensoray]

student lo studente [stoodentay], la studentessa [stoodentessa]

▶ I'm a student sono studente [sono stoodentay]

student discount lo sconto per studenti [skonto per stoodentee]

▶ do you have student discounts? avete degli sconti per studenti? [avaytay delyee skontee per stoodentee]

studio (apartment) il monolocale [monolokalay]

▶ I'm renting a studio apartment ho preso in affitto un monolocale [o prayzo een affeetto oon monolokalay]

style *(manner)* lo stile [steelay]; *(design)* la linea [leenay-a]; *(elegance)* la classe [klassay]

▶ she has a lot of style ha molta classe [a molta klassay]

subway la metropolitana [metropoleetana]

▶ can I have a map of the subway? posso avere una mappa della metropolitana? [posso avayray oona mappa della metropoleetana]

subway train la metropolitana [metropoleetana]

▸ when's the last subway train from this station? **a che ora parte l'ultima metropolitana da questa stazione?** [a kay ora partay loolteema metropoleetana da kwesta statsee-onay]

sudden improvviso(a) [eemprovveezo(a)]

▸ are these sudden changes in temperature common? **sono frequenti questi cambiamenti improvvisi della temperatura?** [sono frekwentee kwestee kambee-amentee eemprovveezee della tempayratoora]

▸ all of a sudden **improvvisamente** [eemprovveezamentay]

sugar lo zucchero [tsookkkayro]

▸ can you pass me the sugar? **mi può passare lo zucchero?** [mee poo-o passaray lo tsookkkayro]

suggest *(propose)* proporre [proporray]

▸ do you have anything else you can suggest? **ha qualcos'altro da proporci?** [a kwalkozaltro da proporchee]

suit *(be convenient for)* andar bene a [andar baynay a]

▸ that suits me perfectly **mi va benissimo** [mee va bayneeseemo]

▸ it doesn't suit me **non mi va bene** [non mee va baynay]

suitcase la valigia [valeeja]

▸ one of my suitcases is missing **manca una delle mie valigie** [manka oona dellay mee-ay valeejay]

▸ my suitcase was damaged in transit **la mia valigia è stata danneggiata durante il trasporto** [la mee-a valeeja ay stata dannejata doorantay eel trasporto]

summer l'estate *f* [estatay]

▸ in (the) summer **d'estate** [destatay]

summer vacation le vacanze estive [vakantsay esteevay]

▸ we've come here for our summer vacation **siamo venuti qui per le vacanze estive** [see-amo vaynootee kwee per lay vakantsay esteevay]

sun il sole [solay]

▸ the sun's very strong at this time of day **il sole è molto forte a quest'ora** [eel solay ay molto fortay a kwestora]

sunburn la scottatura (da sole) [skottatoora (da solay)]

▸ I've got a bad sunburn **ho una brutta scottatura da sole** [o oona brootta skottatoora da solay]

▸ do you have cream for a sunburn? **ha una crema per le scottature da sole?** [a oona krayma per lay skottatooray da solay]

Sunday la domenica [domayneeka]

▸ where can I find a doctor on a Sunday? **dove posso trovare un medico di domenica?** [dovay posso trovaray oon maydeeko dee domayneeka]

▸ are the stores open on Sunday? **i negozi sono aperti la domenica?** [ee negotsee sono apertee la domayneeka]

sun deck il ponte scoperto [pontay skoperto]

▶ how do I get onto the sun deck? come si va sul ponte scoperto? [komay see va sool pontay skoperto]

sunglasses gli occhiali da sole [okkee-alee da solay]

▶ I've lost my sunglasses ho perso gli occhiali da sole [o perso lyee okkee-alee da solay]

sunny *(day)* di sole [dee solay]; *(weather)* bello(a) [bello(a)]; *(place)* soleggiato(a) [solejato(a)]

▶ it's sunny c'è il sole [chay eel solay]

sunrise l'alba *f* [alba]

▶ we got up at sunrise ci siamo alzati all'alba [chee see-amo altsatee allalba]

▶ what time is sunrise? a che ora sorge il sole? [a kay ora sorjay eel solay]

sunset il tramonto [tramonto]

▶ isn't the sunset beautiful? non è bello il tramonto? [non ay bello eel tramonto]

suntan lotion la crema solare [krayma solaray]

▶ I'd like SPF 30 suntan lotion vorrei una crema solare con indice di protezione trenta [vorray-ee oona krayma solaray kon eendeechay dee protetsee-onay trenta]

supermarket il supermercato [soopermerkato]

▶ is there a supermarket nearby? c'è un supermercato nelle vicinanze? [chay oon soopermerkato nellay veecheenantsay]

surcharge il supplemento [supplaymento]

▶ do I have to pay a surcharge? devo pagare un supplemento? [dayvo pagaray oon supplaymento]

sure sicuro(a) [seekooro(a)]

▶ are you sure that's when the train leaves? è sicuro che il treno parta a quell'ora? [ay seekooro kay eel trayn parta a kwellora]

surfboard la tavola da surf [tavola da surf], il surf [surf]

▶ is there somewhere we can rent surfboards? c'è un posto dove possiamo noleggiare dei surf? [chay oon posto dovay possee-amo nolejaray day-ee surf]

surfing il surf [surf]

▶ can we go surfing around here? possiamo fare surf da queste parti? [possee-amo faray surf da kwestay partee]

surprise la sorpresa [sorprayza]

▶ what a nice surprise! che bella sorpresa! [kay bella sorprayza]

surrounding area i dintorni [deentornee]

▶ Siena and the surrounding area Siena e i dintorni [see-ena ay ee deentornee]

swallow inghiottire [eenghee-oteeray]

▶ it hurts when I swallow mi fa male ad inghiottire [mee fa malay ad eenghee-oteeray]

▶ the ATM outside has swallowed my credit card il Bancomat® qui fuori si è mangiato la mia carta di credito [eel bankomat kwee foo-oree see ay manjato la mee-a karta dee kraydeeto]

swim nuotare [noo-otaray] ◆ la nuotata [noo-otata]

▸ is it safe to swim here? è pericoloso nuotare qui? [ay payreekolozo noo-otaray kwee]

▸ to go for a swim andare a farsi una nuotata [andaray a farsee oona noo-otata]

swimming pool la piscina [peesheena]

▸ is there an open-air swimming pool? c'è una piscina scoperta? [chay oona peesheena skoperta]

switch *(for light)* l'interruttore *m* [eenterroottoray]; *(on TV, radio)* il pulsante (di accensione) [poolsantay (dee achensee-onay)]

▸ the switch doesn't work l'interruttore non funziona [leenterroottoray non foontsee-ona]

switch off spegnere [spenyaray]

▸ where do you switch the light off? dove si spegne la luce? [dovay see spenyay la loochay]

▸ my cell was switched off avevo il cellulare spento [avayvo eel celloolaray spento]

switch on accendere [achendayray]

▸ where do I switch this light on? dove si accende questa luce? [dovay see achenday kwesta loochay]

synagogue la sinagoga [seenagoga]

▸ where's the nearest synagogue? dov'è la sinagoga più vicina? [dovay la seenagoga pyoo veecheena]

table il tavolo [tavolo]

▸ I've reserved a table in the name of... ho prenotato un tavolo a nome ... [o praynotato oon tavolo a nomay]

▸ a table for four, please! un tavolo per quattro, per favore! [oon tavolo per kwattro per favoray]

table tennis il ping-pong® [peeng-pong]

▸ are there tables for table tennis? ci sono dei tavoli da ping-pong®? [chee sono day-ee tavolee da peeng-pong]

table wine il vino da tavola [veeno da tavola]

▸ a bottle of red table wine una bottiglia di vino rosso da tavola [oona botteelya dee veeno rosso da tavola]

take *(get hold of, steal)* prendere [prendayray]; *(carry, lead, wear)* portare [portaray]; *(accompany)* accompagnare [akkompanyaray]; *(last)* durare [dooraray]

> someone's taken my bag qualcuno mi ha preso la borsa [kwalkoono mee a prayzo la borsa]

> can you take me to this address? mi può portare a questo indirizzo? [mee poo-o portaray a kwesto eendeereetso]

> are you taking the plane or the train to Rome? prende il treno o l'aereo per Roma? [prenday eel trayno o la-ayray-o per roma]

> which road should I take? che strada devo prendere? [kay strada dayvo prendayray]

> I take a size 8 *(shoes)* porto il trentanove *(di scarpe)* [porto eel trentanovay (dee skarpay)]; *(clothes)* porto la *(taglia)* quarantadue [porto la (talya) kwarantadoo-ay]

> how long does the trip take? quanto dura il viaggio? [kwanto doora eel vee-ajo]

> how long does it take to get to Bologna? quanto ci vuole per andare a Bologna? [kwanto chee voo-olay per andaray a bolonya]

> could you take a photo of us? ci potrebbe fare una foto? [chee potrebbay faray oona foto]

take back *(to store)* riportare [reeportaray]; *(to one's home)* portare a casa [portaray a kaza]

> I'm looking for a present to take back to my son sto cercando un regalo da portare a casa a mio figlio [sto cherkando oon raygalo da portaray a kaza a mee-o feelyo]

take down *(bags, luggage)* tirare giù [teeraray joo]

> could you take these bags down, please? potrebbe portare giù questi bagagli, per favore? [potrebbay portaray joo kwestee bagalyee per favoray]

take in *(bags, luggage)* portare dentro [portaray dentro]

> can you have someone take in my bags, please? mi può far portare dentro i bagagli, per favore? [mee poo-o far portaray dentro ee bagalyee per favoray]

taken *(seat)* occupato(a) [okkoopato(a)]

> sorry, this seat is taken mi dispiace, questo posto è occupato [mee deespee-achay kwesto posto ay okkoopato]

take up *(bags, luggage)* portare su [portaray soo]

> can someone take our bags up to our room? qualcuno può portarci i bagagli su in camera? [kwalkoono poo-o portarchee ee bagalyee soo een kamayra]

talk parlare [parlaray]

> you have no right to talk to me like that non ha il diritto di parlarmi in questo modo [non a eel deereetto dee parlarmee een kwesto modo]

tall *(person, tree, building)* alto(a) [alto(a)]

> what's that tall building over there? cos'è quel palazzo alto laggiù? [kozay kwel palatso alto lajoo]

tank *(for gas)* il serbatoio [serbato-yo]

> is the tank full? è pieno il serbatoio? [ay pee-ayno eel serbato-yo]

tap water l'acqua *f* del rubinetto [akkwa del roobeenetto]

▸ just some tap water, please **solo dell'acqua del rubinetto, per favore** [solo dellakkwa del roobeenetto per favoray]

taste *(flavor)* il gusto [goosto] ✦ *(sense)* sentire un gusto di [senteeray oon goosto dee]; *(try)* assaggiare [assajaray]

▸ I can't taste anything **non sento nessun gusto** [non sento nessoon goosto]
▸ can I taste the wine? **posso assaggiare il vino?** [posso assajaray eel veeno]
▸ it tastes funny **ha uno strano gusto** [a oono strano goosto]
▸ to taste of ... **avere un gusto di ...** [avayray oon goosto dee], **sapere di ...** [sapayray dee]

tax la tassa [tassa]

▸ does this price include tax? **questo prezzo è comprensivo di tasse?** [qwesto pretso ay komprenseevo dee tassay]

taxi il taxi [taxee]

▸ how much does a taxi cost from here to the station? **quanto costa un taxi da qui alla stazione?** [kwanto kosta oon taxee da kwee alla statsee-onay]
▸ I'd like to reserve a taxi to take me to the airport, please **vorrei prenotare un taxi per andare all'aeroporto, per favore** [vorray-ee praynotaray oon taxee per andaray alla-ayroporto per favoray]

taxi driver il/la tassista [tasseesta]

▸ can you ask the taxi driver to wait? **può chiedere al tassista di aspettare?** [poo-o kee-aydayray al tasseesta dee aspettaray]

taxi stand la stazione dei taxi [statsee-onay day-ee taxee]

▸ where can I find a taxi stand? **dove posso trovare una stazione dei taxi?** [dovay posso trovaray oona statsee-onay day-ee taxee]

tea *(drink)* il tè [tay]

▸ tea with milk **tè al latte** [tay al lattay]
▸ tea without milk **tè senza latte** [tay sentsa lattay]

---

taking a taxi

▸ could you call me a taxi, please? **mi può chiamare un taxi, per favore?** [mee poo-o kee-amaray oon taxee per favoray]
▸ to the station/airport, please **alla stazione/all'aeroporto, per favore** [alla statsee-onay/alla-ayroporto per favoray]
▸ stop here/at the lights/at the corner, please **si fermi qui/al semaforo/all'angolo, per favore** [see ferma kwee/al saymaforo/allangolo per favoray]
▸ can you wait for me? **mi può aspettare?** [mee poo-o aspettaray]
▸ how much is it? **quanto fa?** [kwanto fa]
▸ keep the change **tenga pure il resto** [tenga pooray eel resto]

teach insegnare [eensenyaray]
> so, you teach English? maybe you could help me! quindi, insegna l'inglese? forse mi può aiutare! [kweendee eensenya leenglayzay forsay mee poo-o a-yootaray]

teacher l'insegnante *mf* [eensenyantay]
> I'm a teacher sono insegnante [sono eensenyantay]

telephone il telefono [taylayfono] ♦ telefonare (a) [taylayfonaray]
> can I use the telephone? posso usare il telefono? [posso oozaray eel taylayfono]

telephone booth la cabina telefonica [kabeena taylayfoneeka]
> is there a telephone booth near here? c'è una cabina telefonica qui vicino? [chay oona kabeena taylayfoneeka kwee veecheeno]

telephone call la telefonata [taylayfonata]
> I'd like to make a telephone call vorrei fare una telefonata [vorray-ee faray oona taylayfonata]

television *(system, broadcasts)* la televisione [taylayveezee-onay]; *(set)* il televisore [taylayveezoray]
> what's on television tonight? cosa c'è stasera alla televisione? [koza chay stasayra alla taylayveezee-onay]

tell dire [deeray]
> can you tell me the way to the museum? mi può dire qual è la strada per il museo? [mee poo-o deeray kwal ay la strada per eel moozay-o]
> can you tell me what time it is? mi può dire che ora è? [mee poo-o deeray kay ora ay]

temperature *(meteorological)* la temperatura [tempayratoora]; *(fever)* la febbre [febbray]
> what's the temperature? che temperatura c'è? [kay tempayratoora chay]
> I've got a temperature ho la febbre [o la febbray]

ten dieci [dee-aychee]
> there are ten of us siamo in dieci [see-amo een dee-aychee]

tennis il tennis [tennees]
> where can we play tennis? dove possiamo giocare a tennis? [dovay possee-amo jokaray a tennees]

tennis racket la racchetta da tennis [rakketta da tennees]
> can you rent tennis rackets? si possono affittare delle racchette da tennis? [see possono affeettaray dellay rakkettay da tennees]

tent la tenda [tenda]
> I'd like to book space for a tent, please vorrei prenotare un posto tenda, per favore [vorray-ee praynotaray oon posto tenda per favoray]
> can you put up your tent anywhere? la tenda si può montare in qualsiasi posto? [la tenda see poo-o montaray een kwalsee-asee posto]

tent peg il picchetto della tenda [peekketto della tenda]

thanks

The Italian for 'thank you' is *grazie*. If you want to be particularly polite, say *grazie mille* or *la ringrazio* ('thank you very much'). Remember that if someone says *grazie* to you, you should always reply with *prego* ('you're welcome').

- we're short of tent pegs ci mancano dei picchetti della tenda [chee mankano day-ee peekkettee della tenda]

terminal *(for planes)* il terminal(e) [termeenal(ay)]
- where is terminal 1? dov'è il terminal uno? [dovay eel termeenal oono]
- is there a shuttle between terminals? c'è una navetta tra i terminali? [chay oona navetta tra ee termeenalee]

tetanus il tetano [taytano]
- I've been vaccinated for tetanus ho fatto l'antitetanica [o fatto lanteetaytaneeka]

thank ringraziare [reengratsee-aray] ♦ **thanks** grazie [gratsee-ay]
- thanks for everything (you've done) grazie di tutto (quello che ha fatto) [gratsee-ay dee tootto (kwello kay a fatto)]

thank you! grazie! [gratsee-ay]
- thank you very much! grazie mille! [gratsee-ay meellay]

that *(not this)* quello(a) [kwello(a)]; *(which)* che [kay]
- who's that? chi è quello? [kee ay kwello]
- that's right è esatto [ay ayzatto]
- the road that goes to Taormina la strada che va a Taormina [la strada kay va a ta-ormeena]
- I'll have that one prendo quello [prendo kwello]

theater *(for plays)* il teatro [tay-atro]
- where is there a theater? dove c'è un teatro? [dovay chay oon tay-atro]

theft il furto [foorto]
- I'd like to report a theft vorrei denunciare un furto [vorray-ee daynooncharay oon foorto]

then *(at a particular time, in that case)* allora [allora]; *(next)* poi [po-ee]
- I'll see you at six then allora, ci vediamo alle sei [allora chee vaydee-amo allay say-ee]

there là [la], lì [lee]
- you can put my bags down there, thanks può posare i miei bagagli là, grazie [poo-o posaray ee mee-ay-ee bagaglee la gratsee-ay]
- he's over there è laggiù [ay lajoo]
- there is/are ... c'è/ci sono ... [chay/chee sono]
- there's a problem c'è un problema [chay oon problayma]

▶ are there any restrooms near here? ci sono dei bagni qui vicino? [chee sono day-ee banyee qui vicino]

▶ there you are *(handing over something)* ecco [ekko]

thermometer il termometro [termometro]

▶ do you have a thermometer? ha un termometro? [a oon termometro]

▶ the thermometer shows 18 degrees (Celsius) il termometro segna diciotto gradi [eel termometro senya deechotto gradee]

thin *(person)* magro(a) [magro(a)]; *(slice, layer)* sottile [sotteelay]; *(material)* leggero(a) [lejayro(a)]

▶ isn't that jacket too thin for an evening like this? non è troppo leggera quella giacca per una serata come questa? [non ay troppo lejayra kwella jakka per oona sayrata komay kwesta]

thing la cosa [koza] ◆ **things** *(possessions, clothes)* la roba [roba]

▶ what's that thing for? a cosa serve quella cosa? [a koza servay kwella koza]

▶ I don't know what the best thing to do is non so quale sia la miglior cosa da farsi [non so kwalay see-a la meelyor koza da farsee]

▶ could you look after my things for a minute? può dare un'occhiata alla mia roba un momento? [poo-o daray oonokkee-ata alla mee-a roba oon momento]

think pensare [pensaray]

▶ I think (that)... penso che ... [penso kay]

▶ I thought service charge was included pensavo che il servizio fosse compreso [pensavo kay eel serveetsee-o fossay komprayzo]

▶ I don't think so non credo [non kraydo]

third terzo(a) [tertso(a)] ◆ *(fraction)* il terzo [tertso]; *(gear)* la terza [tertsa]

▶ this is my third time in Italy questa è la terza volta che vengo in Italia [kwesta ay la tertsa volta kay vengo een eetalee-a]

thirsty

▶ to be thirsty aver sete [avayr saytay]

▶ I'm very thirsty ho molta sete [o molta saytay]

saying thank you

▶ thank you grazie [gratsee-ay]

▶ thanks, that's very kind of you grazie, è molto gentile da parte sua [gratsee-ay ay molto jenteelay da partay soo-a]

▶ I can't thank you enough non potrò mai ringraziarla abbastanza [non potro ma-ee reengratsee-arla abbastantsa]

▶ thank you for your help grazie per l'aiuto [gratsee-ay per la-yooto]

▶ I wanted to thank you for inviting me volevo ringraziarla per avermi invitato [volayvo reengratsee-arla per avayrmee eenveetato]

three tre [tray]
- there are three of us **siamo in tre** [see-amo een tray]

throat la gola [gola]
- I have a fish bone stuck in my throat **mi si è conficcata in gola una lisca** [mee see ay konfeekkata en gola oona leeska]

throat lozenge la pastiglia per la gola [pasteelya per la gola]
- I'd like some throat lozenges **vorrei delle pastiglie per la gola** [vorray-ee dellay pasteelyay per la gola]

thunderstorm il temporale [temporalay]
- will there be a thunderstorm? **ci sarà un temporale?** [chee sara oon temporalay]

Thursday il giovedì [jovaydee]
- we're arriving/leaving on Thursday **arriviamo/partiamo giovedì** [arreevee-amo/ partee-amo jovaydee]

ticket il biglietto [beelyetto]
- I'd like a ticket to … **vorrei un biglietto per …** [vorray-ee oon beelyetto per]
- how much is a ticket to…? **quanto costa un biglietto per …?** [kwanto kosta oon beelyetto per]
- a book of 10 tickets, please **un carnet da dieci biglietti, per favore** [oon karnay da dee-aychee beelyettee per favoray]
- I'd like to book a ticket **vorrei prenotare un biglietto** [vorray-ee praynotaray oon beelyetto]
- I'd like three tickets for… **vorrei tre biglietti per …** [vorray-ee tray beelyettee per]

tide la marea [maray-a]
- what time does the tide turn? **a che ora cambia la marea?** [a kay ora kambee-a la maray-a]

tight *(piece of clothing)* stretto(a) [stretto(a)]
- these pants are too tight **questi pantaloni sono troppo stretti** [kwestee pantalonee sono troppo strettee]

time il tempo [tempo]; *(by clock)* l'ora *f* [ora]; *(occasion)* la volta [volta]
- do we have time to visit the town? **abbiamo il tempo di visitare la città?** [abbee-amo eel tempo dee veezeetaray la cheetta]
- what time is it? **che ora è?** [kay ora ay]
- what time do you close? **a che ora chiudete?** [a kay ora kee-oodaytay]
- could you tell me if the train from Verona is on time? **mi potrebbe dire se il treno da Verona è in orario?** [mee potrebbay deeray say eel trayno da vayrona ay een oraree-o]
- maybe some other time **magari un'altra volta** [magaree oonaltra volta]
- three times **tre volte** [tray voltay]
- at the same time **allo stesso tempo** [allo stesso tempo]
- the first time **la prima volta** [la preema volta]

timetable l'orario *m* [oraree-o]

> do you have local bus timetables? **avete gli orari degli autobus locali?** [avaytay lyee oraree delyee owtoboos lokalee]

tip *(gratuity)* la mancia [mancha] ✦ *(give gratuity to)* dare la mancia a [daray la mancha a]

> how much should I leave as a tip? **quanto lascio di mancia?** [kwanto lasho dee mancha]

tire *(for vehicle)* la gomma [gomma], lo pneumatico [pnay-oomateeko]

> the tire's flat **la gomma è a terra** [la gomma ay a terra]
> the tire's punctured **la gomma è forata** [la gomma ay forata]

to a [a]

> are you going to the post office? **sta andando all'ufficio postale?** [sta andando alloofeecho postalay]
> I've not been to Italy before **non sono mai stato in Italia prima** [non sono ma-ee stato een eetalee-a preema]
> when is the next train to Trieste? **a che ora è il prossimo treno per Trieste?** [a kay ora ay eel prosseemo trayno per tree-estay]
> it's twenty to nine **sono le nove meno venti** [sono lay novay mayno ventee]

tobacco store la tabaccheria [tabakkayree-a]

> where is the nearest tobacco store? **dov'è la tabaccheria più vicina?** [dovay la tabakkayree-a pyoo veecheena]

today oggi [ojee]

> what's today's date? **quanti ne abbiamo oggi?** [kwantee nay abbee-amo ojee]

toe il dito del piede [deeto del pee-ayday]

> I think I've broken my toe **penso di essermi rotto il dito del piede** [penso dee essermee rotto eel deeto del pee-ayday]

together insieme [eensee-aymay]

> let's go together **andiamoci insieme** [andee-amochee eensee-aymay]

toilet il gabinetto [gabeenetto]

> I need to go to the toilet **devo andare al gabinetto** [dayvo andaray al gabeenetto]
> do you have to pay to use the toilet? **bisogna pagare per usare il gabinetto?** [beezonya pagaray per oozaray eel gabeenetto]

toilet paper la carta igienica [karta eejayneeka]

> there is no toilet paper **non c'è carta igienica** [non chay karta eejayneeka]

toll *(for road, bridge)* il pedaggio [paydajo]

> do you have to pay a toll to use the bridge? **bisogna pagare un pedaggio per usare il ponte?** [beezonya pagaray oon paydajo per oozaray eel pontay]

toll-free *(call)* gratuito(a) [gratoo-eeto(a)] ✦ *(make a call)* gratuitamente [gratoo-eetamentay]

> there's a toll-free number you can call **c'è un numero verde che si può fare** [chay oon noomayro verday kay see poo-o faray]

tomato il pomodoro [pomodoro]
- half a kilo of tomatoes mezzo chilo di pomodori [medzo keelo dee pomodoree]

tomato juice il succo di pomodoro [sookko dee pomodoro]
- I'd like a tomato juice vorrei un succo di pomodoro [vorray-ee oon sookko dee pomodoro]

tomorrow domani [domanee]
- can you hold my reservation until tomorrow? può lasciare in sospeso la mia prenotazione fino a domani? [poo-o lasharay een sospayzo la mee-a praynotatsee-onay feeno a domanee]
- I'm leaving tomorrow morning parto domani mattina [parto domanee matteena]
- see you tomorrow night a domani sera [a domanee sayra]

tonight (evening) stasera [stasayra]; (night) stanotte [stanottay]
- do you have any beds available for tonight? avete dei posti letto per stanotte? [avaytay day-ee postee letto per stanottay]

too (also) anche [ankay]; (excessively) troppo [troppo]
- enjoy your meal! – you too buon appetito! – altrettanto [boo-on appayteeto – altrayttanto]
- she's too tired to... è troppo stanca per ... [ay troppo stanka per]
- it's too expensive è troppo caro [ay troppo karo]
- there are too many people c'è troppa gente [chay troppa jentay]

tooth il dente [dentay]
- I've broken a tooth mi sono rotto un dente [mee sono rotto oon dentay]

toothache il mal di denti [mal dee dentee]
- I have a toothache ho mal di denti [o mal dee dentee]

toothpaste il dentifricio [denteefreecho]
- I'd like to buy some toothpaste vorrei comprare del dentifricio [vorray-ee kompraray del denteefreecho]

toothbrush lo spazzolino da denti [spatsoleeno da dentee]
- I forgot my toothbrush ho dimenticato lo spazzolino da denti [o deementeekato lo spatsoleeno da dentee]

top (of bottle, tube) il tappo [tappo]; (of pen) il cappuccio [kappoocho]; (of jar) il coperchio [koperkee-o] ♦ (floor) ultimo(a) [oolteemo(a)]
- the car drove away at top speed la macchina se n'è andata a tutta velocità [la makkeena say nay andata a tootta vaylocheeta]

tour (of town, country) il giro [jeero]; (of museum) la visita [veezeeta]
- I'm planning to do a two-week tour of the country ho intenzione di fare un giro del paese di due settimane [o eententsee-onay dee faray oon jeero del pa-ayzay dee doo-ay setteemanay]

tourist offices

In large towns, go to the *ufficio turistico* for information. Regional branches (*IAT*, *APT* or *ATL*) that run the *uffici informazioni* can be found all over Italy. In small towns the tourist information offices are called *pro loco*. And you can, of course, always ask the locals for information.

tourist il/la turista [tooreesta] • *(season)* turistico(a) [tooreesteeko(a)]
> do you get many tourists here? vengono molti turisti qui da voi? [vengono moltee tooreestee kwee da vo-ee]

tourist attraction l'attrazione turistica *f* [attratsee-onay tooreesteeka]
> what are the main tourist attractions in the area? quali sono le principali attrazioni turistiche della zona? [kwalee sono lay preencheepalee attratsee-onee tooreesteekay della dzona]

tourist class la classe turistica [klassay tooreesteeka]
> in tourist class, please in classe turistica, per favore [een klassay tooreesteeka per favoray]

tourist guide la guida turistica [gweeda tooreesteeka]
> we have a good tourist guide with a lot of up-to-date information abbiamo una buona guida turistica con molte informazioni aggiornate [abbee-amo oona boo-ona gweeda tooreesteeka kon moltay eenformatsee-onee ajornatay]

tourist office l'ufficio turistico *m* [ooffeecho tooreesteeko]
> I'm looking for the tourist office sto cercando l'ufficio turistico [sto cherkando looffeecho tooreesteeko]
> can I get a street map at the tourist office? posso trovare una piantina della città all'ufficio turistico? [posso trovaray oona pee-anteena della cheetta allooffeecho tooreesteeko]

tow rimorchiare [reemorkee-aray]
> could you tow me to a garage? mi può rimorchiare (la macchina) da un meccanico? [mee poo-o reemorkee-aray (la makkeena) da oon mekkaneeko]

toward *(in the direction of)* verso [verso]
> we're heading toward Naples stiamo andando verso Napoli [stee-amo andando verso napolee]

tow away rimuovere [reemoo-ovayray]
> my car's been towed away mi hanno rimosso la macchina [mee anno reemosso la makkeena]

towel l'asciugamano *m* [ashoogamano]
> we don't have any towels non abbiamo asciugamani [non abbee-amo ashoogamanee]

▸ could we have more towels? **potremmo avere altri asciugamani?** [potremmo avayray altre ashoogamanee]

tower *(of church, castle)* la torre [torray]

▸ can you visit the tower? **si può visitare la torre?** [see poo-o veezeetaray la torray]

town la città [cheetta]

▸ it's a small town in Northern Italy **è una piccola città dell'Italia del nord** [ay oona peekkola cheetta delleetalee-a del nord]

▸ to go into town **andare in centro** [andaray een chentro]

town hall il municipio [mooneecheepee-o]

▸ where is the town hall? **dov'è il municipio?** [dovay eel mooneecheepee-o]

traffic *(vehicles)* il traffico [traffeeko]

▸ is there a lot of traffic on the freeway? **c'è molto traffico in autostrada?** [chay molto traffeeko een owtostrada]

traffic circle la rotatoria [rotatoree-a]

▸ you turn right at the traffic circle **alla rotatoria, giri a destra** [alla rotatoree-a jeeree a destra]

traffic jam l'ingorgo *m* (di traffico) [eengorgo (dee traffeeko)]

▸ we got stuck in a traffic jam **siamo rimasti bloccati in un ingorgo** [see-amo reemastee blokkatee een oon eengorgo]

traffic lights il semaforo [saymaforo]

▸ turn left at the traffic lights **al semaforo, giri a sinistra** [al saymaforo jeeree a seeneestra]

trail *(path)* il sentiero [sentee-ayro]

▸ will this trail take us back to the parking lot? **se prendiamo questo sentiero torniamo al parcheggio?** [say prendee-amo kwesto sentee-ayro tornee-amo al parkejo]

getting around town

▸ which bus goes to the airport? **quale autobus va all'aeroporto?** [kwalay owtoboos va alla-ayroporto]

▸ where does the bus to the station leave from? **da dove parte l'autobus per la stazione?** [da dovay partay lowtoboos per la statsee-onay]

▸ I'd like a one-way (ticket) to ... **vorrei un biglietto di sola andata per ...** [vorray-ee oon beelyetto dee sola andata per]

▸ can I have a book of tickets, please? **posso avere un carnet di biglietti, per favore?** [posso avayray oon karnay dee beelyettee per favoray]

▸ could you tell me where I have to get off for ...? **potrebbe dirmi dove devo scendere per ...?** [potrebbay deermee dovay dayvo shenderay per]

trains

There are discounts available if you travel around Italy or to other European cities on the *Ferrovie dello Stato*. There's the Inter Rail card, of course, but there are also *Prem*'s fares, which are very reasonable if you book in advance (but the tickets can't be exchanged or refunded). The *biglietto chilometrico* is a good buy. For further information and reservations, go to http://www.trenitalia.com.

train *(on railroad)* il treno [trayno]; *(on subway)* la metropolitana [metropoleetana]

▸ when is the next train to Ferrara? a che ora è il prossimo treno per Ferrara? [a kay ora ay eel prosseemo trayno per ferrara]

▸ I'd like a round-trip ticket for the 9 a.m. train to Palermo tomorrow, please vorrei un biglietto di andata e ritorno sul treno per Palermo di domani alle nove, per favore [vorray-ee oon beelyetto dee andata ay reetorno sool trayno per palermo dee domanee allay novay per favoray]

▸ do you have reduced-price train tickets for seniors? avete biglietti ridotti per chi ha più di sessant'anni? [avaytay beelyettee reedottee per kee a pyoo dee sessantannee]

▸ which platform does the train for Bari leave from? da che binario parte il treno per Bari? [da kay beenaree-o partay eel trayno per baree]

▸ the train was fifteen minutes late il treno aveva quindici minuti di ritardo [eel trayno avayva kweendeechee meenootee dee reetardo]

▸ where do international trains leave from? da dove partono i treni internazionali? [da dovay partono ee traynee eenternatsee-onalee]

tram il tram [tram]

▸ can you buy tickets on the tram? si possono comprare i biglietti sul tram? [see possono kompraray ee beelyettee sool tram]

▸ which tram line do we have to take? che linea di tram dobbiamo prendere? [kay leenay-a dee tram dobbee-amo prendayray]

▸ where is the nearest tram stop? dov'è la fermata del tram più vicina? [dovay la fermata del tram pyoo veecheena]

transfer *(of money)* il bonifico [boneefeeko] ♦ *(money)* trasferire [trasfayreeray]

▸ I'd like to transfer some money vorrei trasferire dei soldi [vorray-ee trasfayreeray day-ee soldee]

travel i viaggi [vee-ajee] ♦ *(go on trip)* viaggiare [vee-ajaray]

▸ I'd like a window seat facing the direction of travel vorrei un posto lato finestrino che guardi verso il senso di marcia [vorray-ee oon posto lato feenestreeno kay gwardee verso eel senso dee marcia]

▸ I'm traveling on my own viaggio da solo [vee-ajo da solo]

travel agency l'agenzia *f* di viaggio [ajentsee-a dee vee-ajo]

▸ I'm looking for a travel agency sto cercando un'agenzia di viaggio [sto cherkando oonajentsee-a dee vee-ajo]

traveler's check il traveller's cheque [traveller chek]

▸ do you take traveler's checks? prendete i traveller's cheque? [prendaytay ee traveller chek]

tree l'albero *m* [albayro]

▸ what type of tree is that? che tipo di albero è? [kay teepo dee albayro ay]

trip *(journey)* il viaggio [vee-ajo]

▸ have a good trip! buon viaggio! [boo-on vee-ajo]

trouble *(difficulty)* la difficoltà [deeffeekolta]; *(effort)* il disturbo [deestoorbo]

▸ we didn't have any trouble finding the hotel non abbiamo avuto nessuna difficoltà a trovare l'albergo [non abbee-amo avooto nessoona deeffeekolta a trovaray lalbergo]

▸ I don't want to be any trouble non voglio creare disturbo [non volyo kray-aray deestoorbo]

▸ it's no trouble nessun disturbo [nessun deestoorbo]

trunk *(of car)* il portabagagli [portabagalyee]; *(piece of luggage)* il baule [ba-oolay]

▸ my things are in the trunk of the car la mia roba è nel portabagagli dell'auto [la mee-a roba ay nel portabagalyee dellowto]

▸ I've got two small suitcases and a large trunk ho due piccole valigie e un grosso baule [o doo-ay peekkolay valejay ay oon grosso ba-oolay]

try *(attempt)* provare [provaray]; *(sample)* assaggiare [assajaray]

▸ I'd like to try the local beer vorrei assaggiare la birra locale [vorray-ee assajaray la beerra lokalay]

try on *(dress, shoes)* provare [provaray]

▸ I'd like to try on the one in the window vorrei provare quello in vetrina [vorray-ee provaray kwello een vetreena]

tub *(of ice cream)* la vaschetta [vasketta]

▸ do you sell tubs of ice cream to take home? vendete vaschette di gelato da portare a casa? [vendaytay vaskettay dee jaylato da portaray a kaza]

Tuesday il martedì [martaydee]

▸ we're arriving/leaving on Tuesday arriviamo/partiamo martedì [arreevee-amo/partee-amo martaydee]

tunnel la galleria [gallayree-a]; *(through mountain)* il traforo [traforo]

▸ is there a toll for using the tunnel? c'è un pedaggio per il traforo? [chay oon paydajo per eel traforo]

turn *(in game, order)* il turno [toorno]; *(off road)* la deviazione [dayvee-atsee-onay]
♦ *(change direction)* girare [jeeraray]

▸ let's take turns driving facciamo a turno a guidare [fachamo a toorno a gweedaray]

▸ it's your turn tocca a lei [tokka a lay-ee]
▸ is this the turn for the campground? è questa la deviazione per il campeggio? [ay kwesta la dayvee-atsee-onay per eel kampejo]
▸ turn left at the lights al semaforo, giri a sinistra [al saymaforo jeeree a seeneestra]
▸ you have to turn right deve girare a destra [dayvay jeeraray a destra]

urn down *(radio, volume, gas)* abbassare [abbassaray]; *(bed)* preparare [praypararay]

▸ can we turn the air-conditioning down? possiamo abbassare l'aria condizionata? [possee-amo abbassaray laree-a kondeetsee-onata]
▸ how do you turn the volume down? come si abbassa il volume? [komay see abbassa eel voloomay]
▸ could you please turn down the bed for me? potrebbe prepararmi il letto, per favore? [potrebbay prayprararmee eel letto per favoray]

turn off *(light, radio)* spegnere [spenyayray]; *(faucet)* chiudere [kee-oodayray]

▸ where do you turn the light off? dove si spegne la luce? [dovay see spenyay la loochay]
▸ my cell was turned off avevo il cellulare spento [avayvo eel chelloolaray spento]

turn on *(light, radio, engine)* accendere [achendayray]; *(faucet)* aprire [apreeray]

▸ where do I turn this light on? dove si accende questa luce? [dovay see achenday kwesta loochay]
▸ can you turn on the ignition? può mettere in moto? [poo-o mettayray een moto]

turn up *(sound, central heating)* alzare [altsaray]

▸ how do you turn up the heating? come si alza il riscaldamento? [komay see altsa eel reeskaldamento]

TV la tv [teevoo]

▸ the TV in our room is broken la tv nella nostra camera è rotta [la teevoo nella nostra kamayra ay rotta]

TV lounge la sala tv [sala teevoo]

▸ is there a TV lounge? c'è una sala tv? [chay oona sala teevoo]

twelve dodici [dodeechee] ◆ *(noon)* le dodici [dodeechee]; *(midnight)* la mezzanotte [medzanottay]

▸ there are twelve of us siamo in dodici [see-amo een dodeechee]
▸ it's twelve o'clock *(noon)* sono le dodici [sono lay dodeechee]; *(midnight)* è mezzanotte [ay medzanottay]

twice due volte [doo-ay voltay]

▸ the ferry runs twice a day il traghetto salpa due volte al giorno [eel traghetto salpa doo-ay voltay al jorno]

twin il gemello [jaymello], la gemella [jaymella] ◆ gemello(a) [jaymello(a)]

▸ twin brother fratello gemello [fratello jaymello]
▸ twin sister sorella gemella [sorella jaymella]

twin beds i letti gemelli [lettee jaymellee]

▶ a room with twin beds **una camera con letti gemelli** [oona kamayra kon lettee jaymellee]

two due [doo-ay]

▶ there are two of us **siamo in due** [see-amo een doo-ay]

umbrella l'ombrello *m* [ombrello]

▶ could you lend me an umbrella? **mi può prestare un ombrello?** [mee poo-o prestaray oon ombrello]

unacceptable inaccettabile [eenachettabeelay]

▶ it's completely unacceptable! **è del tutto inaccettabile!** [ay del tootto eenachettabeelay]

underpass il sottopassaggio [sottopassajo]

▶ is the underpass safe at night? **è pericoloso il sottopassaggio di notte?** [ay payreekolozo eel sottopassajo dee nottay]

understand capire [kapeeray]

▶ I can understand Italian, but I can't really speak it **capisco l'italiano, ma non lo parlo molto** [kapeesko leetalee-ano ma non lo parlo molto]
▶ I understand a little **capisco un po'** [kapeesko oon po]
▶ I don't understand a word **non capisco una parola** [non kapeesko oona parola]
▶ do you understand? **capisce?** [kapeeshay]

unit *(of condominium complex)* **l'appartamento** *m* [appartamento]

▶ we'd prefer a unit with air conditioning **preferiremmo un appartamento con l'aria condizionata** [prayfayreeremmo oon appartamento kon laree-a kondeetsee-onata]

---

saying that you have understood/not understood

▶ oh, I see! **ah, capisco!** [a kapeesko]
▶ sorry, but I didn't understand **mi dispiace, ma non ho capito** [mee deespee-achay ma non o kapeeto]
▶ I'm a little confused **sono un po' confuso** [sono oon po konfooza]
▶ I don't understand your question **non capisco la sua domanda** [non kapeesko la soo-a domanda]
▶ sorry, but I still don't understand **mi dispiace, ma continuo a non capire** [mee deespee-achay ma konteenoo-o a non kapeeray]

United States (of America)
- the United States (of America) gli Stati Uniti (d'America) [lyee statee ooneetee (damayreeka)]
- I live in the United States vivo negli Stati Uniti [veevo nelyee statee ooneetee]
- I'm from the United States sono statunitense [sono statooneetensay]
- have you ever been to the United States? è mai stato negli Stati Uniti? [ay ma-ee stato nelyee statee ooneetee]

unleaded *(gas)* verde [verday] ◆ la benzina verde [bendzeena verday]
- is all gas in Italy unleaded? c'è solo benzina verde in Italia? [chay solo bendzeena verday een eetalee-a]

until fino a [feeno a]
- I'm staying until Sunday mi fermo fino a domenica [me fermo feeno a domayneeka]
- until noon fino a mezzogiorno [feeno a medzojorno]

up su [soo] ◆ **up to** fino a [feeno a]
- what's up? *(what's wrong)* qual è il problema? [kwal ay eel problayma]; *(as greeting)* come va? [komay va]
- the apartment can accommodate up to six people? l'appartamento può ospitare fino a sei persone? [lappartamento poo-o ospeetaray feeno a say-ee personay]
- what are you up to tonight? cosa fai stasera? [koza fa-ee stasayra]
- up to now finora [feenora]

urgent urgente [oorjentay]
- it's not urgent non è urgente [non ay oorjentay]

urgently urgentemente [oorjentaymentay]
- I have to see a dentist urgently devo andare urgentemente da un dentista [dayvo andaray oorjentaymentay da oon denteesta]

US(A)
- the US gli USA [lyee ooza]
- I'm from the US vengo dagli USA [vengo dalyee ooza]
- I live in the US vivo negli USA [vevo nelyee ooza]
- have you ever been to the US? è mai stato negli USA? [ay ma-ee stato nelyee ooza]

use usare [oozaray]
- could I use your cellphone? potrei usare il suo cellulare? [potray-ee oozaray eel soo-o chelloolaray]

vacancy la camera libera [kamayra leebayra]
- do you have any vacancies for tonight? **avete delle camere libere per stanotte?** [avaytay dellay kamayray leebayray per stasayra]

vacation la vacanza [vakantsa]
- I'm on vacation **sono in vacanza** [sono een vakantsa]

valid valido(a) [valeedo(a)]
- is this ticket valid for the exhibit too? **questo biglietto è valido anche per la mostra?** [kwesto beelyetto ay valeedo ankay per la mostra]
- how long is this ticket valid for? **quanto tempo è valido questo biglietto?** [kwanto tempo ay valeedo kwesto beelyetto]
- my passport is still valid **il mio passaporto è ancora valido** [eel mee-o passaporto ay ankora valeedo]

vegetable la verdura [verdoora]
- does it come with vegetables? **è servito con delle verdure?** [ay serveeto kon dellay verdooray]

vegetarian vegetariano(a) [vayjaytaree-ano(a)] • il vegetariano [vayjaytaree-ano], la vegetariana [vayjaytaree-ana]
- I'm a vegetarian **sono vegetariano** [sono vayjaytaree-ano]
- do you have vegetarian dishes? **avete dei piatti vegetariani?** [avaytay day-ee pee-attee vayjaytaree-anee]

vending machine il distributore (automatico) [deestreebootoray (owtomateeko)]
- the vending machine isn't working **il distributore non funziona** [eel deestree-bootoray non foontsee-ona]

vertigo le vertigini [verteejeenee]
- I suffer from vertigo **soffro di vertigini** [soffro dee verteejeenee]

very molto [molto]
- I'm very tired **sono molto stanco** [sono molto stanko]
- I'm very hungry **ho molta fame** [o molta famay]
- I like this area very much **mi piace molto questa zona** [mee pee-achay molto kwesta dzona]
- very much **molto** [molto]
- very near **molto vicino** [molto veecheeno], vicinissimo [veecheeneesseemo]

view *(panorama)* la vista [veesta]
- I'd prefer a room with a sea view **preferirei una camera con vista sul mare** [prayfayreeray-ee oona kamayra kon veesta sool maray]

villa la villa [veella]

▸ we'd like to rent a villa for one week **vorremmo affittare una villa per una settimana** [vorremmo affeettaray oona veella per oona setteemana]

virus il virus [veeroos]

▸ I must have picked up a virus **devo aver preso un virus** [dayvo avayr prayzo oon veeroos]

visa il visto [veesto]

▸ do you need a visa? **ci vuole il visto?** [chee voo-olay eel veesto]

visit *(to person)* la visita [veezeeta]; *(to place)* il soggiorno [sojorno] ◆ visitare [veezeetaray]

▸ is this your first visit to Rome? **è la prima volta che viene a Roma?** [ay la preema volta kay vee-aynay a roma]

▸ I'd like to visit the castle **vorrei visitare il castello** [vorray-ee veezeetaray eel kastello]

voicemail la casella vocale [kazella vokalay]

▸ I need to check my voicemail **devo verificare la mia casella vocale** [dayvo vayreefeekaray la mee-a kazella vokalay]

voucher il voucher [vowcher]

▸ I haven't received the voucher **non ho ricevuto il voucher** [non o reechayvooto eel vowcher]

waist la vita [veeta]

▸ it's a little bit tight at the waist **è un po' stretto in vita** [ay oon po stretto een veeta]

wait aspettare [aspettaray]

▸ have you been waiting long? **avete aspettato a lungo?** [avaytay aspettato a loongo]

waiter il cameriere [kamayree-ayray]

▸ are there only two waiters for all the tables? **ci sono solo due camerieri per tutti i tavoli?** [chee sono solo doo-ay kamayree-ayree per toottee ee tavolee]

▸ waiter, could we have the check, please? **mi scusi, possiamo avere il conto, per favore?** [mee skoozee, possee-amo avayray eel konto per favoray]

wait for aspettare [aspettaray]

▸ are you waiting for the bus? **sta aspettando l'autobus?** [sta aspettando lowtoboos]

▸ I'm waiting for them to call back **aspetto che mi richiamino** [aspetto kay mee reekee-ameeno]

▸ don't wait for me **non mi aspettate** [non mee aspettatay]

waiting room la sala d'aspetto [sala daspetto]

▸ is there a waiting room near the platform? **c'è una sala d'aspetto vicino al binario?** [chay oona sala daspetto veecheeno al beenaree-o]

waitress la cameriera [kamayree-ayra]
> the waitress has already taken our order la cameriera ha già preso le nostre ordinazioni [la kamayree-ayra a ja prayzo lay nostray ordeenatsee-onee]

wake svegliare [zvelyaray] ◆ svegliarsi [zvelyarsee]
> could you wake me at 6:45? mi può svegliare alle sei e quarantacinque? [mee poo-o zvelyaray allay say-ee ay kwarantacheenkway]
> I always wake early mi sveglio sempre presto [mee zvelyo sempray presto]

wake up svegliare [zvelyaray] ◆ svegliarsi [zvelyarsee]
> a noise woke me up in the middle of the night un rumore mi ha svegliato in piena notte [oon roomoray mee a zvelyato een pee-ayna nottay]
> I have to wake up very early tomorrow to catch the plane devo svegliarmi molto presto domani per prendere l'aereo [dayvo zvelyarmee molto presto domanee per prendairay la-ayray-o]

walk la passeggiata [passejata] ◆ *(go on foot)* camminare [kammeenaray] ◆ *(distance)* percorrere (a piedi) [perkorrayray (a pee-aydee)]
> let's go for a walk andiamo a fare una passeggiata [andee-amo a faray oona passejata]
> are there any interesting walks in the area? ci sono dei percorsi interessanti da fare a piedi in zona? [chee sono day-ee perkorsee eentayressantee da faray a pee-aydee een dzona]
> how long would it take me to walk it? quanto mi ci vorrà a percorrerlo a piedi? [kwanto mee chee vorra a perkorrerlo a pee-aydee]

walking boots gli scarponi da trekking [skarponee da trekkeeng]
> do you need walking boots? ci vogliono degli scarponi da trekking? [chee volyono delyee skarponee da trekkeeng]

wallet il portafogli [portafolyee]
> I've lost my wallet ho perso il portafogli [o perso eel portafolyee]

want *(wish, desire)* volere [volayray]
> I don't want to go there non ci voglio andare [non chee volyo andaray]
> do you want me to call back later? vuole che richiami più tardi? [voo-olay kay reekee-amee pyoo tardee]

warm caldo(a) [kaldo(a)]
> it's warm fa caldo [fa kaldo]
> where can I buy some warm clothing for the trip? dove posso comprare dei vestiti caldi per il viaggio? [dovay posso kompraray day-ee vesteetee kaldee per eel vee-ajo]

warn avvertire [avverteeray]
> no one warned me about that! non mi ha avvertito nessuno! [non mee a avverteeto nessoono]

wash lavare [lavaray] ◆ lavarsi [lavarsee]
> where can I wash my hands? dove posso lavarmi le mani? [dovay posso lavarmee lay manee]

water

A jug of tap water won't be brought to your table as a matter of course. You can, of course, ask for one, but it is more common to order noncarbonated (*naturale*) or sparkling (*frizzante*) mineral water.

watch l'orologio *m* (da polso) [orolojo (da polso)] ♦ *(look at)* guardare [gwardaray]; *(guard)* sorvegliare [sorvelyaray]

▸ my watch has been stolen mi hanno rubato l'orologio [mee anno roobato lorolojo]
▸ can you watch my bags for a minute? mi può sorvegliare un attimo i bagagli? [mee poo-o sorvelyaray oon atteemo ee bagalyee]

water l'acqua *f* [akkwa]

▸ could I have some hot water, please? potrei avere un po' d'acqua calda, per favore? [potray-ee avayray oon po dakkwa kalda per favoray]
▸ there's no hot water non c'è acqua calda [non chay akkwa kalda]

water ski lo sci d'acqua [shee dakkwa]

▸ can I rent water skis here? posso noleggiare degli sci d'acqua qui? [posso nolejaray delyee shee dakkwa kwee]

water skiing lo sci acquatico [shee akkwateeko]

▸ can I go water skiing anywhere around here? c'è un posto nei dintorni dove posso fare sci acquatico? [chay oon posto nay-ee deentornee dovay posso faray shee akkwateeko]

wave *(of water)* l'onda *f* [onda]

▸ the waves are very big today le onde sono molto alte oggi [lay onday sono molto altay ojee]

way *(means)* il modo [modo]; *(direction)* la direzione [deeretsee-onay]; *(route, path)* la strada [strada]

asking the way

▸ can you show me where we are on the map? mi può far vedere dove siamo sulla mappa? [mee poo-o far vaydayray dovay see-amo soolla mappa]
▸ where is the station/the post office? dov'è la stazione/l'ufficio postale? [dovay la statsee-onay/looffeecho postalay]
▸ excuse me, how do you get to via Veneto? mi scusi, come si va in via Veneto? [mee skoozee komay see va een vee-a vaynayto]
▸ is it far? è lontano? [ay lontano]
▸ is it within walking distance? ci si può andare a piedi? [chee see poo-o andaray a pee-aydee]

▸ what's the best way of getting there? qual è il modo migliore per arrivarci? [kwal ay eel modo meelyoray per arreevarchee]

▸ which way is it to the station? in che direzione è la stazione? [een kay deeretsee-onay ay la statsee-onay]

▸ I went the wrong way ho preso la direzione sbagliata [o prayzo la deeretsee-onay zbalyata]

▸ is this the right way to the cathedral? è la direzione giusta per la cattedrale? [ay la deeretsee-onay joosta per la kattedralay]

▸ on the way per strada [per strada]

▸ no way! neanche per sogno! [nay-ankay per sonyo]

way out l'uscita f [oosheeta]

▸ where's the way out? dov'è l'uscita? [dovay l'oosheeta]

weak *(person)* debole [daybolay]; *(drink)* leggero(a) [lejayro(a)]

▸ I feel very weak mi sento molto debole [mee sento molto daybolay]

▸ could I have a very weak coffee? potrei avere un caffè molto leggero? [potray-ee avayray oon kaffay molto lejayro]

wear *(piece of clothing, glasses)* portare [portaray]

▸ I wear glasses just for reading porto gli occhiali solo per leggere [porto lyee okkee-alee solo per lejayray]

▸ is what I'm wearing all right? va bene come sono vestito? [va baynay komay sono vesteeto]

weather il tempo [tempo]; *(on TV, radio)* le previsioni del tempo [prayveezee-onee del tempo]

▸ what is the weather like today? com'è il tempo oggi? [komay eel tempo ojee]

▸ is the weather going to change? cambierà il tempo? [kambee-ayra eel tempo]

weather forecast le previsioni del tempo [prayveezee-onee del tempo]

▸ what's the weather forecast for tomorrow? come sono le previsioni del tempo per domani? [komay sono lay prayveezee-onee del tempo per domanee]

website address l'indirizzo m del sito web [eendeereetso del seeto web]

▸ can you give me your website address? mi può dare l'indirizzo del suo sito web? [mee poo-o daray leendeereetso del soo-o seeto web]

Wednesday il mercoledì [merkolaydee]

▸ we're arriving/leaving on Wednesday arriviamo/partiamo mercoledì [arreevee-amo/partee-amo merkolaydee]

week la settimana [setteemana]

▸ how much is it for a week? quanto costa per una settimana? [kwanto kosta per oona setteemana]

▸ I'm leaving in a week parto tra una settimana [parto tra oona setteemana]

weekly settimanale [setteemanalay]

▸ is there a weekly rate? c'è una tariffa settimanale? [chay oona tareeffa setteemanalay]

welcome *(greeted with pleasure)* benvenuto(a) [benvaynooto(a)] ◆ *(reception)* il benvenuto [benvaynooto] ◆ *(person)* dare il benvenuto a [daray eel benvaynooto a]

▸ welcome! benvenuto! [benvaynooto]
▸ you're welcome *(in reply to thanks)* prego [praygo]
▸ you're welcome to join us se volete venire con noi, siete i benvenuti [say volaytay vayneeray kon no-ee see-aytay ee benvaynootee]

well bene [baynay]

▸ to be/feel well stare bene [staray baynay]
▸ I'm very well, thank you sto molto bene, grazie [sto molto baynay gratsee-ay]
▸ get well soon! guarisci presto! [gwareeshee presto]
▸ well played! bravo/a! [bravo/a]

well done *(steak)* ben cotto(a) [ben kotto(a)]

▸ well done, please ben cotto, per favore [ben kotto per favoray]

what quale [kwalay] ◆ cosa [koza]

▸ what? *(asking for repetition)* cosa? [koza], come? [komay]
▸ what is it? *(what's this thing?)* (che) cos'è? [(kay) kozay]; *(what's the matter?)* cosa c'è? [koza chay]
▸ what's up? *(what's wrong)* qual è il problema? [kwal ay eel problayma]; *(as greeting)* come va? [komay va]
▸ what's your name? come si chiama? [komay see kee-ama]
▸ what's it called? come si chiama? [komay see kee-ama]
▸ what time is it? che ora è? [kay ora ay]
▸ what day is it? che giorno è? [kay jorno ay]
▸ what desserts do you have? che cosa avete come dessert? [kay koza avaytay komay desser]

wheel la ruota [roo-ota]

▸ could you help me change the wheel? mi potrebbe aiutare a cambiare la ruota? [mee potrebbay a-yootaray a kambee-aray la roo-ota]

when quando [kwando]

▸ when was it built? quando è stato costruito? [kwando ay stato kostroo-eeto]
▸ when is the next train to Florence? a che ora è il prossimo treno per Firenze? [a kay ora ay eel prosseemo trayno per feerentsay]

where dove [dovay]

▸ where do you live? dove abita? [dovay abeeta]
▸ where are you from? di dov'è? [dee dovay]
▸ excuse me, where is the nearest bus stop, please? mi scusi, dov'è la fermata dell'autobus più vicina, per favore? [mee skoozee dovay la fermata dellowtoboos pyoo veecheena per favoray]

which quale [kwalay] ◆ *(that)* che [kay]

▸ which hotel would you recommend for us? quale albergo ci consiglierebbe? [kwalay albergo chee konseelyayrebbay]

- which way should we go? in quale direzione dobbiamo andare? [een kwalay deeretsee-onay dobbee-amo andaray]
- which do you prefer? quale preferisce? [kwalay prayfayreeshay]
- is this the bus which goes to the station? è questo l'autobus che va alla stazione? [ay kwesto lowtoboos kay va alla statseeonay]

while

- a while un po' [oon po]
- I'm only planning to stay for a while intendo fermarmi solo un po' [eentendo fermarmee solo oon po]

white bianco(a) [bee-anko(a)]

- I need a white T-shirt ho bisogno di una maglietta bianca [o beezonyo dee oona malyetta bee-anka]

white wine il vino bianco [veeno bee-anko]

- a glass of white wine, please un bicchiere di vino bianco, per favore [oon beekkee-ayray dee veeno bee-anko per favoray]

who chi [kee]

- who are you? chi è lei? [kee ay lay-ee]
- who should I speak to about the heating? a chi mi devo rivolgere per il riscaldamento? [a kee mee dayvo reevoljayray per eel reeskaldamento]
- who's calling? chi parla? [kee parla]

whole tutto(a) [tootto(a)]

- we spent the whole day walking abbiamo passato tutto il giorno a camminare [abbee-amo passato tootto eel jorno a kammeenaray]
- on the whole we had a good time complessivamente, ci siamo divertiti [komplesseevamentay chee see-amo deeverteetee]

whole-wheat integrale [eentegralay]

- I'd like some whole-wheat bread vorrei del pane integrale [vorray-ee del panay eentegralay]

why perché [perkay]

- why not? perché no? [perkay no]

wide (river, road) largo(a) [largo(a)]

- 2 meters wide largo due metri [largo doo-ay metree]

will

- I'll be arriving at six arriverò alle sei [arreevayro allay say-ee]

win vincere [veenchayray]

- who's winning? chi vince? [kee veenchay]

wind il vento [vento]

- there's a strong west wind c'è un forte vento occidentale [chay oon fortay vento ocheedentalay]

window *(of building)* la finestra [feenestra]; *(of car, plane)* il finestrino [feenestreeno]; *(of store)* la vetrina [vetreena]; *(at station, in post office)* lo sportello [sportello]

▶ I can't open the window non riesco ad aprire la finestra [non ree-esko ad apreeray la feenestra]

▶ I'm cold: could you close your window? ho freddo; potrebbe chiudere il finestrino? [o freddo potrebbay kee-oodayray eel feenestreeno]

▶ I'd like to see the dress in the window vorrei vedere il vestito in vetrina [vorray-ee vaydayray eel vesteeto een vetreena]

▶ where's the window for buying tickets? a quale sportello si comprano i biglietti? [a kwalay sportello see komprano ee beelyettee]

window seat il posto lato finestrino [posto lato feenestreeno]

▶ I'd like a window seat if possible vorrei un posto lato finestrino, se possibile [vorray-ee oon posto lato feenestreeno say posseebeelay]

windshield il parabrezza [parabredza]

▶ could you clean the windshield? può pulire il parabrezza? [poo-o pooleeray eel parabredza]

windsurfing il windsurf [weendsurf]

▶ is there anywhere around here I can go windsurfing? c'è un posto nei dintorni dove posso fare windsurf? [chay oon posto nay-ee deentornee dovay posso faray weendsurf]

windy

▶ it's windy c'è vento [chay vento]

wine il vino [veeno]

▶ this wine is not chilled enough questo vino non è abbastanza fresco [kwesto veeno non ay abbastantsa fresko]

wine list la carta dei vini [karta day-ee veenee]

▶ can we see the wine list, please? possiamo vedere la carta dei vini, per favore? [possee-amo vaydayray la karta day-ee veenee per favoray]

wish *(desire)* il desiderio [dayzeedayree-o] ◆ augurare [owgooraray]

▶ best wishes! tanti auguri! [tantee owgooree]

▶ we wish you good luck le auguriamo buona fortuna [lay owgooree-amo boo-ona fortoona] ▶ see boxes on p. 162

with con [kon]

▶ thanks, but I'm here with my boyfriend grazie, ma sono venuta con il mio ragazzo [gratsee-ay ma sono vaynoota kon eel mee-o ragatso]

withdraw *(money)* ritirare [reeteeraray]

▶ I'd like to withdraw 100 euros vorrei ritirare cento euro [vorray-ee reeteeraray chento ay-ooro]

wishes and regrets

▶ I hope it won't be too busy **spero che non ci sia troppa gente** [spayro kay non chee see-a troppa jentay]

▶ it'd be great if you stayed **sarebbe fantastico se rimanesse** [sarebbay fantasteeko say reemanessay]

▶ if only we had a car! **se solo avessimo una macchina!** [say solo avesseemo oona makkeena]

▶ unfortunately, we couldn't get there in time **purtroppo non siamo riusciti ad arrivare in tempo** [poortroppo non see-amo ree-oosheetee ad arreevaray een tempo]

▶ I'm really sorry you couldn't make it **mi dispiace molto che non sia potuto venire** [mee deespee-achay molto kay non see-a potooto vayneeray]

without senza [sentsa]

▶ a chicken sandwich without mayonnaise **un panino al pollo senza maionese** [oon paneeno al pollo sentsa ma-yonayzay]

woman la donna [donna]

▶ who is the woman he's with? **chi è la donna insieme a lui?** [kee ay la donna eensee-aymay a loo-ee]

▶ where's the women's changing room? **dov'è lo spogliatoio delle donne?** [dovay lo spolyato-yo dellay donnay]

wonderful magnifico(a) [manyeefeeko(a)]

▶ that's wonderful! **è magnifico!** [ay manyeefeeko]

▶ the weather was wonderful **il tempo è stato magnifico** [eel tempo ay stato manyeefeeko]

word la parola [parola]

▶ I don't understand a word **non capisco una parola** [non kapeesko oona parola]

wishing someone something

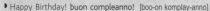

▶ Happy Birthday! **buon compleanno!** [boo-on komplay-anno]

▶ Merry Christmas! **buon Natale!** [boo-on natalay]

▶ Happy New Year! **buon anno (nuovo)!** [boo-onay anno (noo-ovo)]

▶ enjoy your vacation! **buone vacanze!** [boo-onay vakantsay]

▶ enjoy your meal! **buon appetito!** [boo-on appayteeto]

▶ good night! **buonanotte!** [boo-onanottay]

▶ congratulations! **complimenti!** [kompleementee]

▸ I don't know what the word is in Italian non so come si dica in italiano [non so komay see deeka een eetalee-ano]

work *(employment)* il lavoro [lavoro] ♦ *(do job)* lavorare [lavoraray]; *(function)* funzionare [foontsee-onaray]

▸ to be out of work essere disoccupato/a [essayray deezokkoopato/a]

▸ I work in marketing lavoro nel marketing [lavoro nel marketeeng]

▸ the heating's not working il riscaldamento non funziona [eel reeskaldamento non foontsee-ona]

▸ how does the shower work? come funziona la doccia? [komay foontsee-ona la docha]

workday il giorno feriale [jorno fayree-alay]

▸ is tomorrow a workday? domani è un giorno feriale? [domanee ay oon jorno fayree-alay]

world il mondo [mondo]

▸ people from all over the world gente proveniente da tutto il mondo [jentay provaynee-entay da tootto eel mondo]

worried preoccupato(a) [pray-okkoopato(a)]

▸ I'm worried about his health sono preoccupato per la sua salute [sono pray-okkoopato per la soo-a salootay]

worry preoccuparsi [pray-okkooparsee]

▸ don't worry! non si preoccupi [non see pray-okkoopee]

worth

▸ how much is it worth? quanto vale? [kwanto valay]

▸ it's well worth a visit vale la pena di andarlo a vedere [valay la payna dee andarlo a vaydayray]

▸ what's worth seeing in this town? cosa vale la pena di vedere in questa città? [koza valay la payna dee vaydayray een kwesta cheetta]

wound la ferita [fayreeta]

▸ I need something for disinfecting a wound ho bisogno di qualcosa per disinfettare una ferita [o beezonyo dee kwalkoza per deezeenfettaray oona fayreeta]

wrap (up) incartare [eenkartaray]

▸ can you wrap it (up) for me? me lo può incartare? [me lo poo-o eenkartaray]

wrist il polso [polso]

▸ I've sprained my wrist mi sono slogato il polso [mee sono zlogato eel polso]

write scrivere [skreevayray]

▸ I have some letters to write ho delle lettere da scrivere [o dellay lettayray da skreevayray]

wrong sbagliato(a) [zbalyato(a)]

▸ to be wrong *(person)* aver torto [avayr torto]

▸ I'm sorry, but I think you're wrong mi dispiace, ma penso che lei abbia torto [mee deespee-achay ma penso kay lay-ee abbee-a torto]

- sorry, I dialed the wrong number mi scusi, ho sbagliato numero [mee skoozee o sbalyato noomayro]
- you've got the wrong number ha sbagliato numero [a sbalyato noomayro]
- this is the wrong train questo è il treno sbagliato [kwesto ay eel trayno sbalyato]
- what's wrong? cosa c'è che non va? [koza chay kay non va]
- there's something wrong with the switch c'è un problema con l'interruttore [chay oon problayma kon leenterroottoray]

X, y, z

X-ray la radiografia [radee-ografee-a]
- do you think I should have an X-ray? pensa che dovrei fare una radiografia? [pensa kay dovray-ee faray oona radee-ografee-a]

year l'anno *m* [anno]
- we came here last year siamo venuti qui l'anno scorso [see-amo vayroootee kwee lanno skorso]
- I'm 21 years old ho ventun anni [o ventoon annee]

yellow giallo(a) [jallo(a)]
- the yellow one quello giallo [kwello jallo]

Yellow Pages®
- the Yellow Pages®? le Pagine Gialle®? [lay pajeenay jallay]
- do you have a copy of the Yellow Pages®? avete le Pagine Gialle®? [avaytay lay pajeenay jallay]
- why don't you look in the Yellow Pages®? perché non guarda nelle Pagine Gialle®? [perkay non gwarda nellay pajeenay jallay]

yes sì [see]
- yes, please sì, grazie [see gratsee-ay]
- it doesn't matter – yes it does! non importa – invece sì! [non eemporta – eenvaychay see]

yet *(in negatives)* ancora [ankora]; *(in questions)* già [ja]
- I've not been there yet non ci sono ancora stato [non chee sono ankora stato]
- have you been there yet? c'è già stato? [chay ja stato]

yogurt lo yogurt [yogoort]
- do you have any organic yogurt? avete dello yogurt biologico? [avaytay dello yogoort bee-olojeeko]

young man il ragazzo [ragatso]
- who is that young man? chi è quel ragazzo? [kee ay kwel ragatso]

young person il giovane [jovanay]
> ▸ are there any discounts for young people? ci sono sconti per giovani? [chee sono scontee per jovanee]

young woman la ragazza [ragatsa]
> ▸ who is the young woman he's with? chi è la ragazza insieme a lui? [kee ay la ragatsa eensee-aymay a loo-ee]

youth hostel l'ostello *m* della gioventù [ostello della joventoo]
> ▸ I'd like to book two beds for three nights in a youth hostel vorrei prenotare due posti letto per tre notti in un ostello della gioventù [vorray-ee praynotaray doo-ay postee per tray nottee een oon ostello della joventoo]

zoo lo zoo [dzo]
> ▸ is there a zoo nearby? c'é uno zoo qui vicino? [chay oono dzo kwee veecheeno]

Italian language
and culture

Italian around the world:
who speaks it and where?

Italian is spoken by about 70 million people: this makes it something like 24th in the ranking of the world's most spoken languages (Chinese is first, with around 1,200 million speakers and English second, with about 340 million). The vast majority of Italian speakers are the 58 million inhabitants of Italy (which has an area about the same as Arizona). Italian is also the official language of two Swiss cantons that border the north of Italy, Ticino and Grigioni, and of the tiny independent republic of San Marino. Vatican City has two official languages: Italian and Latin. Italian is also spoken in neighboring countries such as Slovenia, Croatia and Albania, and on the Mediterranean island of Malta.

Many Italian speakers are bilingual, since they are fluent both in standard Italian and in the dialect of their area. Some regard their dialect as their first language, since it is the one they normally use in all informal situations.

For most of the 20th century, Italians in the millions migrated to find work. Argentina and the US were the major destinations but European countries such as France, Germany and Great Britain also attracted large numbers. There are 1.5 million Italian speakers in Argentina and half a million in Germany. In the US, 906,000 Italian speakers were recorded in 1989.

Unlike other European countries, Italy never had an empire and consequently Italian is not a world language like English, Spanish and French. Before World War II Italy was a minor colonial power in North Africa, controlling what is now Libya from 1912 until the war, and Ethiopia, Somalia and Eritrea for a brief period in the 1930s. Italian was an official language in Eritrea until 1963, but the use of Italian in Africa has greatly declined.

Who learns Italian?

As a school subject in English-speaking countries Italian is less important than Spanish, French and German. It's a popular language nonetheless, with many adults choosing to study it either because they have family or business connections with Italy, or because they are attracted by the richness and diversity of the country's history and culture, and by the beauty of the language itself.

Where did the Italian language come from?

Italian is a Romance language that, like nearly all the languages spoken in Europe, belongs to the Indo-European family of languages. In pre-Roman times various languages, now extinct – such as Etruscan, Umbrian and Volscian – were spoken by the peoples of the Italian peninsula who were eventually subjugated by the Romans, whose language was Latin, the language of Latium – the central area of Italy. As the language of the Roman Empire (27 BC – 476 AD) Latin became pre-eminent in the peninsula and far beyond. For many centuries after the fall of the Roman Empire Classical Latin continued to be the language of scholarship throughout Europe.

As a spoken language Latin developed into languages such as French, Spanish, Portuguese and Romanian – and Italian, which remains closest to its ancestor. The Latin words for *land, sea, moon* and *star*: **terra, mare, luna** and **stella** are exactly the same in Italian. The Latin **pater** (*father*), **mater** (*mother*), **panis** (*bread*) and **vinum** (*wine*) change slightly in Italian, becoming **padre, madre, pane** and **vino**.

Italian dialects

What is now standard Italian has only quite recently been spoken by the majority of people who live in Italy – in part because Italy has existed as a political entity for a relatively short time. Not until 1861 did Italy become a unified country – until then, in the words of the Austrian chancellor Metternich, Italy was merely a 'geographical expression.'

In 1861 most Italians spoke only their local dialect and many were unable to read or write. There were innumerable dialects, which had developed from Latin in very different ways: a Sicilian farm worker would have been unable to communicate with one from Piedmont since their dialects were (and still are) mutually incomprehensible.

There was, however, a written language common to most literate Italians, that had developed from the Florentine dialect. The prestige of Florentine Italian was greatly enhanced by the fact that Dante wrote his great work **La Divina Commedia** in this 'vulgar' language (i.e. language of the people) rather than in Latin. Boccaccio and Petrarch followed his example.

After unification, Italy's seat of government was Rome, but the official language was Florentine. This did not mean that Sicilian and Piedmontese farm workers started speaking it – for several decades most uneducated people continued to speak only their own dialect. They rarely left their native town or village and so had no need to make themselves understood in any other part of the country.

How Italian became the national language

Things began to change in the 20th century: all children went to school, and were taught standard Italian (though many didn't speak it at home). The population became more mobile, with men being conscripted in the two world wars and whole families moving from south to north to find work. Trade unions urged workers to speak standard Italian rather than dialect, to avoid making themselves targets for discrimination. Cinema and television were two other potent factors in the greatly increased use of standard Italian. Despite this, however, dialects continue to be spoken much more in Italy than in other European countries. From an Italian perspective the differences between English as spoken in Detroit and that spoken in Denver are minuscule, compared with the very different language you hear on the streets if you go, for example, from Turin to Florence.

Regional variations

Even when people are speaking standard Italian their pronunciation varies according to where they are from: in Tuscany, for example, people tend to pronounce the **c** of words such as **casa** (*house*) and **cosa** (*thing*) like an h. The question **quanto costa una coca cola?** (*how much does a coca cola cost?*) can sound something like **hwanto hosta una hoha hola?** – the grammar of the question is standard, but the pronunciation is not.

The old and the new

Italian is a language that goes both ways – it retains much of the grammar of Latin, but readily adopts new words, most of which are English. In France the **Académie française** fights unceasingly against English borrowings and Anglicisms, but the equivalent body in Italy – the **Accademia della Crusca** is less vociferous.

Unlike English-speaking children, Italian **bambini** have no difficulty in reading or spelling their language, since every letter is pronounced, and words are spelled phonetically. This leaves them free to worry about the present, perfect, imperfect and pluperfect subjunctives – like their Roman forebears!

Italian loanwords in English

Italian culture has been hugely influential in the US, especially in the areas of food and classical music.

Italian words for Italian foods

For Americans, as for Italians, pasta, pizza and coffee are three necessities of life, and innumerable Italian words to do with them are used every day in kitchens, stores and eateries: spaghetti, ravioli, macaroni (spelled **maccheroni** in Italian), lasagna (spelled **lasagne** in Italian), mozzarella, parmigiano, cappuccino, espresso, to name but a few.

English speakers have adopted the pasta dishes – and also **zucchini** – but not their grammar: in Italian **zucchini, spaghetti, lasagne** etc. are plural, so if you want to comment on them you say, for example, **gli spaghetti sono buoni** (*the spaghetti are good*). Two endings **-ini**, and **-oni**, which you see in words for some types of pasta, for example **tortellini**, and **tortelloni**, give a clue about what they're like, **-ino** being a diminutive, and **-one** suggesting something big. In the same way, **un minestrone** is a heartier soup than **una minestra**, and **panettone** is rich and sweet, unlike ordinary **pane** (*bread*).

New meanings for borrowed words

Outside Italy, **latte**, the Italian for *milk*, has been borrowed quite recently as a name for milky coffee – but **latte** never has this meaning in Italy, where **caffellatte** is used for milky breakfast coffee. There is also a difference of meaning in the case of **confetti**, which in Italy are sugared almonds, prettily packaged and given to guests at weddings, rather than bits of colored paper thrown over the bride and groom.

Italian: the language of music

Italian has always been the international language of music: it has provided the names of musical instruments, for example violin, viola, cello, piccolo (which means *small*). The pianoforte was so called because it could play both soft (**piano**) and loud (**forte**). Composers still write the instructions about how works should be performed in Italian – **pianissimo, adagio, allegro ma non troppo, con brio, legato.** Some musical terms, such as **staccato, crescendo** and **solo** have taken on more general meanings. Types of composition too have Italian names – **opera, concerto, sonata, aria, largo,** as do types of performer – **maestro, diva, primadonna, soprano, contralto.**

Striking a discordant note

To descend to a less elevated plane, English has borrowed **bimbo** (which means *little child* in Italian), **bordello, gigolo, graffiti** and **mafia**.

English loanwords in Italian

Italians love their national style, but they like to use English to talk about it: **il made in Italy** is a favorite phrase used to refer to Italian products, especially those of the fashion industry. At **uno show,** where creations are worn by **le top model,** you'll see **il design** and **lo styling** that translate into **il look** of the moment. Afterwards you may be lured into **lo shopping**.

IT and science

As well as in the world of fashion, English words are heavily used in the fields of science, information technology, business, entertainment and sports. While the French have their own words for *computer* and *mouse*, Italians use **il computer, il Pc** (Italianized by the lower-case **c**) and **il mouse.** What you do with a mouse is **cliccare,** what you do in a chat room is **chattare** or **ciattare** (the Italian spelling). Other such thinly disguised English verbs are **interfacciare, listare** and **scrollare. L'e-mail** exists alongside la **posta elettronica:** you can send **un messaggio di posta elettronica,** or – less Italian, but snappier, **una mail;** *junk mail* and *snail mail* are **posta spazzatura** and **posta lumaca.** A person who works for **una software house** is a **softwarista.**

Economics and business

US economic theory and business practice have been very influential in Italy and many terms have been imported, such as **il management, i manager, manageriale, il training, il turnover, il break even, il trust, il target** – not to mention **il business** itself. Innumerable concepts have been translated into Italian, for example, **la produttività, la redittività** (*profitability*), **l'incentivazione, il controllo della qualità, la comunicazione organizzazionale** – and the hotly debated **globalizzazione** and **sostenibilità**.

Popular culture

American popular culture has always been well-loved by Italians, especially music and the movies, and many words have been borrowed in those fields: **il blues, il jazz, la musica pop, il rock, il rapper, la break dance, il fan, lo showbusiness, il talk show, le star**. In an interview in a recent issue of the Italian newspaper **La Repubblica** a singer is asked if she thinks the Italian premier is **un presidente rock. Si rockissimo**, she replies.

In the case of those most popular of garments, **i jeans**, Italians are merely taking back a word that came from Italy in the first place, since *jean* derives from the name of the city of Genoa (at one time known as Jennes), where **blu di Genova**, a hard-wearing blue cloth, was manufactured from the 16th century onwards. Another word Italians have borrowed back is *studio*. This is obviously of Italian origin, but it meant *study* in Italian – not a place where movies are made. Now the word has both meanings.

Sports

Lo sport is a major area for English loanwords: **il golf, il tennis, il rugby, l'hockey, lo squash, il baseball**. Basketball is called both **il basket** and **la pallacanestro**. The national passion **il calcio** (*soccer*) was originally known as **il football**.

The sports pages of newspapers are full of English: **dribblare, crossare, sprintare. Il favorito**, backed by **i supporter**, could achieve **qualificazione**, might establish **un record mondiale** and become **il champion**, dreads **un flop** or **la squalifica**, and may or may not stick to the principles of **il fair play**.

English words all'italiana

Italian borrows words, but not grammar such as the *s* that makes English words plural, so two top models are **due top model**, three goals are **tre gol**, and sweaters and trench coats are **gli sweater** and **i trench**. Italian adjectives come after the noun, so that's where borrowed English adjectives go too: **una donna sexy** (*a sexy woman*) **un dossier top-secret** (*a top-secret dossier*), **la musica soft** (*soft music*).

In Italian, English verbs and adjectives can become nouns, and nouns become verbs: **un relax** is *a rest*, **un optional** *an optional extra*; to **snobbare** someone's offer is *to reject* it. Other times words take on whole new identities: who would guess that **un golf** is *a sweater*, **uno smoking** *a tuxedo*, **un lifting** *a face-lift*, **un night** *a night club*, **un box** *a garage*, **un flipper** *a pinball machine*, **un jolly** *a joker* and **un holding** *a holding company*?

Making it snappy

Italian is a musical language with few monosyllables; Italians seem to enjoy short English words such as *big, boss, club, fast, soft, check-in* and *password*, which are snappier and more staccato than their Italian counterparts: **grande, padrone, circolo, veloce, morbido, accetazione bagagli, parola d'ordine**. Many English words are optional extras, but some – such as **lo stress**, **la privacy** and **gay** – have become essentials.

False friends

Luckily for English speakers learning Italian, lots of Italian words look very much like English words, and have the same meaning. Sometimes though, Italian look-alikes are **falsi amici** (*false friends*) that mean something quite different from what one would expect. For example, **una fattoria** isn't a *factory*, but *a farm*, and **una delusione** is not a *delusion*, but *a disappointment*.

The difference in meaning between apparently identical words means that you might end up with something you don't want, for example, **una camera** is not something you take pictures with, but *a bedroom* and **gasolio** is not *gasoline*, but *diesel fuel*.

Here are some more examples of words that might give you the wrong idea:

un box	*a garage*
una macchina	*a car*
un'incidente	*an (auto) accident*
una patente	*a driver's license*
il pavimento	*the floor*
una firma	*a signature*
un'agenda	*a diary*
la stampa	*the press*
un parente	*a relative*
tremendo	*terrible*
simpatico	*nice*
eventuale	*possible*
attuale	*current*
sensibile	*sensitive*
annoiare	*to bore*
pretendere	*to expect*

Don't worry too much about **amici falsi** — most Italian words that seem like English ARE like English — they're **amici veri** (*real friends*).

Slang and youth culture

I ragazzi have to learn English at school, but they also voluntarily use English words, such as *cool*, *trendy* and *good*, and their own versions of English words such as **kesh** (*money*); **skeitare** (*to skateboard*) and **roflare** (*to roll on the floor laughing*) and **fashion**, used to mean *fashionable* – as in **come sei fashion!** (*you're so trendy!*). **Forever!** is used to express enthusiasm and congratulations – for example, **abbiamo vinto la partita – forever!** (*we won the match – great!*). **Airbag** (pronounced erbeg) is used to comment on your girlfriend's large bust: **che airbag che hai!**

A **B-boy** is a rapper – the feminine equivalent being **una fly-girl**.

Nobody likes you if you're **un loser** or **un nerdz** – note that **un nerdz** is just one geeky person, **nerdz** being the same in the singular as in the plural. You can see why **alien** means ugly – but it's less obvious why **testa di quiz** (*quiz head*) means stupid. **Un Krusty** is someone like the Simpsons character – outwardly smiling, inwardly sad.

Home-grown slang

There is also plenty of Italian slang – **un quarz** is a pimply kid (the word allegedly represents the sound of a squashed pimple), un **paolotto** is a goody-goody who works hard at school and goes to church, **un pappone** is the classic **figlio di papà** (*daddy's boy*), an idle rich kid. **Oc** are types who appear on the beach in garish bermudas and flowered shirts. **Truzzi** are rough-looking kids who hang around in packs, wear Lonsdale and listen to techno music.

Bella cumpa! is how you greet a group of friends; **raga** is short for **ragazzi**, as in **raga, andiamo al cinema?** (*hey guys, should we go to the movies?*).

Playing hooky

While slang of English origin is used all over Italy, much home-grown slang varies according to region. There are dozens of variants, for example, on the standard Italian **marinare la scuola** (*to play hooky*): in Rimini it's **fare puffi**, in Verona **fare berna**, in Milan **bigiare la scuola**, in Ferrara **fare fuoco**, in Parma **fare fogone**, in Sardinia **fare vela**, in Bergamo **fare filotto**. In Florence it's generally **fare sega** – but in the area near the Boboli Gardens (a public park) it's **andare a Boboli!**

Text messaging

The two must-haves of the Italian teenager are the small motorbike – **il motorino**, and **il cellulare** (*cellphone*), also known as **il trillino**. Standard Italian is rather too polysyllabic for text messaging – **gli sms.** Here are some examples of abbreviations in common use:

k	che	*that*
x	per	*for*
xke	perché	*why/because*
d	di	*of*
t	ti	*you*
tu6	tu sei	*you are*
+ tardi	più tardi	*later*
+o-	più o meno	*more or less*
bn	bene	*well*
qd	quando	*when*
qc	qualcosa	*something*
doma	domani	*tomorrow*
pome	pomeriggio	*afternoon*
TVB	ti volgio bene	*I love you*
TVTB	ti voglio tanto bene	*I love you so much*
okp	oh che palle!	*what a pain!*

What matters

Music, the discotheque, drugs and style are important elements in Italian youth culture. Alcohol is less prominent than in the US and there are fewer slang expressions to do with being drunk (e.g. **prendere una cassa** *to get paralytic*), as compared with the vast number concerned with sex and drugs. A small sample of the latter are **split, joint, canna, erba, farsi un cannone** (*to smoke a joint*), **fumato**, (*high*), **mangiare un trip** (*to take a tablet*), **sprinz** (*syringe*), **raglia** (*line of cocaine*).

Another difference between Italy and the US is the greater interest in politics shown by young people. Although much less often than in the 70s, school students still sometimes occupy their schools to protest against educational policies. Many young people also feel strongly about globalization and the G8 – in July 2001 many thousands of young Italians joined the demonstrations in Genova against the G8 meeting being held there. There is even a word for such protesters – **giotini** (*G-eighters*).

What's so special about Italy?

Italy is unique in its enormous wealth of art and architecture, two main sources of which are the civilizations of ancient Rome, and the city states dating from the Middle Ages, such as Venice, Milan, Florence and Siena. Nowhere else in the world does such a small area as the Italian Peninsula have such a concentration of beautiful and historic cities – or of such icons as the Coliseum, the Leaning Tower of Pisa, the Grand Canal, Michelangelo's statue of David and Sistine Chapel frescoes and Leonardo's Last Supper.

Imperial Rome

Rome is the imperial city par excellence: for five centuries it was the hub of the Roman Empire and for two millennia it has been the center of the Roman Catholic Church. The city has a vast array of ancient remains – theaters, stadia, temples, palaces, baths, aqueducts, bridges and the enormous **forum**. Seeing these huge and sophisticated structures gives one a vivid feeling of the wealth, power and technical expertise of the people who built them. There are, of course, classical remains all over Italy – for a very poignant view of life in a 1st century Roman town one can walk the perfectly preserved streets of Pompeii, which was buried in ash when Vesuvius erupted in 79 AD. Excavation only began in the 18th century.

Designed to impress

The hugeness and splendor of the classical buildings in Rome are also found in its multitudinous churches, most notably in the Basilica of **San Pietro**. The Vatican museums are full of treasures. Splendor is a very Italian quality: throughout the peninsula there are churches designed by the foremost architects of their age and whose mosaics, frescoes, pictures and statues were made by outstanding artists. Cities were designed to impress: the Gothic center of Siena, for instance – the **Piazza del Campo** – has amazing grandeur, Venice is legendary and even if the Leaning Tower was perfectly perpendicular, the **Piazza dei Miracoli** of Pisa would still be stunning.

Traditional events

21st century Italians are proud of the historic cities they live in and their traditional events – many of which offer wonderful opportunities for dressing up. In February **Carnevale** is an opportunity to enjoy gorgeous costumes, masks, parades and dancing before the rigors of

Lent. The **Carnevale** of Venice is the most famous, but it is celebrated all over Italy.

You get to choose your own costume for **Carnevale**, but for other traditional festivals, such as **il Calcio in Costume** (soccer played in costume: Florence), **la Giostra del Saracino** (jousting competition between the four areas of town: Arezzo) and **il Palio** (horse race around the **Campo**: Siena) carefully re-created medieval costumes are worn. Local organizations devote much time and money to ensuring they have perfect reproductions of weapons, banners, drums, trumpets and the trappings for horses. Before events begin you see 21st century people smoking and talking on their cellphones, but when they don their helmets or plumed hats and throw away their cigarettes, they immediately look as if they have stepped out of a fresco by Ghirlandaio.

Il Palio

The Sienese **Palio** is not the only **palio** – there are several others, including one in Querceta where a race is run by donkeys – if they can be persuaded to face the right way and get moving. The Sienese event, however, is no joking matter – the 17 **contrade** (areas) of the city each enter a horse, and their desperate desire to win has seven centuries of bitter neighborly rivalry behind it. The race happens twice a year, in July and August: it is the climax of a day of glittering pageantry watched by thousands. The notion of fair play was quite absent from medieval Siena, and in this respect too, the modern race preserves perfect authenticity.

Spectacle, elegance and style

The Italian gift for staging drama and spectacle did not of course end with the Middle Ages: the electric atmosphere of Milan's **La Scala** is well-known, and the operas performed in the Verona festival are heightened by their setting in the Roman amphitheater. The care with which medieval costumes are re-created is one aspect of a much wider passion for beautiful clothes, which underpins the famous Milan fashion industry and is evident on the street. More than Anglo-Saxons, Italians look at what people are wearing and expect to be looked at: their style and elegance is often wonderful to behold.

Life all'italiana

Family life

The Italian family is traditionally seen as large and tight-knit, with **la mamma** doting on her children and running around after them (even when they are middle-aged), and old people being lovingly cared for by their relatives.

Compared with the US, fewer Italians leave home to go to university, or to find jobs, and it is indeed quite normal for unmarried thirty-somethings to continue living with their parents, sometimes for financial reasons, but often because they don't feel any desire for a home of their own. Being independent of one's parents is not seen as any particular virtue – and the word **privacy** was only borrowed from English fairly recently. In other ways, however, the Italian family is not what it was – for one thing, it's no longer large: Italy has the lowest birthrate in Europe (1.28 children per woman, as compared with 2.08 per woman in the US). The Italian population is aging, with 20% over 65, but a growing number of women are employed – which makes it harder for them to care for elderly relatives.

The street scene

A visitor may not see much of family life, but anyone walking around an Italian city can observe characteristic aspects of Italian social life. The word *walking* here is important – cities are places to walk around, places where you look in shop windows, look at passers-by and at what they're wearing, and stop to shake hands with friends and acquaintances and exchange the time of day with them. Some **piazza** in the center of town – maybe in front of the main church – will be the place where people (mainly men) congregate to talk, with the roar of human voices drowning the noise of traffic. Later in the day, before dinner, couples have traditionally taken part in the **passeggiata** – promenading arm-in-arm along the main street, seeing people and being seen, and chatting. The advent of the cellphone has further increased the volume of talk on the street.

Il bar

Aside from the street and the piazza, another favorite meeting place is **il bar**, which is more like a café than an American bar. In the morning, people on their way to work stop at a bar to have a cup of coffee and maybe a little pastry – they mostly stand at the counter, rather than sitting at a table, which takes longer and costs more. Later, people may sit together over a coffee or possibly a beer – but **un bar** sells far less alcohol than its US namesake. The **pizzeria** and **gelateria** are two other places where friends meet – **il gelato** has long been an Italian passion.

Local pride

Italians are often deeply attached to their village or city, sometimes excessively so. The pejorative word **campanilismo** denotes a parochial outlook that does not go beyond the **campanile** of the village church. It must generally be positive though, and foster community solidarity, that people enjoy living in their native place, and are proud of its history and traditions. Many citizens of historic cities take part in events which have been enacted for centuries, such as **il Palio** in Siena and **la Giostra del Saracino** in Arezzo.

Local food

Food is one area of life where faithfulness to tradition, attachment to local products and appreciation of quality are very evident. People understand, for example that Parma ham and Parmesan cheese take time to make and are therefore expensive. Italians love to talk about food and wine, and to taste the specialties of an area – but they generally do so very moderately, especially in the case of wine. They are equally interested and discriminating with regard to everyday things – an espresso is not just a cup of coffee. Most Italians, having swallowed the tiny thimbleful, will have reached a judgement on it which may include consideration of the type of water, and whether the **caffettiera** has been cleaned incorrectly.

The slow food movement

Such attitudes go against the standardization, blandness and emphasis on quantity rather than quality that are typical of fast food. It was in Italy that the notion of **slow food** was born in 1986 – a movement dedicated to the preservation of tastes and smells, to diversity and to the belief that eating is about much more than simply satisfying hunger. The organization **Slow Food** now has thousands of members world-wide, including in the US.

Popular leisure activities

Il calcio

The main spectator sport in Italy is soccer. Three top teams in the A division are AC Milan (whose chairman is Silvio Berlusconi), Inter Milan, and Juventus, the Turin team which was for a long time controlled by the **Agnelli** family, who own **Fiat**. Rivalry between the two Milan teams, and between Inter and Juventus is particularly intense. As is the case with all top European clubs, many of the players are talented foreigners, from countries such as Argentina and Brazil. Although far behind soccer, rugby is growing in popularity, and since 2000 Italy has taken part in the Six Nations Championship.

Cycling

Il ciclismo is another important sport: the **Giro d'Italia** (inspired by **Le Tour de France**) is one of the three most important road races for professional riders. It takes place in May and lasts for three weeks. The course varies from year to year, and may start outside Italy. The total distance is about 3,500 km. Cycling is also a very popular leisure activity in Italy – and in areas that aren't too hilly it's a good way to get around, especially in cities that ban cars from the town center to reduce pollution.

Hunting

In rural areas the shooting season (**la caccia**) begins in September. Many small birds are shot, as well as larger animals such as deer and wild boar. At this time of year people also hunt for mushrooms such as the delicious **porcini**. In town **lo shopping** takes the place of **la caccia** all year round – Italians, even Italian children, are addicted to it.

Travel

Now that there are cheap flights all over Europe, Italians travel abroad much more than they used to. In past years the classic choice for **la villeggiatura** (*vacation*) was **il mare o la montagna** (*the seaside or the mountains*). With 7,600 km of coastline there is plenty of sea to choose from and a great diversity of resorts. In the summertime walking and climbing in the Alps and Dolomites is popular, and in winter many go skiing in these areas.

Understandably, many Italians like to visit the galleries, museums and historic places of their own country, either on organized day trips or on longer tours.

Italian–English dictionary

a

a [a] *prep (movement)* to; *(place, time)* at; *(town, city)* in

abbastanza [abbastantsa] *adv* enough; quite

abbazia [abbatsee-a] *f* abbey

abbigliamento [abbeelyamento] *m* clothes, clothing ▸ 'abbigliamento uomo' 'menswear'

abbondante [abbondantay] *adj (meal)* big ▸ un chilo abbondante just over a kilo

abbronzante [abbrondzantay] *m* suntan lotion

abbronzatura [abbrondzatoora] *f* suntan

abito [abeeto] *m (woman)* dress; *(man)* suit ◆ **abiti** [abiti] *mpl* clothes, clothing

abitudine [abeetoodeenay] *f* habit ▸ per abitudine out of habit

accademia [akkademee-a] *f (cultural institute)* academy ▸ accademia di belle arti art school

accanto [akkanto] *adv* nearby ◆ *adj* next

accendere [achendayray] *v (cigarette)* to light; *(engine)* to turn on

accendino [achendeeno] *m (cigarette)* lighter

accento [achento] *m* accent

acceso, a [achayzo] *adj (light)* on; *(color)* bright

accesso [achesso] *m* access

acciaio [acha-yo] *m* steel

accidenti [acheedentee] *excl (in annoyance)* damn!; *(in surprise)* wow!

acciuga [achooga] *f* anchovy

accoglienza [akkolyentsa] *f* welcome

accogliere [akkolyayray] *v* to welcome

accomodarsi [akkomodarsee] *v* to sit down ▸ s'accomodi! sit down!; *(at door)* come in!

accompagnatore, trice [akkompan-yatoray] *m, f* companion

acconto [akkonto] *m* deposit

accordo [akkordo] *m* agreement ▸ d'accordo! OK!

accorgersi di [akkorjersee dee] *v* to notice

accumulare [akkoomoolaray] *v* to accumulate

acerbo, a [acherbo] *adj (fruit)* unripe

aceto [achayto] *m* vinegar

acidità [acheedeeta] *f* ▸ acidità di stomaco heartburn

acido, a [acheedo] *adj* sour ◆ *m* acid

acqua [akkwa] *f* water ▸ acqua dolce/salata fresh/salt water ▸ acqua minerale (gassata/naturale) (sparkling/non-carbonated) mineral water ▸ 'acqua non potabile' 'non-potable water'

acquario [akkwaree-o] *m* aquarium

acquavite [akkwaveetay] *f* brandy

acquedotto [akkwaydotto] *m* aqueduct

acquerello [akkwayrello] *m* watercolor

acquisto [akkweesto] *m* purchase ▸ fare acquisti to go shopping

acuto, a [akooto] *adj* acute; *(person)* perceptive

ad [ad] = a

adagio [adajo] *adv* slowly ▸ 'entrare/uscire adagio' 'very slow'

agriturismi

Agriturismi, farm cottages or rural guesthouses, are often the place for a really unique vacation. Living in the farmhouse, or in a self-contained cottage, you can enjoy being part of an Italian family, help with work in the fields (fruit or grape-picking, harvesting, etc.) or take part in various sports. Some *agriturismi* are like luxury guesthouses, especially those in Tuscany.

adatto, a [adatto] *adj* suitable

addetto, a [addetto] *m, f* person in charge

addio [addee-o] *excl* goodbye

addirittura [addeereettoora] *adv* even ✦ *excl* really!

addome [addomay] *m* abdomen

addormentare [addormentaray] *v (baby)* to put down to sleep ✦ **addormentarsi** [addormentarsee] *v* to go to sleep

addosso [addosso] *adv* ▸ mi è venuto addosso he bumped into me

aderente [adayrentay] *adj (dress)* tight-fitting

adesso [adesso] *adv* now ▸ gli ho parlato proprio adesso I spoke to him just now

Adriatico [adreeateeko] *m* ▸ l'Adriatico, il mar Adriatico the Adriatic (Sea)

aereo, a [a-ayray-o] *adj* air ✦ *m* plane ▸ aereo da turismo light aircraft

aeroporto [a-ayroporto] *m* airport

afa [afa] *f* sultriness

affanno [affanno] *m* breathlessness

affare [affaray] *m (business)* deal; *(matter)* affair; *(object)* thing

affatto [affatto] *adv* at all ▸ niente affatto not at all

affettare [affettaray] *v* to slice

affidare [affeedaray] *v* to entrust

affinché [affeenkay] *conj* so that

affissione [affeesseeonay] *f* billposting

▸ 'divieto di affissione' 'billposters will be prosecuted'

affittare [affeettaray] *v* to rent ▸ 'affittasi appartamento' 'apartment for rent'

affitto [affeetto] *m* rental; *(money)* rent

affogare [affogaray] *v* to drown

affogato [affogato] *m* ▸ un affogato al caffè ice cream with coffee poured over it

affollato, a [affollato] *adj* crowded

affrancatura [affrankatoora] *f* postage

affresco [affresko] *m* fresco

affumicato, a [affoomeekato] *adj* smoked

afoso, a [afozo] *adj* sultry

Africa [afreeka] *f* ▸ l'Africa Africa

agenzia [ajentsee-a] *f* agency ▸ agenzia immobiliare real estate agency ▸ agenzia di viaggi travel agency

aggiungere [ajoonjayray] *v* to add

aggiustare [ajoostaray] *v* to repair

agitare [ajeetaray] *v* to shake ✦ **agitarsi** [ajeetarsee] *v* to get worked up

aglio [alyo] *m* garlic

agnello [anyello] *m* lamb

ago [ago] *m* needle

agosto [agosto] *m* August

agriturismo [agreetooreesmo] *m* farm vacations; farm cottage, rural guesthouse

AIDS [a-eeds] *mf* AIDS

air-terminal [ayr-termeenal] *m* air terminal

aiutare [a-yootaray] *v* to help

aiuto [a-yooto] *m* help ▸ aiuto! help! ▸ chiedere aiuto to ask for help

al [al] *prep (movement)* to the; *(place)* at the ▸ al supermercato to/at the supermarket

ala [ala] *f* wing

alba [alba] *f* dawn

albergatore, trice [albergatoray] *m, f* hotelier

albergo [albergo] *m* hotel

albero [albero] *m* tree ▸ albero genealogico family tree

albicocca [albeekokka] *f* apricot

albume [alboomay] *m* egg white

alcuni [alkoonee] *adj & pron* some ▸ alcuni di noi some of us

aliante [alee-antay] *m* glider

alice [aleechay] *f* anchovy

alimentari [aleementaree] *mpl* foodstuffs

alla [alla] *prep (movement)* to the; *(place)* at the ▸ questo sentiero porta alla spiaggia this path leads to the beach

allacciare [allacharay] *v (shoes)* to tie; *(belt, coat)* to fasten

alle [allay] *prep (movement)* to the; *(place)* at the ▸ alle sette di sera at seven in the evening

alleanza [allay-antsa] *f* alliance

allegato, a [allaygato] *adj (with letter)* enclosed; *(with e-mail)* attached ◆ *m (with letter)* enclosure; *(with e-mail)* attachment

allegria [allegree-a] *f* cheerfulness

allegro, a [allegro] *adj* cheerful

allentare [allentaray] *v (screw, knot)* to loosen

allestire [allesteeray] *v (exhibit)* to

mount; *(show)* to put on

alloggio [allojo] *m* accommodations

allontanare [allontanaray] *v* to take away ◆ **allontanarsi** [allontanarsee] *v* to move away

allora [allora] *adv & conj* then ▸ da allora since then

alluce [alloochay] *m* big toe

alluvione [alloovee-onay] *f* flood

almeno [almayno] *adv* at least

Alpi [alpee] *fpl* ▸ le Alpi the Alps

alt [alt] *excl* stop!

altalena [altalayna] *f* seesaw

altare [altaray] *m* altar

alterno, a [alterno] *adj* ▸ a giorni alterni every other day

altezza [altetsa] *f* height

alto, a [alto] *adj* high; *(person, animal)* tall

Alto Adige [alto adeejay] *m* ▸ l'Alto Adige the Alto Adige

altoparlante [altoparlantay] *m* loudspeaker

altrimenti [altreementee] *adv* otherwise

altro, a [altro] *adj* other ▸ un altro caffè? would you like another coffee?

altronde [altronday] ◆ **d'altronde** [daltronday] *adv* on the other hand

altrove [altrovay] *adv* elsewhere

alzare [altsaray] *v* to raise ◆ **alzarsi** [altsarsee] *v* to get up

amaca [amaka] *f* hammock

amare [amaray] *v* to love

amarena [amarayna] *f* sour black cherry

amaretto [amaretto] *m* amaretto cookie; amaretto liqueur

amaro, a [amaro] *adj* bitter ◆ *m* bitters

amatriciana [amatreechana]

• all'amatriciana [allamatreechana] *adv* in a tomato and bacon sauce

ambasciata [ambashata] *f* embassy

ambiente [ambeeentay] *m* environment

ambulanza [amboolantsa] *f* ambulance

America [amayreeka] *f* ▸ l'America America ▸ l'America del Nord North America ▸ l'America del Sud South America ▸ l'America latina Latin America

americano, a [amayreekano] *adj & m, f* American

amico, a [ameeko] *m, f* friend

ammalato, a [ammalato] *m, f* sick person; *(in hospital)* patient

ammazzare [ammatsaray] *v* to kill

ammobiliato, a [ammobeeleeato] *adj* furnished

ammorbidente [ammorbeedentay] *m* fabric softener

ammortizzatore [ammorteedzatoray] *m* shock absorber

amore [amoray] *m* love

ampio, a [ampee-o] *adj* large; *(piece of clothing)* loose

analcolico, a [analkoleeko] *adj* non-alcoholic **♦** *m* soft drink

anatra [anatra] *f* duck

anca [anka] *f* hip

anche [ankay] *conj* also, too; even ▸ anch'io me too ▸ anche se even if

ancora [ankora] *f* anchor

ancora [an-kora] *adv* again; still; yet; more

andare [andaray] *v* to go ▸ come va? how are you? ▸ va bene OK **♦ andarsene** [andarsaynay] *v* to go away

andata [andata] *f* one-way ticket

anello [anello] *m* ring

anfiteatro [anfeetay-atro] *m* amphitheater; lecture hall

angolo [angolo] *m* corner; angle

anguilla [angweella] *f* eel

anguria [angooree-a] *f* watermelon

anice [aneechay] *m (plant)* anise; *(seed)* aniseed

annegare [annaygaray] *v* to drown

anniversario [anneeversaree-o] *m* anniversary

anno [anno] *m* year

annuale [annooalay] *adj* annual

annullare [annoollaray] *v* to cancel

annuncio [annooncho] *m* announcement ▸ annunci economici classified ads

annuo, a [annoo-o] *adj* annual

ansia [ansee-a] *f* anxiety

Antartide [antarteeday] *f* ▸ l'Antartide the Antarctic

anteprima [antaypreema] *f* preview

anteriore [antayree-oray] *adj (event)* previous; *(leg)* front

anticipo [anteecheepo] *m* advance ▸ in anticipo *(arrive)* early; *(be paid)* in advance

antico, a [anteeko] *adj (times)* ancient; *(furniture)* antique

anticoncezionale [anteekonchetseeonalay] *adj* contraceptive

anticorpo [anteekorpo] *m* antibody

antifurto [anteefoorto] *m* alarm

antincendio [anteenchendee-o] *adj (door, alarm)* fire

antinebbia [anteenebbee-a] *adj (light)* fog

antipasto [anteepasto] *m* hors d'oeuvre ▸ antipasto di mare seafood hors d'oeuvres ▸ antipasto misto assorted hors d'oeuvres

antiquariato [anteekwaree-ato] *m* antiques trade; antiques

antipasti

You can make an entire meal of these wonderful hors d'oeuvres: *mazzancolle* (king-sized prawns), *calamari* (squid) *alla romana*, *carpaccio* (marinated raw meat), *supplì di riso* (rice croquettes), *vitello tonnato* (roast veal in a sauce of mayonnaise, tuna and capers), and, of course, all those salamis and cooked meats, and grilled vegetables marinated in olive oil.

antiruggine [anteeroojeenay] *adj* rust-proof

antitetanica [anteetaytaneeka] *f* tetanus injection

antivipera [anteeveepera] *m* antivenom

anulare [anoolaray] *m* ring finger

anzi [antsee] *conj* or rather; on the contrary

anziano, a [antsee-ano] *m, f* elderly person

ape [apay] *f* bee

aperto, a [aperto] *adj* open ◆ *m* all'aperto outdoors

apertura [apertoora] *f* opening

apnea [apnay-a] *f* ◗ immersione in apnea diving without a breathing apparatus

apparecchio [apparekkee-o] *m* device

appassionato, a [appassee-onato] *adj* passionate

appena [appayna] *adv* hardly; only; just ◗ *conj* as soon as ◗ sono appena arrivato ve just arrived ◗ non appena as soon as

appendicite [appendeecheetay] *f* appendicitis

Appennini [appenneenee] *mpl* ◗ gli Appennini the Apennines

appetito [appayteeto] *m* appetite buon appetito! enjoy (your meal)!

appiccicoso, a [appeecheekozo] *adj (substance)* sticky; *(person)* clingy

applauso [applowzo] *m* applause

appoggiare [appojaray] *v* to lean; to support ◆ **appoggiarsi a** [appojarsi a] *v* to lean on

apposito, a [appozeeto] *adj* appropriate

apposta [apposta] *adv* deliberately

approfittare di [approffeetaray dee] *v* to take advantage of

approssimativo, a [approsseematee-vo] *adj* approximate

approvare [approvaray] *v* to approve of

appuntamento [appoontamento] *m* appointment

appunto [appoonto] *adv* just; *(in replies)* exactly

apribottiglie [apreebotteelyay] *m* bottle-opener

aprile [apreelay] *m* April

aprire [apreeray] *v* to open ◆ **aprirsi** [apreersee] *v* to open

apriscatole [apreeskatolay] *m* can-opener

aquila [akweela] *f* eagle

aquilone [akweelonay] *m* kite

aragosta [aragosta] *f* lobster

arancia [arancha] *f* orange

aranciata [aranchata] *f* orangeade, orange soda

arancione [aranchonay] *adj* bright orange

arazzo [aratso] *m* tapestry

architettura [arkeetettoora] *f* architecture

archivio [arkeevee-o] *m* archives; *(on computer)* file

arcipelago [archeepaylago] *m* archipelago

arco [arko] *m* bow; *(period of time)* space ▸ nell'arco di tre anni in the space of three years

arcobaleno [arckobalayno] *m* rainbow

area [aray-a] *f* area ▸ 'area di servizio' 'service plaza', 'rest area'

argento [arjento] *m* silver ▸ d'argento silver

aria [aree-a] *f* air ▸ aria condizionata air-conditioning

ariete [aree-aytay] *m* ram

aringa [areenga] *f* herring

arista [areesta] *f* roast saddle of pork

Arlecchino [arlekkeeno] *m* Harlequin

arma [arma] *f* weapon ▸ arma da fuoco firearm

armadio [armadee-o] *m* closet ▸ armadio a muro walk-in closet

armatura [armatoora] *f* armor

aroma [aroma] *m* aroma ◆ **aromi** [aromi] *mpl* herbs and spices

arrabbiarsi [arrabbee-arsee] *v* to get angry

arrabbiata [arrabbee-ata] ◆ **all'arrabbiata** [allarrabbee-ata] *adv   in a spicy sauce*

arrangiarsi [arranjarsee] *v* to manage

arredamento [arraydamento] *m (action)* furnishing; *(furniture)* furnishings

arrestare [arrestaray] *v* to arrest

arrivederci [arreevayderchee]   *excl* goodbye!

arrivederla [arreevayderla] *excl (formal)* goodbye!

arrivo [arreevo] *m* arrival ▸ 'arrivi (nazionali/internazionali)' '(domestic/international) arrivals'

arrosto [arrosto] *m* roast

arrotolare [arrotolaray] *v* to roll up

arrugginito, a [arroojeeneeto] *adj* rusty

arte [artay] *f* art

arteria [artayree-a] *f* artery

articolo [arteekolo] *m* article ▸ 'articoli da regalo' 'gifts'

Artide [arteeday] *f* ▸ l'Artide the Arctic

artigianato [arteejanato] *m* crafts

artigiano, a [arteejano] *m, f* craftsman craftswoman

arto [arto] *m* limb

ascella [ashella] *f* armpit

ascensore [ashensoray] *m* elevator

ascesso [ashesso] *m* abscess

asciugacapelli [ashoogakapellee]   *m* hairdryer

asciugamano [ashoogamano] *m* towel

asciutto, a [ashootto] *adj* dry

ascoltare [askoltaray] *v* to listen to

asfalto [asfalto] *m* asphalt

Asia [azee-a] *f* ▸ l'Asia Asia

asilo [azeelo] *m* preschool; asylum ▸ asilo nido day care center

asino [azeeno] *m* donkey, ass

asma [azma] *f* asthma

asparago [asparago] *m* asparagus

aspettare [aspettaray] *v* to wait for

aspetto [aspetto] *m* appearance; aspect

aspirapolvere [aspeerapolvayray]   *m* vacuum cleaner

aspro, a [aspro] *adj (fruit)* sour; *(smell)* pungent

assaggiare [assajaray] *v* to taste

asse [assay] *m* axis; axle

assegno [assenyo] *m* check

assente [assentay] *adj* absent

assetato, a [assaytato] *adj* thirsty

assicurazione [asseekooratsee-onay] *f* insurance ▸ assicurazione sulla vita life insurance

assistente [asseestente] *mf* assistant

▸ assistente di volo flight attendant

asso [asso] *m (card)* ace

assolutamente [assolootamentay] *adv* absolutely

assorbente [assorbentay] *adj* absorbent ◆ *m* ▸ assorbente (igienico) sanitary napkin/pad ▸ assorbente interno tampon

assurdo, a [assoordo] *adj* absurd

asta [asta] *f* auction ▸ all'asta at auction

astratto, a [astratto] *adj* abstract

astuccio [astoocho] *m (for jewelry)* box; *(for glasses)* case

atlante [atlantay] *m* atlas

Atlantico [atlanteeko] *adj* ▸ l'(oceano) Atlantico the Atlantic (Ocean)

atletica [atlayteeka] *f* track and field

atmosfera [atmosfayra] *f* atmosphere

attaccapanni [attakkapannee] *m* hook

attaccare [attakkaray] *v* to attach; to attack; *(disease, illness)* to transmit ◆ **attaccarsi** [attakkarsee] *v* to cling

attacco [attakko] *m* attack; *(for bulb)* socket

atteggiamento [attejamento] *m* attitude

attendere [attendayray] *v* to wait for

attento, a [attento] *adj* careful ▸ stai attento be careful

attenzione [attentsee-onay] *f* attention ◆ *excl* look out!

atterraggio [atterrajo] *m* landing

attesa [attayza] *f* wait

attimo [atteemo] *m* moment

attivo, a [atteevo] *adj* active; *(balance)* credit

atto [atto] *m* act

attore [attoray] *m* actor

attorno [attorno] *adv* around ▸ attorno a around

attraversare [attraversaray] *v* to cross

▸ 'vietato attraversare i binari' 'do not cross tracks'

attrezzo [attretso] *m* tool

attrice [attreechay] *f* actress

attuale [attoo-alay] *adj* current

attualità [attoo-aleeta] *f* current affairs

audace [owdachay] *adj (undertaking)* risky; *(person)* daring

auguri [owgooree] *mpl* wishes ◆ *excl* best wishes

aula [owla] *f* classroom; lecture room; courtroom

aumentare [owmentaray] *v* to increase

aurora [owrora] *f* dawn

Austria [owstree-a] *f* ▸ l'Austria Austria

autista [owteesta] *mf* driver; chauffeur

autoadesivo, a [owto-adayzeevo] *adj* sticky

autoambulanza [owto-amboolantsa] *f* ambulance

autocontrollo [owtocontrollo] *m* self-control

autodromo [owtodromo] *m* racetrack

automatico, a [owtomateeko] *adj* automatic

automobile [owtomobilay] *f* automobile

autonomia [owtonomee-a] *f* independence

autorevole [owtorayvolay] *adj* authoritative

autorimessa [owtoreemessa] *f* garage

autorizzazione [owtoreedzatsee-onay] *f* authorization

autoscuola [owtoscoo-ola] *f* driving school

autostrada [owtostrada] *f* freeway

autunno [owtoonno] *m (season)* fall

avanti [avantee] *adv* forward ▸ 'avanti!' 'enter'; *(at traffic lights)* 'go'; *(in a line)* 'next!'

avere [avayray] *v* to have ▸ non ho

capito I didn't understand ▸ quanti anni hai? how old are you?

avorio [avoree-o] *m* ivory

avvelenamento [avvaylaynamento] *m* poisoning

avvelenare [avvaylaynaray] *v* to poison

avvenimento [avvayneemento] *m* event

avversario, a [avversaree-o] *m, f* opponent

avvertenze [avvertentsay] *fpl* instructions

avviare [avvee-aray] *v* to start (up) ◆ **avviarsi** [avvee-arsee] *v* to set off

avviso [avveezo] *m* notice ▸ a mio

avviso in my opinion

avvistare [avveestaray] *v* to sight

avvitare [avveetaray] *v (object)* t● screw

avvocato [avvokato] *m* lawyer

avvolgibile [avvoljeebeelay] *m* window shade

azienda [adzee-enda] *f* compan● ▸ azienda agricola farm

azionare [atsee-onaray] *v* to operate

azione [atsee-onay] *f* action

azzannare [adzannaray] *v* to maul

azzurro, a [adzoorro] *adj* blue

b

babà [baba] *m* rum baba

babbo [babbo] *m (familiar)* dad, daddy

baccalà [bakkala] *m* salt cod ▸ baccalà alla vicentina *salt cod with anchovies, onions, parsley, and Parmesan, cooked in milk and served with polenta*

baciare [bacharay] *v* to kiss ◆ **baciarsi** [bacharsee] *v* to kiss (each other)

bacio [bacho] *m* kiss; chocolate and hazelnut ice cream ▸ bacio di dama *two little hazelnut pastries with chocolate cream in between*

baffi [baffee] *mpl* mustache

bagaglio [bagalyo] *m* piece of baggage/ luggage ▸ bagaglio a mano piece of carry-on luggage

bagnare [banyaray] *v* to wet ◆ **bagnarsi** [banyarsee] *v (in ocean)* to bathe; *(in rain)* to get wet

bagnino, a [banyeeno] *m, f* lifeguard

bagno [banyo] *m* bathtub; bathroom

▸ fare il bagno to take a bath; *(i● ocean)* to go for a swim ◆ **bagn●** [banyee] *mpl* seaside resort; spa

bagnoschiuma [banyoskyooma] *n● (soap)* bubble bath

baita [ba-eeta] *f* mountain hut

ballare [ballaray] *v* to dance

ballerino, a [ballayreeno] *m, f* dancer

balneazione [balnay-atseeonay] ▸ 'divieto di balneazione' 'no swimming

balsamo [balsamo] *m (for hair)* conditioner

bambino, a [bambeeno] *m, f* chil● (little) boy, (little) girl; baby ◆ **bam●** **bini** [bambeenee] *mpl* children

bambola [bambola] *f* doll

bancarella [bankarella] *f* stand

banchina [bankeena] *f* quay, whar● ▸ 'banchina non transitabile' 'sof● shoulder' ▸ 'banchina spartitraffic●' 'median strip'

la bandiera tricolore

The Tricolor, the Italian flag, has one green, one white, and one red vertical stripe. It was adopted in 1946, the year Italy became a republic. The colors are sometimes said to represent Italy's green hills, snowy peaks, and the blood its people shed for their country.

banco [banko] *m (of store, bar)* counter; *(in market)* stand

Bancomat® [bankomat] *m* ATM; ATM card

bancone [bankonay] *m* counter

banconota [bankonota] *f (paper money)* bill

banda [banda] *f* band

bandiera [bandee-ayra] *f* flag

barattolo [barattolo] *m (glass)* jar; *(metal)* can; *(plastic)* pot

barbiere [barbee-ayray] *m* barber

barbone, a [barbonay] *m, f* tramp

barca [barka] *f* boat ▸ barca a remi rowboat ▸ barca a vela sailboat

barista [bareesta] *mf* bartender

Barocco [barokko] *m* ▸ il Barocco the Baroque

basilico [bazeeleeko] *m* basil

basso, a [basso] *adj* low; *(person)* short; *(tree)* small; *(water)* shallow

basta [basta] *excl* (that's) enough! ▸ basta con le chiacchiere! that's enough talking!

bastare [bastaray] *v* to be enough ▸ per prenotare, basta telefonare to book, you just have to phone up

battere [battayray] *v* to hit; to type; *(defeat)* to beat

battito [batteeto] *m (of clock)* ticking; heartbeat

baule [ba-oolay] *m (luggage, part of car)* trunk

Befana [bayfana] *f imaginary old woman similar to Santa Claus*

bel [bel] *adj* beautiful ▸ un bel regalo a beautiful present

bellezza [belletsa] *f* beauty ▸ che bellezza! fantastic!

bello [bello] *adj (woman, child, object)* beautiful; *(man)* handsome; *(movie)* good ▸ belle arti fine arts ▸ una bella idea a good idea ▸ una bella serata a lovely evening

bene [baynay] *adv* well ▸ va bene OK ▸ avete mangiato bene in albergo? was the food good in the hotel? ▸ bene! good!

la Befana

The *Befana* is a kindly old witch who is supposed to fly around on a broomstick on January 5th, the night before Epiphany, delivering presents. The next morning, good children find these in the stockings they've hung from their mantlepieces. Naughty children used to get coal instead of presents, but nowadays they get black sugar candy instead.

benvenuto, a [benvaynooto] *adj* welcome

benzina [bendzeena] *f* gas(oline)

benzinaio, a [ben-dzeena-yo] *m, f* gas pump attendant

bere [bayray] *v* to drink

bevanda [bayvanda] *f* drink

biancheria [bee-ankayree-a] *f* linen

bianco, a [bee-anko] *adj* white

biblioteca [beeblee-otayka] *f* library; bookcase

bicchiere [beekkee-ayray] *m (for drinking)* glass

bici [beechee] *n* bike

bicicletta [beecheecletta] *f* bicycle

bigiotteria [beejottayree-a] *f* costume jewelry store

biglietteria [beelyettayree-a] *f* ticket office; box office ▸ biglietteria automatica ticket machine

biglietto [beelyetto] *m* ticket ▸ biglietto intero full-price ticket ▸ biglietto ridotto discounted ticket

bignè [beenyay] *m* cream puff

biliardo [beelee-ardo] *m* billiards

binario [beenaree-o] *m* platform ▸ 'ai binari' ' this way to platforms'

biondo, a [bee-ondo] *adj (man)* blond; *(woman)* blonde

birra [beerra] *f* beer ▸ birra chiara lager ▸ birra scura stout ▸ birra alla spina draft beer

birreria [beerrayree-a] *f* bar

biscotto [beeskotto] *m* cookie

bisognare [beezonyaray] *v* to be necessary ▸ bisogna confermare you need to confirm

bisogno [beezonyo] *m* need

bistecca [beestekka] *f* steak ▸ bistecca al sangue rare steak ▸ bistecca alla fiorentina T-bone steak

bivio [beevee-o] *m* fork (in the road)

blocco [blokko] *m* block

blu [bloo] *adj* blue

boa [boa] *f* buoy

bocca [bokka] *f* mouth ▸ in bocca al lupo! good luck!

bolla [bolla] *f* blister

bollito, a [bolleeto] *adj* boiled ◆ *m* ≃ boiled beef

bombolone [bombolonay] *m doughnut filled with flavored egg custard*

bontà [bonta] *f* goodness

bordo [bordo] *m* edge ▸ vietato fumare a bordo della nave no smoking on board ship

borotalco® [borotalko] *m* talcum powder

borraccia [borracha] *f* water bottle

borsa [borsa] *f* bag ◆ Borsa [borsa] *f* Stock Exchange

borseggio [borsejo] *m* pickpocketing

borsetta [borsetta] *f* handbag, purse

bosco [bosko] *m* wood

botte [bottay] *f* barrel

bottega [bottayga] *f* store; *(of artist)* workshop

bottiglia [botteelya] *f* bottle

bottone [bottonay] *m* button

braccio [bracho] *m (of person)* arm

bracciolo [bracholo] *m (of chair)* arm

brace [brachay] *f* embers

braciola [brachola] *f* chop ▸ braciola di maiale pork chop

bresaola [brayza-ola] *f* bresaola, *air-dried thinly sliced salted beef*

briciola [breechola] *f* crumb

brindisi [breendeezee] *m* toast

britannico, a [breetanneekoo] *adj* British

brivido [breeveedo] *m* shiver

brodo [brodo] *m* broth; *(for cooking)* stock

bruciare [broocharay] *v* to burn

bruno, a [broono] *adj* brown

bruschetta [broosketta] *f* bruschetta, *toasted bread rubbed with garlic and drizzled with olive oil*

brutto, a [brootto] *adj* ugly; *(weather, news)* bad

buca [booka] *f* hole

buccia [boocha] *f (of banana, peach, potato)* skin; *(of orange, apple)* peel

budino [boodeeno] *m* pudding ▸ budino di riso rice pudding

bufera [boofayra] *f* storm

buffo, a [booffo] *adj* funny

buio, a [boo-yo] *adj & m* dark

buonanotte [boo-onanottay] *excl* good night!

buonasera [boo-onasayra] *excl* good evening!

buongiorno [boo-onjorno] *excl* good morning!; good afternoon!

buono, a [boo-ono] *adj* good ▸ buon viaggio! have a good trip!

burattino [booratteeno] *m* puppet

burrasca, che [boorraska] *f* storm

burro [boorro] *m* butter

burrone [boorronay] *m* ravine

bussola [boossola] *f* compass

busta [boosta] *f* envelope

buttafuori [boottafoo-oree] *m* bouncer

buttare [boottaray] *v* to throw

C

cabina [kabeena] *f* cabin ▸ cabina telefonica telephone booth

caccia [kacha] *f* hunting

cacciavite [kachaveetay] *m* screwdriver

cadere [kadayray] *v* to fall

caduta [kadoota] *f* fall ▸ 'caduta massi' 'falling rocks'

caffè [kaffay] *m* coffee ▸ caffè freddo iced coffee ▸ caffè corretto coffee with liqueur ▸ caffè lungo weak espresso ▸ caffè macchiato espresso with a dash of milk

caffellatte [kaffayllattay] *m* coffee with milk

calare [kalaray] *v* to lower

calcio [kalcho] *m* kick; *(sport)* soccer

calcolo [kalkolo] *m* calculation

caldo, a [kaldo] *adj* warm, hot ◆ *m* heat

---

il calcio

In Italy, you have to know how to talk about soccer, which is a real national passion. *Tifosi* (supporters) bet on the results of games each week using the *Totocalcio* betting form, whether their team is playing at home (*in casa*) or away (*in trasferta*), in the early matches (*gli anticipi*) or in the late ones (*i posticipi*). This goes on right up to the moment the *scudetto* (championship) is decided.

calendario [kalendaree-o] *m* calendar

calmante [kalmantay] *m* painkiller; sedative

calmo, a [kalmo] *adj* calm

calpestare [kalpestaray] *v* to trample ▸ 'non calpestare le aiuole/l'erba' 'keep off the grass'

calza [kaltsa] *f (of woman)* stocking; *(of man)* sock

calzoncini [kaltsoncheenee] *mpl* shorts

cambiare [kambee-aray] *v* to change

cambio [kambee-o] *m (of car)* gears; *(of currency)* exchange

camera [kamayra] *f* (bed)room ▸ camera con bagno en suite room ▸ camera matrimoniale double room ▸ camera singola single room

cameriere, a [kamayree-ayray] *m, f* waiter, waitress ▸ cameriere! waiter!

camicia [kameecha] *f (of man)* shirt; *(of woman)* blouse

camminare [kammeenaray] *v* to walk

camorra [kamorra] *f* Camorra, *Southern Italian Mafia*

campanello [kampanello] *m* bell ▸ 'suonare il campanello' 'please ring the bell'

campanile [kampaneelay] *m* bell tower

campeggio [kampejo] *m* campground

camper [kamper] *m (vehicle)* camper

campione, essa [kampee-onay] *m, f* champion ◆ *m* sample

campo [kampo] *m* field

canale [kanalay] *m* canal; *(TV)* channel

cancellare [kanchellaray] *v* to erase; to cross out; to delete; *(reservation)* to cancel

cancello [kanchello] *m* gate

candela [kandayla] *f* candle

candito [kandeeto] *m* candied fruit

cane [kanay] *m* dog

canna [kanna] *f* reed; *(for smoking)* joint

cannolo [kannolo] *m* pastry filled with flavored egg custard ▸ cannolo siciliano pastry filled with ricotta, candied fruit, and chocolate chips

cannone [kannonay] *m* cannon

canottiera [kanottee-ayra] *f* undershirt

cantante [kantantay] *mf* singer

cantare [kantaray] *v* to sing

canzone [kantsonay] *f* song

C.A.P. [kap] *abbr of* codice di avviamento postale postal code

capacità [kapacheeta] *n* capacity

capello [kapello] *m* hair

capire [kapeeray] *v* to understand ▸ non capisco I don't understand ▸ si capisce of course

capitaneria [kapeetanaree-a] *f* harbor master's office

capitello [kapeetello] *m (on column)* capital

capitolo [kapeetolo] *m* chapter

capitone [kapeetonay] *m* eel

capo [kapo] *m (of person, department, government)* head; *(extremity)* end

Capodanno [kapodanno] *m* New Year

capolavoro [kapolavoro] *m* masterpiece

capolinea [kapoleenay-a] *m* terminus

capoluogo [kapoloo-ogo] *m* ▸ capoluogo di regione regional capital

capostazione [kapostatsee-onay] *mf* station master

cappella [kappella] *f* chapel

cappello [kappello] *m* hat

cappero [kappero] *m (for eating)* caper

cappotto [kappotto] *m* coat

capra [kapra] *f* goat

capriolo [kapree-olo] *m* roe deer

capsula [kapsoola] *f* capsule

il carnevale

In the two weeks before Lent, there are carnival celebrations all over Italy. The most famous carnivals are those of Venice, Viareggio, Ivrea, and Putignano. There are parades with floats and costume parties for children and adults alike.

carabiniere [karabeenee-ayray] *m* carabiniere, *Italian military police officer*

caramella [karamella] *f* (piece of) candy

carbone [karbonay] *m* coal

carcere [karcheray] *m* prison

carciofo [karchofo] *m* artichoke ▸ carciofi alla romana *fried or roasted artichoke hearts with parsley, garlic and mint*

carica [kareeka] *f* (job) position

carico, a [kareeko] *adj* loaded

carie [karee-ay] *n* (tooth) decay

carino, a [kareeno] *adj* pretty; (kind) nice

carne [karnay] *f* meat ▸ carne macinata/tritata ground meat

carnevale [karnayvalay] *m* carnival

caro, a [karo] *adj* dear

carota [karota] *f* carrot

carreggiata [karrejata] *f* roadway

carrozza [karrotsa] *f* (horse-drawn) carriage; (on train) car

carta [karta] *f* (material) paper; map; menu; (for payment, membership) card ▸ carta d'identità identity card ▸ carta d'imbarco boarding pass ▸ carta verde *international car insurance certificate*

cartaviaggio [kartavee-ajo] *m* card entitling holder to travel by rail at reduced prices and to collect rail miles

cartello [kartello] *m* sign ▸ cartello stradale road sign

cartina [karteena] *f* map

cartoleria [kartolayree-a] *f* stationery store

cartolina [kartoleena] *f* postcard

casa [kaza] *f* house; home ▸ a casa di Stefano at Stefano's (house)

cascata [kaskata] *f* waterfall

cascina [kasheena] *f* farmhouse

casco [kasko] *m* helmet

casello [kazello] *m* tollbooth

casino [kazeeno] *m* (familiar) mess

caso [kazo] *m* case ▸ per caso by chance ▸ 'in caso d'emergenza rompere il vetro' 'in case of emergency, break glass'

cassa [kassa] *f* (container) box; (in bank) window; (in supermarket) checkout; (in store) cash register; (money) cash; (building) bank

cassaforte [kassafortay] *f* safe

cassata [kassata] *f* cassata, *ice-cream cake*

cassetta [kassetta] *f* box; cassette

castagna [kastanya] *f* chestnut

castello [kastello] *m* castle

catacomba [katakomba] *f* catacomb

catastrofe [katastrofay] *f* catastrophe

catena [katayna] *f* chain

catrame [katramay] *m* tar

cattedrale [kattaydralay] *f* cathedral

cattivo, a [katteevo] *adj* bad

causa [kowza] *f* cause

cava [kava] *f* quarry

cavalcavia [kavalkaveea] *m* overpass

cavallo, a [kavallo] *m, f* horse

cavatappi [kavatappee] *m* corkscrew

caverna [kaverna] *f* cave

caviale [kaveeaylay] *m* caviar

caviglia [kaveelya] *f* ankle

cavo [kavo] *m* cable

cavolfiore [kavolfee-oray] *m* cauliflower

cavolo [kavolo] *m* cabbage

ceci [chaychee] *mpl* chickpeas

cedro [chedro] *m* cedar; citron, *citrus fruit resembling a lemon*

celeste [chaylestay] *adj* sky blue

celibe [chayleebay] *adj* single

cella [chella] *f* cell

cellulare [chelloolaray] *m* cellphone

cemento [chaymento] *m* cement

cena [chayna] *f* dinner

cenere [chaynayray] *f* ash

cenone [chaynonay] *m* Christmas Eve *or* New Year's Eve dinner

centesimo, a [chentayzeemo] *num* hundredth ◆ *n* cent

centinaio [chenteena-yo] *m* ▸ un centinaio (di) about a hundred

cento [chento] *num* a/one hundred

centomila [chentomeela] *num* a/one hundred thousand

centralino [chentraleeno] *m* switchboard

centro [chentro] *m* center ▸ centro storico old town ▸ centro commerciale shopping center

cera [chayra] *f* wax; polish

cercare [cherkaray] *v* to look for

cerchio [cherkee-o] *m* circle

cerimonia [chayreemonee-a] *f* ceremony

cerotto [chayrotto] *m* Band-Aid®

certo [cherto] *adj* certain ◆ *adv* certainly

▸ un certo signor Rossi a (certain) Mr. Rossi

certosa [chertoza] *f* charterhouse

cervello [chervello] *m* brain

cesso [chesso] *m* (*familiar*) can, john

cetriolo [chetree-olo] *m* cucumber

che [kay] *pron & adj* what? ▸ che cosa desidera? what would you like? ▸ che ore sono? what time is it

chi [kee] *pron* who? ▸ chi è? who is it?

chiacchierare [kee-akkee-ayraray] *v* to chat

chiamare [kee-amaray] *v* to call ✦ **chiamarsi** [kee-amarsee] *v* to be called ▸ come ti chiami? what's your name? ▸ mi chiamo Lucia my name's Lucia

chiaro, a [kee-aro] *adj* clear

chiave [kee-avay] *f* key

chiedere [kee-aydayray] *v* to ask for

chiesa [kee-ayza] *f* church

chilo [keelo] *m* kilo

chilometro [keelometro] *m* kilometer

chiodo [kee-odo] *m* nail ▸ chiodi di garofano cloves

chiosco [kee-osko] *m* kiosk

chiostro [kee-ostro] *m* cloister

chitarra [keetarra] *f* guitar

chiudere [kee-oodayray] *v* to close, to shut ▸ 'si chiude da sé' 'door closes automatically'

chiuso, a [kee-oozo] *adj* closed ▸ 'chiuso per ferie' 'closed for vacation' ▸ 'chiuso per riposo settimanale' 'closed today'

chiusura [kee-oozoora] *f* closing

ci [chee] *adv* here ▸ c'è/ci sono there is/there are ▸ c'è gente there are people there ▸ ci si può andare a piedi you can go there on foot ▸ ci penso io I'll see to it

cibo [cheebo] *m* food

cieco, a [chayko] *m, f* blind person

Cinecittà

Founded in 1937 and located on a vast site on the outskirts of Rome, the *Cinecittà* studios are Italy's answer to Hollywood. In fact, many major American movies such as 'Ben Hur' were made there. Famous names of Italian cinema such as Fellini, Visconti and Pasolini made their masterpieces there, and today Nanni Moretti and Roberto Benigni follow in their footsteps.

cielo [chaylo] *m* sky; heaven

ciglio [cheelyo] *m (of road)* edge; eyelash

ciliegia [cheelee-ayja] *f* cherry

cima [cheema] *f* top ▸ cima alla genovese *boiled stuffed breast of veal served cold and sliced*

cimitero [cheemeetayro] *m* cemetery

Cinecittà [cheenaycheetta] *f* Cinecittà

cinese [cheenayzay] *adj* Chinese

cinghiale [cheenghee-alay] *m* (wild) boar

cinquanta [cheenkwanta] *num* fifty

cinque [cheenkway] *num* five

cinta [cheenta] *f* city walls

cintura [cheentoora] *f* belt ▸ cintura di sicurezza seat belt, safety belt ▸ allacciare le cinture di sicurezza fasten your seat belts

cioccolata [chokkolata] *f* chocolate ▸ cioccolata (calda) hot chocolate

cioè [cho-ay] *conj* that is

cipolla [cheepolla] *f* onion

circa [cheerka] *adv* about, around

circo, chi [cheerko] *m* circus

circolare [cheerkolaray] *adj* circular ♦ *v (vehicle)* to go

circolazione [cheerkolatsee-onay] *f* traffic ▸ circolazione stradale (road) traffic

circondare [cheerkondaray] *v* to surround

circuito [cheerkoo-eeto] *m* circuit

citofono [cheetofono] *m* intercom

città [cheetta] *f* city; town ▸ la Città del Vaticano Vatican City

cittadino, a [cheettadeeno] *m, f (of town, city)* inhabitant; *(of country)* citizen ♦ *adj* city; town

civiltà [cheeveelta] *f* civilization

classe [klassay] *f* class ▸ classe turistica tourist class

cliccare [kleekkaray] *v* to click

cliente [klee-entay] *mf* customer; *(of hotel)* guest

clima [kleema] *m* climate

clinica [kleeneeca] *f* clinic

cocco [kokko] *m* coconut palm

cocomero [kokomayro] *m* watermelon

coda [koda] *f* tail; *(of people)* line ▸ fare la coda to stand in line

codice [kodeechay] *m* code ▸ codice di avviamento postale postal code

cofano [kofano] *m (of car)* hood

cognato, a [konyato] *m, f* brother-in-law, sister-in-law

cognome [conyomay] *m* surname, last name

coincidenza [ko-eencheedentsa] *f* coincidence; *(on public transportation)* connection ▸ perdere la coincidenza to miss one's connection

colazione [kolatsee-onay] *f* breakfast; lunch

la comitiva

The word *comitiva* is used in spoken language to refer to a group of friends from the same neighborhood, often young people, who meet up every day and hang out together. In some cases they even have their own private slang (*gergo*).

collana [kollana] *f* necklace

colle [kollay] *m* hill

collegare [kollaygaray] *v* to connect

collezione [kolletseeonay] *f* collection

collirio [kolleeree-o] *m* eyedrops

collo [kollo] *m* neck

colomba [kolomba] *f* dove ▸ colomba (pasquale) *dove-shaped cake eaten at Easter*

colonia [kolonee-a] *f* colony; camp

colonna [kolonna] *f* column

colore [koloray] *m* color ▸ a colori (movie, TV, photo) color

Colosseo [kolossay-o] *m* ▸ il Colosseo the Colosseum

colpa [kolpa] *f* fault

colpo [kolpo] *m* blow

coltello [koltello] *m* knife

comando [komando] *m* command

combinazione [kombeenatsee-onay] *f* combination

come [komay] *adv* as ▸ come no? of course! ▸ come ti chiami? what's your name?

cominciare [komeencharay] *v* to start, to begin

comitiva [komeeteeva] *f* group

commedia [kommaydee-a] *f* play; comedy

commercio [kommercho] *m* commerce ▸ fuori commercio not for sale

commesso, a [kommesso] *m, f* sales clerk

commissario [kommeessaree-o] *m* (police) captain

commissione [kommeessee-onay] *f* committee; errand; (money) commission

comodità [komodeeta] *f* comfort

comodo, a [komodo] *adj* comfortable ▸ faccia con comodo take your time

compartimento [komparteemento] *m* compartment

compenso [kompenso] *m* payment; compensation

compiere [kompee-ayray] *v* to carry out

compleanno [komplayanno] *m* birthday ▸ buon compleanno! happy birthday!

complessivo, a [komplesseevo] *adj* overall

complesso, a [komplesso] *adj* complex ◆ *m* (of musicians) group

complicato, a [kompleekato] *adj* complicated

complimento [kompleemento] *m* compliment

comprare [kompraray] *v* to buy

comprendere [komprendayray] *v* to understand

compreso, a [komprayzo] *adj* included ▸ tutto compreso all-inclusive

compressa [kompressa] *f* tablet, pill

comunale [komoonalay] *adj* municipal

comune [komoonay] *m* city council; town hall; town ◆ *adj* common; (friend) mutual ▸ in comune shared

comunicare [komooneekaray] *v* to communicate

con [kon] *prep* with ▸ con piacere! with pleasure!

concerto [koncherto] *m* concert

condire [kondeeray] *v (salad)* to dress

condizionatore [kondeetsee-onatoray] *m* air conditioner

condizione [kondeetsee-onay] *f* condition

condominio [kondomeenee-o] *m* condominium

conducente [kondoochentay] *m* driver ▸ 'non parlare al conducente' 'do not speak to the driver'

confermare [konfermaray] *v* to confirm

confetto [konfetto] *m* Jordan almond

confezione [konfetsee-onay] *f* pack

confine [konfeenay] *m* border

conflitto [konfleetto] *m* conflict

confondere [konfondayray] *v* to confuse

confortevole [konfortayvolay] *adj* comfortable

confronto [konfronto] *m* comparison ▸ in confronto a in comparison to/with

confusione [konfoozee-onay] *f* confusion; noise

congelare [konjaylaray] *v* to freeze

congratulazioni [kongratoolatsee-onee] *fpl* congratulations

congresso [kongresso] *m* conference

coniglio [koneelyo] *m* rabbit ▸ coniglio in salmi *half-roasted rabbit finished in wine sauce*

cono [kono] *m* cone

conoscere [konoshayray] *v* to know

consegna [konsenya] *f* delivery

conseguenza [konsaygwentsa] *f* consequence

consenso [konsenso] *m* consent

consentire [konsenteeray] *v* to allow

conserva [konserva] *f* purée; preserve

consigliare [konseelyaray] *v* to advise

consiglio [konseelyo] *m* advice; council

consolato [konsolato] *m* consulate

consumare [konsoomaray] *v* to consume ◆ **consumarsi** [konsoomarsee] *v* ▸ 'da consumarsi preferibilmente entro' 'best before'

consumazione [konsoomatsee-onay] *f* drink; snack

contadino, a [kontadeeno] *m, f* farmer

contante [kontantay] *m* cash ▸ pagare in contanti to pay (in) cash

contare [kontaray] *v* to count

contattare [kontattaray] *v* to contact

contemporaneamente [kontemporanay-amentay] *adv* at the same time

contento, a [kontento] *adj* pleased

continente [konteenentay] *m* continent; mainland

continuare [konteenoo-aray] *v* to continue

conto [konto] *m* calculation; *(in restaurant)* check; *(in hotel)* bill

contorno [kontorno] *m* side dish

contrabbando [kontrabbando] *m* contraband

contraccettivo [kontrachetteevo] *m* contraceptive

contrassegno [kontrassenyo] *m* mark ▸ spedire in contrassegno to send COD

contrattempo [kontrattempo] *m (difficulty)* hitch

contratto [kontratto] *m* contract

contravvenzione [kontravventseeonay] *f* infringement; fine

contro [kontro] *prep* against

controllare [kontrollaray] *v* to check ▸ 'controllare il resto' 'check your change'

controllo [kontrollo] *m* control ▸ 'controllo elettronico della velocità' 'speed trap'

controllore [kontrolloray] *m* conductor

contromano [kontromano] *adv* the wrong way

convalidare [konvaleedaray] *v* to stamp ▸ 'convalidare all'inizio del viaggio' 'stamp your ticket before traveling'

convenire [konvayneeray] *v* to be advisable

convento [konvento] *m* convent; monastery

conversazione [konversatsee-onay] *f* conversation

convincere [konveenchayray] *v* to convince

coperchio [koperkee-o] *m* cover; lid

coperta [koperta] *f* blanket; *(on ship)* deck

coperto [koperto] *m* cover charge; place setting

copia [kopee-a] *f* copy

coppa [koppa] *f* glass; bowl; cured neck of pork ▸ coppa dell'olio *(in car)* oil pan

coppia [koppee-a] *f* couple

coprire [kopreeray] *v* to cover

corallo [korallo] *m* coral

corda [korda] *f* rope; string

cordialmente [cordialmentay] *adv* warmly

coriandoli [koree-andolee] *mpl* confetti

coriandolo [koree-andolo] *m* cilantro

cornetto [kornetto] *m* croissant; *(ice cream)* cone

cornicione [korneechonay] *m* cornice

corno [korno] *m* horn; antler

coro [koro] *m* chorus; choir

corona [korona] *f* crown

corpo [korpo] *m* body

corrente [korrentay] *f* current; draft

correre [korrayray] *v* to run

corridoio [korreedo-yo] *m* corridor

corriera [korree-ayra] *f* bus

corriere [korree-ayray] *m* courier

corrimano [korreemano] *m* handrail

corsa [korsa] *f* run; race; *(on public transportation)* trip ▸ faccio una corsa al supermercato I'm just heading over to the supermarket

corsia [korseea] *f* *(on road)* lane; *(in hospital)* ward ▸ corsia preferenziale bus lane ▸ 'corsia d'emergenza' 'shoulder' ▸ 'corsia chiusa' 'lane closed'

Corsica [korseeka] *f* la Corsica Corsica

corso [korso] *m* course ▸ corsi di lingua language course

cortile [korteelay] *m* courtyard; playground

corto, a [korto] *adj* short

cosa [koza] *f* thing ▸ cosa? what? ▸ cosa c'è? what is it?

coscia [kosha] *f* *(of person)* thigh; *(piece of meat)* leg

cosciotto [koshotto] *m* *(of lamb)* leg

così [kozee] *adv* like this/that ▸ meglio così it's all for the best ▸ proprio così! exactly! ▸ e così via and so on

coso [kozo] *m* *(familiar)* thing

costa [kosta] *f* coast

costare [kostaray] *v* to cost

costata [kostata] *f* chop

costituzione [kosteetootsee-onay] *f* constitution

costo [kosto] *m* cost ▸ a tutti i costi at all costs

costola [kostola] *f* rib

costoletta [kostoletta] *f* cutlet

costoso, a [kostozo] *adj* expensive

costringere [kostreenjayray] *v* to force

costruire [kostroo-eeray] *v* to build

costume [kostoomay] *m* costume; custom ▸ **costume da bagno** *(for woman)* swimsuit; *(for man)* swimming trunks

cotechino [kotaykeeno] *m large pork sausage generally eaten with lentils at New Year*

cotoletta [kotoletta] *f* chop; cutlet ▸ **cotoletta alla milanese** Wiener schnitzel

cotone [kotonay] *m* cotton

cotto, a [kotto] *adj* cooked ▸ **ben cotto** well done

cottura [kottoora] *f* cooking

cozza [kotsa] *f* mussel

credere [kraydayray] *v* to believe

credito [kraydeeto] *m* credit

crema [krayma] *f* cream; custard

criminale [kreemeenalay] *mf* criminal

cripta [kreepta] *f* crypt

crisi [kreezee] *f* crisis ▸ **in crisi** in crisis

cristallo [kreestallo] *m* crystal

cristiano, a [kreestee-ano] *adj & m, f* Christian

Cristo [kreesto] *m* Christ ▸ **avanti Cristo** B.C. ▸ **dopo Cristo** A.D.

critica [kreeteeca] *f* criticism; critique; review

Croazia [kroatsee-a] *f* ▸ **la Croazia** Croatia

crocchetta [krokketta] *f* croquette

croce [krochay] *f* cross ▸ **la Croce Rossa** the Red Cross

crociera [krochayra] *f* cruise

crostaceo [krostachay-o] *m* crustacean

crostata [krostata] *f* tart

crostino [krosteeno] *m* canapé ▸ **crostini di fegato** *small pieces of toast spread with a chicken liver, anchovy, and caper pâté and served hot*

crudo, a [kroodo] *adj* raw; underdone

cuccetta [koochetta] *f* *(on train)* sleeping berth; *(on ship)* bunk

cucchiaio [kookkee-a-yo] *m* spoon

cucina [koocheena] *f* kitchen; cooking

cucinare [koocheenaray] *v* to cook

cuffia [kooffee-a] *f* swimming cap ▸ '**è obbligatorio l'uso della cuffia**' 'swimming caps must be worn'

cugino, a [koojeeno] *m, f* cousin

cultura [kooltoora] *f* culture

cuocere [koo-ochayray] *v* to cook

cuoco, a [koo-oco] *m, f* chef; cook

cuoio [koo-o-yo] *m* leather ▸ **cuoio capelluto** scalp

cuore [koo-oray] *m* heart

cura [koora] *f* care ▸ **cura dimagrante** diet

curva [koorva] *f* curve ▸ '**curva pericolosa**' 'dangerous curve'

cuscino [koosheeno] *m* cushion; pillow

custode [koostoday] *mf* janitor; *(in museum)* curator

d

da [da] *prep* from; by

dai [da-ee] *excl* come on (now)!

dal [dal] *prep* from the; by the ▸ lontano dal paese far from the village ▸ dal medico at the doctor ▸ dal finestrino through the window

danno [danno] *m* damage

danza [dantsa] *f* dance

dappertutto [dappertootto] *adv* everywhere

dare [daray] *v* to give

data [data] *f* date ▸ data di nascita date of birth

dato [dato] *m* piece of information ▸ dato che given that

davanti [davantee] *m* front ▸ davanti a in front of

davvero [davvayro] *adv* really

debole [daybolay] *adj* weak

decaffeinato, a [daykaffay-eenato] *adj* decaffeinated

decidere [daycheedayray] *v* to decide

decimo, a [decheemo] *num* tenth

decina [daycheena] *f* ten

decisione [daycheezee-onay] *f* decision

decollare [daykollaray] *v* to take off

definizione [dayfeeneetsee-onay] *f* definition

delicato, a [dayleekato] *adj* delicate

delitto [dayleetto] *m* murder; crime

delizioso, a [deleetsee-ozo] *adj* delicious

delusione [dayloozee-onay] *f* disappointment

democratico, a [daymokrateeko] *adj* democratic

denaro [daynaro] *m* money ▸ denaro contante cash

denominazione [daynomeenatsee-onay] *f* denomination

dente [dentay] *m* tooth

dentifricio [denteefreecho] *m* toothpaste

dentro [dentro] *adv* inside ▸ là dentro in there

denunciare [daynooncharay] *v* to report

deposito [daypozeeto] *m* deposit ▸ deposito bagagli baggage room

desiderare [dayzeedayraray] *v* to want

destinazione [desteenatsee-onay] *f* destination

destra [destra] *f* right

detergente [dayterjentay] *adj* cleansing

detersivo [dayterseevo] *m* detergent

dettaglio [dettalyo] *m* detail

deviazione [dayvee-atsee-onay] *f* detour

di [dee] *prep* of ▸ di notte at night ▸ statua di marmo marble statue ▸ al piano di sopra on the floor above

diagnosi [dee-anyozee] *f* diagnosis

dialetto [dee-aletto] *m* dialect

diarrea [dee-array-a] *f* diarrhea

dicembre [deechembray] *m* December

dichiarare [deekee-araray] *v* to declare

diciannove [deechannovay] *num* nineteen

diciannovesimo, a [deechannovayzeemo] *num* nineteenth

diciassette [deechassettay] *num* seventeen

diciassettesimo, a [deechassettay-zeemo] *num* seventeenth

diciottesimo, a [deechottayzeemo] *num* eighteenth

diciotto [deechotto] *num* eighteen

dieci [dee-aychee] *num* ten

dieta [dee-ayta] *f* diet ▪ sono a dieta I'm on a diet

dietro [dee-aytro] *adv* behind ▪ dietro pagamento on payment

difesa [deefayza] *f* defense

difetto [deefetto] *m* defect

differenza [deeffayrentsa] *f* difference ▪ a differenza di unlike

difficile [deeffeecheelay] *adj* difficult ▪ è difficile che it's unlikely that

diga [deega] *f* dam

digitale [deejeetalay] *adj* digital

digiuno [deejoono] *m* fasting

dimagrire [deemagreeray] *v* to lose weight

dimenticare [deementeekaray] *v* to forget

dintorni [deentornee] *mpl* surrounding area ▪ nei dintorni di around

dio [dee-o] *m* god

dipendere [deependayray] *v* to depend ▪ dipende it depends

dipinto [deepeento] *m* painting

diplomatico [deeplomateeko] *m* diplomat; *whipped cream and liqueur puff pastry*

dire [deeray] *v* to say ▪ dica pure can I help you? ▪ a dir poco to say the least

diretto, a [deeretto] *adj* direct ◆ *n* direct train ▪ il diretto per Bologna the direct train to Bologna

direzione [deeretsee-onay] *f* direction

dirottare [deerottaray] *v* to hijack

disabitato, a [deezabeetato] *adj* uninhabited

disagio [deezajo] *m* inconvenience; discomfort ▪ mi sento a disagio I feel uncomfortable

discarica [deeskareeka] *f* dump

discesa [deeshayza] *f* descent ▪ 'discesa a mare' 'to beach'

disco [deesko] *m* disk ▪ disco orario *type of parking permit showing arrival time of vehicle*

discoteca [deeskotayka] *f* (night)club

disdire [deesdeeray] *v* to cancel

disegnare [deezenyaray] *v* to draw; to design

disegno [deezenyo] *m* drawing; design

disinfettante [deezeenfettantay] *adj* disinfectant

disoccupato, a [deezokkoopato] *m, f* unemployed person

disonesto, a [deezonesto] *adj* dishonest

disordine [deezordeenay] *m* mess

dispari [deesparee] *adj (number)* odd

disperso, a [deesperso] *m, f* missing person ▪ è stato dato per disperso he's been reported missing

dispiacere [deespee-achayray] *v* ▪ mi dispiace I'm sorry

disposto, a [deesposto] *adj* ▪ disposto a tutto desperate

dissestato, a [deessestato] *adj (road)* uneven

distante [deestantay] *adj* far

distanza [deestantsa] *f* distance

distendere [deestendayray] *v (legs)* to stretch

distintivo [deesteenteevo] *m* badge

distorsione [deestorsee-onay] *f* sprain

distributore [deestreebootoray] *m* ▪ distributore automatico ATM ▪ distributore (di benzina) gas pump

distruzione [deestrootsee-onay] *f* destruction

disturbare [deestoorbaray] *v* to disturb
▸ 'non disturbare il conducente' 'do not speak to the driver' ▸ disturbo se fumo? do you mind if I smoke?

disturbo [deestoorbo] *m* inconvenience

dito [deeto] *m* finger ▸ dito del piede toe

ditta [deetta] *f* firm

diventare [deeventaray] *v* to become

diversi, e [deeversee] *adj* several

diverso, a [deeverso] *adj* different

divertente [deevertentay] *adj* entertaining

dividere [deeveedaray] *v* to divide

divieto [deevee-ayto] *m* prohibition
▸ 'divieto di accesso' 'no entry'
▸ 'divieto di transito' 'no thoroughfare'

divisa [deeveeza] *f* uniform

dizionario [deetsee-onaree-o] *m* dictionary

doccia [docha] *f* shower

documento [dokoomento] *m* document
▸ documenti, per favore your papers, please

dodicesimo, a [dodeechayzeemo] *num* twelfth

dodici [dodeechee] *num* twelve

dogana [dogana] *f* customs

dolce [dolchay] *adj* sweet ◆ *m* dessert; cake

dolcificante [dolcheefeekantay] *m* sweetener

Dolomiti [dolomeetee] *fpl* ▸ le Dolomiti the Dolomites

dolore [doloray] *m* pain

domanda [domanda] *f* question

domandare [domandaray] *v* to ask

domani [domanee] *adv* tomorrow

domenica [domayneeka] *f* Sunday

donna [donna] *f* woman ▸ donna di servizio maid

dono [dono] *m* gift

dopo [dopo] *adv* afterward ◆ *prep* after
▸ a dopo! see you later

dopodomani [dopodomanee] *adv* the day after tomorrow

doposci [doposhee] *m* snowboot

doppio, a [doppee-o] *adj & adv* double

dorato, a [dorato] *adj* golden

dosso [dosso] *m* bump

dott. *abbr of* **dottore** Dr.

dottore, essa [dottoray] *m, f* doctor

dove [dovay] *adv* where ▸ dov'è? where is it? ▸ dove andate? where are you going?

dovere [dovayray] *v* to have to

dovunque [dovoonkway] *adv* wherever; everywhere

dozzina [dodzeena] *f* ▸ una dozzina a dozen

dritto [dreetto] *adj* straight ▸ andate sempre dritto keep on going straight

droga [droga] *f* drug

dubbio [doobbee-o] *m* doubt

due [doo-ay] *num* two

duemila [doo-aymeela] *num* two thousand

dunque [doonkway] *conj* so

duomo [doo-omo] *m* cathedral

durante [doorantay] *prep* during

duro, a [dooro] *adj* hard

e [ay] *conj* and ▸ e io? what about me?

è [ay] *v* is ▸ è tardi it's late

ebbrezza [ebbretsa] *f* ▸ in stato di ebbrezza inebriated

eccesso [echesso] *m* excess ▸ eccesso di velocità speeding

eccezione [echetsee-onay] *f* exception ▸ salvo eccezioni with some exceptions

ecco [ekko] *adv* here's/there's ▸ ecco a lei *(in a store)* here/there you are ▸ ecco fatto! there you go! ▸ eccolo! *(person)* here he is; *(thing)* here it is

eccome [ekkomay] *adv* and how

edera [aydayra] *f* ivy

edicola [aydeekola] *f* newsstand

edificio [aydeefeecho] *m* building

effetto [effetto] *m* effect ▸ in effetti in fact

elastico, a [aylasteeko] *adj* elastic; *(body)* flexible

Elba [èlba] *f* ▸ l'isola d'Elba the island of Elba

elenco [aylenko] *m* list ▸ elenco telefonico telephone directory

elicottero [ayleekottero] *m* helicopter

emergenza [aymerjentsa] *f* emergency

emicrania [aymeekranee-a] *f* migraine

emorragia [aymorajee-a] *f* hemorrhage

ennesimo, a [aynnayzeemo] *adj* umpteenth

enoteca [aynotayka] *f* wine store

ente [entay] *m (organization)* body

entrambi, e [entrambee] *pron* both

entrare [entraray] *v* to go/come in ▸ (questo) non c'entra niente that's got nothing to do with it

entrata [entrata] *f* entrance

entro [entro] *prep* in ▸ entro una settimana in a week

Eolie [ayolee-ay] *fpl* ▸ le (isole) Eolie the Aeolian Islands

eppure [eppooray] *conj* and yet

equipaggiamento [aykweepajamento] *m* equipment

equivoco [aykweevoko] *m* misunderstanding

erba [erba] *f* grass

eredità [ayraydeeta] *f* inheritance

errore [erroray] *m* mistake, error ▸ per errore by mistake

eruzione [ayrootsee-onay] *f* eruption

esame [ayzamay] *m* examination ▸ esame del sangue blood test

esatto, a [ayzatto] *adj* exact

esclusivo, a [eskloozeevo] *adj* exclusive

escursione [eskoorsee-onay] *f* trip

esempio [ayzempee-o] *m* example ▸ ad/per esempio for example

esercito [ayzercheeto] *m* army

esercizio [ayzerchetsee-o] *m* exercise; *(store, restaurant etc.)* business

esistere [ayzeestayray] *v* to exist

esperienza [espayree-entsa] *f* experience

esperimento [espayreemento] *m* experiment

esperto, a [esperto] *m, f* expert

esplodere [esplodayray] *v* to explode

espressione [espressee-onay] *f* expression

espresso [espresso] *m* espresso

essenziale [essentsee-alay] *adj* essential

essere [essayray] *v* to be ▸ c'è/ci sono there is/there are

estate [estatay] *f* summer

esterno, a [esterno] *adj* external

estero [estayro] *m* ▸ l'estero foreign countries ▸ all'estero abroad

estintore [esteentoray] *m* extinguisher

estivo, a [esteevo] *adj* summer

estraneo, a [estranay-o] *m, f* stranger ▸ 'vietato l'ingresso agli estranei' 'authorized personnel only'

estremo, a [estraymo] *adj* extreme

età [ayta] *f* age ▸ raggiungere la maggiore età to come of age

eterno, a [ayterno] *adj* eternal

ettaro [ellaro] *m* hectare

etto [etto] *m* hundred grams ▸ due etti di prosciutto two hundred grams of ham

europeo, a [ay-ooropayo] *adj* European

evento [ayvento] *m* event

evitare [ayveetaray] *v* to avoid

extracomunitario, a [extrakomoonee-taree-o] *m, f* non-EU citizen

fa [fa] *adv* ago ▸ due ore fa two hours ago

fabbrica [fabbreeka] *f* factory

faccenda [fachenda] *f* matter

faccia [facha] *f* face

facciata [fachata] *f* front

fagiano [fajano] *m* pheasant

fagiolino [fajoleeno] *m* green bean

fagiolo [fajolo] *m* bean ▸ fagioli all'uccelletto *beans in a tomato and sage sauce*

fai da te [fa-ee da tay] *m* do-it-yourself

falò [falo] *m* bonfire

fama [fama] *f* fame

fame [famay] *f* hunger

famiglia [fameelya] *f* family

famoso, a [famozo] *adj* famous

fanale [fanalay] *m* (of vehicle) light

fango [fango] *m* mud

fantasma [fantasma] *m* ghost; (sexual) fantasy

faraona [faraona] *f* guinea fowl

farcito, a [farcheeto] *adj* stuffed; (pastry, cake) filled

fare [faray] *v* to do; to make ▸ quanto fa? how much is it? ▸ fa caldo/freddo it's hot/cold

farfalla [farfalla] *f* butterfly

farinata [fareenata] *f* flat bread made from chickpeas

fascia [fasha] *f* sash ▸ fascia elastica elastic bandage ▸ fascia oraria time slot

fastidio [fasteedee-o] *m* trouble ▸ le dà fastidio se fumo? do you mind if I smoke?

fatica [fateeka] *f* effort ▸ a fatica hardly

fatto, a [fatto] *m* fact ◆ *adj* ▸ fatto in casa homemade ▸ sono fatti miei that's my business

favore [favoray] *m* favor ▸ fare un favore to do a favor ▸ per favore please

febbraio [febbra-yo] *m* February

febbre [febbray] *f* temperature; fever

Ferragosto

August 15th in Italy is known as *Ferragosto*, from the Latin *feriae augusti*, 'August holidays.' It is a public holiday and people traditionally enjoy a day out at the seaside, in the country, by the lake, or in the mountains.

fegato [faygato] *m* liver ▸ fegato alla veneziana liver and onions

felice [fayleechay] *adj* happy

felpa [felpa] *f* sweatshirt

femmina [femmeena] *f (child)* girl; *(animal)* female

femminile [femmeeneelay] *adj* feminine; female

feriale [fayree-alay] *adj* weekday

ferie [fayree-ay] *fpl* vacation

ferita [fereeta] *f* injury

fermare [fermaray] *v* to stop

fermata [fermata] *f* stop ▸ 'fermata prenotata' 'stop requested' ▸ 'fermata a richiesta' *stop at which bus halts only by request of a dismounting or boarding passenger*

fermo, a [fermo] *adj* still

ferragosto [ferragosto] *m August 15th holiday*

ferro [ferro] *m (metal)* iron ▸ ferro battuto wrought iron ▸ toccare ferro to knock on wood

ferrovia [ferrovee-a] *f* railroad

festa [festa] *f* holiday ▸ 'buone feste' 'happy holidays'

festival [festeeval] *f* festival

festivo, a [festeevo] *adj* festive

fetta [fetta] *f* slice

fettuccine [fettoocheenay] *fpl* fettuccine

fiamma [fee-amma] *f* flame

fianco [fee-anko] *m* side ▸ di fianco alla chiesa next to the church

fico [feeko] *m* fig ▸ fico d'India prickly pear

fidanzato, a [feedantsato] *m, f* boyfriend, girlfriend

fidarsi [feedarsee] *v* ▸ fidarsi di to trust ▸ non fidarti di lui don't trust him

fiducia [feedoocha] *f* confidence

fiera [fee-ayra] *f* fair

figlio, a [feelyo] *m, f* child, son, daughter ▸ hanno tre figli they have three children

fila [feela] *f (of people)* line; *(in theater)* row ▸ fare la fila to stand in line

filetto [feeletto] *m* fillet ▸ filetti di pollo chicken fillets

filo [filo] *m* thread ▸ filo spinato barbed wire

il Festival di Sanremo

Held annually in the town of San Remo, in Liguria, the Sanremo Festival has been one of Italy's most popular musical events since 1951. It is a song contest for pop and easy-listening music and is broadcast live on the main radio and TV channels, attracting huge audiences every year.

filone [feelonay] *m large long baguette*

filtro [feeltro] *m* filter ▸ con filtro filter-tipped

finalmente [feenalmentay] *adv* finally

finché [feenkay] *conj* as long as

fine [feenay] *f* end ▸ fine settimana weekend ▸ alla fine sono rimasto I stayed in the end

finestra [feenestra] *f* window

finestrino [feenestreeno] *m (of car)* window

finire [feeneeray] *v* to finish ▸ dov'è finito il mio cellulare? what happened to my cell?

fino [feeno] *prep* ▸ fino a as far as

finocchio [feenokkee-o] *m* fennel

finto, a [feento] *adj* false

fiore [fee-oray] *m* flower ▸ a fior d'acqua on the surface of the water

firma [feerma] *f* signature

fisso, a [feesso] *adj* fixed

fiume [fee-oomay] *m* river

focaccia [fokacha] *f* focaccia, *flat salty bread made with olive oil*

foce [fochay] *f (of river)* mouth

foglio [folyo] *m* sheet

fogna [fonya] *f* sewer

folla [folla] *f* crowd

follia [follee-a] *f* madness

fondo [fondo] *m* bottom ▸ in fondo at the bottom ▸ fino in fondo alla strada right to the end of the street

fonduta [fondoota] *f* fondue

fontana [fontana] *f* fountain

fonte [fontay] *f* spring

fontina [fonteena] *f* fontina, *whole-milk hard cheese*

forbici [forbeechee] *fpl* scissors

forchetta [forketta] *f* fork

foresta [foresta] *f* forest

formaggio [formajo] *m* cheese

formica [formeeka] *f* ant

fornello [fornello] *m* burner ▸ fornello da campeggio camping stove

forno [forno] *m* oven; bakery ▸ forno a legna wood-fired oven ▸ pizza cotta nel forno a legna pizza cooked in a wood-fired oven ▸ in forno in the oven

foro [foro] *m* hole; *(Roman)* forum

forse [forsay] *adv* perhaps, maybe

fortezza [fortetsa] *f* fortress

fortuna [fortoona] *f* luck ▸ per fortuna luckily

forza [fortsa] *f* strength; *(violence)* force ▸ forza! come on!

foschia [foskee-a] *f* mist

foto [foto] *f* photo

fotografia [fotografee-a] *f* photography; photograph

fototessera [fototessayra] *f* passport-sized photograph

fra [fra] *prep* in ▸ fra cinque minuti in five minutes

fragola [fragola] *f* strawberry

frana [frana] *f* landslide

francese [franchayzay] *adj* French

Francia [francha] *f* ▸ la Francia France

francobollo [frankobollo] *m* stamp

frappè [frappay] *m* milk shake

frate [fratay] *m* monk

fratello [fratello] *m* brother

frattempo [frattempo] *m* ▸ nel frattempo in the meantime

frattura [frattoora] *f* fracture

frazione [fratsee-onay] *f* hamlet

freccia [frecha] *f* arrow; turn signal

freddo, a [freddo] *adj* cold

frenare [fraynaray] *v (vehicle)* to brake

freno [frayno] *m* brake

fresco, a [fresko] *adj* fresh

fretta [fretta] *f* hurry ▸ vado di fretta I'm in a hurry

i fumetti

Comic books and graphic novels are enormously popular in Italy, and not just with children. Some have even been adapted for film or television. Characters like Lupo Alberto, Tex, Corto Maltese, Dylan Dog, Julia, Diabolik, Martin Mystère, Zagor, Nathan Never and Mister No have huge cult followings.

frigorifero [freegoreefayro] *m* refrigerator

frittata [freettata] *f* omelette

frittella [freettella] *f* fritter

fritto, a [freetto] *adj* fried ▸ fritto misto alla piemontese *giblet and vegetable fritters* ▸ fritto misto di pesce mixed fried fish

frizzante [freedzantay] *adj* fizzy

fronte [frontay] *f* forehead ▸ di fronte opposite

frullato [froollato] *m* *drink made from puréed fruit or vegetables*

frutta [frootta] *f* fruit

fulmine [foolmeenay] *m* lightning

fumatore, trice [foomatoray] *m, f* smoker

fumetti [foomettee] *mpl* comic books

fumo [foomo] *m* smoke

fungo [foongo] *m* mushroom

funivia [fooneevee-a] *f* cable car

funzionare [foontsee-onaray] *v* to work

fuoco [foo-oco] *m* fire ▸ al fuoco! fire! ▸ mettere a fuoco *(camera)* to focus

fuori [foo-oree] *adv* outside ▸ 'fuori servizio' out of order ▸ fuori mano out of the way

fuoristrada [foo-oreestrada] *m* off-road vehicle

furto [foorto] *m* robbery

fuso [foozo] *m* ▸ fuso orario time zone

g

gabinetto [gabeenetto] *m* bathroom

galleria [gallayree-a] *f* tunnel ▸ galleria d'arte art gallery ▸ 'in galleria accendere i fari' 'turn headlights on in tunnel'

Galles [galles] *n* ▸ il Galles Wales

gallese [gallayzay] *adj* Welsh

gallina [galleena] *f* hen

gallo [gallo] *m* rooster

gamba [gamba] *f* leg

gamberetto [gambayretto] *m* shrimp

gambero [gambayro] *m* crayfish

gamberoni [gambayronee] *m* Norway lobsters

gara [gara] *f* competition

garanzia [garantsee-a] *f* guarantee

Garda [garda] *m* ▸ il lago di Garda Lake Garda

gas [gas] *m* gas

gasolio [gazolee-o] *m* diesel

gassato, a [gassato] *adj* fizzy

il Giro d'Italia

First held in 1909, the *Giro d'Italia* is a 3,500 km cycle race in 21 stages around the Italian peninsula that attracts an international field of competitors. The winner gets to wear the famous *maglia rosa* (pink jersey).

gatto, a [gatto] *m, f* cat

gazzosa [gassosa] *f* soda

gelare [jaylaray] *v* to freeze

gelateria [jaylatayree-a] *f* ice-cream parlor

gelato [jaylato] *m* ice cream, gelato

gelo [jaylo] *m* frost

genere [jaynayray] *m* kind ▸ generi alimentari foodstuffs ▸ in genere generally

genio [jaynee-o] *m* genius

genitore [jayneetoray] *m* parent

gennaio [jenna-yo] *m* January

Genova [jaynova] *f* Genoa

gente [jentay] *f* people

genuino, a [jaynoo-eeno] *adj (food)* natural

gergo [jergo] *m* slang

Germania [jermanee-a] *f* ▸ la Germania Germany

gettare [jettaray] *v* to throw

ghiacciaio [ghee-acha-yo] *m* glacier

ghiaccio [ghee-acho] *m* ice

già [ja] *adv* already ♦ *excl* yes (of course) ▸ di già? already?

giacca [jakka] *f* jacket ▸ giacca a vento windbreaker

giallo, a [jallo] *adj* yellow

gianduiotto [jandoo-yotto] *m chocolate filled with chocolate and hazelnut paste*

giardino [jardeeno] *m* garden

ginocchio [jeenokkee-o] *m* knee

giocare [jokaray] *v* to play

gioco [joko] *m* game

gioiello [jo-yello] *m* jewel

giornale [jornalay] *m* (news)paper

giornalista [jornaleesta] *mf* reporter

giornata [jornata] *f* day ▸ oggi è una bella giornata it's a lovely day today

giorno [jorno] *m* day ▸ giorno feriale weekday ▸ a giorni alterni every other day

giovane [jovanay] *adj* young

giovedì [jovaydee] *m* Thursday ▸ giovedì grasso Maundy Thursday

girare [jeeraray] *v* to turn

giro [jeero] *m* turn; *(journey)* trip ▸ nel giro di un mese in the space of a month

gita [jeeta] *f* trip

giù [joo] *adv* down ▸ i bambini dai dieci anni in giù children under ten

giugno [joonyo] *m* June

giunta [joonta] *f* council

giusto, a [joosto] *adj* right ▸ al momento giusto at the right time ▸ giusto in tempo just in time

gnocchi [nyokkee] *mpl* gnocchi ▸ gnocchi alla bava *gnocchi with butter and cheese*

gola [gola] *f* throat; greed

goloso, a [golozo] *adj* greedy

gomito [gomeeto] *m* elbow

gomma [gomma] *f* tire; *(material)* rubber ▸ gomma a terra flat tire ▸ gomma (da masticare) (chewing) gum

gonfiare [gonfee-aray] *v* to inflate

gonna [gonna] *f* skirt

governo [governo] *m* government

gradevole [gradayvolay] *adj* pleasant

gradino [gradeeno] *m* step

grado [grado] *m* degree

grana [grana] *m* *hard cheese similar to Parmesan*

Gran Bretagna [gran bretanya] *f* ▸ la Gran Bretagna Great Britain

granchio [grankee-o] *m* crab

grande [granday] *adj* big, large ▸ un gran bugiardo a terrible liar ▸ fa un gran caldo it's very hot

grandine [grandinay] *f* hail

granita [graneeta] *f* Italian ice, granita

grano [grano] *m* grain

grappa [grappa] *f* grappa

grasso, a [grasso] *adj* fat; *(food)* fatty; *(skin)* greasy

grazie [gratsee-ay] *excl* thanks ▸ grazie mille thanks a lot

Grecia [graycha] *f* ▸ la Grecia Greece

grido [greedo] *m* shout

grigio, a [greejo] *adj* gray

griglia [greelya] *f (of vehicle)* grille; *(for cooking)* grill ▸ alla griglia grilled

grigliata [greelyata] *f* grilled food

grissini [greesseenee] *mpl* bread sticks

grosso, a [grosso] *adj* big

groviera [grovee-ayra] *mf* gruyère (cheese)

gruppo [grooppo] *m* group ▸ gruppo sanguigno blood type

guaio [gwa-yo] *m* trouble

guardare [gwardaray] *v* to look at

guardaroba [gwardaroba] *m* closet; *(in restaurant, theater)* coat check

guardia [gwardee-a] *f* guard ▸ guardia medica emergency doctor service (with doctors on call)

guasto, a [gwasto] *adj* out of order

guglia [goolya] *f* spire

guida [gweeda] *f* guide

guidare [gweedaray] *v* to drive

gusto [goosto] *m* taste

i

idea [eedaya] *f* idea ▸ ho cambiato idea I've changed my mind

ieri [ee-ayree] *adv* yesterday ▸ ieri notte last night ▸ l'altro ieri the day before yesterday

il [eel] *art* the ▸ il lago the lake

illuminare [eelloomeenaray] *v* to light

imbarco [eembarko] *m* boarding

imbocco [eembokko] *m* entrance ▸ imbocco dell'autostrada entrance to the freeway

imbroglio [eembrolyo] *m* swindle

immagine [eemmajeenay] *f* image

immersione [eemmersee-onay] *f* diving

immondizia [eemmondeetsee-a] *f* garbage

impacco [eempakko] *m* compress

impalcatura [eempalkatoora] *f* scaffolding

imparare [eempararay] *v* to learn

impedire [eempaydeeray] *v* to prevent

impermeabile [eempermayabeelay] *adj* waterproof

impero [eempayro] *m* empire

impianto [eempee-anto] *m* installation

‣ impianto di riscaldamento heating system ‣ impianto sportivo sports complex ‣ impianti di risalita ski lifts

impiegato, a [eempee-aygato] *m, f* employee

imponente [eemponentay] *adj* imposing

importanza [importantsa] *f* importance

importare [eemportaray] *v* to import ‣ non importa! it doesn't matter! ‣ non mi importa it's all the same to me

importo [emporto] *m* sum of money

impresa [eemprayza] *f* venture; firm

imprevisto, a [eemprayveesto] *adj* unforeseen

impronta [eempronta] *f* mark ‣ impronta digitale fingerprint

improvviso, a [eemprovveezo] *adj* sudden ‣ all'improvviso suddenly

impulso [eempoolso] *m* impulse ‣ d'impulso on an impulse

in [een] *prep* in; to ‣ in città in town ‣ in primavera in spring

inaspettato, a [eenaspettato] *adj* unexpected

incantevole [eenkantayvolay] *adj* charming

incapace [eenkapachay] *adj* incapable

incaricato, a [eenkareekato] *m, f* person responsible

incendio [eenchendee-o] *m* fire

incertezza [eenchertetsa] *f* uncertainty

inchiesta [eenkee-esta] *f* inquiry

incidente [eencheedentay] *m* accident ‣ incidente stradale road accident

incirca [eencheerka] *adv* ‣ all'incirca about

incisione [eencheezee-onay] *f* engraving

incivile [eencheeveelay] *adj* rude

incluso, a [eenkloozo] *adj* included ‣ incluso nel prezzo included in the price

incollare [eenkollaray] *v* to stick

incompiuto, a [eenkompyooto] *adj* unfinished

inconfondibile [eenkonfondeebeelay] *adj* unmistakable

incredibile [eenkraydeebeelay] *adj* incredible

incrociare [eenkrocharay] *v* to cross

incrocio [eenkrocho] *m* crossroads

incustodito, a [eenkoostodeeto] *adj* unattended

indagine [eendajeeny] *f* investigation

indicare [eendeekaray] *v* to show

indicazione [eendeekatsee-onay] *f* piece of information

indice [eendeechay] *m* index; index finger

indietro [eendee-aytro] *adv* back ‣ dovete tornare indietro you have to go back; *(in vehicle)* you have to back up ‣ vada indietro, per favore move back, please

indimenticabile [eendeementeekabeelay] *adj* unforgettable

indirizzo [eendeereetso] *m* address ‣ indirizzo e-mail e-mail address

indomani [eendomanee] *m* ‣ l'indomani the next day

indovinare [eendoveenaray] *v* to guess

indovinello [eendoveenello] *m* riddle

indubbiamente [eendoobbee-amentay] *adv* without doubt

indumento [eendoomento] *m* garment

inefficiente [eeneffeechentay] *adj* inefficient

inesperto, a [eenesperto] *adj* inexperienced

infantile [eenfanteelay] *adj* children's

infarto [eenfarto] *m* heart attack

infatti [eenfattee] *conj* in fact

inferiore [eenfayree-oray] *adj* lower

infermeria [eenfermayree-a] *f* infirmary

inferno [eenferno] *m* hell

infezione [eenfetsee-onay] *f* infection

infiammabile [eenfee-ammabeelay] *adj* flammable ▸ 'materiale infiammabile' 'flammable material'

infiammazione [eenfee-ammatsee-onay] *f* inflammation

influenza [eenflooentsa] *f* influence; flu

informatica [eenformateeka] *f* information technology

informazione [eenformatsee-onay] *f* information

infrangibile [eenfranjeebeelay] *adj* unbreakable

ingenuo, a [eenjaynoo-o] *adj* naive

Inghilterra [eengheelterra] *f* ▸ l'Inghilterra England

inglese [eennglayzay] *adj* English

ingorgo [eengorgo] *m* traffic jam

ingranaggio [eengranajo] *m* gear

ingrandimento [eengrandeemento] *m* enlargement

ingrassare [eengrassaray] *v* to put on weight

ingresso [eengresso] *m* entrance ▸ 'ingresso gratuito' 'free admission' ▸ 'ingresso libero' 'free admission'

iniezione [eenyetsee-onay] *f* injection

ininterrottamente [eeneentayrotta-mentay] *adv* continuously

iniziare [eeneetsee-aray] *v* to start, to begin

inizio [eeneetsee-o] *m* start, beginning ▸ all'inizio at the start/beginning

innamorarsi [eennamorarsee] *v* to fall in love

innamorato, a [eennamorato] *adj* in love

innanzitutto [eennantseetootto] *adv* first of all

innocuo, a [eennokoo-o] *adj* harmless

inoltre [eenoltray] *adv* moreover

inondazione [eenondatsee-onay] *f* flood

inquinamento [eenkweenamento] *m* pollution

insaccati [eensakkatee] *m* sausage

insalata [eensalata] *f* salad; lettuce ▸ insalata mista mixed salad ▸ insalata di riso rice salad

insegna [eensenya] *f* sign

insegnante [eensenyantay] *mf* teacher

insenatura [eensaynatoora] *f* inlet

inserire [eensayreeray] *v* to insert

inserzione [eensertsee-onay] *f* advertisement

insetto [eensetto] *m* insect

insieme [eensee-aymay] *adv* together ▸ insieme a Marcella with Marcella ▸ nell'insieme on the whole

insolito, a [eensoleeto] *adj* unusual

insomma [eensomma] *adv* in short

insonnia [insonnee-a] *f* insomnia

inspiegabile [eenspee-aygabeelay] *adj* inexplicable

intanto [eentanto] *adv* meanwhile

intatto, a [eentatto] *adj* intact

integrale [eentaygralay] *adj* full; whole wheat

intercity [eenterseetee] *m* ▸ (treno) intercity intercity (train)

interesse [eentayressay] *m* interest

interiora [eentayree-ora] *fpl* offal

interno, a [eenterno] *adj* internal

intero, a [eentayro] *adj* whole ▸ per intero in full

interrompere [eenterrompayray] *v* to interrupt

interruttore [eenterroottoray] *m* switch

intervallo [intervallo] *m* break; *(at theater)* intermission

intervento [eentervento] *m* intervention

intervista [eenterveesta] *f* interview

inteso, a [eentayzo] *adj* ▸ intesi! agreed!

intestino [eentesteeno] *m* intestine

intimo, a [eenteemo] *adj (friend)* close ◆ *n* underwear

intorno [eentorno] *adv* around

intossicazione [eentosseekatsee-onay] *f* poisoning

intrigo [eentreego] *m* intrigue

introdurre [eentrodoorray] *v* to introduce ▸ 'vietato introdurre cani' 'no dogs'

introvabile [eentrovabeelay] *adj* unobtainable

intuito [eentoo-eeto] *m* intuition

invano [eenvano] *adv* in vain

invece [eenvaychay] *adv* instead ▸ invece di instead of

inverno [eenverno] *m* winter ▸ d'inverno in winter

inverosimile [eenvayroseemeelay] *adj* unlikely

inversione [eenversee-onay] *f* U-turn

inverso, a [eenverso] *adj* opposite ▸ all'inverso upside down, back to front

invertire [eenverteeray] *v* to reverse

investire [eenvesteeray] *v (pedestrian)* to run over

inviare [eenvee-aray] *v* to send

invio [eenvee-o] *m* mailing

invito [eenveeto] *m* invitation

involtino [eenvolteeno] *m slice of meat rolled up around a filling* ▸ involtino primavera spring roll

inzuppare [eendzoopparay] *v* to soak

io [ee-o] *pron* I ▸ sono io it's me ▸ io stesso I myself

Ionio [ee-onee-o] *m* ▸ lo Ionio, il Mar Ionio the Ionian (Sea)

Ipotesi [eepotayzee] hypothesis

Irlanda [eerlanda] *f* ▸ l'Irlanda Ireland

irlandese [eerlandayzay] *adj* Irish

irraggiungibile [eerraajoonjeebeelay] *adj* inaccessible

irregolare [eerraygolaray] *adj* irregular

irrilevante [eerreelayvantay] *adj* insignificant

irritare [eerreetaray] *v* to irritate

iscrizione [eeskreetsee-onay] *f* enrollment; inscription

isola [eezola] *f* island ▸ isola pedonale pedestrian mall

isolato, a [eezolato] *adj* isolated ◆ *m* block

ispettore [eespettoray] *m* inspector

ispirare [eespeeraray] *v* to inspire

istantanea [eestantanay-a] *f* snapshot

istante [eestantay] *m* instant

istinto [eesteento] *m* island

istituto [eesteetooto] *m* institute

istruttore, trice [eestroottoray] *m, f* instructor ▸ istruttore di nuoto swimming instructor

istruzioni [eestrootsee-onee] *n* instructions ▸ istruzioni (per l'uso) instructions (for use)

Italia [eetalee-a] *f* ▸ l'Italia Italy

italiano, a [eetalee-ano] *adj* Italian

itinerario [eeteenayraree-o] *m* route

IVA [eeva] *f* VAT

l

la [la] *pron* you ▸ la prego! please!

là [la] *adv* there ▸ di là next door

labbro [labbro] *m* lip

lacca, che [lakka] *f* hairspray

lacrima [lakreema] *f* tear ▸ in lacrime in tears

ladro, a [ladro] *m, f* thief

laggiù [lajoo] *adv* down there

lago [lago] *m* lake

lametta [lametta] *f* razor blade

lampada [lampada] *f* lamp ▸ fare la lampada to go tanning

lampadina [lampadeena] *f* (light) bulb ▸ lampadina tascabile flashlight

lampo [lampo] *m* flash of lightning

lampone [lamponay] *m* raspberry

lana [lana] *f* wool ▸ 'pura lana vergine' 'pure virgin wool'

lancetta [lanchetta] *f* (of watch) hand; (of instrument) needle

largo, a [largo] *adj* wide ▸ (fate) largo! make room!

lasciare [lasharay] *v* to leave; (allow) to let ▸ prendere o lasciare take it or leave it

lassativo [lassateevo] *m* laxative

latitudine [lateetoodeenay] *f* latitude

lato [lato] *m* side ▸ a lato del museo next to the museum

latte [lattay] *m* milk ▸ latte detergente cleanser ▸ latte scremato skim milk

latticini [latteecheenee] *mpl* dairy products

lattina [latteena] *f* can

lattuga [lattooga] *f* lettuce

lavanderia [lavandayreea] *f* laundry ▸ lavanderia automatica Laundromat®

lavandino [lavandeeno] *m* kitchen sink; bathroom sink

lavare [lavaray] *v* to wash

lavorativo, a [lavorateevo] *adj* working

lavoro [lavoro] *m* work ▸ 'lavori in corso' 'roadwork ahead'

le [lay] *pron* (to) you ▸ le spiace se apro il finestrino? do you mind if I open the window?

legare [laygaray] *v* to tie (up)

legge [lejay] *f* law

leggere [lejayray] *v* to read

leggero, a [lejayro] *adj* light

legittimo, a [lejeetteemo] *adj* legal

legno [lenyo] *m* wood

legumi [laygoomee] *mpl* legumes

lei [lay-ee] *pron* she; her; (formal) you

lente [lentay] *f* lens ▸ lenti a contatto contact lenses

lenticchie [lenteekkee-ay] *fpl* lentils

lento, a [lento] *adj* slow

lenzuolo [lentsooolo] *m* sheet

lepre [lepray] *f* hare ▸ lepre in salmì half-roasted hare finished in wine sauce

lesso, a [lesso] *adj* boiled

lettera [lettayra] *f* letter ▸ alla lettera to the letter

letto [letto] *m* bed ▸ letti a castello bunk beds ▸ letto matrimoniale/a due piazze double bed

levare [layvaray] *v* to take off

lezione [letseeonay] *f* lesson

lì [lee] *adv* there ▸ **da lì in poi** from then on ▸ **lì per lì** there and then

liberare [leebayraray] *v* to release

libero, a [leebayro] *adj* free

libreria [leebrayree-a] *f* bookstore; bookcase

libretto [leebretto] *m* booklet ▸ **libretto degli assegni** checkbook ▸ **libretto di circolazione** vehicle registration ▸ **libretto d'istruzioni** instruction booklet

libro [leebro] *m* book

liceo [leechayo] *m* ≃ high school

lieto, a [lee-ayto] *adj* happy ▸ **molto lieto!** pleased to meet you! ▸ **lieto di conoscerla!** pleased to meet you!

limite [leemeetay] *m* edge; limit ▸ **al limite** if worse comes to worst ▸ **limite di velocità** speed limit

limonata [leemonata] *f* lemonade; soda

limone [leemonay] *m* lemon

linea [leenay-a] *f* line ▸ **resti in linea** stay on the line ▸ **'linee urbane'** 'city bus routes'

lingua [leengwa] *f* tongue; language

lino [leeno] *m* linen

liquirizia [leekweereetsee-a] *f* licorice

liquore [leekworay] *m* liqueur

liscio, a [leesho] *adj* smooth; *(with no ice)* straight up ◆ *m* ballroom dancing

lista [leesta] *f* list ▸ **è in lista d'attesa?** are you on the waiting list? ▸ **lista dei vini** wine list

listino [leesteeno] *m* ▸ **listino (dei) prezzi** price list

lite [leetay] *f (quarrel)* row

litorale [leettoralay] *m* coast

litro [leetro] *m* liter

livello [leevello] *m* level ▸ **livello del mare** sea level

livido [leeveedo] *m* bruise

lo [lo] *pron* him; it ▸ **lo vuoi?** do you want it?

locale [lokalay] *m* room; *(bar, restaurant)* place ▸ **locale notturno** (night) club

locanda [lokanda] *f* inn

lontano, a [lontano] *adj* distant ▸ **è lontano?** is it far?

lordo, a [lordo] *adj* gross

loro [loro] *adj* their ◆ *pron* they; them; theirs ▸ **il loro padre** their father ▸ **un loro amico** a friend of theirs ▸ **è (il) loro** it's theirs

lotta [lotta] *f* fight

lotteria [lottayree-a] *f* lottery

lotto [lotto] *m* lottery

lubrificante [loobreefeekantay] *m* lubricant

luce [loochay] *f* light ▸ **a luci rosse** *(movie)* adult

lucido, a [loocheedo] *adj* shiny ▸ **lucido da scarpe** shoe polish

luglio [loolyo] *m* July

lui [loo-ee] *pron* he; him

lumaca [loomaka] *f* snail

luna [loona] *f* moon ▸ **luna park** fairground ▸ **luna piena** full moon

lunedì [loonaydee] *m* Monday

lungo, a [loongo] *adj* long

lungofiume [loongofyoomay] *m* embankment

lungomare [loongomaray] *m* seafront

luogo [looogo] *m* place

lupo [loopo] *m* wolf

lusso [loosso] *m* luxury

lutto [lootto] *m* mourning ▸ **'chiuso per lutto'** 'closed due to bereavement'

m

ma [ma] *conj* but

maccheroni [makkayronee] *mpl* macaroni

macchia [makkee-a] *f* stain

macchina [makkeena] *f* car; machine

macedonia [machaydonee-a] *f* fruit salad

macelleria [machellayree-a] *f* butcher shop

macinare [macheenaray] *v (coffee, meat)* to grind

Madonna [madonna] *f* Madonna

madre [madray] *f* mother

madrelingua [madrayleengwa] *f* mother tongue

madreperla [madrayperla] *f* mother-of-pearl

maestro, a [ma-estro] *m, f* teacher ▸ maestro di nuoto swimming instructor ▸ maestro di sci skiing instructor

magari [magaree] *excl* ▸ vai in vacanza? – magari! are you going on vacation? – I wish! ▸ magari potessi venire! if only I could come!

maggio [majo] *m* May

maggioranza [majorantsa] *f* majority ▸ nella maggioranza dei casi in the majority of cases

maggiore [majoray] *adj* greater; *(price, temperature)* higher ▸ la sorella maggiore the elder sister ▸ raggiungere la maggiore età to come of age ▸ la maggior parte the majority

maggiorenne [majorennay] *adj* adult

mago, a [mago] *m, f* magician

magro, a [magro] *adj* thin

mai [ma-ee] *adv* never

maiale [ma-yalay] *m* pig; pork

maionese [ma-yonayzay] *f* mayonnaise

malapena [malapayna] ◆ **a malapena** *adv* barely

malato, a [malato] *adj* sick ▸ essere malato di cuore to have a bad heart

malattia [malattee-a] *f* illness

male [malay] *m* evil ▸ ti fa male? does it hurt? ▸ si sente male? are you sick? ▸ non c'è male! not bad!

maleducato, a [malaydookato] *adj* rude

malessere [malessayray] *m* slight illness

malgrado [malgrado] *prep* in spite of ◆ *conj* even though

malinconia [maleenkonee-a] *f* melancholy

malincuore [maleenkoo-oray] ◆ **a malincuore** *adv* reluctantly

malore [maloray] *m* sudden illness

malridotto, a [malreedotto] *adj* in a bad state

maltempo [maltempo] *m* bad weather

mamma [mamma] *f* mom ▸ mamma mia! good heavens!

mancare [mankaray] *v* to be missing ▸ mancano ancora due euro you're still two euros short ▸ manca un quarto alle quattro it's a quarter to four

mancia [mancha] *f* tip

mandarancio [mandarancho] *m* clementine

mandare [mandaray] *v* to send

mandarino [mandareeno] *m* mandarin orange

mandorla [mandorla] *f* almond

mangiare [manjaray] *v* to eat

manica [maneeka] *f* sleeve

maniera [manee-ayra] *f* way, manner

mano [mano] *f* hand ▸ **fatto a mano** handmade ▸ **man mano che** as ▸ **di seconda mano** secondhand

manuale [manooalay] *m* manual

manutenzione [manootentsee-onay] *f* maintenance

manzo [mandzo] *m* young bull; beef

maratona [maratona] *f* marathon

marchio [markee-o] *m* mark ▸ **marchio registrato** registered trademark

marcia [marcha] *f* march; *(of vehicle)* gear ▸ **deve fare marcia indietro** you have to back up

marciapiede [marchapee-ayday] *m* sidewalk; *(at station)* platform

marcio, a [marcho] *adj* rotten

mare [maray] *m* sea

marea [maray-a] *f* tide ▸ **alta marea** high tide

marinara [mareenara] *adj* ▸ **alla marinara** seafood

marito [mareeto] *m* husband

marmellata [marmellata] *f* jam

marmitta [marmeetta] *f* *(on vehicle)* muffler

marmo [marmo] *m* marble

martedì [martayday] *m* Tuesday

martello [martello] *m* hammer

marzapane [mardzapanay] *m* marzipan

marzo [martso] *m* March

mascarpone [maskarponay] *m* mascarpone (cheese)

mascella [mashella] *f* jaw

maschera [maskayra] *f* mask ▸ **ballo in maschera** masked ball

maschile [maskeelay] *adj* male ▸ **spogliatoio maschile** men's changing room

maschio, a [maskee-o] *adj* & *m* male

massiccio, a [masseecho] *adj* solid

massimo [masseemo] *m* maximum

masso [masso] *m* boulder

materasso [matayrasseeno] *m* air mattress

materasso [matayrasso] *m* mattress

materiale [matayree-alay] *m* material

matita [mateeta] *f* pencil

matrimonio [matreemonee-o] *m* marriage

mattino [matteeno] *m* morning

matto, a [matto] *adj* crazy ▸ **vado matto per il gelato** I just love ice cream

maturo, a [matooro] *adj* ripe

me [may] *pron* me ▸ **secondo me** in my opinion ▸ **me ne vado** I'm off

media [maydee-a] *f* average

medicare [maydeekaray] *v (wound)* to dress; *(patient)* to treat

medicina [maydeecheena] *f* medicine

medicinale [medeecheenalay] *m* medicine

medico [maydeeko] *m* doctor ▸ **medico di guardia** doctor on duty

medio, a [maydee-o] *adj* average; medium

medioevo [maydee-o-ayvo] *m* Middle Ages

Mediterraneo [maydeeterranay-o] *m* ▸ **il (mar) Mediterraneo** the Mediterranean (Sea)

meglio [melyo] *adv* & *adj* better; best ▸ **va meglio?** is that better? ▸ **è meglio prenotare** it's better to book

mela [mayla] *f* apple

melagrana [maylagrana] *f* pomegranate

melanzana [maylandzana] *f* eggplant ▸ **melanzane alla parmigiana** eggplant Parmesan

il Mezzogiorno

This is the name for southern Italy, including Sicily and Sardinia. Despite its natural beauty and rich cultural and artistic heritage, the South is less industrially developed and has much higher unemployment than the North. National and local government agencies are constantly trying new initiatives to help reduce the north-south divide.

memoria [maymoree-a] *f* memory

meno [mayno] *adv* less ◆ *prep* except ▸ più o meno more or less ▸ le nove meno un quarto a quarter to nine ▸ meno male (che) thank goodness (that) ▸ 'tutti i giorni meno il sabato' every day except Saturday'

menta [menta] *f* mint

mente [mentay] *f* mind

mentre [mentray] *conj* while; whereas

meraviglioso, a [mayraveelyozo] *adj* wonderful

mercato [merkato] *m* market

merce [merchay] *f* goods ▸ 'la merce non si cambia' 'goods cannot be exchanged'

mercoledì [mercolaydee] *m* Wednesday

meringa [mayreenga] *f* meringue

merletto [merletto] *m* lace

merluzzo [merlootso] *m* cod

mese [mayzay] *m* month

meta [mayta] *f* destination

metà [mayta] *f* half ▸ metà fetta half a slice ▸ a metà strada halfway

metro [metro] *m* meter ▸ metro quadrato square meter

metropolitana [metropoleetana] *f* subway

mettere [mettayray] *v* to put ▸ ci si mette un'ora it takes an hour

mezzanotte [medzanottay] *f* midnight

mezzo, a [medzo] *adj* half ◆ *m* half; middle ▸ mezza pensione *system in which the price of a room includes breakfast and one main meal* ▸ mezza stagione mid-season ▸ in mezzo a in the middle of ▸ mezzi pubblici public transportation

mezzogiorno [medzojorno] *m* Southern Italy

mezzora [medzora] *f* half hour

mi [mee] *pron* (to) me ▸ mi scusi excuse me

mica [meeka] *adv* ▸ non sono mica scemo I'm not stupid ▸ mica male not bad at all

miei [mee-ayee] *adj* my ◆ *pron* mine ▸ i miei amici my friends

migliaio [meelya-yo] *m* thousand

migliorare [meelyoraray] *v* to improve

migliore [meelyoray] *adj* better; best

millefoglie [meellayfolyay] *m* millefeuille

millesimo, a [meellayzeemo] *num* thousandth

milza [meeltsa] *f* spleen

minestra [meenestra] *f* soup ▸ minestra di verdure vegetable soup

minigonna [meeneegonna] *f* miniskirt

minimo [meeneemo] *m* minimum

minoranza [meenorantsa] *f* minority

minore [meenoray] *adj* lesser; *(price, temperature)* lower ▸ il mio fratello minore my little brother

minorenne [meenorennay] *mf* minor

minuto [meenooto] *m* minute

mio [meeo] *adj* my ◆ *pron* mine ▸ mio padre my father ▸ un mio amico a friend of mine ▸ è (il) mio it's mine

miscela [meeshayla] *f* mixture

misto [meesto] *m* mixture

misura [meezoora] *f* size; measurement; *(action)* measure

mittente [meettentay] *mf* sender

mobile [mobeelay] *m* piece of furniture

moda [moda] *f* fashion ▸ alla moda fashionable ▸ l'alta moda haute couture

modello, a [modello] *m, f* model

modifica [modeefeeka] *f* modification

modo [modo] *m* way ▸ è un modo di dire it's an expression ▸ di modo che so that ▸ in ogni modo anyway ▸ in qualche modo somehow

modulo [modoolo] *m* form

moglie [molyay] *f* wife

moltiplicare [molteepleekaray] *v* to multiply

molto, a [molto] *adj & pron* much; many ◆ *adv* a lot, much ▸ mi piace molto *(thing)* I like it a lot; *(person)* I like him/her a lot ▸ è molto presto/tardi it's very early/late

momento [momento] *m* moment

moneta [monayta] *f* coin ▸ moneta spicciola small change

monolocale [monolokalay] *m* studio (apartment)

monte [montay] *m* mountain ▸ monte premi jackpot

montone [montonay] *m* ram; mutton

montuoso, a [montoo-ozo] *adj* mountainous

mora [mora] *f* blackberry

morbido, a [morbeedo] *adj* soft

morbillo [morbeello] *m* measles

morire [moreeray] *v* to die

moro, a [moro] *adj* dark

morso [morso] *m* bite

mosaico [moza-eeko] *m* mosaic

mosca [moska] *f* fly

moscato [moskato] *m* muscatel

mosso, a [mosso] *adj (ocean)* choppy

mostarda [mostarda] *f* mustard

mostra [mostra] *f* exhibit

mostro [mostro] *m* monster

motivo [moteevo] *m* reason

motore [motoray] *m* engine

motorino [motoreeno] *m* moped

motoscafo [motoskafo] *m* motorboat

mozzarella [motsarella] *f* mozzarella ▸ mozzarella in carrozza *mozzarella sandwich dipped in egg and fried*

mucca [mookka] *f* cow

mucchio [mookkee-o] *m* pile

muffa [mooffa] *f (fungus)* mold

mulino [mooleeno] *m* mill

mulo [moolo] *m* mule

multa [moolta] *f* fine

municipio [mooneecheepee-o] *m* town hall

muovere [moo-ovayray] *v* to move

mura [moora] *fpl* walls

muscolo [mooskolo] *m* muscle

museo [moozay-o] *m* museum

musica [moozeeka] *f* music

mutande [mootanday] *fpl (of woman)* panties, underpants; *(of man)* underwear

mutilato, a [mooteelato] *m, f* ▸ mutilato di guerra *disabled war veteran*

muto, a [mooto] *adj* unable to speak

n

nafta [nafta] *f* diesel fuel

nano, a [nano] *adj* dwarf

narice [nareechay] *f* nostril

nascere [nashayray] *v* to be born

nascita [nasheeta] *f* birth ▸ data di nascita date of birth ▸ luogo di nascita place of birth

nascosto, a [naskosto] *adj* hidden

naso [nazo] *m* nose

Natale [natalay] *m* Christmas

nato, a [nato] *adj* born ▸ Dante è nato a Firenze Dante was born in Florence

navata [navata] *f* nave

nave [navay] *f* ship ▸ nave traghetto ferry

ne [nay] *pron* of him/her/it/them ▸ non ne ho idea I have no idea

né [nay] *conj* ▸ né ... né neither ... nor ▸ non voglio né questo né quello I don't want either

neanche [nayankay] *conj* & *adv* not even ▸ neanch'io me neither ▸ non l'ho neanche visto I haven't even seen it ▸ neanche per sogno/per idea! not on your life

nebbia [nebbee-a] *f* fog

necessario, a [naychessaree-o] *adj* necessary ▸ è necessario farlo it has to be done

negare [naygaray] *v* to deny

negozio [naygotsee-o] *m* store

nel [nel] *prep* in the ▸ nel centro storico in the old town

nemico, a [naymeeko] *m, f* enemy

neo [nay-o] *m* mole

neonato, a [nay-onato] *m, f* newborn

neorealismo [nay-oray-aleezmo] *m* neorealism

nero, a [nayro] *adj* black

nervo [nervo] *m* nerve

nessuno, a [nessoono] *adj* no ✦ *pron* no one ▸ da nessuna parte nowhere ▸ non lo sa nessuno no one knows

netto, a [netto] *adj* clear; net ▸ 'peso netto' 'net weight'

neve [nayvay] *f* snow

nevicare [nayveekaray] *v* ▸ nevica it's snowing

nevischio [nayveeskee-o] *m* sleet

niente [nee-entay] *pron* nothing ✦ *adv* at all ▸ è una cosa da niente it's nothing ▸ non è per niente furbo he's not at all smart ▸ un bel niente nothing at all

nipote [neepotay] *mf* nephew, niece;

---

il Neorealismo

Postwar Italian cinema of the late 1940s and early 1950s tried to depict social and economic problems through a new movement called neorealism. Two of the most famous movies of this period are *Ladri di biciclette* (Bicycle Thieves) by Vittorio de Sica and *Riso amaro* (Bitter Rice) by Giuseppe De Santis starring Silvana Mangano.

grandchild, grandson, granddaughter

no [no] *adv* no ▸ lo vuoi o no? do you want it or not? ▸ no di certo of course not ▸ no davvero not at all

nobile [nobeelay] *adj* noble

nocciola [nochola] *f* hazelnut

nocciolina [nocholeena] *f* peanut

noce [nochay] *f* walnut ▸ noce di cocco coconut

nodo [nodo] *m* knot

noi [no-ee] *pron* we; us ▸ da noi at our house ▸ noi stessi/stesse we ourselves

noia [no-ya] *f* boredom

noioso, a [no-yozo] *adj* boring; annoying

noleggiare [nolejaray] *v* to rent

nome [nomay] *m* name

non [non] *adv* not ▸ non è venuto he didn't come

nonna [nonna] *f* grandmother

nonno [nonno] *m* grandfather

nono, a [nono] *num* ninth

nonostante [nonostantay] *prep* despite ◆ *conj* even though

non vedente [none vaydentay] *mf* vision-impaired person

norma [norma] *f* rule ▸ di norma as a rule

nostro, a [nostro] *adj* our ◆ *pron* our ▸ nostro padre our father ▸ un nostro amico a friend of ours ▸ è (il) nostro it' ours

notizia [noteetsee-a] *f* news

notte [nottay] *f* night ▸ notte in bianco sleepless night

notturno, a [nottoorno] *adj* night

novanta [novanta] *num* ninety

novantesimo, a [novantayzeemo] *num* ninetieth

nove [novay] *num* nine

novembre [novembray] *m* November

novità [noveeta] *f* news

nozze [notsay] *fpl* wedding ▸ nozze d'oro golden wedding

nube [noobay] *f* cloud

nubile [noobeelay] *adj* single

nuca [nooka] *f* nape (of the neck)

nudo, a [noodo] *adj* naked

numeroso, a [noomayrozo] *adj (family group)* large

nuoto [noo-oto] *m* swimming

nuovo, a [noo-ovo] *adj* new

nuraghe [nooragay] *m* *prehistoric stone structure in Sardinia*

nuvola [noovola] *f* cloud

o [o] *conj* or

obbligo [obbleego] *m* duty

oca [oka] *f* goose

occhiali [okkee-alee] *mpl* glassses ▸ occhiali da sole sunglasses

occhiata [okkee-ata] *f* look ▸ vuole dare un'occhiata? do you want to have a look?

occhio [okkee-o] *m* eye ▸ a occhio nudo to/with the naked eye ▸ occhio al portafoglio! watch your wallet!

occorrere [okkorrayray] *v* to be needed ▸ occorre aspettare you need to wait

odiare [odee-aray] *v* to hate

odore [odoray] *m* smell

offendere [offendayray] *v* to offend

l'olio di oliva

Italy is the second-biggest producer – and top consumer – of olive oil in the world. In the South you'll see hundreds of *frantoi* (olive presses) and *aziende agricole* or *fattorie* (farms) producing extra-virgin olive oil.

offensivo [offenseevo] *adj* offensive

offerta [offerta] *f* offer ▸ offerta speciale special offer

oggetto [ojetto] *m* object ▸ (ufficio) oggetti smarriti lost and found

oggi [ojee] *adv* today

ogni [onyee] *adj* every, each ▸ ogni volta che every time that ▸ in ogni caso in any case ▸ ogni tanto every so often

Ognissanti [onyeessantee] *m* All Saints' Day

ognuno, a [onyoono] *pron* everyone, everybody; each (one) ▸ ognuno di voi each of you

olimpiadi [oleempee-adee] *fpl* ▸ le olimpiadi the Olympics

olio [olee-o] *m* oil

oliva [oleeva] *f* olive ▸ olive all'ascolana *large olives stuffed with meat or fish and fried in breadcrumbs*

oltre [oltray] *prep* beyond ▸ oltre a lui apart from him

oltrepassare [oltraypassaray] *v* to exceed

omaggio [omajo] *m* gift ▸ 'copia omaggio' 'complimentary copy'

ombelico [ombayleeko] *m* navel

ombrellone [ombrellonay] *m* beach umbrella

omogeneizzato [omojaynay-eedzato] *m* baby food

onda [onda] *f* wave

onesto, a [onesto] *adj* honest

onomastico [onomasteeko] *m feast day of saint for whom one is named*

opera [opayra] *f* work; opera ▸ opera d'arte work of art ▸ opere pubbliche public works

opposto, a [opposto] *adj* opposite

oppure [oppooray] *conj* or; otherwise

ora [ora] *f* hour; time ◆ *adv* now ▸ a che ora parte il treno? what time does the train leave? ▸ ora legale daylight saving time

orario [oraree-o] *m* timetable ▸ orario di arrivo arrival time ▸ orario di partenza departure time ▸ 'orario d'apertura' 'business hours'

orata [orata] *f* sea bream

ordinare [ordeenaray] *v* to order

ordine [ordeenay] *m* order

orecchiette [orekkee-ettay] *fpl type of*

l'Opera

The first opera was performed in Italy in the early 17th century. Opera was at its peak in the 19th century with composers such as Rossini, Bellini, Donizetti, and Verdi. Later composers like Puccini brought opera to a wider audience, and it continues to enjoy great popularity in Italy today.

small round pasta

orecchio [orekkee-o] *m* ear

orecchioni [orekkee-onee] *mpl* mumps

oreficeria [orayfeechayree-a] *f* jewelry store

organizzazione [organeedzatsee-onay] *f* organization

orientamento [oree-entamento] *m* position

orizzonte [oreedzontay] *m* horizon

ormai [orma-ee] *adv* already

oro [oro] *m* gold ▸ d'oro gold

orrendo, a [orrendo] *adj* awful

orso [orso] *m* bear

ortaggio [ortajo] *m* vegetable

ortica [orteeka] *f* nettle

orticaria [orteekaree-a] *f* urticaria

orto [orto] *m* vegetable garden

orzo [ordzo] *m* barley

oscuro, a [oskooro] *adj* dark

ospedale [ospaydalay] *m* hospital

ospite [ospeetay] *mf* guest; host

osservatorio [osservatoree-o] *m* observatory

ossigeno [osseejayno] *m* oxygen

osso [osso] *m* bone

ostacolo [ostakolo] *m* obstacle

ostello [ostello] *m* ▸ ostello (della gioventù) youth hostel

osteria [ostayree-a] *f* bistro

ostrica [ostreeka] *f* oyster

ottanta [ottanta] *num* eighty

ottantesimo, a [ottantayzeemo] *num* eightieth

ottavo, a [ottavo] *num* eighth

ottenere [ottaynayray] *v* to get

ottimo, a [otteemo] *adj* excellent

otto [otto] *num* eight

ottobre [ottobray] *m* October

ottone [ottonay] *m* brass

ovest [ovest] *m* west ▸ a ovest (to the) west

ovvero [ovvayro] *conj* that is

ovvio, a [ovvee-o] *adj* obvious

pacchetto [pakketto] *m* package

pacco [pakko] *m* package ▸ un pacco regalo a giftwrapped package

pace [pachay] *f* peace

pacifico, a [pacheefeeko] *adj* peaceful

padella [padella] *f* frying pan

Padova [padova] *f* Padua

padre [padray] *m* father

padrino [padreeno] *m* godfather

padrone, a [padronay] *m, f* owner; boss

paesaggio [pa-ayzajo] *m* landscape

paese [pa-ayzay] *m (nation)* country; village

pagare [pagaray] *v* to pay ▸ pagare in contanti/con il Bancomat® to pay cash/by card

pagina [pajeena] *f* page

paio [pa-yo] *m* pair

palazzo [palatso] *m* palace; apartment building ▸ palazzo di giustizia courts of law

palco [palko] *m (for performers)* stage; *(for audience members)* box

palestra [palestra] *f* gym

Palio [palee-o] *m* Palio

palla [palla] *f* ball ▸ che palle! *(vulgar)* what a bummer!

il Palio di Siena

Twice a year, in July and August, people from the 17 *contrade* (districts) of Siena parade in the *Piazza del Campo* in Renaissance costume. Horsemen from each *contrada* then compete to win the *palio*, a banner bearing a picture of the Virgin Mary. The winner is carried around in triumph by the people from his *contrada*.

pallido, a [palleedo] *adj* pale

pallone [pallonay] *m* ball

palude [palooday] *f* marsh

pancarrè [pankarray] *m* sliced bread

pancetta [panchetta] *f* bacon

pancia [pancha] *f* stomach

pandolce [pandolchay] *f* type of cake from Genoa, similar to panettone and traditionally eaten at Christmas

pandoro [pandoro] *m* type of sponge cake traditionally eaten at Christmas

pane [panay] *m* bread; loaf ▸ pan di Spagna sponge cake

panetteria [panettayree-a] *f* bakery

panettone [panettonay] *m* panettone, type of cake containing dried white grapes and candied fruit, traditionally eaten at Christmas

panforte [panfortay] *m* type of flat cake from Siena containing dried fruit and nuts

panino [paneeno] *m* sandwich; roll

▸ panino (imbottito/ripieno) sandwich/ (filled) roll

paninoteca [paneenotayka] *f* sandwich bar

panna [panna] *f* cream ▸ panna cotta *cold dessert made by heating cream with sugar and gelatin* ▸ panna da cucina *cream with a long shelf life for cooking* ▸ panna (montata) whipped cream

pannolino [pannoleeno] *m* diaper

papa [papa] *m* Pope

papà [papa] *n* dad(dy)

pappardelle [pappardellay] *fpl* wide pasta strips

paracadute [parakadootay] *m* parachute

paralizzare [paraleedzaray] *v* to paralyze

parcheggiare [parkejaray] *v* to park

parcheggio [parkejo] *m* parking lot; parking ▸ parcheggio a pagamento *parking lot that charges fees* ▸ 'par-

il pane

Each region has its own bread: crunchy *carasau* from Sardinia, *cudurra* (foccaccia) and sesame *mafalda* from Sicily, the thin *sfilatino* from Lazio, *ferrarese* made with young wheat from Emilia Romagna, the long, pointed *struzza* from Friuli-Venezia Giulia, the small round *michetta* from Lombardy, the flat, unsalted *pane sciocco* from Tuscany, and the *pane di Altamura* (country-style bread) from Puglia.

la pasta

It is hard for an Italian to imagine a meal without pasta, whether cooked plain, with a sauce, in a soup, or baked. Pasta may be fresh or dried, made with egg, or from durum wheat. It comes in all shapes and sizes and each region has its specialties. Learn to recognize the different types: *bavette* (long and flat), *penne* (short tubes cut diagonally), *bucatini* (long hollow tubes), *rigatoni* (short fluted tubes), *fusilli* (spirals), *orecchiette* (little concave discs), *gnocchi* (made from potatoes), and the many different sorts of filled pasta: *tortellini, agnolotti* and, of course, *ravioli*.

cheggio privato' 'private parking' ‣ 'parcheggio riservato a cicli e moto-cicli' 'bicycle and motorcycle parking only' ‣ 'parcheggio riservato ai clienti' 'customer parking only'

parchimetro [parkeemetro] *m* parking meter

parco [parko] *m* park ‣ parco giochi playground

parecchio, a [parekkee-o] *adj* quite a lot of ‣ c'è parecchia gente there are quite a lot of people there

parere [parayray] *m* opinion ✦ *v* to seem ‣ che te ne pare? what do you think? ‣ fate come vi pare do as you like ‣ mi pare di sì/no I think so/I don't think so

pari [paree] *adj* equal; (*number*) even ‣ alla pari au pair ‣ siamo pari we're even

parlare [parlaray] *v* to speak, to talk

parmigiano [parmeejano] *m* Parmesan

parola [parola] *f* word ‣ parole crociate crossword

parte [partay] *f* part; (*direction*) way ‣ la maggior parte (di) most (of) ‣ a parte questo apart from this ‣ dall'altra parte della città on the other side of town ‣ in parte in part

partenza [partentsa] *f* departure ‣ il treno per Milano è in partenza al

binario due the train for Milan is about to leave from platform two

particolare [parteekolaray] *adj* particular ✦ *m* detail

partita [parteeta] *f* (*of sport*) game

partito [parteeto] *m* (*political*) party

Pasqua [paskwa] *f* Easter

Pasquetta [paskwetta] *f* Easter Monday

passaggio [passajo] *m* passage ‣ passaggio a livello railroad/grade crossing

passato, a [passato] *adj* past ✦ *m* soup ‣ passato di verdura vegetable soup

passeggero, a [passejayro] *m, f* passenger

passeggiata [passejata] *f* walk

passo [passo] *m* step; pace; (*in mountains*) pass ‣ 'passo carrabile/carraio' 'no parking: busy entrance' ‣ a passo d'uomo at a walking pace

pasta [pasta] *f* pasta; cake; pastry ‣ pasta frolla pie crust

pastasciutta [pastashoota] *f* pasta

pasticceria [pasteechayree-a] *f* pastry shop

pasticcino [pasteecheeno] *m* petit four

pasticcio [pasteecho] *m* pie; mess

pastiglia [pasteelya] *f* tablet ‣ pastiglia dei freni brake pad

pasto [pasto] *m* meal

pastore [pastoray] *m* shepherd ‣ pastore tedesco German shepherd

patata [patata] *f* potato ▸ patate fritte (French) fries

patente [patentay] *f* license ▸ patente di guida driver's license

patrono [patrono] *n* patron saint

paura [pa-oora] *f* fear

pausa [powza] *f* break

pazienza [patsee-entsa] *f* patience

pazzo, a [patso] *m, f* madman, madwoman

peccato [pekkato] *m* sin ▸ è un peccato che ... it's a pity that ...

pecorino [paykoreeno] *m* pecorino, *ewe's milk cheese*

pedaggio [paydajo] *m* toll

pedone [paydonay] *m* pedestrian

peggio [pejo] *adv & adj* worse; worst ▸ il peggio è che... the worst thing is that...

peggiorare [pejoraray] *v* to make worse; to get worse

peggiore [pejoray] *adj* worse; worst

pelle [pellay] *f* skin; leather ▸ avere la pelle d'oca to have goose bumps

pena [payna] *f* sadness ▸ mi fa pena I feel sorry for him/her

pendio [pendee-o] *m* slope

penna [penna] *f* pen; feather ▸ penne all'arrabbiata *penne pasta in a spicy tomato sauce*

pennarello [pennarello] *m* felt-tip pen

pensare [pensaray] *v* to think ▸ ci penso io! I'll see to it

pensione [pensee-onay] *f (money)* pension; guest house ▸ mezza pensione *system in which the price of a room includes breakfast and one main meal*

penultimo, a [penoolteemo] *adj* second-last

pepe [paypay] *m* pepper

peperonata [paypayronata] *f* peperonata, *peppers, onions, and tomatoes stewed in olive oil*

peperoncino [paypayroncheeno] *m* chili

peperone [paypayronay] *m* pepper

per [per] *prep* for; by ▸ per sempre for ever ▸ per telefono by phone ▸ per caso by chance

pera [payra] *f* pear

percentuale [perchentooalay] *f* percentage

perché [perkay] *adv* why ◆ *conj* because ▸ perché no? why not? ▸ chissà perché who knows why?

perciò [percho] *conj* so

percorso [percorso] *m* route ▸ percorso di visita tour route

perdere [perdayray] *v* to lose; to waste

perfetto, a [perfetto] *adj* perfect

pericolante [payreekolantay] *adj* unsafe

pericolo [payreekolo] *m* danger ▸ 'pericolo (di morte)' 'danger'

permanente [permanentay] *adj* permanent

però [payro] *conj* but

pertanto [pertanto] *conj* therefore

Perugia [payrooja] *f* Perugia

pesante [paysantay] *adj* heavy

pesca [pesca] *f* peach ▸ pesche ripiene *peach halves filled with a mixture of amaretto cookies and almonds and baked in white wine*

pesce [payshay] *m* fish

peso [payzo] *m* weight ▸ peso lordo/netto gross/net weight

pessimo, a [pesseemo] *adj* terrible

pesto [pesto] *m* pesto

petto [petto] *m* chest ▸ petto di pollo chicken breast

pezzo [petso] *m* piece; *(component)* part ▸ pezzo di ricambio spare part

la pizza

Pizzas were first made in the poorest parts of Naples. Dock workers put whatever they had available (oil, tomato, cheese...) onto pieces of dough. When touring the town in 1889, Queen Margaret of Savoy developed a liking for this 'poor man's dish' and the *pizza margherita*, the queen of pizzas, was born.

piacere [pee-achayray] *m* pleasure ◆ *v* ▸ mi piace il mare I like the ocean ▸ mi piacciono gli spaghetti I like spaghetti ▸ per piacere please ▸ piacere (di conoscerla)! pleased to meet you ▸ piacere mio! my pleasure!

piacevole [pee-achayvolay] *adj* pleasant

piano [pee-ano] *adv* slowly ◆ *m (story)* floor ▸ piano piano gradually ▸ il piano di sopra/di sotto the floor above/below

pianoterra [pee-anoterra] *m* first floor

pianterreno [pee-anterrayno] *m* first floor

pianura [pee-anoora] *f* plain ▸ la pianura padana the Po valley

piatto [pee-atto] *m (for food)* plate; *(food)* dish ▸ piatto del giorno today's special ▸ primo piatto first course ▸ secondo piatto second/main course

piazza [pee-atsa] *f* square

piazzale [pee-atsalay] *m* (large) square

picchiare [peekkee-aray] *v* to hit

piccione [peechonay] *m* pigeon

piccolo, a [peekkolo] *adj* small

piede [pee-ayday] *m* foot ▸ a piedi on foot

pieno, a [pee-ayno] *adj* full

pietà [pee-ayta] *f* pity

pietra [pee-aytra] *f* stone ▸ pietra preziosa precious stone

pila [peela] *f* pile; battery ▸ pila (tascabile) flashlight

pinacoteca [peenakotayka] *f* art gallery

pineta [peenayta] *f* pine forest

pinolo [peenolo] *m* pine nut

pinzimonio [peentseemonee-o] *m dip of olive oil, salt, and pepper for crudités*

pioggia [pee-oja] *f* rain

piombo [pee-ombo] *m* lead ▸ 'senza piombo' 'unleaded'

piovere [pee-ovayray] *v* to rain ▸ piove it's raining

pisello [peezello] *m* pea

pista [peesta] *f* track; *(for skiing)* run; runway ▸ pista ciclabile bike lane

pistacchio [peestakkio] *m* pistachio

pittore, trice [peettoray] *m, f* painter

pittura [peettoora] *f* painting; paint ▸ 'pittura fresca' 'wet paint'

più [pyoo] *adv* more; most ▸ per di più what's more ▸ più volte several times

piuttosto [pyoottosto] *adv* rather

pizza [peetsa] *f* pizza

pizzaiola [peetsa-yola] *f* ▸ alla pizzaiola *with a tomato, garlic, and oregano sauce*

placcare [plakkaray] *v* ▸ placcato d'oro gold-plated

plastica [plasteeka] *f* plastic

pneumatico [pnay-oomateeko] *m* tire

po' [po] *n* ▸ un po' di sale a little salt

poco, a [poko] *adj* not much; not many ▸ tra poco farà buio it'll soon be dark

poi [po-ee] *adv* then

poiché [po-eekay] *conj* since

polenta [polenta] *f* polenta ▸ polenta pasticciata alla veneta *polenta cooked in the oven with meat juices, tomato sauce, and pieces of sausage*

polizia [poleetsee-a] *f* police

poliziotto, a [poleetsee-otto] *m, f* police officer

pollo [pollo] *m* chicken

polmone [polmonay] *m* lung

polmonite [polmoneetay] *f* pneumonia

polo [polo] *m* ▸ il polo Nord/Sud the North/South Pole

polpetta [polpetta] *f* meatball

polpettone [polpettonay] *m* meatloaf

polpo [polpo] *m* octopus

polvere [polvayray] *f* ▸ in polvere powdered

pomata [pomata] *f* ointment

pomeriggio [pomayreejo] *m* afternoon

pomodoro [pomodoro] *m* tomato

pompelmo [pompelmo] *m* grapefruit

ponte [pontay] *m (across river)* bridge; *(on ship)* deck

porcellana [porchellana] *f* porcelain

porchetta [porketta] *f* roast pork

porcino [porcheeno] *m* cep

porco [porko] *m* pork

porro [porro] *m* leek

portare [portaray] *v* to carry; to take; to bring

portata [portata] *f (of meal)* course ▸ alla portata di tutti within everyone's means

portatile [portateelay] *adj* portable

portico [porteeko] *m* portico ▸ i portici di via Roma the arcades of Via Roma

porto [porto] *m* port

Portogallo [portogallo] *n* ▸ il Portogallo Portugal

portoghese [portogayzay] *adj* Portuguese

portone [portonay] *m* main door

porzione [portsee-onay] *f* portion

posta [posta] *f* mail; post office ▸ posta aerea airmail

posteriore [postayree-oray] *adj* back; later

posto [posto] *m* place ▸ posto di blocco roadblock ▸ posto letto bed

potabile [potabeelay] *adj* drinkable ▸ 'acqua non potabile' 'non-potable water'

potente [potentay] *adj* powerful

potere [potayray] *v* to be able to ▸ non potete parcheggiare qui you can't park here ▸ può darsi maybe, perhaps

povero, a [povayro] *adj* poor

pozzo [potso] *m* well

pranzo [prandzo] *m* lunch

precedenza [praychaydentsa] *f* right of way ▸ dare la precedenza (a) *(in vehicle)* to give way to

precipitare [praycheepeetaray] *v* to fall

pregare [praygaray] *v* to pray

pregiato, a [prayjato] *adj* fine

prego [praygo] *excl (as reply)* you're welcome ▸ prego, si sieda please sit down

premere [praymayray] *v* to press

premio [premee-o] *m* prize ▸ see box on p. 48

prendere [prendayray] *v* to take

prenotare [praynotaray] *v* to book

preoccupare [pray-okkooparay] *v* to worry

presepe [prayzaypay] *m* Nativity scene

presepio [prayzaypee-o] *m* Nativity scene

preservativo [prayzervateevo] *m* condom

presso [presso] *prep* near

prestare [prestaray] *v* to lend

i premi letterari

There are more than 1,300 literary awards in Italy. The most prestigious is the *Strega* prize, which was first awarded in 1947. Other major awards are the *Viareggio-Répaci* prize, the *Campiello* prize, and the *Bagutta* prize.

presto [presto] *adv* early; soon ▸ **fai presto!** hurry up! ▸ **a presto!** see you soon ▸ **al più presto** as soon as possible

prevedere [prayvaydayray] *v* to expect

previsione [prayveezee-onay] *f* prediction ▸ **previsioni del tempo/meteorologiche** weather forecast

prezioso, a [pretsee-ozo] *adj* precious

prezzo [pretso] *m* price ▸ **il prezzo è comprensivo del servizio** the price includes service charge ▸ **a buon prezzo** cheaply

prigione [preejonay] *f* prison

prima [preema] *adv* before ▸ **prima di tutto** first of all

primavera [preemavayra] *f* spring

primo, a [preemo] *num* first ◆ *m* first course ▸ **di prima qualità** first-class

principiante [preencheepee-antay] *mf* beginner

principio [preencheepee-o] *m* beginning, start; principle ▸ **per principio** on principle

privato, a [preevato] *adj* private

prodotto [prodotto] *m* product

produttore, trice [prodoottoray] *m, f* producer

profumeria [profoomayree-a] *f* perfumery

proibire [pro-eebeeray] *v* to ban ▸ **è proibito fumare** there's no smoking

pronto, a [pronto] *adj* ready ◆ *excl (on phone)* hello! ▸ **pronto soccorso** first aid, emergency room

proposta [proposta] *f* proposal

proprietà [propree-aytà] *f* property

proprio, a [propree-o] *adj* exact ◆ *adv* really ▸ **proprio così** exactly

prosciutto [proshootto] *m* ham ▸ **prosciutto cotto** cooked ham ▸ **prosciutto crudo** raw ham

prossimo, a [prosseemo] *adj* next ▸ **avanti il prossimo!** next!

prova [prova] *f* try

provare [provaray] *v* to try

proveniente [provaynee-entay] *adj* ▸ **proveniente da** from

provincia [proveencha] *f* province

provinciale [proveenchalay] *adj* provincial

prudenza [proodentsa] *f* prudence ▸ **'prudenza'** 'caution'

prugna [proonya] *f* plum

pubblicare [poobbleekaray] *v* to publish

Puglia [poolya] *f* ▸ **la Puglia** Puglia

pugno [poonyo] *m* fist; punch

pulire [pooleeray] *v* to clean

pulito, a [pooleeto] *adj* clean

pulizia [pooleetsee-a] *f* cleaning ▸ **fare le pulizie** to do the cleaning

pullman [poollman] *m* bus

pulsante [poolsantay] *m* button

punto [poonto] *m* point ▸ **punto di ritrovo** meeting point ▸ **punto vendita** *a store that is licensed to sell a certain product* ▸ **a tal punto che** so much so that ▸ **le tre in punto** three o'clock exactly

puntuale [poontooalay] *adj* punctual

puntura [poontoora] *f (of mosquito)* bite; *(of bee, wasp)* sting; *(medical)* injection

purché [poorkay] *conj* provided (that)

pure [pooray] *adv* also ▸ faccia pure! please do!

purtroppo [poortroppo] *adv* unfortunately

puzzare [pootsaray] *v* to stink

q

qua [kwa] *adv* here ▸ ecco qua there you are ▸ questo qua this one here ▸ per di qua this way

quadrato [kwadrato] *m* square

quadro [kwadro] *m* picture

qualche [kwalkay] *adj* a few; some qualche volta sometimes ▸ in qualche modo somehow

qualcosa [kwalkoza] *pron* something ▸ qualcosa da bere something to drink ▸ qualcos'altro something else

qualcuno [kwalkoono] *pron* someone, somebody ▸ qualcun altro someone else

quale [kwalay] *adj* which ▸ quale vuole? which (one) do you want?

qualsiasi [kwalsee-asee] *adj* any ▸ uno qualsiasi any one at all

qualunque [kwaloonkway] *adj* any ▸ qualunque cosa succeda whatever happens ▸ uno qualunque anyone at all

quando [kwando] *adv* when ▸ da quando sono qui since I've been here

quanto, a [kwanto] *adj* how much; how many ◆ *adv* how much ▸ quanto costa? how much is it? ▸ quanto tempo ci vuole? how long does it take? ▸ quanti anni hai? how old are you? ▸ quanto prima as soon as possible ▸ in quanto as, since

quaranta [kwaranta] *num* forty

quarantesimo, a [kwarantayzeemo] *num* fortieth

quaresima [kwarayzeema] *f* Lent

quarto, a [kwarto] *num* fourth ◆ *m* quarter ▸ le tre e un quarto a quarter past three

quasi [kwazee] *adv* almost

quattordicesimo, a [kwattordeechayzeemo] *num* fourteenth

quattordici [kwattordeechee] *num* fourteen

quattro [kwattro] *num* four ▸ in quattro e quattr'otto in less than no time

quello, a [kwello] *adj* that ◆ *pron* that

---

i quotidiani

The biggest-selling daily newspapers are Milan's *Corriere della Sera*, Rome's *La Repubblica*, and Turin's *La Stampa*. There are also popular sports dailies: *La Gazzetta dello Sport*, *Tuttosport* and *Corriere dello Sport*. *Il Sole 24 Ore* is the main financial daily.

(one) ▸ abito in quella casa I live in that house ▸ la mia macchina è quella my car's that one

questo, a [kwesto] *adj* this ◆ *pron* this (one) ▸ questa finestra è aperta this window's open ▸ questo è Franco this is Franco

questura [kwestoora] *f* police station

qui [kwee] *adv* here ▸ di/da qui from here ▸ da qui in avanti from now on

quindi [kweendee] *conj* so

quindicesimo, a [kweendeechayzeemo] *num* fifteenth

quindici [kweendeechee] *num* fifteen

quinto, a [kweento] *num* fifth

quota [kwota] *f* altitude

quotidiano [kwoteedee-ano] *m* daily (newspaper) ▸ see box on p. 49

rabarbaro [rabarbaro] *m* rhubarb

rabbia [rabbee-a] *f* anger; rabies

raccogliere [rakkolyayray] *v (from ground)* to pick up; *(fruit, flowers)* to pick

raccolta [rakkolta] *f* collection; harvest ▸ raccolta differenziata *waste separation with different bags for different types*

raccomandare [rakkomandaray] *v* to recommend ▸ mi raccomando remember

raccomandata [rakkomandata] *f* registered letter

racconto [rakkonto] *m* story; *(in literature)* short story

raccordo [rakkordo] *m* ramp ▸ raccordo anulare beltway

radicchio [radeekkee-o] *m* radicchio

radice [radeechay] *f* root

raffreddare [raffreddaray] *v* to cool

raffreddore [raffreddoray] *m* cold

ragazza [ragatsa] *f* girl; girlfriend

ragazzo [ragatso] *m* boy; boyfriend

raggio [rajo] *m* ray

raggiungere [rajoonjayray] *v* to catch up to; *(place)* to reach

ragione [rajonay] *f* reason

ragno [ranyo] *m* spider

ragù [ragoo] *m* meat sauce

RAI [ra-ee] *f Italian state television and radio company*

rallentare [rallentaray] *v* to slow down ▸ 'rallentare!' 'slow'

rame [ramay] *m* copper

ramo [ramo] *m* branch

rana [rana] *f* frog

rapa [rapa] *f* turnip

rapina [rapeena] *f* robbery

rasoio [razo-yo] *m* razor

rassegna [rassenya] *f* exhibit ▸ rassegna di film film festival ▸ la rassegna degli spettacoli event listings

ravanello [ravanello] *m* radish

re [ray] *m* king

reale [rayalay] *adj* real

realtà [ray-alta] *f* reality

reato [rayato] *m* crime

recente [raychentay] *adj* recent

recitare [raycheetaray] *v (in play, movie)* to act

reclamo [rayklamo] *m* complaint

regalare [raygalaray] *v* to give

regalo [raygalo] *m* present

reggere [rejayray] *v* to hold

reggia [reja] *f* palace

reggiseno [rejeesayno] *m* bra

regia [rayjeea] *f* direction

regina [rayjeena] *f* queen

regione [rayjone] *f* region

regista [rayjeesta] *mf* director

registrare [rayjeestraray] *v* to record

regno [renyo] *m* kingdom; reign ▸ il Regno Unito the United Kingdom

regolamento [raygolamento] *m* regulations

regolare [raygolaray] *adj* regular ♦ *v* to regulate

reliquia [rayleekwee-a] *f* relic

rendere [rendayray] *v* to give back

reparto [rayparto] *m* department

repubblica [raypoobbleeka] *f* republic

residenza [rayzeedentsa] *f* residence

respirare [respeeraray] *v* to breathe

restare [restaray] *v* to stay

restauro [restowro] *m* restoration

restituire [resteetoo-eeray] *v* to return

resto [resto] *m* rest; *(money)* change ▸ del resto what's more

restringere [restreenjayray] *v* to restrict

rete [raytay] *f* net; *(of roads)* network

retro [retro] *m* back ▸ 'vedi retro' 'see reverse' ▸ sul retro on the back

retromarcia [retromarcha] *f* reverse

rettile [retteelay] *m* reptile

rianimazione [ree-aneematsee-onay] *f* intensive care

riapertura [ree-apertoora] *f* reopening

riassunto [ree-assoonto] *m* summary

ribes [reebess] *m* currant

ricambi [reekambee] *mpl (for car)* spare parts

ricamo [reekamo] *m* embroidery

ricchezza [reekketsa] *f* wealth

riccio, a [reecho] *adj* curly ♦ *n* ▸ riccio di mare sea urchin

ricciolo [reecholo] *m* curl

ricco, a [reekko] *adj* rich

ricerca [reecherka] *f* research

ricetta [reechetta] *f* recipe ▸ ricetta medica prescription

ricevimento [reechayveemento] *m* reception

ricevuta [reechayvoota] *f* receipt

richiesta [reekee-esta] *f* request ▸ 'fermata a richiesta' stop at which bus halts only by request of a dismounting or boarding passenger

riciclare [reecheeclaray] *v* to recycle

riconoscenza [reekonoshentsa] *f* gratitude

riconoscere [reekonoshayray] *v* to recognize

ricoprire [reekopreeray] *v* to cover

ricordare [reekordaray] *v* to remember

ricordo [reekordo] *m* memory; souvenir

ricoverare [reekovayraray] *v* to admit

ridere [reedayray] *v* to laugh

riduzione [reedootsee-onay] *f* reduction

riempire [ree-empeeray] *v* to fill

riferimento [reefayreemento] *m* reference

rifiuti [reefyootee] *mpl* garbage

rifiuto [reefyooto] *m* refusal

riflesso [reeflesso] *m* reflection

riflettere [reeflettayray] *v* to reflect

rifugiato, a [reefoojato] *m, f* refugee

rifugio [reefoojo] *m* shelter

riga [reega] *f* line ▸ a righe *(fabric, piece of clothing)* striped

rigido, a [reejeedo] *adj* rigid; *(climate)* harsh

rilassare [reelassaray] *v* to relax

il Rinascimento

The transition from medieval to modern art known as the Renaissance was a unique period in the history of art, lasting from the 15th century to the end of the 16th. It saw Italy produce many of the world's greatest artists, including Leonardo da Vinci, Michelangelo and Raphael.

rilevante [reelayvantay] *adj* significant

rilievo [reelee-ayvo] *m* relief

rimandare [reemandaray] *v* to postpone

rimanere [reemanayray] *v* to remain

rimborsare [reemborsaray] *v* to reimburse

rimedio [reemaydee-o] *m* cure

rimettere [reemettayray] *v* to put back

rimorchio [reemorkee-o] *m* towing; trailer

rimorso [reemorso] *m* remorse

rimozione [reemotsee-onay] *f* removal ▸ 'zona rimozione' 'tow-away zone'

rimpiangere [reempee-anjayray] *v* to regret

Rinascimento [reenasheemento] *m* ▸ il Rinascimento the Renaissance

rinfrescante [reenfreskantay] *adj* refreshing

rinfresco [reenfresko] *m* reception

ringhiera [reenghee-ayra] *f* railing; banister

ringraziare [reengratsee-aray] *v* to thank

rinomato, a [reenomato] *adj* famous

rinunciare a [reenooncharay a] *v* to give up

rinviare [reenvee-aray] *v* to postpone

rione [ree-onay] *m* district

riparare [reepararay] *v* to protect; to repair; to make amends for

riparo [reeparo] *m* shelter

ripetere [reepaytayray] *v* to repeat

ripido, a [reepeedo] *adj* steep

ripieno, a [reepee-ayno] *adj* stuffed; filled ◆ *m* stuffing; filling

riportare [reeportaray] *v* to take back; to bring back ▸ riportare una ferita to suffer an injury

riposare [reepozaray] *v* to rest

riposo [reepozo] *m* rest ▸ 'riposo settimanale' 'closed today'

riprendere [reeprendayray] *v* to take again

ripresa [reeprayza] *f* ▸ a più riprese several times

riproduzione [reeprodootsee-onay] *f* reproduction

ripulire [reepooleeray] *v* to clean

risalire [reesaleeray] *v* to go back up

risarcimento [reesarcheemento] *m* compensation

risata [reezata] *f* laugh

riscaldamento [reeskaldamento] *m* heating

rischio [reeskee-o] *m* risk

riserva [reezerva] *f* reservation

riservato, a [reezervato] *adj* reserved ▸ 'parcheggio riservato' 'reserved parking'

riso [reezo] *m* rice ▸ risi e bisi *rice and pea soup*

risolvere [reezolvayray] *v* to resolve

risorsa [reezorsa] *f* resource

risotto [reezotto] *m* risotto ▸ risotto alla

milanese saffron risotto

risparmiare [reesparmee-aray] *v* to save

rispettare [reespettaray] *v* to respect

rispetto [reespetto] *m* respect

rispondere [reespondaray] *v* to answer, to reply

risposta [reesposta] *f* answer, reply

rissa [reessa] *f* brawl

ristorante [reestorantay] *m* restaurant

risultato [reezooltato] *m* result

risveglio [reezvelyo] *m* awakening

ritardare [reetardaray] *v* to be late

ritardo [reetardo] *m* delay

ritirare [reeteeraray] *v* to withdraw

rito [reeto] *m* rite

ritornare [reetornaray] *v* to return

ritratto [reetratto] *m* portrait

ritrovare [reetrovaray] *v* to find; to meet

ritrovo [reetrovo] *m* meeting place

rituale [reetoo-alay] *adj* ritual

riuscire [ree-oosheeray] *v* to succeed

riva [reeva] *f* bank; shore

rivendita [reevendeeta] *f* ▸ rivendita di giornali newsstand

rivenditore, trice [reevendeetoray] *m, f* ▸ rivenditore autorizzato authorized dealer

riviera [reevee-ayra] *f* coast

rivista [reeveesta] *f* magazine

rivoluzione [reevolootsee-onay] *f* revolution

roba [roba] *f* things

rocca [rokka] *f* fortress

roccaforte [rokkafortay] *f* fortress

roccia [rocha] *f* rock

rognone [ronyonay] *m* kidney ▸ rognoni alla romana *kidneys in white wine and parsley*

rogo [rogo] *m* stake

romanico, a [romaneeko] *adj* Romanesque

romano, a [romano] *adj* Roman

romanzo [romandzo] *m* novel

rompere [rompayray] *v* to break

rondine [rondeenay] *f* swallow

rosone [rozonay] *m* rose window; ceiling rose

rossetto [rossetto] *m* lipstick

rosso, a [rosso] *adj* red

rosticceria [rosteechayree-a] *f* *store or restaurant selling roast meats*

rotonda [rotonda] *f* terrace; traffic circle

rotondo, a [rotondo] *adj* round

rotto, a [rotto] *adj* broken

roulotte [roolot] *f* trailer

rovescio [rovesho] *m* back ▸ al rovescio back to front

rovina [roveena] *f* ruin

rovinare [roveenaray] *v* to ruin

rubare [roobaray] *v* to steal

rubinetto [roobeenetto] *m* faucet

rubino [roobeeno] *m* ruby

rucola [rookola] *f* arugula

rumore [roomoray] *m* noise

ruota [roo-ota] *f* wheel ▸ ruota di scorta spare wheel

ruscello [rooshello] *m* stream

le sagre

Sagre are local festivals. Some celebrate the patron saint of a town or the anniversary of the founding of a church with processions, fairs, and carnivals. Others are organized to celebrate a local product with stands where you can sample local wine, truffles, chestnuts etc.

S

sabato [sabato] *m* Saturday ▸ **sabato scorso** last Saturday ▸ **di sabato** on Saturdays

sabbia [sabbee-a] *f* sand

sacco [sakko] *m* bag ▸ **un sacco di** a lot of ▸ **sacco a pelo** sleeping bag ▸ **pranzo al sacco** bag lunch

sacro, a [sakro] *adj* sacred

saggio [sajo] *m* sample; essay

sagra [sagra] *f* festival

sala [sala] *f* room ▸ **sala d'aspetto/d'attesa** waiting room ▸ **sala da tè** tearoom

salame [salamay] *m* salami

salatini [salateenee] *mpl* crackers

salato, a [salato] *adj* salty; salted

saldo [saldo] *m* balance ▸ **in saldo** on sale ▸ **'saldi' 'sale'**

sale [salay] *m* salt ▸ **sale grosso** rock salt

salire [saleeray] *v* to go up; to come up

salita [saleeta] *f* ascent ▸ **in salita** uphill

salmì [salmee] *n half-roasted game or poultry finished in wine sauce*

salmone [salmonay] *m* salmon

salsa [salsa] *f* sauce ▸ **salsa di pomodoro** tomato sauce

salsiccia [salseecha] *f* sausage

saltare [saltaray] *v* to jump; to sauté

salumi [saloomee] *mpl* cold cuts

salute [salootay] *f* health

saluto [salooto] *m* greeting

salvagente [salvajentay] *m* life buoy; life preserver

salvare [salvaray] *v* to save

salve [salvay] *excl* hi!; bye!

salvo, a [salvo] *adj* safe ◆ *m* ▸ **mettersi in salvo** to get to safety

sangue [sangway] *m* blood ▸ **a sangue freddo** in cold blood ▸ **al sangue** rare

San Marino [san mareeno] *f* San Marino

sano, a [sano] *adj* healthy ▸ **sano e**

sale da tè

Sale da tè (tearooms) are often pastry shops (*pasticcerie*) which serve *paste* (pastries) and also thick hot chocolate (*la cioccolata*), which is not to be confused with *il cioccolato* (chocolate to eat). In Turin, they also sell the famous *gianduiotti*, chocolates made with hazelnuts from Piedmont.

i Santi

Every town and city in Italy has its own patron saint. The patron saint's feast day, which is different for every saint, is a local and school holiday with religious processions and fairs. Some towns put up lights for the day.

---

salvo safe and sound ▸ **sano come un pesce** (as) fit as a fiddle

santo, a [santo] *adj* Saint ▸ San Francesco Saint Francis ▸ Santo Stefano Boxing Day

santuario [santoo-aree-o] *m* sanctuary

sapere [sapayray] *v* to know

sapone [saponay] *m* soap

sapore [saporay] *m* flavor

Sardegna [sardenya] *f* ▸ la Sardegna Sardinia

savoiardi [savo-yardee] *mpl* ladyfingers

sbagliare [zbalyaray] *v* to get wrong ▸ ho sbagliato strada I've taken the wrong road

sbaglio [zbalyo] *m* mistake

sbarco [zbarko] *m* disembarkation

sbattere [zbattayray] *v* ▸ sbattere contro (*wall*) to bump into

sbocco [zbokko] *m* end ▸ 'strada senza sbocco' 'no through road'

sbrigarsi [zbreegarsee] *v* to hurry up

scacchi [skakkee] *mpl* chess ▸ a scacchi checked

scadere [skadayray] *v* to expire

scala [skala] *f* ladder ▸ scala mobile escalator ▸ scale stairs

scaldare [skaldaray] *v* to heat

scalino [skaleeno] *m* step

scaloppina [skaloppeena] *f* (*meat*) scallop

scambio [skambee-o] *m* exchange

scampi [skampee] *mpl* Norway lobsters

scapolo [skapolo] *m* bachelor

scappare [skapparay] *v* to run away

scarico [skareeko] *m* dumping ▸ 'divieto di scarico' 'no dumping'

scarpa [skarpa] *f* shoe

scarso, a [skarso] *adj* insufficient ▸ un chilo scarso just under a kilo

scatola [skatola] *f* box

scatto [skatto] *m* click ▸ di scatto suddenly

scavi [skavee] *mpl* excavation

scelta [shelta] *f* choice ▸ 'dolce o frutta a scelta' 'choice of dessert or fruit'

scelto, a [shelto] *adj* first-class

scena [shayna] *f* scene

scendere [shendayray] *v* to go down; to come down

scheda [skayda] *f* card ▸ scheda (magnetica) magnetic-strip card

scheletro [skayletro] *m* skeleton

---

il teatro alla Scala

La Scala, which first opened its doors in 1778, is one of the world's most famous venues for opera and ballet. Its productions feature many of the greatest opera singers, ballet dancers, musicians, and conductors in the world.

schermo [skermo] *m* screen

scherzo [skertso] *m* joke

schiacciare [skee-acharay] *v* to crush

schiaffo [skee-affo] *m* slap

schiavo, a [skee-avo] *m, f* slave

schiena [skee-ayna] *f* back

schifo [skeefo] *m* disgust ▸ che schifo! how disgusting!

schiuma [skyee-ooma] *f* foam ▸ schiuma da barba shaving cream

sci [shee] *m* skiing; ski ▸ sci d'acqua water skiing

sciacquare [shakkwaaray] *v* to rinse

sciare [shee-aray] *v* to ski

scimmia [sheemmee-a] *f* monkey

scioccare [shokkaray] *v* to shock

sciocco, a [shokko] *adj* silly

sciopero [shopero] *m* strike

scippo [sheeppo] *m* mugging

scivolare [sheevolaray] *v* to slip

scogliera [skolyayra] *f* rocks

scoglio [skolyo] *m* rock

scommessa [skommessa] *f* bet

sconfitta [skonfeetta] *f* defeat

scongelare [skonjaylaray] *v* to defrost

sconosciuto, a [skonoshooto] *adj* unknown

scontato, a [skontato] *adj* discounted ▸ prezzi scontati sale prices

sconto [skonto] *m* discount ▸ 'sconti' 'sale'

scontrino [skontreeno] *m* receipt ▸ 'munirsi dello scontrino alla cassa' *sign in a bar asking customers to pay for their order at the cash register and then take the receipt to the counter to get served*

scontro [skontro] *m* collision

scoperta [skoperta] *f* discovery

scopo [skopo] *m* aim

scordare [skordaray] *v* to forget

scorso, a [skorso] *adj* last ▸ l'estate scorsa last summer

scossa [skossa] *f (electric)* shock

scottare [skottaray] *v* to burn

Scozia [skotsee-a] *f* ▸ la Scozia Scotland

scozzese [skotsaysay] *adj* Scottish

scritta [skreetta] *f* (piece of) writing

scritto, a [skreetto] *adj* written

scrittore, trice [skreettoray] *m, f* writer

scultore, trice [skooltoray] *m, f* sculptor, sculptress

scultura [skooltoora] *f* sculpture

scuola [skoo-ola] *f* school

scuro, a [skooro] *adj* dark

scusa [skooza] *f* apology; excuse ▸ chiedo scusa I apologize

scusare [skoozaray] *v* to excuse ▸ (mi) scusi, dov'è la stazione? excuse me, where's the station? ▸ scusi! excuse me!

se [say] *conj* if ▸ se non sbaglio ... if I'm not mistaken ...

secco, a [sekko] *adj* dry

secolo [saykolo] *m* century

seconda [saykonda] *f* ▸ seconda classe second class

secondo, a [saykondo] *num* second ◆ *m (part of minute)* second; *(part of meal)* main course ▸ secondo me in my opinion ▸ di seconda mano secondhand

sede [sayday] *f* office

sedere [sayderay] *m* bottom ▸ posti a sedere seats

sedersi [saydersee] *vr* to sit down ▸ si sieda sit down

sedia [saydee-a] *f* chair

sedicesimo, a [saydeechayzeemo] *num* sixteenth

sedici [saydeechee] *num* sixteen

sedile [saydeelay] *m* seat

seggiovia [sejovee-a] *f* chairlift

segnalare [saynyalaray] *v* to signal

segnale [saynyalay] *m* signal; *(on road)* sign ▸ segnale d'allarme alarm bell

segnaletica [saynyalayteeka] *f* signs ▸ 'segnaletica in rifacimento' 'no road markings'

segno [senyo] *m* sign

segreteria [saygraytayree-a] *f (in government)* secretariat

seguire [saygweeray] *v* to follow

seguito [saygweeto] *m* continuation ▸ due giorni di seguito two days running ▸ in seguito then

sei [say-ee] *num* six ▸ ha sei anni he/she is six (years old) ▸ sono le sei it's six (o'clock)

seicento [say-eechento] *num* six hundred ♦ *m* ▸ il Seicento the seventeenth century

selezionare [sayletsee-onaray] *v* to select

semaforo [semaforo] *m* traffic lights

sembrare [sembraray] *v* to seem

semifreddo [saymeefreddo] *m* ice-cream dessert

semplice [sempleechay] *adj* simple

sempre [sempray] *adv* always ▸ da sempre always

senape [saynapay] *f* mustard

sennò [senno] *adv* otherwise

seno [sayno] *m (of person)* breast

senso [senso] *m* sense; meaning; direction ▸ senso vietato no entry ▸ in senso orario clockwise

sentire [senteeray] *v* to feel; to hear

senza [sentsa] *prep & conj* without ▸ senz'altro of course ▸ senza dubbio without a doubt

seppia [seppee-a] *f* cuttlefish

sera [sayra] *f* evening ▸ di sera in the evening

serio, a [sayree-o] *adj* serious ▸ sul serio seriously

servizio [serveetsee-o] *m* service ▸ servizio escluso gratuity not included

sessanta [sessanta] *num* sixty

sessantesimo, a [sessantayzeemo] *num* sixtieth

sesso [sesso] *m* sex

sesto, a [sesto] *num* sixth

seta [sayta] *f* silk

sete [saytay] *f* thirst

settanta [settanta] *num* seventy

settantesimo, a [settantayzeemo] *num* seventieth

sette [settay] *num* seven

settecento [settaychento] *num* seven hundred ♦ *m* ▸ il Settecento the eighteenth century

settembre [settembray] *m* September ▸ all'inizio di settembre at the beginning of September

settentrionale [settentree-onalay] *adj* northern

settimana [setteemana] *f* week

settimanale [setteemanalay] *adj* weekly

settimo, a [setteemo] *num* seventh

severamente [sayvayramentay] *adv* strictly ▸ 'è severamente vietato attraversare i binari' 'do not attempt to cross the tracks'

sformato [sformato] *m cheese or vegetable soufflé*

sfortuna [sfortoona] *f* bad luck

sgombro [zgombro] *m* mackerel

sgonfiare [zgonfee-aray] *v* to deflate

si [see] *pron* oneself; *(impersonal)* one ▸ si sono conosciuti a Roma they met in Rome ▸ si dice che ... it is said that ... ▸ 'si prega di non fumare' 'no smoking'

sì [see] *m* yes

siccome [seekkomay] *conj* as

Sicilia [seecheelee-a] *f* ▸ la Sicilia Sicily

la Smorfia

The *Smorfia* is a book, originally from Naples, that offers a way of interpreting dreams and the events of daily life by assigning each feature of them a number between 1 and 90. For example, 90 is associated with fear. People often use it to help them choose their lottery numbers.

sicurezza [sicooretsa] *f* security; safety

sicuro, a [seekooro] *adj* secure, safe; sure, certain ◆ *adv* of course

sigaretta [seegaretta] *f* cigarette

signora [seenyora] *f* woman; *(form of address)* M'am ▸ la signora Poli Mrs. Poli, Ms. Poli

signore [seenyoray] *m* man; *(form of address)* Sir ▸ il signor Martini Mr. Martini

signorina [seenyoreena] *f* young woman; *(form of address)* Miss

silenzio [seelentsee-o] *m* silence

simile [seemeelay] *adj* similar

sinagoga [seenagoga] *f* synagogue

sindaco [seendaco] *m* mayor

single [seengol] *mf* single person

singolo, a [seengolo] *adj* individual

sinistra [seeneestra] *f* left

ski-lift [skee-leeft] *m* ski lift

ski-pass [skee-pass] *m* ski pass

slavina [zlaveena] *f* snowslide

smalto [zmalto] *m* enamel

smarrimento [zmarreemento] *m* loss

smettere [zmettayray] *v* to stop ▸ smettila! stop it!

smorfia [zmorfee-a] *f* grimace

soccorso [sokkorso] *m* help ▸ soccorso stradale breakdown service

socio, a [socho] *m, f (of club)* member; *(in company)* partner

soddisfatto, a [soddeesfatto] *adj* satisfied

soffiare [soffee-aray] *v* to blow

soffocare [soffokaray] *v* to suffocate

soffrire [soffreeray] *v* to suffer

soffritto [soffreetto] *m onions, herbs and bacon or ham fried in oil or butter*

soggetto [sojetto] *m* subject

soggiorno [sojorno] *m* stay; living room

sogliola [solyola] *f (fish)* sole

sogno [sonyo] *m* dream

soldi [soldee] *mpl* money

sole [solay] *m* sun

solito, a [soleeto] *adj* usual ▸ di solito usually

sollevare [sollayvaray] *v* to lift

sollievo [sollee-ayvo] *m* relief

solo, a [solo] *adj* alone ◆ *adv* only ▸ da solo on one's own ▸ ho solo due euro I only have two euros

soltanto [soltanto] *adv* only

sonnifero [sonneefero] *m* sleeping pill

sonno [sonno] *m* sleep

sopra [sopra] *prep* on

soprannome [soprannomay] *m* nickname

soprattutto [soprattootto] *adv* above all

soprelevata [sopraylayvata] *f* overpass

sordo, a [sordo] *adj* deaf

sordomuto, a [sordomooto] *adj* hearing and speech impaired

sorella [sorella] *f* sister

sorgere [sorjayray] *v (sun)* to rise

sorpassare [sorpassaray] *v (in vehicle)* to pass

sorpresa [sorprayza] *f* surprise

sorriso [sorreezo] *m* smile

sospeso, a [sospayzo] *adj* hanging

sospetto, a [sospetto] *adj* suspicious

sosta [sosta] *f* stop ▸ 'sosta consentita solo per carico e scarico' 'parking permitted for passenger pick-up and drop-off only' ▸ 'sosta vietata' 'no parking'

sostanza [sostantsa] *f* substance

sostenere [sostaynayray] *v* to support

sostituire [sosteetoo-eeray] *v* to replace

sottaceti [sottachaytee] *mpl* pickles

sotterraneo, a [sotterranay-o] *adj* underground

sottile [sotteelay] *adj* thin

sottinteso, a [sotteentayzo] *adj* understood

sotto [sotto] *prep* under ▸ al piano di sotto on the floor below ▸ sott'olio in oil

sottopassaggio [sottopassajo] *m* underpass ▸ 'servirsi del sottopassaggio' 'use underpass'

sottosopra [sottosopra] *adj* upside down

sottosuolo [sottosoo-olo] *m* subsoil

sottovoce [sottovochay] *adv* quietly

sottovuoto [sottovoo-oto] *adv* vacuum-packed

spaccare [spakkaray] *v* to split

spaghetteria [spaghettayree-a] *f* restaurant specializing in pasta dishes

spaghetti [spaghettee] *mpl* spaghetti ▸ spaghetti aglio, olio e peperoncino *spaghetti with garlic, olive oil and chili peppers* ▸ spaghetti alle vongole *spaghetti with clam sauce*

Spagna [spanya] *f* ▸ la Spagna Spain

spagnolo, a [spanyolo] *adj* Spanish

spalla [spalla] *f* shoulder ▸ di spalle from the back

spaventare [spaventaray] *v* to frighten

spazio [spatsee-o] *m* space

spazzatura [spatsatoora] *f* trash

specchio [spekkee-o] *m* mirror

specie [spechay] *f* kind ▸ una specie di a kind of

spegnere [spenyayray] *v (fire)* to put out; *(light, TV)* to switch off

spendere [spendayray] *v* to spend

spese [spayzay] *fpl* expenses ▸ spese postali mailing charges

spesso, a [spesso] *adj* thick ◆ *adv* often

spettacolo [spettakolo] *m* show

spezzatino [spetsateeno] *m* stew

spia [spee-a] *f* warning light

spiacente [spee-achentay] *adj* sorry ▸ sono spiacente I'm sorry

spiaggia [spee-aja] *f* beach ▸ spiaggia privata private beach

spiccioli [speecholee] *mpl (money)* change

spiedino [spee-aydeeno] *m* kabob

spiedo [spee-aydo] *m (cooking)* spit ▸ allo spiedo on a spit

spinaci [speenachee] *mpl* spinach

spingere [speenjayray] *v* to push

spirito [speereeto] *m* mind; spirit

spogliatoio [spolyato-yo] *m* changing room

sporcare [sporkaray] *v* to dirty

sporco, a [sporko] *adj* dirty

sportello [sportello] *m (in bank)* counter; *(of building, vehicle)* door

spremuta [spraymoota] *f* ▸ spremuta di arancia freshly squeezed orange juice

spumante [spoomantay] *m* sparkling wine

spuntino [spoonteeno] *m* snack ▸ fare uno spuntino to have a snack

squadra [skwadra] *f* team

stabilimento [stabeeleemento] *m* complex ▸ **stabilimento balneare** *area of beach offering a number of services and activities*

stadio [stadee-o] *m* stadium

stagionale [stajonalay] *adj* seasonal

stagionato, a [stajonato] *adj* mature

stagione [stajonay] *f* season ▸ **alta/bassa stagione** high/low season

stamattina [stamatteena] *adv* this morning

stampa [stampa] *f* press

stancare [stancaray] *v* to tire

stanco, a [stanko] *adj* tired

stanotte [stanottay] *adv* tonight; last night

stanza [stantsa] *f* room

stare [staray] *v* to stay; to be ▸ **come sta?** *(formal)* how are you? ▸ **come stai?** *(informal)* how are you?

stasera [stasayra] *adv* this evening

statale [statalay] *adj* state

stato [stato] *m* state ▸ **gli Stati Uniti (d'America)** the United States (of America)

stazione [statsee-onay] *f* station ▸ **'ferma in tutte le stazioni'** 'stops at all stations'

stella [stella] *f* star

stesso, a [stesso] *adj* same ◆ *pron* same one ▸ **fa/è lo stesso** it doesn't matter

stoccafisso [stokkafeesso] *m* salted cod

stoffa [stoffa] *f* fabric

storia [storee-a] *f* history; story

stracciatella [strachatella] *f* vanilla ice cream with grated chocolate

strada [strada] *f* road; street ▸ **strada panoramica** scenic route ▸ **'strada deformata'** 'uneven road surface' ▸ **'strada transitabile con catene'** 'snow chains required'

straniero, a [stranee-ayro] *adj* foreign

strano, a [strano] *adj* strange

stretto, a [stretto] *adj* narrow ◆ *n* ▸ **lo stretto di Messina** the Strait of Messina

stringere [streenjayray] *v* to hold tight

striscia [streesha] *f* stripe ▸ **strisce (pedonali)** crosswalk

studente, essa [stoodentay] *m, f* student

studiare [stoodee-aray] *v* to study

studio [stoodee-o] *m (of doctor)* office

stufato [stoofato] *m* stew

stupendo, a [stoopendo] *adj* stupendous

su [soo] *prep* on ▸ **dai 18 anni in su** 18 and up

subacqueo, a [soobakkway-o] *adj* underwater

subito [soobeeto] *adv* immediately

successo [soochesso] *m* success ▸ **di successo** successful

succo [sookko] *m* juice ▸ **succo di frutta** fruit juice

sufficiente [sooffeechentay] *adj* sufficient

suggerimento [soojayreemento] *m* suggestion

sugo [soogo] *m* sauce ▸ **sugo di pomodoro** tomato sauce

suo [soo-o] *adj* his/her/its/their; *(formal)* your ◆ *pron* his/hers/its/theirs; *(formal)* yours ▸ **suo padre** his/her/your father ▸ **un suo amico** a friend of his/hers/yours ▸ **è (il) suo?** is it his/hers/yours?

suolo [soo-olo] *m* ground

suonare [soo-onaray] *v (bell)* to ring; *(musical instrument, piece of music)* to play

suono [soo-ono] *m* sound

suora [soo-ora] *f* nun

superare [soopayraray] *v* to pass

superficie [sooperfeechay] *f* surface

supermercato [soopermerkato] *m* supermarket

superstrada [sooperstrada] *f* freeway

susina [soozeena] *f* plum

svantaggio [zvantajo] *m* disadvantage ▸ a svantaggio di to the detriment of

svegliare [zvelyaray] *v* to wake

svelto, a [zvelto] *adj* quick ▸ alla svelta quickly

svendita [zvendeeta] *f* clearance sale

svincolo [zveenkolo] *m* (on road) junction

svoltare [zvoltaray] *v* to turn ▸ svoltare a sinistra to turn left

tabaccheria [tabakkayree-a] *f* tobacconist

tacchino [takkeeno] *n* turkey

tagliare [talyaray] *v* to cut

tale [talay] *adj* such ▸ quel tale that man ▸ un tale signor Rossi a Mr. Rossi

talmente [talmentay] *adv* so

tangenziale [tanjentsee-alay] *f* beltway

tanto, a [tanto] *adj* so much; so many ◆ *adv* so much ▸ ti ringrazio tanto thank you so much ▸ tanti saluti best wishes ▸ di tanto in tanto, ogni tanto every now and again ▸ non tanto not too much

tappa [tappa] *f* stage

tappo [tappo] *m* lid; cork

tardi [tardee] *adv* late ▸ al più tardi at the latest

targa [targa] *f* license plate

tariffa [tareeffa] *f* fare; rate ▸ tariffa ridotta reduced rate

tartufo [tartoofo] *m* (mushroom) truffle; *chocolate ice cream dessert*

tasca [taska] *f* pocket

tassa [tassa] *f* tax

tasto [tasto] *m* (on keyboard) key

tavolo [tavolo] *m* table

tè [tay] *m* tea

teatro [tayatro] *m* theater

tedesco, a [taydesko] *adj* German

telefono [taylefono] *m* (tele)phone ▸ telefono cellulare cellphone

Telepass® [taylaypass] *m automatic freeway toll system*

temere [temayray] *v* to fear

tempesta [tempesta] *f* storm

tempo [tempo] *m* time; weather ▸ tempo fa some time ago ▸ allo stesso tempo at the same time

temporale [temporalay] *m* storm

tenere [taynayray] *v* to hold

tenero, a [taynayro] *adj* tender

tentare [tentaray] *v* to attempt

teoria [tay-oree-a] *f* theory ▸ in teoria in theory

terme [termay] *fpl* thermal baths

termine [termeenay] *m* end

terrazza [terratsa] *f* terrace

terremoto [terraymoto] *m* earthquake

terreno [terrayno] *m* ground, land

terzo, a [tertso] *num* third

terzultimo, a [tertsoolteemo] *m, f* third-last

tessera [tessayra] *f* card ▸ tessera

magnetica swipe card

testa [testa] *f* head

testimone [testeemonay] *mf* witness

testo [testo] *m* text

Tevere [tayvayray] *m* ▸ il Tevere the Tiber

ti [tee] *pron* (to) you ▸ ti piace? do you like it?

tifoso, a [teefozo] *m, f* supporter

timbrare [teembraray] *v* to stamp

tipo [teepo] *m* type

tiramisù [teerameesoo] *m* tiramisu

tirare [teeraray] *v* to pull; to throw

tiro [teero] *m* shooting

Tirreno [teerrayno] *m* ▸ il (Mar) Tirreno the Tyrrhenian Sea

titolo [teetolo] *m* title

tizio, a [teetsee-o] *m, f* person

toast [tost] *m* toasted ham-and-cheese sandwich

toccare [tokkaray] *v* to touch

togliere [tolyayray] *v* to remove

tombola [tombola] *f* bingo

tonnellata [tonnellata] *f* ton

tonno [tonno] *m* tuna

topo [topo] *m* mouse

tornare [tornaray] *v* to return

torneo [tornayo] *m* tournament

torre [torray] *f* tower ▸ la torre di Pisa the Leaning Tower of Pisa

torrone [torronay] *m* nougat

torta [torta] *f* cake; tart ▸ torta gelato ice-cream cake

torto [torto] *m* wrong ▸ a torto unjustly

tosse [tossay] *f* cough

tossico, a [tosseeko] *adj* toxic

totano [totano] *m* squid

totocalcio [totokalcho] *m Italian system for betting on soccer games*

tra [tra] *prep* between ▸ tra breve/poco soon

tradizione [tradeetsee-onay] *f* tradition

traffico [traffeeko] *m* traffic

traforo [traforo] *m* tunnel

traghetto [traghetto] *m* ferry

tramezzino [tramedzeeno] *m* sandwich

tramonto [tramonto] *m* sunset

transitabile [tranzeetabeelay] *adj* negotiable

transito [tranzeeto] *m* transit ▸ 'divieto di transito' 'no entry'

trasgressore [trasgressoray] *m* trespasser ▸ 'i trasgressori saranno puniti' 'trespassers will be prosecuted'

trasportare [trasportaray] *v* to transport

trattare [trattaray] *v* to treat ▸ si tratta di it's a question of

tratto [tratto] *m (of pen)* stroke ▸ ad un tratto suddenly ▸ un bel tratto di strada a good stretch of road

trattoria [trattoree-a] *f* restaurant

tre [tray] *num* three

tredicesimo, a [traydeechayzeemo] *num* thirteenth

tredici [traydeechee] *num* thirteen

tremare [traymaray] *v* to tremble

tremendo, a [traymendo] *adj* terrible

Tremiti [traymeetee] *fpl* ▸ le (isole) Tremiti the Tremiti Islands

treno [trayno] *m* train ▸ treno espresso express train ▸ 'treni in partenza/in arrivo' 'departures/arrivals'

trenta [trenta] *num* thirty

trentesimo, a [trentayzeemo] *num* thirtieth

Trentino [trenteeno] *m* ▸ il Trentino-Alto Adige Trentino-Alto Adige

triangolo [tree-angolo] *m* triangle

trifolato, a [treefolato] *adj* ▸ funghi trifolati *mushrooms cooked in garlic, oil, and parsley*

triglia [treelya] *f (fish)* mullet

trippa [treeppa] *f* tripe

tritare [treetaray] *v (meat)* to grind; *(vegetables)* to chop

troppo, a [troppo] *adj & pron* too much; too many ◆ *adv & pron* too, too much

▸ parla troppo velocemente he speaks too quickly

trota [trota] *f* trout

trovare [trovaray] *v* to find

truffare [trooffaray] *v* to swindle

trullo [troollo] *n round house made of stone with a pointed roof, often found in Puglia*

tuo [too-o] *adj* your ◆ *pron* yours ▸ tuo padre your father ▸ un tuo amico a friend of yours ▸ è (il) tuo? is it yours?

turista [tooreesta] *mf* tourist

tutto, a [tootto] *adj* all ◆ *pron* everything ◆ *adv* completely ▸ tutti everyone, everybody ▸ tutto esaurito completely sold out ▸ in tutti i casi in any case ▸ tutto sommato all things considered ▸ tutt'al più if worse comes to worst ▸ tutt'altro not at all

U

ubriaco, a [oobree-ako] *adj* drunk

uccello [uchello] *m* bird

uccidere [ucheedayray] *v* to kill

uffa [ooffa] *excl* oh!

ufficiale [ooffeechalay] *adj* official ▸ pubblico ufficiale public official

ufficio [ooffeecho] *m* office ▸ ufficio informazioni information office ▸ ufficio turistico tourist office

Uffizi [ooffeetsee] *mpl* ▸ gli Uffizi the Uffizi (Gallery)

uguale [oogwalay] *adj* equal ◆ *adv* the same

ultimo, a [oolteemo] *adj* last

Umbria [oombree-a] *f* ▸ l'Umbria Umbria

umido, a [oomeedo] *adj* humid; damp ◆ *m* ▸ in umido stewed

undicesimo, a [oondeechayzeemo] *num* eleventh

undici [oondeechee] *num* eleven

unità [ooneeta] *f* unit; unity

uno, a [oono] *num & pron* one

uomo [oo-omo] *m* man ▸ da uomo *(clothes)* men's

---

l'Unità d'Italia

The first step toward the unification of Italy was the victory in 1859 of the alliance between Cavour's Piedmont and Napoleon III's France over Austria, which had until then controlled much of what is now Italy. Garibaldi then liberated the Kingdom of the Two Sicilies with his famous Expedition of the Thousand, before entering Naples in triumph. Victor Emmanuel II became king of a united Italy on March 17th 1861, with Rome and Venice being annexed a few years later.

uovo [oo-ovo] *m* egg ▸ uovo in camicia poached egg ▸ uovo sodo hard-boiled egg ▸ uova strapazzate scrambled eggs

USA [ooza] *mpl* ▸ gli USA the USA

usare [oozaray] *v* to use

uscire [oosheeray] *v* to go out; to come out

uscita [oosheeta] *f* exit ▸ 'uscita di emergenza/di sicurezza' 'emergency exit'

uso [oozo] *m* use ▸ 'per uso esterno' 'for external use only'

utente [ootentay] *mf* user

uva [oova] *f* grapes

uvetta [oovetta] *f* raisin

vacanza [vakantsa] *f* vacation

vagone [vagonay] *m (on train)* car; freight car ▸ vagone letto sleeping car ▸ vagone ristorante dining car

valanga [valanga] *f* avalanche

valere [valayray] *v* to be worth; *(ticket)* to be valid ▸ vale a dire that is

valico [valeeko] *m* pass

valido, a [valeedo] *adj* valid

valigia [valeeja] *f* suitcase

valle [vallay] *f* valley ▸ la Valle d'Aosta the Valle d'Aosta

valore [valoray] *m* value

valuta [valoota] *f* currency

vaniglia [vaneelya] *f* vanilla

vantaggio [vantajo] *m* advantage

vapore [vaporay] *m* steam ▸ cotto a vapore steamed

vaporetto [vaporetto] *m* steamboat

vario, a [varee-o] *adj* various

Vaticano [vateekano] *m* ▸ il Vaticano the Vatican

vecchio, a [vekkee-o] *adj* old

vedere [vaydayray] *v* to see ▸ ci vediamo! see you!

veduta [vaydoota] *f* view

veglione [velyonay] *m* New Year's Eve party

veleno [vaylayno] *m* poison

velenoso, a [vaylaynozo] *adj* poisonous

veloce [vaylochay] *adj* fast

velocità [vaylocheeta] *f* speed ▸ moderare la velocità to reduce speed

vendere [vendayray] *v* to sell ▸ 'vendesi' 'for sale'

vendita [vendeeta] *f* sale

venerdì [vaynerdee] *m* Friday

Venezia [vaynetsee-a] *f* Venice

---

il Vaticano

Vatican City is an independent state just 0.44 km² in size situated inside the city of Rome on the right bank of the Tiber. It prints its own stamps and uses the euro as its currency. It is under the Pope's authority and contains St Peter's and the Vatican Museum.

la Vespa

In 1946, the engineer Corradino D'Ascanio came up with the idea of a two-wheeled vehicle that was cheaper than a car but more practical than a motorcycle, and equipped with a spare wheel. This was the *Vespa*, which enjoyed meteoric success and has become one of the symbols of Italy.

venire [vayneeray] *v* to come ▸ viene tre euro it's 3 euros

ventesimo, a [ventayzeemo] *num* twentieth

venti [ventee] *num* twenty

vento [vento] *m* wind ▸ 'forte vento laterale' 'strong side-winds'

veramente [vayramentay] *adv* really; *(introducing an admission)* to tell the truth

verde [verday] *adj* green

verdura [verdoora] *f* vegetables

verificare [vayreefeekaray] *v* to check

vernice [verneechay] *f* paint ▸ 'vernice fresca' 'wet paint'

verso [verso] *prep* toward ▸ deve andare verso Bologna you have to head toward Bologna

vespa [vespa] *f* wasp

vestiario [vestee-aree-o] *m* clothes

vestito [vesteeto] *m* dress; *(for man)* suit ▸ vestiti clothes

Vesuvio [vayzoovee-o] *m* ▸ il Vesuvio Vesuvius

via [vee-a] *f* street; route; way ▸ via! go

away! ▸ andiamo via! let's go! ▸ e così via and so on

viaggiare [vee-ajaray] *v* to travel

viaggio [vee-ajo] *m* trip; journey

viale [vee-alay] *m* avenue

vicino, a [veecheeno] *adj* near ♦ *prep* ▸ vicino a near (to) ▸ da vicino up close

vicolo [veekolo] *m* alley ▸ vicolo cieco blind alley

vietato, a [vee-aytato] *adj* forbidden ▸ 'vietato l'accesso' 'no entry' ▸ 'è vietato fare il bagno nelle ore notturne' 'no swimming after dark' ▸ 'vietato fumare' 'no smoking'

vigile [veejeelay] *m* ▸ vigile (urbano) municipal police officer ▸ vigile del fuoco firefighter

vigilia [veejeelee-a] *f* eve ▸ la vigilia di Natale Christmas Eve

vincere [veenchayray] *v* to win

vino [veeno] *m* wine

viso [veezo] *m* face

vista [veesta] *f* sight; view ▸ a prima vista at first sight

visto [veesto] *m* visa

il vino

Almost all the Italian regions produce fine wines, whether red, white, or rosé. Their names often come from the region they are produced in, e.g. *Chianti*. Other famous wines are *Barolo* from Piedmont, *Valpolicella* from the Veneto, *Lambrusco* from Emilia Romagna, and *Primitivo* from Puglia.

vita [veeta] *f* life; waist

vitello [veetello] *m* calf; veal; calfskin
▸ **vitello tonnato** *cold veal with a tuna mayonnaise*

vittima [veetteema] *f* victim

vitto [veetto] *m* food ▸ **vitto e alloggio** room and board

vivere [veevayray] *v* to live

vivo, a [veevo] *adj* alive

voce [vochay] *f* voice

voglia [volya] *f* desire ▸ **contro voglia** against one's will

voi [vo-ee] *pron* you

volentieri [volentee-ayray] *adv* willingly; gladly

volere [volayray] *v* to want

volo [volo] *m* flight

volta [volta] *f* time ▸ **uno alla volta** one at a time ▸ **una volta** once ▸ **a sua volta** in his/her turn

volto [volto] *m* face

vongola [vongola] *f* clam

vostro, a [vostro] *adj* your ◆ *pron* yours ▸ **vostro padre** your father ▸ **un vostro amico** a friend of yours ▸ **è (il) vostro?** is it yours?

vulcano [voolkano] *m* volcano

vuoto, a [voo-oto] *adj* empty

W, Y, Z

würstel [voorstel] *m* frankfurter

yogurt [yogoort] *m* yogurt

zabaione [dzaba-yonay] *m* dessert made from egg yolks, sugar, and Marsala

zafferano [dzaffayrano] *m* saffron

zaino [dza-eeno] *m* backpack

zampone [dzamponay] *m* pig's foot stuffed with ground meat

zanzara [dzandzara] *f* mosquito

zenzero [dzendzayro] *m* ginger

zia [dzee-a] *f* aunt

zingaro, a [dzeengaro] *m, f* gypsy

zio [dzee-o] *m* uncle

zitto, a [dzeetto] *adj* quiet ▸ **state zitti!** be quiet!

zona [dzona] *f* area ▸ **'zona industriale'** 'industrial park' ▸ **zona pedonale** pedestrian mall

zucchero [dzookkayro] *m* sugar

zuppa [dzooppa] *f* soup ▸ **zuppa inglese** dessert consisting of sponge cake soaked in liqueur and covered in custard and chocolate